# BUSINESS SPEAKING AND WRITING

Hugh Fellows
and
Fusaye Ikeda

Prentice-Hall, Inc., Englewood Cliffs, New Jersey 07632

*Library of Congress Cataloging in Publication Data*

FELLOWS, HUGH PRICE.
   Business speaking and writing.

   Includes bibliographies and index.
   1. Communication in management.  2. Commercial
correspondence.  3. Public speaking.  I. Ikeda, Fusaye.
II. Title.
HF5718.F45     651.7     81-15435
ISBN  0-13-107854-2     AACR2

Editorial/production supervision
   and interior design by Anne Armeny
Cover design by Miriam Recio
Manufacturing buyer: Edmund W. Leone

Acknowledgments for the use of copyrighted material
   appear on page xviii.

Printed in the United States of America

10  9  8  7  6  5  4  3  2  1

ISBN 0-13-107854-2

Prentice-Hall International, Inc., *London*
Prentice-Hall of Australia Pty. Limited, *Sydney*
Prentice-Hall of Canada, Ltd., *Toronto*
Prentice-Hall of India Private Limited, *New Delhi*
Prentice-Hall of Japan, Inc., *Tokyo*
Prentice-Hall of Southeast Asia Pte. Ltd., *Singapore*
Whitehall Books Limited, *Wellington, New Zealand*

*To W. W. Post, Jr.*
*whose wide business experience has been*
*of great help in preparing this text*

18   INTERNAL CORRESPONDENCE: MINUTES, MEMORANDA, AND REPORTS   271

19   EXTERNAL CORRESPONDENCE: SPECIAL REQUESTS, SALES, COMPLAINTS, AND CREDIT   292

APPENDIX A, Meetings   328

APPENDIX B, Parliamentary Procedure   336

APPENDIX C, Answers   352

AUTHOR INDEX   357

SUBJECT INDEX   360

# The Authors

HUGH FELLOWS, Ph.D. (New York University), M.A. (Northwestern University), has taught speech, drama, and literature in colleges and universities for more than forty years. During World War II, he served as an aviation psychologist and speech intelligibility officer at various U.S. Naval Air Stations. After the war he became speech coordinator at The City College of New York's Baruch School of Business, servicing communication needs of advertising, foreign trade, credits and collections, sales, and business management.

After accepting a Fulbright Scholarship in the British Isles, he returned to New York University as a Fellow in the School of Education and also worked as a communication consultant for such firms as Johns-Manville Corporation, Western Electric, New York Port Authority, and First Federal Savings and Loan Association.

He has directed professional theatre at several summer stock companies and was guest professor at Tokyo Medical and Dental University in Japan and University of the East in Manila (Philippines).

He is the recipient of New York University's Founder's Day Award for outstanding service in pedagogy, awards as "outstanding teacher" from three other universities, and a citation from the Library of Congress for recording *Talking Books* (28 volumes) for international distribution to blind people. He has published feature articles in such divergent magazines as *Theatre Arts Monthly, Boy's Life,* and *Today's Health*. He is the author of *The Art and Skill of Talking with People* (Prentice-Hall, 1964, now in its sixteenth printing).

FUSAYE IKEDA, B.A. (University of California at Berkeley) has had many years of business experience. For seven years she was in charge of office operations for the Intensive Business Training Center of the City College of New

York (now the Baruch School of Business), where her duties included interviewing, testing and hiring of all non-teaching staff members. She headed the Order Department of Donmoor Knitwear for thirteen years, one of the nation's largest manufacturers of boys' knitwear, where she interviewed, tested, hired and trained office personnel. She was an interviewer for almost twenty years for the New York State Department of Labor. Miss Ikeda has almost always "moonlighted" in a second job, including such occupations as work in a florist shop, "Girl Friday" to a prominent sports columnist, modeling for The Arts Students League, and night cashier in the most prominent Greenwich Village coffee house.

# Foreword

In a sense I helped create the text of *Business Speaking and Writing*, so I'm happy to see it in print. Hugh Fellows was an instructor of mine in a graduate program at New York University. Later he recruited Fusaye Ikeda and me as colleagues in an intensive business training program at New York City's Baruch School of Business. The communications program there was boldly experimental, innovative, and stimulating for we were faced with the task of servicing the spoken and written communication needs of five different departments: Advertising, Business Management, Credits and Collections, Foreign Trade, and Sales Training.

Under Fellows's direction, the staff* met the challenge with success. We experimented and often failed. We experimented and *succeeded* more often than we failed. Fusaye Ikeda was the focal point around which all written communication revolved. From the time she took over the stenographic pool at C.C.N.Y., work that would have normally taken two weeks to process was done within two days, and the employment turnover dropped from 33 percent in six months to only 10 percent for the same time period. Her organization, her assessment of a task, and the time-motion process involved was nothing short of astounding. She employed a staff of "eclectic" people who might be regarded as "rejects" in a conservative business firm, but the *work was done well*, and all of her employees loved "Saye."

Other colleagues and I urged Fellows to write for publication this empiric experiment in business communications, but he was too busy with his leisure

*Louis Lauro, Frank O'Neill, Harry Rockberger, Arthur Schoenfelt, Clyde Stitt, and Richard Wells.

time: aviation (a licensed pilot); theater (both a professional actor and director); art (a good "Sunday painter" in oils); creative writing (a book of poetry and many feature articles, published in a variety of magazines), and other Epicurean delights which shall be nameless. Somehow he managed to find time to record 28 books for the blind *(Talking Books)*, and to finish work on his Ph.D. He never thought of sleep.

When Hugh Fellows left the Baruch School of Business to accept a Fulbright Scholarship, I left the field of education to go into the business world. I took with me many of the communication skills and depth of experience which we shared in that admirable experiment of intensive business training at C.C.N.Y. I took, also, some of the enthusiasm which Fellows infused into students and colleagues alike. Both have served me well.

In the years intervening between 1950 and 1980, I have kept in touch with Ikeda and Fellows. I was certain that advancing years would have slowed them down. Not so! Fellows has written two other books, has taught in Japan, the Philippines, and Great Britain, traveled over five continents, and has been communication consultant for such firms as Johns-Manville Corporation, General Foods, First Savings and Loan Association of New York City, New York State Labor Board, and others.

I hope that you will read—and *enjoy*—this textbook by two people who believe that learning can be *fun* and an *adventure,* and who have never stopped pursuing that adventure. Fellows's writing is often "corny," and sometimes shocking, but his and Ikeda's *ideas* are from people who have witnessed a broad spectrum of life, and who *know* whereof they speak. They have also done their library research thoroughly. Miss Ikeda, with her usual equanimity, is still holding down *two* jobs!

One thing I am sure of: You will not want to sell this volume as a "second-hand" book!

Sincerely,

Richard G. Wells
Former Vice President—Sales
Minnesota Rubber Company
Minneapolis, Minnesota

November, 1981

# Preface

This book is designed for the college business and professional major who will enroll for a terminal course in business speech and writing; therefore, it is short on theory and long on practice. However, the theory is based upon current research, and the practice is based on more than thirty years of pedagogical and business experience. We make no apology for its being pragmatic, prescriptive, and authoritative.

Basic skills in oral communication have not changed *radically* in more than 2,500 years. We set that date arbitrarily because that was about the time Aristotle (384–322 B.C.) wrote his *Rhetoric*. It is hardly logical to assume that Aristotle *invented* the principles that govern effective speaking among men; the precepts must have been in existence for at least several decades before Aristotle interpreted them and set them down.

Current research has given us refinements of those precepts as well as fresh insight. That same research has burdened us with such terms as encoding, decoding, auditory response, interpersonal and intrapersonal communication, nonverbal communication, sociometrics, kinesics, proxemics, "sociopedal" (standing face-to-face), "sociofugal" (standing back-to-back), and cognitive dissonance. We have no quarrel with such terms; indeed, it is necessary to use many of them in this text. However, we have made an earnest attempt to eliminate academic jargon as much as possible.

We have also tried to avoid being grandiose in our "style." Styles of speaking and writing have changed greatly within our culture over a relatively short period of time. Consider Abraham Lincoln's Gettysburg Address, for example.

Lincoln spoke after the speech of Senator Edward Everett (1794–1865), a famous orator, scholar, former Governor of Massachusetts, and former President of Harvard University, whose oration lasted *two hours* and was filled with flowery phrases and dramatic figures of speech. Lincoln spoke for only *two minutes,* and his speech was scoffed at for its simplicity and brevity by all of the newspapers except one; it went against the *style* of public address at the time. Senator Everett's speech made the front page of most newspapers, while Lincoln's speech was relegated to the inside pages as "hardly worth noting."*
Today, Senator Everett's speech would probably be as out of style as Lincoln's was when he delivered it. So we have tried to write simply and briefly.

The basic skills in business and professional speaking do not differ radically from those in other forms of oral communication; the *situations* encountered by a business and professional person may differ a great deal. After having taught and counseled both business and professional persons for more than thirty years and having used or examined a number of texts on the subject, we believe that the professional person gets shortchanged in many textbooks; texts are almost entirely concerned with the business world, with "professional" tacked on as an afterthought—perhaps as a sales inducement. We have tried to meet the needs of men and women in business and the professions (such as law, medicine, and the clergy) by including chapters on conversation, voice and diction, and vocabulary study. From experience we have found that these are of prime importance to professionals who lack them. For both the business and professional person such matters rank high in *personal gratification.*

There is a rationale for the form of the vocabulary exercises at the beginning of each chapter. Looking up a word in the dictionary, one tends to forget it after the passage which contains it has been understood. Often one *guesses* its meaning from the context. However, one who receives the added stimulus of a game, or discovers the *exact* meaning from multiple choices, tends to remember it more easily.

We would like to thank Prentice-Hall, Inc. for permission to borrow material from *The Art & Skill of Talking with People* by Hugh Fellows, 1964. This material was used extensively in Chapter 15.

There are few textbooks on communication which can satisfy any one individual instructor or even a department head teaching the same sections of the same course. The instructor with initiative will pick and choose from the various chapters of a text, saying, "This chapter *lacks* something that I can supply from my *own* graduate instruction and research," or, "That chapter has no value in my scheme of instruction, so I'll skip it entirely." *No* textbook author can encompass all of the experiences and *emphases* placed upon instruction by the

---

*Oliver, Robert T., *History of Public Speaking in America*. Boston: Allyn and Bacon, 1965.

many graduate schools and the varied professions; we do not offer this textbook as gospel.

We *do* believe that with our combined pedagogical and practical business experiences we have encompassed a large enough balance among research, theory, and workable situations to make this text worthwhile.

Hugh Fellows
Fusaye Ikeda

# Acknowledgments

We acknowledge gratefully the aid of the persons listed below. Not only have they helped us select the topics that they considered essential to a book of this sort, but they have also contributed materials for our use, and in many instances read and made helpful comments on portions of the unfinished manuscript:

Jack Watson, training director, P. Lorillard Corporation, New York City.

Richard G. Wells, vice president, Minnesota Rubber Company, Minneapolis, Minnesota.

Nancy Webb, account executive, Young and Rubicam Advertising Agency, New York City.

LaVange Richardson, Ph.D. Diplomate, American Psychological Association, San Diego, California.

H. M. Benedek, former president, General Dynamics Corporation, New York City.

The late Stella McCullough, R.N., American Tuberculosis Association, Austin, Texas.

Harry Rockberger, Ph.D., clinical psychologist, West Orange, New Jersey.

Janice Bennett, M.A., realtor, Tampa, Florida.

Walter Cutter, Ph.D., LL.D., former director, New York University's Center for Safety Education, Dunedin, Florida.

Russell B. Smith, Ph.D., former director of New York University's Office of Special Services for Business and Industry, White Plains, New York.

Edith Jurka, M.D., New York City.

Edward (Ted) Hodgkins, vice president, Paul Revere Insurance Company, Worcester, Massachusetts.

The Rev. Frank Beall, pastor, Trinity Presbyterian Church, Pensacola, Florida, and moderator for the Presbyterian churches in Florida.

Don Martinetti, illustrator, Livingston, New Jersey.

Steve Dalphin, acquisitions editor, Prentice-Hall, Inc., Englewood Cliffs, New Jersey.

Anne Armeny, production editor, Prentice-Hall, Inc., Englewood Cliffs, New Jersey.

Gert Glassen, supplemental books editor, Prentice-Hall, Inc., Englewood Cliffs, New Jersey.

The quotations at the beginning of Chapters 5, 6, 7, and 8 are reprinted from *Dictionary of Humorous Quotations*, edited by Evan Esar, copyright 1949, by permission of the publisher, Horizon Press, New York.

The quotation at the beginning of Chapter 11 is reprinted from Neil Postman, *Crazy Talk, Stupid Talk* (New York: Delacorte Press, 1972). Used by permission.

The quotation at the beginning of Chapter 17 is reprinted from Dorothy Sarnoff, *Speech Can Change Your Life* (New York: Dell Publishing Co., Inc., 1970). Used by permission.

# I | BUSINESS SPEAKING

# VOCABULARY STUDY FOR CHAPTER ONE

Following are some words with which you may not be familiar; they are all used in this chapter. Try to select the correct meaning of each word from the multiple-choice definitions.

1. AGHAST — A. An open ventilator   B. Shock or amazement   C. Filled with gas.

2. ABSTRUSE — A. A condensation   B. Esoteric   C. Hard to understand.

3. CONNOTATION — A. The sum of all parts   B. An insult   C. An implied meaning.

4. DEMAGOGUE — A. One who arouses prejudice or passion   B. A half-god   C. A temple for demon worship.

5. DENOTATION — A. The process of taking notes   B. The exact meaning of a word for most people speaking a language   C. Denial.

6. DEROGATORY — A. A derivative   B. Demonstrative   C. Disparaging, tending to detract.

7. HYPERCRITICAL — A. Deceitful   B. To find fault with, even on minor points   C. A state of crisis.

8. INCINERATE — A. To make snide remarks   B. To perfume with incense   C. To reduce to ashes.

9. KINESICS — A. The study of one's ancestors   B. The study of body motion as related to speech   C. The study of touch in fingerprinting.

10. POLYSYLLABIC — A. The sounds made by a parrot   B. A many-sided geometrical figure   C. Containing many syllables.

11. PROXEMICS — A. The study of "personal space" needed by people   B. The practice of voting by proxy   C. A word coined by Edward T. Hall.

12. REJOINDER — A. A hyphenated word   B. A counterreply   C. An annex.

13. REPERTORY — A. Clever conversation   B. A place of safety   C. A store or stock of things available.

14. SENSORY — A. Passing judgment upon something   B. A monk's haircut   C. Pertaining to the five senses.

# 1 | Basic Principles of Business Speech

The business of America is business.
President Calvin Coolidge (1872–1933)

Rules won't work when talking with people. Oh, yes, we once *thought* that they would; for example, two books[1] published at the turn of this century set down absolute rules for a business or professional man to follow when speaking before an audience (women did very little speaking at the time). Here are some of them:

1. A man must always stand with his feet at an angle of 45 degrees, one foot slightly in advance of the other, with his weight resting on the balls of his feet.
2. When there is a change of thought, or transition from one topic to another, the speaker should always take one step (but not more than one) backwards.
3. When a major point is to be emphasized strongly, the speaker should always take one step forward (again, no more than one), after which he returns to "home position."
4. A speaker's arms and hands are to remain in a relaxed position at his sides, except when making a gesture:
   A. A derogatory gesture should always be made below the waist; an emotional gesture should be made in the region of the heart; an inspirational gesture must be made above the line of the eyes (Heavenward, it would seem!).
   B. The wrist should always lead the arm in making a gesture, and a little "ictus" (snap of the wrist) should end it. A gesture should be made in a curved line, and so forth.

Why won't rules work when people talk with one another? Because each person is different. Yet, people in a specific culture are more alike than their differences, and they form clubs to express their similarities of interests. Those clubs have rules, and the members obey them; but in a democracy those clubs generally do not have rules that infringe too deeply upon an individual's personal freedom, and the rules are based upon *principles* to which all members subscribe.

So it is with this textbook. It is based upon *principles* which are broad enough to include most people who have an interest in presenting their ideas before others, principles that have worked in times past and are still working. Those principles are narrow enough, however, to act as a guide. However, if you violate a principle and find that your presentation *works*, then continue to violate that principle; perhaps you'll come up with a *new* one! We have no desire to stifle your creativity or your individuality. However, since these principles have worked over many years and with many businesses and professions, we suggest that you try them before striking out in an uncharted wilderness.

### *PRINCIPLE NUMBER ONE:* BUSINESS PRESENTATIONS MUST BE PURPOSEFUL

Once I was called upon to consult with a state senator about his speechmaking problem. He wanted me to teach him how to make a speech on any occasion without preparation, an obviously impossible task. When I suggested that an effective "statesman" or businessman have a repertory of speeches that could be given on certain occasions and that the type of speech depended upon its intended purpose, he was aghast.

"Do you mean to tell me that I've got to have a *motive* for giving every speech I deliver?" he asked. Apparently the word *motive* had an unclean connotation to him.

"Of course," I replied. "What have you been doing all of your political life?" (I wanted to add, "and why are you in trouble *now?*" but did not.)

"Well, I've always tried to stand up and say a few well-chosen words," he answered, "and that's about it."

And that person was the senate minority leader in the state of New York!

It occurred to me that a politician's speech might *avoid* having a purpose; it should be *pleasant* enough to make people vote for him, but *vague* enough so that those same voters cannot hold him to any promises.

Business and professional speech must have a purpose: A business conference is not usually called to congratulate an executive on his new baby; it is called to solve a problem. A lawyer isn't in court to get acquainted socially with the judge and jury; he is there to win his lawsuit. A manufacturing firm's quality control staff does not ordinarily call a meeting to plan a party on company time;

it is usually concerned about how to make its product better, or maintain its standards, while expanding at the same time.

In business if you're ever unable to answer the question, "Why am I talking?" you'd better stop! If you don't know why, it is certain no one else will, and you have lost all hope of giving a clear-cut message to your listeners. Messages that are unclear, and thereby open to misinterpretation, are unbusinesslike, and can even be dangerous.

### PRINCIPLE NUMBER TWO: THE BUSINESS AND PROFESSIONAL SPEAKER HAS A HEALTHY ATTITUDE TOWARD HIMSELF AND OTHERS

We at times make ridiculous assumptions about other people such as, "She feels that she is better than I," or "They're going to be hypercritical of me when I start talking," or "I can sense that they don't like the way I'm dressed." The worst attitude of all to take is, "I'll say what I have to say, because I've been assigned to say it, and then sit down; these people don't mean anything to me anyway."

Why not assume instead that your listeners are honest, intelligent, generous, cheerful people whom you'd like to know because there is something interesting about each one. You'll feel much better if you make such assumptions, and you will also not be disillusioned as often as you might think.

One's self-attitude is equally important. There is not one of us who has not made mistakes; most of us have at times known shame, guilt, fear, and a feeling of inadequacy. That is no reason for us to continue to allow those feelings to control us.

Chapter Three will more precisely explore what provides each person's self-image.

### PRINCIPLE NUMBER THREE: A BUSINESS OR PROFESSIONAL PRESENTATION RECOGNIZES AND USES THE COMMUNICATION PROCESS IN BOTH ITS VERBAL AND NONVERBAL ASPECTS

Simplified, this principle states, "The *way* you say it is just as important as *what* you say." Learning to read has always been one of life's great mysteries; making sense out of those meaningless squiggles of ink is truly amazing! Yet, learning to talk is equally mystifying. George Bernard Shaw once said, "There are fifty ways of saying Yes, and five hundred of saying No, but only one way of writing them down."

When communicating *in person* with others (please note that we did not say "communicating *orally*"), we communicate with our entire body. Sometimes this body language is more eloquent than words. Here is an example:

Bill Tilden, the outstanding tennis star of his day, had a manner of intimidating both his opponents and officials without saying a word: He would simply turn and stare at the offending person with the utmost contempt. "Big Bill" literally incinerated them.

This weapon was considered unfair by less imposing figures, so the U.S. Lawn Tennis Association actually proposed a rule to forbid a "dirty look" at its 1928 convention.

Tilden heard about the proposal, and made a special trip to the convention. He stood up and suggested that the manner in which a player looked at his opponents or the judges had nothing to do with that player's skill at the game. As the proponents of the rule stood up to protest, Tilden simply glared at them, and they wilted. The proposal never came to a vote![2]

Actors are frequently accused of "acting from the neck up" when they fail to use their entire body. The vocal clues are also important. Physicians are taught that speaking in a rapid, high-pitched voice will only increase the anxiety of their patients, so the good physician speaks in a calm, soothing, low-pitched voice to relieve that anxiety. Prospective business and professional people should learn that technique, which is why we have included the chapter on "verbalization."

### PRINCIPLE NUMBER FOUR: A BUSINESS PRESENTATION MUST BE ADAPTABLE TO ITS LISTENERS AND IMMEDIATELY RELATE TO THEM

If a group of scientists tells you that a polar ice cap will cover your home in five thousand years, it may *relate* to you. If a reliable meteorologist warns that your home is in the track of a tornado that may strike within three hours, it has *immediacy* for you.

An interesting phenomenon struck the giant Chrysler Corporation in 1979. After the 1973–74 oil crisis the other "Big Three" in the automotive industry started retooling to produce smaller automobiles that would burn less fuel and pollute the air with fewer harmful emissions. Chrysler continued to turn out luxury "gas guzzlers," which nobody in 1979 would buy. Suddenly Chrysler asked the U.S. Government to loan them *one billion dollars* so that they would not add more than 100,000 auto workers to the number of unemployed in this country. The 1973–74 fuel shortages surely *related* to *all* automobile manufacturers, but Chrysler apparently thought themselves exempt from it until they found themselves in an immediate crisis.

If an earthquake kills 2,000 people in Peru, it relates to you as a compassionate human being; if your family, who are visiting Peru on vacation, are in the path of the earthquake, it has much more immediacy for you.

The same is true of adaptability. If you are to give a progress report to a newly appointed staff officer in your business firm, your first question is apt to be, "What is that individual like?" so that you can adapt your report for his or her approval.

The *content* of your presentation may not vary, but its adaptability should—especially if the report is to be given to listeners who differ widely. If you are an estate planner (an insurance broker with a high degree of tax knowledge) and are making a presentation to a college faculty, you will use examples with which that faculty are familiar; you may even use *words* with which *only* its members are familiar. If you are required to make a presentation to the blue-collar workers in a small electronics plant, you will *change* your examples to those with which your blue-collar workers are familiar; you may even include some workers' jargon to show that you know something about their jobs.

*Two points* need emphasis: 1. You must not try to "talk up" to the college faculty by using polysyllabic words, and you must not "talk down" to the blue-collar workers. Both practices are insulting to your listeners. 2. It requires research and *hard work* to adapt your presentation to groups that vary as widely as those two groups.

You must also adapt your presentation to the time allotted to you.

Suppose you have ten minutes in which to make your presentation: You would certainly make the main points and try to give each main point at least one piece of supportive material (statistics, specific examples, quotations from authorities). You may need to omit some of the *minor* points, hoping that there will be a question-and-answer period or a discussion period afterward. However, you must stay within the time limits assigned to you unless it is absolutely impossible, in which case you should request more time.

On the other hand, if you have twenty minutes for your presentation, you may bring up those minor points, always being careful to emphasize the *main* ones. You may also give additional support to your main points.

In summary, your presentation must be adaptable to (a) the average *age* of your listeners, (b) their occupation, (c) their intellectual level, (d) their membership in groups, (e) their immediate interests, and (f) the time allotted to you.

## PRINCIPLE NUMBER FIVE: AN *EFFECTIVE* BUSINESS PRESENTATION USES MORE THAN ONE MEDIUM AND ALWAYS RECEIVES "FEEDBACK"

Behaviorists tell us that sight is more important than sound in remembering things, but that a *combination* of the two is far more effective than either one alone.[3] The *more* senses that are involved in a presentation, the stronger the impression will be. Talking is one sensory medium; listening is another; sight is still another; and smell, kinesics,* and proxemics are still others. Perhaps the most important media in making a presentation are (a) talking, (b) listening, (c) showing, and (d) talking as feedback.

Several years ago a toy manufacturer in one of my adult classes objected to my mandate, "When giving instructions orally, always ask for feedback."

"That is ridiculous!" he said. "Do you mean to tell me that when I give instructions to my employees, I must always ask them to repeat what I've said?"

"Why not?" I asked.

"First of all, it would take too much of *my* time, and second, I'd be insulting the intelligence of the employees if I thought they couldn't understand plain English!"

I rejoined, "Then I take it that you never have any trouble with having employees follow your instructions?"

"Of *course* I do—all the time, *all* the time!" he snorted, "But it's just because they weren't listening in the *first* place!"

The toy manufacturer might have saved a great deal of time if he had asked for feedback instead of correcting the mistakes his employees made. His concern about insulting the employees' intelligence need not have bothered him, because he could easily have said, "Charley, I'm not sure that I've covered everything I intended to, so please just go over it as you understand it:" or, "Susan, I may have overlooked something, so you won't mind if I ask you to repeat what I've said as you understand it, will you?" The Armed Forces have tried to circumvent misunderstanding by putting everything into *written* directives and memoranda; unfortunately these are often worded in such abstruse language that they are difficult to understand and often need an interpreter:

> "It has been determined that a number of military personnel on this base who are entitled to privileges of the Non-Commissioned Officers' Club have made their appearance in the aforementioned facility with their pedal extremities showing an insufficient amount of covering, or without outer covering at all. Henceforth, personnel entitled to the privileges of that particular recreational facility will not be admitted without the proper attire heretofore referred to."
>
> Translation: You must wear shoes and socks in the N.C.O. Club.
> —N.C.O. Club, MacBill AFB

In addition, the directive or memorandum is always "communicating down" and leaves no opportunity for feedback.

In their book *Handling Barriers in Communication*[4] Irving and Laura Lee write that information passed on to others tends to *lose something* most of the

---

*Used here in the sense of writing, or taking notes. Def: "The study of body motion as related to speech."

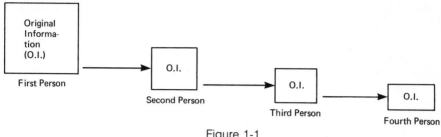

Figure 1-1

time, as shown in Figure 1-1. Lee also suggests that people tend, not only to *omit* parts of the original information, but also to *change* it or *add* to it, presumably to "pad" the information to its original size. In any case, little of the original information gets through, as shown in Figure 1-2. To summarize, in passing information from one person to another, one should (1) try to reduce the number of levels through which the information is passed, (2) use more than one medium if possible, and (3) get feedback from the person to whom the information is being passed.

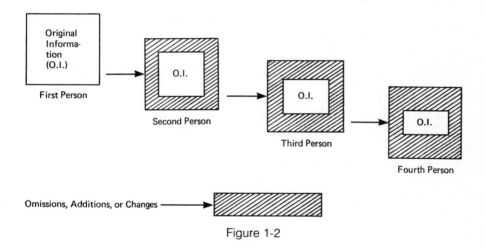

Figure 1-2

## *PRINCIPLE NUMBER SIX:* AN EFFECTIVE BUSINESS PRESENTATION MUST BE LOGICAL AND APPEALING

Professional people in all fields pride themselves on their logic and reasoning. Yet, they are subject to the same visual and emotional appeals as other people.

Although a presentation must first be logical and reasonable, it should also appeal to people's basic drives, such as self-preservation, sex, ego, altruism, desire for change, and desire to maintain the *status quo*. The man who loses himself in the study of electronics may be just as emotional as the man who cheers for his football team to win the homecoming game at his alma mater.

None of these principles is new. They apply to talking with people and the responses you are apt to get if you use them in business and professional situations.

## SUGGESTED CLASSROOM EXERCISE

### Passing on Information

Your instructor will divide the class into groups of four or five (not more than five), with each group bearing a letter of the alphabet, and the members of each group numbered consecutively. For example, Group "A" will have students numbered 1, 2, 3, 4, and Group "B" will also have students numbered 1, 2, 3, 4, and possibly 5.

The procedure is the same for each group: The instructor will give No. 1 in each group a card upon which some information has been written. *No one else in the group sees the card except No. 1*. No. 1 reads the card (more than once if desired) and returns it to the instructor. Then, No. 1 calls aside No. 2 and gives the information to No. 2 *privately*. No. 2 then gives the information to No. 3 privately, and so on to the end of the group. The class is reassembled, and No. 4 (or 5) in each group is asked to give the information he has received; No. 3 verifies it or corrects it. No. 2 does the same for No. 3, and No. 1 tells what he passed on to No. 2. The instructor then reads the card, noting on the chalkboard (a) changes, (b) omissions, and (c) additions.

Each card carries different information and each is structured. See Instructor's Manual for examples and suggestions for the structure.

## FOOTNOTES FOR CHAPTER ONE

[1]No authors listed. *The Complete Speaker* (Philadelphia: David McKay, 1899). *The Orator's Handbook with Quotations* (London: The Henslow Press, 1909).

[2]Condensed from Frank Deford's *Big Bill Tilden* (New York: Simon and Schuster, 1978). Used by permission.

[3]Randall P. Harrison, *Beyond Words* (Englewood Cliffs, N.J.: Prentice-Hall, 1974).

[4]Irving and Laura Lee, *Handling Barriers in Communication* (New York: Harper and Brothers, 1957).

# VOCABULARY STUDY FOR CHAPTER TWO

Following are some words with which you may not be familiar; most of them are used in this chapter. Test yourself to see if you can select the correct meaning of each word from the multiple-choice definitions. We suggest that you look up each word in a good dictionary so that you learn the *connotations* as well as the *denotations* of the words.

1. ABSTRACT

A. Conceived apart from concrete realities or actual instances   B. Flavoring for pastry   C. Mentally ill, "daffy."

2. AVERSION

A. To state the truth   B. Abnormal sex habits   C. Strong feeling of dislike.

3. CONDUCIVE

A. To contribute or help   B. Poor conduct   C. Term used in electricity.

4. DEPLORABLE

A. Subject for grief or regret   B. Process of giving a deposition   C. The opposite of *adorable*.

5. DYAD

A. A wood-nymph   B. Communication between two people   C. A unit of electricity.

6. EMANATE

A. To be in the immediate future   B. To take precautions against a disease   C. To flow out, as from a source.

7. INCREMENT

A. Excretions from the body   B. Automatic increase in pay as time goes on   C. Unpleasant weather.

8. INFLECTION

A. The rise or fall in pitch in a single word   B. The image in a mirror   C. Distortion caused by water.

9. INTONATION

A. To be "in tune with"   B. The opposite of detonation   C. The overall melody or "tune" of one's voice.

10. JARGON

A. Vocabulary peculiar to a profession or trade   B. Gibberish   C. The language spoken on the Isle of Jarga.

11. PARAMETER

A. An instrument for measuring sound   B. Within a certain area or limits   C. Two concentric circles.

12. PLETHORA

A. A sore throat, laryngitis   B. A musical instrument   C. Too much of anything; superabundance.

13. RECAPITULATE

A. To review or summarize what one has said   B. To surrender   C. To replace corks with metal caps on bottles.

14. SEMANTICS

A. An advanced form of algebra   B. The study of various word meanings   C. The study of marine plants.

15. SPATIAL

A. Pertaining to space   B. Pertaining to sputum   C. A type of spasm.

16. TENET(S)

A. French, meaning "to own," as a landlord   B. One who plays close to the net in tennis   C. Principles, or doctrine, held by some to be true.

17. TRIAD

A. The Holy Trinity   B. Communication among three persons   C. A three-wheeled cart.

18. VIABLE

A. Vicious, venal   B. Capable of living and growing.   C. The flow of traffic on a viaduct.

# The Process
# 2 of Oral
# Communication

The gods gave us two ears, but only one mouth.
Does this mean that we should listen twice as
much as we talk?

Attributed to Socrates (470?–399, B.C.)

In spite of what was once widely believed, animals can and do *think*. They can solve simple problems, and it also appears that they have certain sounds by which they communicate to others of their species. Even a chicken is capable of this and can be clearly understood by other chickens. A mother hen will make certain sounds to her baby chicks when there is food at hand, certain other sounds when there is danger present, and still other sounds to express her disapproval of their behavior.

The mother hen can only communicate one sound at a time and then without a *condition* to that meaning. She can signal, "There's food here," or "There's danger for us," but she cannot communicate, "There's food here, but you'd better be careful, because there's danger in getting to the food." Because her language has limitations, we refer to it as a *closed* language.

Animals, so far as we know, cannot talk in abstract terms. This is also true of human beings when they first try to communicate with someone who speaks a foreign tongue.

> During World War II, I was sent to fly anti-submarine patrol from a tiny atoll in the South Pacific. The natives were friendly, but had had little contact with the outside world, and knew no formal, classified language. I soon developed a friendship with the tallest of these Micronesians and called him Willie. Willie and I could communicate fairly well on almost any tangible and concrete subject: He wanted to know if I would like a house, instead of the pup-tent I was sleeping in; when I said "yes" he rounded up several natives and they built one for me. We "talked" about the weather, food, gardening, airplanes and even sex. I missed learning about what those gentle people on the Isle of Uvia believed about God, or justice, or any of those abstract things that separate animals from man.
> —Recounted by Comdr. Judson Davis.

Given more time, Judd and Willie might have been able to communicate with each other on a great many other levels, perhaps eventually learning to communicate about abstract matters. Human language allows us to describe events and objects, to express and describe emotions in a variety of ways, and to combine sounds into complicated structures. Our communication is an *open* language, almost boundless in its limitations, and yet precise in its meanings.

But you wouldn't think so—not with the misunderstandings that arise when we "speak plain English" to another person who also "speaks plain English."

## BASIC PROCESS OF INTERPERSONAL COMMUNICATION

Let us see what is involved in a simple dyadic situation: You have just been promoted to the position as head of the stenographic pool in a large company. The steno pool furnishes personnel to take dictation and handle correspondence for all minor executives who do not have a full-time secretary; it handles all duplicating, types reports for a certain branch of the corporation, and gathers and distributes all interoffice memos and mail. You have a full-time messenger and mailman, and five typists, three of whom can take shorthand. Your immediate supervisor is the Assistant Personnel Director for Staff, Curly Sanders. He asks to see you early in the day.

CURLY:    Peter, I wish you'd get an inventory of our office supplies. Your predecessor did not maintain a very careful inventory and we were always running out of things when we needed them.

YOU:    Yes, Curly. Shall I do it today?

Nothing unusual about that request and the response to it, is there? However, let us examine it in minute terms of oral communication:

1. Curly has had to put his thoughts into words (called *encoding*) and he transmits them to you. He is the SENDER and you are the RECEIVER.
2. With your response, "Yes, Curly," you indicate that you have heard his words and have understood him (called *decoding*). You next *encode* the question, "Shall I do it today?" and transmit it. *You* are now the sender and *he* is the receiver.

Still simple, eh? But suppose there is a sudden noise interference—a truck rumbling past outside, combined with the clatter of typewriters and a sudden upsurge in volume from the Muzak speaker in his office? You may have difficulty hearing him, or he you, so one of you may need to repeat some of your transmissions. This is still a relatively simple matter, and a diagram of it might look something like this:

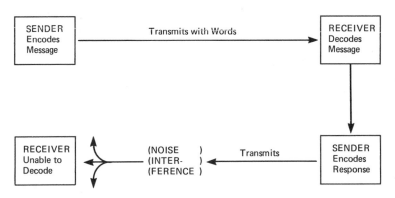

Figure 2-1

Suppose that, when you enter his office, Curly leans forward, places the palms of his hands flat on the surface of his desk, arms akimbo, and says in an injured tone of voice, "Peter, I *w-i-s-h* you'd get an *inventory* of our office supplies," as if he had asked you to do so a dozen times before. He continues, with a scornful curl of his lips, "Your *predecessor* did *not* maintain a very careful inventory, and we were *always* running out of things when we needed them."

This is an entirely different communication from that simple request for you to take inventory and the explanation of why it should be done. Curly is now using *paralinguistics*, or *nonverbal* communication, which may be stronger than the words themselves. Consequently if you should diagram his *total* communication to you, the diagram would be more complicated. (See Figure 2-2)

Suppose that you respond with the same words, but this time you let your shoulders drop with a sigh and cock your head to one side with a negative motion. "Y-e-e-s-s, Curly," you say, and your voice takes on the tone which means, "You're nagging me again!" Then your shoulders go back and you look at him with an expression of disbelief on your face as you ask, "Shall I do it *today?*" implying that you have dozens of things to do that are more important than taking inventory. If Figure 2-1 tries to reflect more than the mere words used, it becomes more complicated.

Oral communication involves more than mere words and their meanings; the words themselves may be inflected, emphasized, and set into an intonation pattern that changes their meanings more than slightly. Furthermore we communicate by facial expressions, gestures, and physical tensions and relaxations

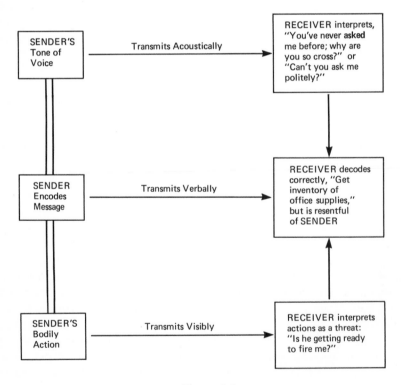

Figure 2-2

(often called "body language") that add to—or detract from—the meanings of words alone. Judge Frank Turkenheimer declared that the transcript of a trial, being reread to jurors in the jury room, is far from being totally accurate; the jurors cannot reconstruct the physical behavior or the vocal expression of either a witness or the lawyer examining the witness. They have only the *words* to depend upon for meaning. [1]

If a mere four sentences of oral interpersonal communication can be so complicated, you may wonder how we ever accomplish anything more complex than taking inventory. After all, in the business and professional world there are goods to manufacture, lawsuits to disentangle, and illnesses to heal.

To summarize thus far, in a dyadic communication situation the process is a circle of stimulus and response. Speaker A transmits something to Speaker B; this stimulates a response from Speaker B, who then transmits something to Speaker A, who in turn is stimulated by what B has transmitted. Anything that breaks the circuit, as shown in Figure 2-1, can imperil further communication.

There have been many other attempts to diagram the process of interpersonal communication* in order to bring it to a visual level, most of them far more complicated than these presented in Figures 2-1 and 2-2. They range anywhere from a simple, funnel-shaped spiral by Frances E. X. Dance[2] to an immensely complicated one in Berko, Wolvin, and Wolvin. [3] Some of them are described in an article by Ronald L. Smith, "Theories and Models of Communication Processes," in the book *Speech Communication Behavior*. [4] None of them seems to have taken into account the *reasons* for such behavior: that is, the part that the two lobes of the brain play in the entire communication process.

## Relationship of the Right and Left Lobes of the Brain

In a dyadic communication the Receiver responds to the literal meanings of the words (verbal) with the *left* lobe of the brain and will not even notice such things as tone of voice, inflection, facial expression, and body language (nonverbal). On the other hand, the Receiver's *right* lobe of the brain hardly notices the *words*, but responds to the nonverbal communication of the Sender. So it would *seem* that when two people interact they actually form two separate relationships, as in Figure 2-3. [5] Thus the mother about to punish her child

---

*For example, the Barker-Wiseman Communication Model, the Shannon-Weaver Model (mathematical), the Wendel Johnson Model (similar to ours), and the Barnlund Model (transactional).

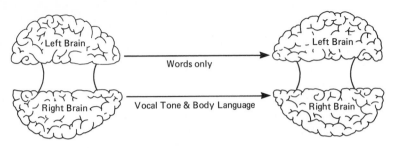

Figure 2-3

might say the words, "I want to do the right thing for *you*, because I *love* you, dear," while the child, detecting a harsh note in the mother's voice and the mother's menacing body language, interprets the message, "You *hate* me, and you'll *kill* me if you can!"

Of course, the brain does not operate under such a complete dichotomy. The *corpus callosum*, which connects the two hemispheres of the brain, has about 200 million fibers that telegraph impulses from one lobe of the brain to the other.[6] If we suppose that each fiber carries a frequency of twenty impulses per second (which is slow for an electronic computer), that is approximately *four billion* impulses per second! We coordinate verbal and nonverbal impressions so quickly that we are not aware of them.

Recent research has shown that neither the right nor left hemisphere of the brain works independently of the other. Even when the *corpus callosum* is severed (as is sometimes done in severe cases of epilepsy), the two halves of the brain still appear to cooperate. For example, when Roger Sperry experimented on such patients in the sixties, he found that the *informed* half of the brain tended to correct the *uninformed* half in such things as estimating the comparative length of two straight bars. In one instance when a male patient was presented with pictures of nude females on the *right* hemisphere of vision, the patient reported seeing nothing, but the *left* hemisphere corrected this and caused a broad grin to spread over the patient's face.[7,8] Whenever aphasia results from a stroke or any injury to that part of the brain that controls speech, another part appears to take over, and recovery of speech is often possible.[9]

While the two hemispheres of the brain are *not* rigidly compartmentalized, the brain *does* seem to have areas of "priority."[10] It assigns those priorities to various departments in both the left and right hemispheres, as shown in Figure 2-4.[11]

Various models and theories of interpersonal communication have advised us to consider both the Sender's and the Receiver's experiences, attitudes, fears, expectations, and intuition—most of which we have no way of knowing. We also do not know whether the Sender or Receiver is stronger in perceiving verbal or nonverbal symbols. Therefore it is *fundamental* to interpersonal communication to use both. Restak has demonstrated that meaningful gestures which normally accompany speech cannot be made if speech itself is blocked by a short-acting anesthetic, even though there is no paralysis in the arms and hands and they can move at command. When the anesthetic wears off, the normal gestures return. [12]

Nierenberg states in *Meta Talk* [13] that "Meaning is in the speaker, listener and circumstance." We hasten to add that "circumstance" includes both verbal and nonverbal symbols, as set forth in our Principle Number Three:

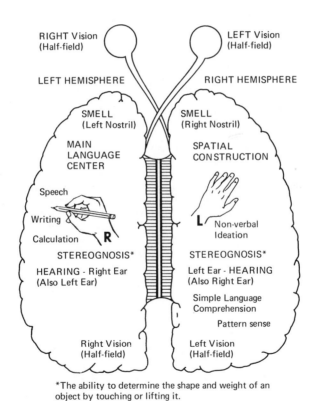

RIGHT Vision (Half-field)   LEFT Vision (Half-field)

LEFT HEMISPHERE   RIGHT HEMISPHERE

SMELL (Left Nostril)   SMELL (Right Nostril)

MAIN LANGUAGE CENTER   SPATIAL CONSTRUCTION

Speech
Writing
Calculation   **R**

Non-verbal Ideation   **L**

STEREOGNOSIS*   STEREOGNOSIS*

HEARING - Right Ear (Also Left Ear)   Left Ear - HEARING (Also Right Ear)

Simple Language Comprehension

Pattern sense

Right Vision (Half-field)   Left Vision (Half-field)

*The ability to determine the shape and weight of an object by touching or lifting it.

Figure 2-4

Business and professional presentations recognize and use the communication process in both its verbal and nonverbal aspects.

## SUGGESTED CLASSROOM EXERCISE

### Verbal and Nonverbal Communication

These assignments may serve for both this chapter and Chapter Three. While they seem calculated to amuse rather than teach, they can demonstrate forcefully the interrelation between words and body language. The students may work as individuals or as teams:

1. A student demonstrates *one* thing while giving directions for doing something totally different. For instance, the student may write on the chalkboard the proper form for a business letter, while telling how to make a pizza.

2. A team of students may take turns giving directions for sailing a boat; meanwhile, they are demonstrating how to make a clay pot: One mixes the clay with water and kneads it; another shapes it on a potter's wheel (or by hand); the third puts it into the kiln, adjusting the temperature carefully; the fourth takes it from the kiln and glazes or paints it, then returns it to the kiln for further baking.

The rest of the class is never told what the *demonstrations* are supposed to be, but receive only the words. The instructor then asks a few questions at random about what the performers were actually *doing,* as opposed to what they were saying.

Two students chose to experiment with this assignment: one impersonated a dentist, and the other his patient. The "dentist" hung a large print of "Washington Crossing the Delaware" from the chalkboard. Then he proceeded to demonstrate drilling and filling the "patient's" tooth, meanwhile vividly and accurately describing the print on the chalkboard, even to the number of people in the boat. When the demonstration finished, the "dentist" removed the print and asked questions about it. The "audience" had empathized so strongly with the poor "patient" in the dentist's chair that they could not answer a single question about the picture.

## FOOTNOTES FOR CHAPTER TWO

[1]Judge Frank Turkenheimer, from interview on the *Dick Cavett Show,* PBS-TV, June 12, 1979.

[2]Frank E. X. Dance and Carl E. Larson, *Speech Communication: Concepts and Behavior.* New York: Holt, Rinehart and Winston, 1976.

[3]Roy M. Berko, Andrew D. Wolvin, and Darlyn R. Wolvin, *Communicating: a Social and Career Focus* (Boston: Houghton-Mifflin Co., 1977) p. 7.

[4]L. L. Barker and R. J. Kibler, eds., *Speech Communication Behavior.* (Englewood Cliffs, NJ: Prentice-Hall, 1971) pp. 16–43.

[5]Thomas Blakeslee *The Right Brain* (Garden City, NY: The Anchor Press/ Doubleday, 1980) p. 120.

[6]Richard Restak M.D., *The Brain: the Last Frontier* (Garden City, NY: Doubleday & Company, 1979) p. 172.

[7]Roger W. Sperry, "The Great Cerebral Commissure," *Scientific American* (1964) 210 (I): 42.

[8]——— "Hemisphere deconnection and unity in conscious awareness." *American Psychologist* (1968), 23: 723–33.

[9]Peter Russell, *The Brain Book* (New York: Hawthorn Books, Inc., 1979) p. 54.

[10]Gordon Rattray Taylor, *The Natural History of the Mind* (New York: E. P. Dutton, 1979) p. 126.

[11]Sir John Carew Eccles, *The Understanding of the Brain* (New York: McGraw Hill, 1973) p. 207.

[12]Richard Restak, M. D., *The Brain: the Last Frontier,* pp. 322–23.

[13]Gerard I. Nierenberg and Henry H. Calero, *Meta Talk* (New York: Trident Press, 1973) p. 178.

# VOCABULARY STUDY FOR CHAPTER THREE

Below are some words that appear in this chapter with which you may not be familiar. No mix-and-match here. They are offered as a straight glossary.

1. COAGULATION (noun) — A thick, congealed mass originally in fluid form.
2. CULINARY — Pertaining to cookery or the kitchen.
3. EXPLOIT (verb) — Utilize for profit; turn to practical account.
4. FRAUGHT — Full of, or charged with.
5. HORTICULTURE — The science and art of cultivating trees, shrubs, vegetables, and fruit.
6. JUGGERNAUT — Large, overpowering destructive force or object.
7. LEWD — Lecherous; obscene or indecent.
8. MANIFESTLY — Readily perceived; obvious, apparent.
9. OBSOLETE — No longer in general use; discarded, outmoded.
10. PARLANCE — Way or manner of speaking; vernacular, idiom.
11. PEJORATIVE — Having a disparaging effect.

# 3 | Verbalization

More matter, with less art.

*Hamlet,* Act II, Sc. 2

This text is concerned primarily with words; words are supposed to carry meaning. You note that we say "supposed to" because, as shown in the preceding chapter, words alone are not enough to convey meaning.

English is a rich and varied language with about 750,000 words in its everyday usage. English is viable, and we add three or four hundred words to the language every year, and drop (or stop using) about the same number. The figure 750,000 does not include technical words and professional jargon, which, when included, put the figure closer to five million.

The very richness of the language often causes misunderstandings. It is fraught with connotations as well as denotations, multiple meanings, meanings that change with time, and words that mean different things in different sections of the country. Furthermore English is not a phonic language,* and it is almost impossible for a foreign-born person to learn to *pronounce* it correctly. For instance, there are *sixteen* different ways of pronouncing the combination of letters "ough". But there are ways to conquer this juggernaut.

---

*Unlike most other modern languages, English does not have an alphabet symbol for each of its sounds; there are forty sounds in English but only twenty-six letters in its alphabet, three of which are duplications of other alphabet sounds.

## VOCABULARY BUILDING

Throughout your school life your English teachers have nagged you about building a large vocabulary; we add our harangue. The world is expanding, and you cannot be a successful business or professional person without a broad knowledge of social, political, and cultural interests. Looking up the meanings of words in a dictionary is not enough; you must also know how to *use* them.

For several years I shared an office with three other speech instructors at the Baruch College of Business. One of them, Frank Roberts, spent all of his spare time with his head buried in an unabridged dictionary. He would look up words and copy them into a large looseleaf notebook for hours at a time.

The Dean of Academics requested our department to prepare a detailed syllabus, in synopsis form, for the fundamental course in speech, which all of us taught. As chairman, I delegated the work among the four of us.

When Frank Roberts turned in his portion to me, I could hardly believe it. To put it generously, his writing had the quality of an eighth grader in junior high school! As Queen Christina of Sweden said of the scholar Salmasius, "He knows the word for 'chair' in seven languages, but doesn't know how to sit in one."

—From a lecture given by Prof. Earl Ryan at the College of the City of New York, March 24, 1975.

Many scholars agree that only wide reading about a variety of subjects will provide you with a good vocabulary and teach you its proper usage. However, there is an obstacle: The vocabularly of *writing* is often different from the vocabulary of *speaking*. The late Professor Lucinda Bukeley, who taught successful courses in "Foreign Accent Correction" and "English as a Second Language" at New York University for fifteen years, offers this suggestion:

There is no substitute for reading if one wishes to improve one's vocabulary. But to suggest that a student stop and look up every word whose meaning he does not know *exactly* will spoil the pleasure of his reading. He can usually understand the meaning of the word from the context.

I ask the student to read from a popular magazine which carries a variety of subjects, and one whose vocabulary is close to that used in speaking. I use *The Reader's Digest*, in spite of what scholarly opinion of it may be. The student is asked to read only *one* article per day, pencil in hand, and simply circles the words whose *exact* meaning he may not know. After he has *finished* the article, he looks up in the dictionary the words he has circled, and goes back to the article to see how those words are used. He then writes down each word in a notebook—but *not* the definition.

The following day, the student reviews the words in his notebook. If he has forgotten their meanings, he once again looks them up in his dictionary, and notes the way they are used in the article he read the previous day. Then he reads another article, following the same procedure.

The reason for not allowing the student to write the definitions in his notebook is that he is forced to try to *recall* its meaning, and this extra effort reinforces that meaning. If he must go to the trouble of looking it up again, that also helps, because we are just normally lazy![1]

I have used this method for many years, and it works better than any other I have tried.

## Denotations and Connotations

The denotation of a word is its *literal* meaning; the connotation is the meaning it has taken on after several generations have *associated* it with something else. For instance, what associations do *you* have with the words *"politics"* and *"exploit?"* Are the associations pleasant or unpleasant? Good or bad? Perhaps you'd better look them up in a dictionary if you have formed a pejorative opinion about them. (You might also look up *"pejorative"!*)

The word *"home"* literally means one's dwelling place; yet, to most of us *"home"* connotes a place of warmth, love, and refuge. *"An orphan's home"* or *"a home for the aged"* take on quite different connotations, and *"home"* to a baseball player is still another matter. When a host greets his guests with "Everything in my home is yours," he is obviously not including his wife!

Computers are incapable of using connotations. A computer which was supposed to translate English into any foreign language and then retranslate it into English was given this sentence from the Scriptures to be translated into Russian and then back into English: "The spirit is willing, but the flesh is weak" (Mark 14:38). It turned out, "The wine is agreeable, but the meat is spoiled."

## Usage

Striving for a large vocabulary on a variety of subjects should be more for your *understanding* than for your use in speaking. Always use a *simple* word rather than an esoteric one *if* it conveys the same meaning. Among the good guides to usage that are available is a reasonably priced paperback, *A Dictionary of American-English Usage* by Margaret Nicholson.[2] To illustrate usage: You must not say 'a herd of sharks,' because sharks travel in 'schools' and not 'herds,' and even *fish* have their specific group nouns.*

---

*While usage forms a part of rhetoric, rhetoric itself concerns the overall effectiveness of speech, including figures of speech and imagery.

# A BRIEF TRIP INTO GENERAL SEMANTICS

General Semantics has been defined by S. I. Hayakawa, former President of San Francisco State University and currently in the U. S. Senate, as "the study of how *not* to be a damn' fool!" The English language is complicated but fascinating, and some of its peculiarities are:

## Multiple Meanings

Here are some of the meanings the word *"salt"* may have:

Sodium chloride (NaCl)

An old salt (meaning a sailor)

To salt away (meaning "to save")

To salt a mine (Meaning to place ore at strategic spots to deceive others into believing the mine is productive)

To use salty language (slang or profanity)

"Ye are the salt of the earth" (meaning character)

"Not worth his salt" (meaning *no* character)

A Salty Dog (A drink prepared with grapefruit juice and either gin or vodka; no salt and no dog in it!)

SALT (Strategic Arms Limitation Treaty)

The words *sodium chloride* have only one meaning, the chemical we use as a preservative or to flavor our food; however, *sodium chloride* is a *technical* expression, and such definite words are comparatively few in our language. It is estimated that there are only about 150,000 technical expressions in English. If you subtract that number from the 750,000 words in common usage, that leaves 600,000 words which are capable of being misunderstood because of multiple meanings. Here are a few unusual ones:

| | |
|---|---|
| *Mother—* | The cloudy coagulation which sometimes forms in vinegar |
| *Soda—* | In the card game Faro, the card that is turned face up before the game begins. |
| *Low—* | The sound emitted by cattle: Moo. |
| *Sister—* | In seamanship, a splint or reinforcement for a broken spar; also used as a verb, "to sister it up." |

The *Random House Unabridged Dictionary* lists fifty-three definitions (or usages) for the simple word *low*, ninety-one for the word *hand*, and 172 for the word *run*.

When you as Sender start to communicate, make sure that your Receivers understand the word in the sense which you mean it to have.

## Word Changes

Because English is a growing language, words have a peculiar habit of changing in meaning over a period of time. If I remark, "He is a large and silly man," you may conjure up a picture of a big guy who is frivolous. Not so in times past. The word *silly* comes from *selig,* and it at one time meant *blessed,* while the word *large* at one time had nothing to do with size; it once meant *generous.* We still use one form of that original meaning in our word *largess.* So what the speaker of a couple of centuries ago meant by saying, "He is a large and silly man," could be translated, "He is a generous and blessed man."

Here are some other words for which the meanings have changed drastically over the ages:

| | |
|---|---|
| *Obese*— | Once meant lean, thin, wasted away |
| *Fool*— | Was once a term of endearment |
| *Villa*— | Once meant a lowly hovel, a serf's hut; not the luxury dwelling it has come to mean today |
| *Villain*— | Had no connection of evil; simply one who lived in a villa |
| *Gossip*— | Originally meant a kinsman, one "related in God," and had no relation to talebearing |
| *Gorgeous*— | Once meant proud. |

Even during the authors' lifetimes some meanings of words have changed: In the late thirties and early forties roadside accommodations for an overnight stay were called *tourist camps;* now they are known as "motels" or "motor hotels."

## Regional Differences

Along with radio and television have come a more universal meaning and pronunciation of words; more and more midwesterners are now pronouncing the word for a small flowing body of water as "creek" instead of "crick," and more southerners now refer to a frying pan as a "skillet" instead of a "spider." We're somewhat sorry to see these regional differences become obsolete because they added color to our language. However, they were constantly interfering with clear communication.

No longer does one hear the friendly greeting in the south, "C'mon, and I'll buy you a dope!" The word *"dope"* meant Coca-Cola, and the Candler family in Atlanta spent thousands of dollars to stamp out the use of that word for their product, Coca-Cola. Yet the English language still contains different names for a soft drink: pop, soda, coke, squash.

The regional differences are not so great in the United States as they are in other countries where English is spoken:

In Australia, when a pretty girl refuses to go out with you because "Friday is her day to get screwed," she is not being lewd; it simply means that she must go across town to draw her weekly salary.

In England, when a young woman confides to you that she is "knocked up," she does not mean that she is even slightly pregnant—only that she is fatigued.

## Slang and Jargon

There is no way in which we can help you communicate with a person, or persons, whose talk is largely slang. The expressions change rapidly, and have little relevance to understandable English. Slang has little place in effective business and professional speech.

Jargon, however, is different. In making a presentation, you should learn some of the jargon that the members of your audience use in their everyday work. This is a *priceless* ingredient of your speech, but it must not be faked. You must understand what the term means and how it is used in the person's work.

Let's assume that you are an estate planner, and are talking with a college faculty on the desirability of planning their income for its maximum benefits. You will use terms such as "As your increment increases, you can put more into your tax-sheltered annuity."

Now, let's assume that you must make the same presentation to workers in a factory which manufactures nylon thread. "Increment" would mean nothing to them, but a "raise in pay" would. Furthermore, if you have studied the process of producing nylon even slightly, you might speak of "hydrogenation workers" or "spinneret re-pairmen" just as you have referred to "instructors" and "assistant professors" in your previous presentation to the college faculty.

Actually, the *content* of your presentation is essentially the same, but you should make some attempt to adapt it to the *interests* of various groups. A little jargon can be useful. However, beware of using the jargon of one occupation in speaking to a group from an entirely different occupation; it will be incomprehensible.

"Kill the baby!" a stagehand yells, and I shiver and shake with fright
At the prospect of murder, but all that occurs is that someone turns off a light.
"Burn one!" calls the restaurant counter-man, and I picture a blackened steak,
But the soda-jerk calmly empties a spoonful of malt in a "shake."
The printer says "Thirty!" and "Put her to bed!" and I wonder who's in distress:
Thirty drinks? No wonder she's sleepy! But he simply means "Start up the press."
The bartender quietly says, "Eighty-six." Is he giving a baseball score?
Oh, no, he's telling the bouncer to toss some drunk through the door.
Ah, the strange and wonderful meanings in the world of jargonese

Are a mystery to a layman; won't someone "update" me, please?

—Hugh P. Fellows[3]

Teen-age slang and jargon is even more of a mystery. Someone has estimated that such a vocabulary changes meaning almost completely about every four years, the time it takes the average freshman in high school to become a senior.

Mario Pei writes that "The only way to make the same word mean the same thing to all men is to subject all people to the selfsame life experience, which is manifestly impossible. Even if it could be done, there is no guarantee that everyone would view the same experiences and occurrences in quite the same way and react alike to the words which symbolize those experiences and occurrences."[4]

In any oral communication, you should try to understand that meanings may vary with differences in time, regions, slang, and jargon. In the parlance of 1979, "Know where *they're* 'coming from,' and make sure that they know where *you're* 'coming from.' "

## SUGGESTED CLASSROOM EXERCISE

### Jargon

Jargon is interesting because many words which have a common meaning for most of use take on a completely different meaning in certain occupations and professions. It is estimated that there are about 2 million such words in our vocabulary (and that does not include *technical terms*).

In the following exercises are listed fifty-one of these words in groups of ten or eleven. Your instructor may wish to divide the class into two or more groups to determine which team can match the specialized words with their "peculiar" meanings in the shortest length of time. In parentheses alongside the words themselves are the figures of speech (such as verb, noun, adjective) in which sense they are most commonly used. In the definitions, also in parentheses, are listed the professions or occupations that use those words in a special sense. Answers are found in Appendix C.

LIST I

1. AIR BRUSH (v. or n.)      A. (Transportation) Steward's quarters on a ship, usually located between decks aft (at the rear).

2. BUMP (v.)      B. (Cosmetology) To remove all color from one's hair.

3. GLORY HOLE (n.)      C. (Decorating) Excessive ornamentation. Originally, carved decorations on exterior of a ship.

4. FADE (v.)

D. (Business) Cash on hand, versus all liabilities, to determine if a firm can meet its immediate debts.

5. GINGERBREAD (n.)

E. (Photography or art) An atomizer to spray paint or ink to give a blurred effect.

6. KITING (v.)

F. (Transportation) To have one's reservation on a plane flight cancelled to make room for a more important person.

7. PAYLOAD (n.)

G. (Transportation) The number of freight cars, passenger cars, and tankers a railroad has.

8. RATIO LIQUIDITY (n.)

H. (Arms) The explosive energy of the warhead of a missile, for example, 50 megatons.

9. ROLLING STOCK (n.)

I. (Banking) To obtain illegal loans from two banks by alternately depositing checks and withdrawing them.

10. STRIP (v.)

J. (Football) When a player moves back toward his own goal with intent to pass.

## LIST II

1. AIR LAYER (v.)

A. (Business) One who believes that corporate stocks will increase.

2. BLEEP (v. or n.)

B. (Nautical) Single circle of a coiled rope. (I = fake, 2 or more = tier, total = coil.)

3. BULL (n.)

C. (Radio-TV) To obliterate with a high-pitched sound words that might be offensive.

4. CAST (n.)

D. (Business) In an auction to bring down the gavel to signify that a sale has been made.

5. EQUITY (n.)

E. (Advertising) The arrangement of print and photos (or drawings) on a page.

6. FAKE (n.)

F. (Business) The central locations in a *grain* exchange for buying and selling.

7. FLOAT (v.)

G. (Business) Calculation, particularly addition.

8. KNOCK DOWN (v.)

H. (Banking) Writing a check to one's self on a distant bank and depositing it into one's local account. By the time the check has been returned, one has had the use of the money for a few days. Banks now protect themselves from this practice.

9. LAYOUT (n.)

I. (Horticulture) To propagate plants by cutting a thin strip of bark from around the circumference of a branch, and applying moist moss enclosed in a bag; the roots will grow on the living plant.

10. PITS (n.)

J. (Real estate) The portion of a property which is already paid for.

## LIST III

1. ACID TEST (n.)

A. (Plumbing) A short pipe that is cast in the shape of the letter "L".

2. BIT (n.)

B. (Mining) Nitroglycerine.

3. BLEED (n.)

C. (Veterinarian) The training of a pet not to excrete in the house or on a specific space.

4. DIBBLE (v.)

D. (Computers) Binary digit—either "zero" or "one."

5. ELBOW (n.)

E. (Business) The line (or hierarchy) of formal authority, running from top to bottom of an organization.

6. FISHYBACK (n. or adj.)

F. (Horticulture) To transplant barely-sprouted seedlings into larger pots or compartments of "trays" for sale.

7. GOLDBRICKING (v. or adj.)

G. (Printing) To deliberately run the edge of a photograph off the edge or corner of a page.

8. HOUSEBREAK (v.)

H. (Transportation) The hauling of trucks or freight cars on barges, boats, or ships.

9. SCALAR CHAIN (n.)

I. (Business) The ratio of liabilities to cash receivable plus marketable securities to equal solvency.

10. SOUP (n.)

J. (Business) Shirking one's work while pretending to be busy.

## LIST IV

1. ARRANGEMENT (n.)

A. (1) (Transportation) Railroad cars or trucks carrying other cars in layers of two or three; (Radio-TV) (2) To run commericals on radio or TV "back to back."

2. BEAR (n.)

B. (Law) Property; especially a trust estate or a trust fund.

3. FEATHERBEDDING (v. or adj.)

C. (Business) Location in a *cotton* exchange for buying and selling.

4. PIGGYBACK (n. or adv.)

D. (Business) Pessimist; one who believes that the value of stocks will decline.

E. (Business) Rumor; originally, talk heard around a navy drinking fountain.

5. REPLEVIN (n.)

6. RES (n.)

F. (Business) Training offered in location *away* from where skills will be performed but in location resembling it.

7. RING (n.)

G. (Law) Wrongful act (*other* than breach of contract), resulting in injury to person, property, or reputation.

8. SCUTTLEBUT (n.)

H. (Law) Petition filed to avoid bankruptcy for mutual advantage of petitioner and creditors.

9. TORT (n.)

I. (Law) Legal suit where buyer has failed to make prescribed payments, or where someone is holding property rightfully belonging to another.

10. TORTE (n.)

J. (Business) Using more workers than the task requires.

11. VESTIBULE TRAINING (n. or v.)

K. (Culinary) Sweet cake, using very little flour, but lots of egg whites, ground nuts, and sugar.

## LIST V

1. BROADSIDE (n.)

A. (Business) To place a piece of unfinished business where it will be remembered on a certain date; a "tickler file."

2. BULLDOG (v.)

B. (Business) An act (or to act) exceeding the rights of a legal charter; therefore, null and void.

3. DRESS STAGE (v.)

C. (Cosmetology) To "frizzle" hair by combing strands of it against its normal growth to give it bulk.

4. LEAN (n.)

D. (Business) Fundamental motions in performing an operation or "cycle of work." Frank and Lillian ___formulated and named it; it is their name spelled backwards!

5. SCISSOR(S) (n. or adj.)

E. (C.B. Radio) Meaning "I understand you."

6. STIPPLE (v. or adj.)

F. (Rodeo) To throw a calf or a steer to the ground by seizing its horns and twisting its neck.

7. TEASE (v.)

G. (Theater) One actor moves laterally to the left or right as another actor moves in the opposite direction, to achieve "balance."

8. TEN-FOUR (v.)

H. (Advertising) A large advertising poster turned to face the flow of traffic.

9. TICKLE (v.)

I. (Wrestling) When one wrestler uses his legs to squeeze another wrestler's head or body.

10. THERBLIG(S) (n.)

J. (Painting) To paint with dots of different colors to achieve an overall blend or texture.

11. ULTRA VIRES ACT (n.)

K. (Printing) Matter difficult to set because of complexity or intermixed fonts.

# FOOTNOTES FOR CHAPTER THREE

[1]Lucinda Bukeley, "English for the Foreign-Born," (unpublished manuscript, copyright, 1977, by Nancy Webb, New York).

[2]Margaret Nicholson, *A Dictionary of American-English Based on Fowler's Modern English Usage* (New York: Signet Books, 1958).

[3]Hugh Fellows, *The Art and Skill of Talking With People* (Englewood Cliffs, N.J.: Prentice-Hall, 1964) p. 30.

[4]Mario Pei, "Problems in Semantics," *Language Today,* Mario Pei and others, (New York: Funk & Wagnalls, 1967) p. 96.

# VOCABULARY STUDY FOR CHAPTER FOUR

Following are some words with which you may not be familiar; they are all used in this chapter. Try to select the correct meaning of each word from the multiple-choice definitions.

1. ACUITY      A. Acting   B. Sharpness, keenness   C. Cuteness.

2. ADMONISH      A. Caution, advise, counsel   B. Polish   C. Bewilder.

3. ANALOGY      A. An itch   B. Symbolic story   C. Similarity, agreement.

4. CELESTIAL      A. Sex with member of the family   B. Heavenly, divine   C. Choosing carefully.

5. CHRONOLOGICAL      A. Chronic condition   B. Crowning of a monarch   C. Arranged according to time.

6. DECADE      A. Deck worker   B. Period of ten years   C. Decay.

7. EQUATE      A. Regard or treat as equal   B. Imaginary line around the globe   C. Odd, peculiar.

8. FLICKER      A. Quarrel   B. Unsteady flame or light   C. A movie.

9. INTERMITTENT      A. Loss of one glove   B. Including all religions   C. Stopping and starting.

10. YORE      A. Belonging to another person   B. Long ago, time past   C. A sore that will not heal.

# 4 | Listening

My notion was that you had been
(Before she had this fit)
An obstacle that came between
Him, and ourselves, and it.
                Lewis Carroll, (1832–1898) *Alice in Wonderland*

Does the above verse make about as much sense as some of the notes you may have taken at a recent class lecture? Don't put all of the blame on the professor; perhaps you simply have not learned to listen well.

Listening to a speaker is not a natural bodily function such as eating and sleeping; it is a *skill* which can be developed. This chapter will try to explain that skill and show you how to enhance your listening ability.

Two friends and I were having coffee at a lunch counter when a man entered and sat on my left. The waiter placed a glass of water in front of him and handed him a menu, returning shortly afterwards to take his order.

"Bacon and eggs and whole wheat toast," the man ordered.

"Yessir, ham and eggs with wheat. How'd you like those eggs?"

"I said *bacon* and eggs," the man repeated. "I'll have the eggs scrambled."

The waiter thanked the man and left. I turned to the friend who was farthest away from me. "Ronnie, did you hear that man when he ordered the first time?"

"Sure. He ordered bacon and the waiter thought he said ham. Happens all the time."

The waiter was directly across the counter from the stranger, and was looking directly at him as he gave his order, while Ronnie was three bodies away and had his eyes on his coffee cup. Perhaps the waiter thought that the stranger *looked* like a ham eater, so he heard what he expected to hear. Or, perhaps he was only half listening.

"Aw, it was a petty thing, and no harm was done," you may think. However, such things, involving more serious matters, happen every day to most of us.

Until a decade or two ago little attention was given to the skill of listening. However, during World War II it was discovered that one of the primary causes of combat fatigue (even above *fear*) among aviators was the strain caused by trying to hear and be heard over interplane radios against a noisy background,[1] so the Armed Forces conducted studies and experiments on speech intelligibility and listening ability. Those studies showed that a person's listening ability can be improved. This skill is quite apart from an individual's hearing acuity.*

## HEARING AND LISTENING

There is a difference between hearing and listening. The person whose hearing is impaired should obtain medical aid. But hearing alone is not enough for comprehension. Someone has said, "You hear with your ears, but you listen with your brain."

## THE PERIL OF POOR LISTENING

We spend about 70 percent of our waking hours in some form of communication. Communication experts agree that it breaks down somewhat as follows:

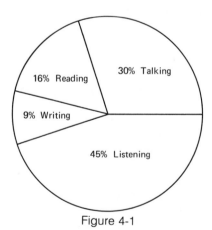

Figure 4-1

*This author was one of the officers helping to conduct those experiments at U.S. Naval Air Stations in Atlanta and Pensacola, 1945–46.

Yet, throughout one's educational training the major emphasis is placed on reading and writing. Listening and speaking now receive more attention, but such courses are not generally offered until high school and are usually electives. By that time, poor listening and speaking habits have become so deeply ingrained that they are difficult to overcome. Although there have been public speaking courses for more than a hundred years, until about thirty-five years ago no one questioned whether or not listening skills could be improved. Listening was equated with paying attention or intelligence. But paying attention in class is not necessarily *listening;* sometimes it only *appears* to be so.

## ACTIVE LISTENING

There is a difference between hearing and listening. The average preschool child has an extremely acute ability to listen. Progressing in school, the child gains increased reading ability, but listening ability *decreases*.[2] Some evidence suggests that high school graduates have poorer listening ability than they had in the first grade. First grade students depend entirely upon their five senses for their knowledge of the world around them. They hear not only *words,* but also the emotional tone of voice, the inflections, and the overall intonation pattern of those words. They use other senses, such as body language, facial expressions, and even a sensitivity to clothing, in order to listen. They are masters of nonverbal communication, which many of us lose as we become adults. We aren't sure why. Perhaps it is because students are constantly admonished in school to "Pay attention to what teacher says!" Or, perhaps it is because students are trained to shut out impressions that seem less important than words, until they become nontotal Receivers.

To listen effectively, one must listen for vocal clues, bodily tensions and relaxations, and gestures, as well as to words.

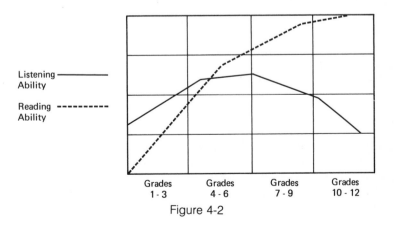

Figure 4-2

Psychological counselors use the term "active listening" in a different sense. Their theory is that the way a client reacts *emotionally* to an event or situation may be more important than the event itself. The couselor focuses on the *emotion* of the client, rather than on the story the client is telling or the facts being reported. Then the counselor *reflects* that emotion back to the client, so that the client may clarify and sort out those emotions in order to choose alternatives as a means of making a decision.[4] For example:

CLIENT: Joey took *my* idea for streamlining the procedure in the mailroom to his supervisor, and pretended it was *his* idea!

COUNSELOR: You resent that, don't you?

CLIENT: You bet I do! But little Joey will *get* his, one of these days . . .

COUNSELOR: I can hear that you're really angry at Joey.

## Concentration and Energy

Effective listening requires concentration and expending physical energy. I was teasing a psychiatrist friend who specializes in psychoanalysis: "What a racket you have! No lesson plans to prepare, no grades to give, no academic red tape to wade through. All you do is to sit in your air-conditioned office all day and listen!"

"Except for the pay, I'd exchange jobs with you any day," he replied. "By the end of six hours, I'm exhausted—absolutely drained of energy. Truly listening to my clients and making mental notes—or actually taking notes for future reference—is the most difficult work I know of."

Several years ago I conducted a survey among two hundred business executives enrolled in oral communication classes at New York University's Office of Special Services to Business and Industry. Each executive agreed to have his secretary log (for one week only) the exact amount of time the executive spent in listening, talking, and writing. The results were startling: Those executives spent an average of 77 percent of their time listening. One of them remarked, "I wouldn't have believed it! My company pays me $60,000 a year, just to *listen?*" Another was not surprised. "That's about the amount of time I spend listening in order to make decisions, and—believe me!—it's not the decisions that are the tough part of my job; it's the *listening!*"

## Distractions and "Blackout Areas"

To study a book, one can usually find a quiet spot where the temperature and light are just right; that is rarely true in a listening situation. The room is too hot or too cold. There is traffic noise coming from an open window. The speakers around the conference table tend to mumble. One should try to remove the distractions if possible—even asking those who are talking to "speak up," if necessary. When the distraction cannot be removed, one must concentrate to overcome it—and that requires physical energy.

Incidentally, researchers have found that a *steady* noise is not as distracting (provided it does not actually bar *hearing*) as are *intermittent* noises, even those of low volume.[3] This is why many libraries pipe in soft music for their reading rooms; it drowns out the unexpected noises of shuffling feet, books being dropped, and whispered conversations.

However, there is a "built-in" distraction for most people; we call it our "blackout area," and there are apt to be more than one. These are words, phrases, or even ideas, that have had some personal unpleasant association in the past, and which one still resents hearing. Upon hearing them, one immediately stops listening and starts thinking:

1. That speaker is attacking me personally by using that word (or idea).
2. What can I do to refute the speaker or get revenge?
3. What will the speaker's reaction be when I counterattack?

Peculiarly enough, most of our blackout areas are not concerned with inflammatory ideas or namecalling, such as *spic, nigger, red-neck, pervert*, etc. A random sampling from students revealed that some of them disliked hearing such words as *dawn, chicken, Bible, rape, flicker*, and *explore*. The late Edward R. Murrow (1908–1965), one of the most famous newsmen and commentators of his day, and head of the United States Information Agency from 1961 to 1964, was never allowed to use "hello" as a greeting during his childhood because his mother had an aversion to the "hell" in it.[5]

What can be done about this listening barrier? First, try to *identify* the words, phrases, or ideas that block your listening. (After all, there should be no taboos on any subject if discussed in an adult manner.) Write them down and discuss them with a friend; you don't need a psychiatrist, rabbi, priest, or even a college professor for this discussion. Then, be on the alert when you hear them, and remind yourself that you must concentrate to keep from becoming defensive, rather than listening to the speaker. Whoever the speaker may be, he probably has a few hang-ups of his own!

## LISTENING TRAINING

While training in listening should begin in the early grades, it is never too late to start. Here are some suggestions for helping you to listen more acutely:

1. *Selective listening.*

    A. For about two minutes each day, go to a relatively quiet surrounding, close your eyes, and try to listen to every sound. Try to identify the source of the sound and the direction from which it comes. Practice listening to *all* sounds. Repeat this procedure for at least five days in the same surroundings.

B. For another two minutes each day, try to find surroundings that are *noisy*, such as a busy street intersection or an airport. Select a sound that is *not* predominant (not the sound of motors starting up or planes taking off) and concentrate on that one minor sound. Try to shut out the predominant sound.

The key to this practice is to learn how to *control* your listening ability. You can either take in *all* the sounds you wish to, or shut out those which you do not wish to concentrate upon.

## 2. *Anticipatory listening*.
For at least three times a week, listen to a speaker and try to anticipate what he or she is going to say before the speaker is halfway through the sentence. Radio or television news commentators are good subjects for this. Don't be surprised if you cannot *always* anticipate the ending of the sentence. Usually, however, you can.

## 3. *Listening for note taking*.
In a longer speech (perhaps one of your professors') practice anticipatory listening, and then try to recapitulate what the speaker has said at the end of each sentence. This is fairly easy to do, since we generally *speak* at a rate of 150 words per minute but *think* at a rate of more than twice that speed. Try this for a while before you begin to take notes. Then, after you have had some practice at recapping what has been said, use your judgment to decide what is worth taking down on paper and what is *not* worth taking down.

Usually, professional speakers will let you know when they have finished one topic and are going on to another by using a transitional phrase such as:

"Moving on, we find that . . ." "To pursue the matter further . . ."
"Now, let's see what happens . . ." "On the other hand . . ."
"So far, we have found that . . ." "In addition to these facts . . ."
"To summarize . . ." "So far, so good, but . . ."

## 4. *Listening for the central idea*.
Experiments by the late Irving Lee[6] at Northwestern University indicated that less than 25 percent of college students could get the central idea from listening to a ten-to-fifteen-minute speech. Most of them picked out a trivial incident or an idea that interested them but that was used for *support* of the main idea, rather than the main idea itself.

Some speakers, however, seem determined to *avoid* making themselves clear, and their central ideas are buried in a plethora of meaningless phrases. Witness this account by Mark Twain of an interview with the humorist Artemus Ward. Ward is asking Twain a "simple" question about silver mining:

Now, what I want to get at is—is, well, the way the deposits of ore are made, you know. For instance: Now, as I understand it, the vein which contains the silver is sandwiched in between casings of granite, and runs along the ground, and sticks up like a curbstone. Well, take a vein forty feet thick, for example, or eight, or even a hundred—say you go down on it with a shaft, straight down, you know, or with what you call "incline," maybe you go down five hundred feet, or maybe you don't go down but two hundred—anyway you go down, and all the time this vein grows narrower, when the casings come nearer or approach each other, you may say—that is, when they do approach, which, of course, they don't always do, particularly in cases where the nature of the formation is such that they stand apart wider than they otherwise would, and which geology has failed to account for, although everything in that science goes to prove that, all things being equal, it would if it did not, or would not certainly if it did, and then, of course, they are. Don't you think it is?

Mark Twain, *Sketches Old and New*

Of course Ward was spoofing with the young reporter, Twain, but there are people who talk like that!

**5.** *Listening for structure.*
Most good speakers use one of several structures in making a presentation. The structure will vary with the content of the presentation. Some of them are:

A. Simple enumeration. The main topics should be limited to three—certainly not more than five—with a summary at the close of the presentation.

B. Chronological order. Useful in describing incidents that lead up to a main event. The incidents should be brief, and not more than four or five of them should be given as contributing to the important event.

C. Geographical or spatial order. These are really the same, except for the area covered. In describing conditions in the United States, the speaker may divide the country into four geographical areas. In describing your college campus, the speaker might begin with the northeast corner and go clockwise around the entire campus.

D. The problem-solution order. Briefly, the speaker states a problem and gives possible solutions to it, usually recommending a solution. Sometimes a short history of the events leading up to the existing problem is given, but this is not always necessary.

E. The cause-to-effect or the effect-to-cause structure. Closely related to the problem-solution structure, this involves presenting causes of the problem. The listener should listen with a critical ear when this structure is used; it is rare that a *single* cause brings about a particular effect.

Since many speakers are not well organized, you may find none of the foregoing structures—or any other—in their presentations. If you cannot determine *early* in the presentation what sort of structure is being used, stop searching for one and try to listen for ideas, concepts, and figures or statistics. You can sort them into some sort of order after the speaker has finished.

In summary, to be an effective listener, one must realize that (a) listening requires physical energy and concentration; (b) one must listen with one's eyes as well as ears to obtain nonverbal clues for meaning; (c) one must anticipate a speaker's sentences in order to evaluate them and take notes, and (d) one must listen for structures and the central idea.

## SUGGESTED CLASS EXERCISE

### Recognizing Central Ideas

Each of the following passages contains five sentences. One of the sentences is the central idea and the others are subordinate to it. Each sentence is consecutively numbered. Try to select the sentence that serves as the central idea. If you wish to test your *listening ability,* have a classmate *read* the passage to you, rather than reading it yourself.

## I. "The Florist Business"

(1) Christmas brings good sales for poinsettias and evergreens, but not much else. (2) Chrysanthemums sell well during the football season, if your business is near a college or a university. (3) The florist business is extremely seasonal. (4) Violets and sweetheart roses are a big item for St. Valentine's day, but they're hard to get. (5) Easter lilies don't sell well in certain neighborhoods, no matter what the season.

## II. "Tuberculosis in the U.S.A."

(1) The Southern states had the largest number of reported cases last year. (2) The West Coast states and adjoining states had the fewest number of reported cases last year. (3) America's largest cities (Atlanta, Chicago, Detroit, Los Angeles, New Orleans, and New York) reported the highest per capita number of cases of the disease. (4) Tuberculosis seems to thrive in slum areas and ghettos. (5) Tuberculosis is still undefeated in the U.S.A.

## III. "The Travel Agency Business"

(1) Travel agents in the Far West inform us that 80 percent of their foreign and domestic travel comes from Seattle, Los Angeles, and San Francisco. (2) Agents from New York City, Philadelphia, and Hartford claim they sell more tickets to residents of their own cities than to travelers from anywhere else. (3) Boston travel agents report that 45 percent of their travelers live in rural New England. (4) People from the large cities, rather than from rural areas, comprise the bulk of all travel, both foreign and domestic. (5) Travel agents in the South inform us that 85 percent of their tourists come from Houston, Birmingham, New Orleans, and Atlanta.

## IV. "Television As a Sales Medium"

(1) Charles Siepmann, former member of the Federal Communications Commission and one of the authors of the "Bluebook" regulating television and radio practices, stated that the main difference between radio and television is that "radio *advertises,* but television *sells* products." (2) Wealthy people are affected

less by television advertising than any other class. (3) Children are affected by television advertising and try to influence their parents' buying habits. (4) People from the lowest economic scale would be the largest potential buyers of products advertised on television if they had the means to do so. (5) Television advertising is targeted in the U.S. to the large middle class.

## V. "Solar Energy"

(1) A physics professor at the University of Florida and his two sons built and installed a solar hot water system for their family of six; the cost, aside from labor, was only $290.00, and it has paid for itself in two years. (2) The ancient Incas of Peru are believed to have harnessed the power of the sun in order to move and put into place the 80-ton granite stones used in the building of Machu Picchu. (3) Taking his cue from the sundial, a professor of thermodynamics at Miami University has perfected a clock powered by solar energy that is 95 percent accurate and works twenty-four hours a day. (4) Skylab depended upon the sun to recharge its batteries, generating millions of energy units. (5) There is still a vast untapped source of energy in the sun, and no nation has a monopoly on it.

## VI. "American Initiative"[7]

(1) An old adage says that "Necessity is the mother of invention," and while they are not really necessary to our existence, many of our treats are the results of American inventiveness. (2) Arnold Feuchtwanger, a Bavarian immigrant who sold piping-hot sausages on the streets of St. Louis in 1904, could not afford to serve them with silverware or dishes; he slipped them into a slit on a long bread roll so that his customers would not burn their fingers—and invented the frankfurter. (3) George Crum, an American Indian chef at a plush hotel in Saratoga Spa, N.Y., could not satisfy a difficult diner who complained that his french fried potatoes were too thick; angrily Crum grabbed a knife and sliced the potatoes paper-thin before frying them—thereby initiating potato chips, which were called "Saratoga Chips" for a long time after Crum fried his first one in 1853. (4) In 1912 Clarence Crane hired a local pillmaker to press hard candy mints for him to sell, but the machinery was defective and stamped out mints with round holes in their centers; Crane turned this liability into an asset and called them "Life Savers"; since then, 29 *billion* rolls have been sold! (5) Ernest A. Hamwi, a Damascus-born pastry maker, sold thin sweet hot pancakes (crepes) at the St. Louis World's Fair in 1904; when a neighboring ice cream vendor ran out of dishes, Hamwi rolled one of his pancakes into a

cone, allowed it to cool, and plopped a scoop of ice cream on top; the ice cream cone was an immediate success.

## VII. "Older Women"*

(1) *La Belle Poitrine,* the French singer and dancer, had—at age seventy-eight— a string of lovers, all under the age of thirty, who vied for her favors by sending her flowers, candy, and jewelry. (2) Certain older women have always fascinated men much younger than themselves. (3) Lady Delia Howard-Duff, an *impoverished* English noblewoman, married three consecutive husbands in her late fifties and early sixties, all of them in their twenties—and *wealthy.* (4) One of Hollywood's successful marriages has lasted for twenty-five years; the husband is forty-five, and the wife thirty years his senior. (5) Baroness Maria von Papendorf was, at the age of seventy-six, the subject of a duel for her affection; the duelists were ages twenty-six and thirty-five.

### *ANSWERS to the exercise on SELECTING THE CENTRAL IDEA at the end of this chapter:*

I - (3) The florist business is extremely seasonal.

II - (5) Tuberculosis is still undefeated in the U.S.A.

III - (4) People from the large cities, rather than from rural areas, comprise the bulk of all travel, both foreign and domestic.

IV - (5) Television advertising is targeted in the U.S.A. to the large middle class.

V - (5) There is still a vast untapped source of energy in the sun, and no nation has a monopoly on it.

VI - (1) An old adage says that "Necessity is the mother of invention," and while they are not really necessary to our existence, many of our treats are the results of American inventiveness.

VII - (2) Certain older women have always fascinated men much younger than themselves.

If you found it difficult to locate the central idea in the foregoing paragraphs, refer to the BUSINESS WRITING section of this book and you will realize that placing the topic sentence either at the beginning or the end of the paragraph makes the central idea easier to identify.

## FOOTNOTES FOR CHAPTER FOUR

[1]Max Steer, "Speech Intelligibility and Noise" (unpublished bulletin, U.S. Navy, 1945).
[2]Ralph G. Nichols and Leonard A. Stevens, *Are You Listening?* (New York: McGraw Hill, 1957).

*All names in this exercise are fictitious, but the facts are accurate.

[3]Karl D. Kryter, *The Effects of Noise on Man* (New York: Academic Press, 1970).

[4]Condensed from a training program for volunteer counselors offered by Hillsborough County Suicide and Crisis Center, Tampa, Florida.

[5]Recounted by Howard K. Smith, a close friend of Murrow's, in an interview on PBS-TV, July 25, 1979.

[6]Irving Lee, *How to Talk With People* (New York: Harper & Brothers, 1952).

[7]Paraphrased from Bruce Felton and Mark Fowler, *Famous Americans You Never Knew Existed* (Briarcliff Manor, N.Y.: Stein & Day, Scarborough House, 1979). Used by permission.

# VOCABULARY STUDY FOR CHAPTER FIVE

Following are some words used in this chapter with which you may not be familiar. Select the meaning of each word from the multiple-choice definitions.

1. AMPUTEE — A. A measurement of electricity  B. An Eskimo's leather boot  C. A person who has lost one or more limbs, usually by surgery.

2. APOCRYPHAL — A. Concerning an age or epoch  B. Of doubtful authenticity  C. A skin condition.

3. CATEGORICALLY — A. Sarcastically  B. Absolute; unqualified and unconditional  C. Rarely found.

4. EQUIVOCATION — A. An algebraic equation  B. From *equine,* the capers of a horse  C. The use of unclear expressions, often to avoid or mislead.

5. FACET — A. One of the small flat surfaces of a cut and polished stone  B. A water tap  C. From "facetious"— a witty person.

6. HIERARCHY — A. The highest arch in a structure  B. A system of persons or things ranked one above another  C. One's natural (though not legal) rights.

7. INEXTRICABLE — A. Incapable of being untangled, undone, or solved  B. One who pretends to be an expert  C. A trick that is easily figured out.

8. INTROSPECTION — A. Inspecting a stranger when introduced  B. The act of looking within one's self thoughtfully  C. Speculation on the stock market.

9. LUCRATIVE — A. Profitable, moneymaking  B. From the Spanish *luz* (light), enlightened  C. Any gumlike substance.

10. PATHOLOGICAL — A. Incapable of telling the truth  B. Referring to the lines or "paths" on a weather map  C. Any deviation from a healthy, normal, or efficient condition.

11. SPASMODIC — A. Concerns space modules  B. Reflecting light  C. Sudden, violent, but brief.

12. STIGMALT — A. One who is disgraced  B. No such word  C. Type of printer's ink.

# 5 | Intrapersonal Communication

The best way to study human nature is when nobody
else is present.

Tom Masson (1866–1934)

The process of communication is so inextricably intertwined with psychology
that in recent years the term *intrapersonal communication* has become an
integral part of communication studies.

All of us see ourselves in many ways. We find ourselves cast in numerous
roles as we grow older, but our self-image is often shaped in our formative
years by three influences or forces:

1. The comments and criticisms of our parents, our teachers, and our peers.

2. Our *comparison* of ourselves with others, usually our peers, but not always; this
   depends upon whether or not we have a strong and influential adult whom we
   wish to "be like." That adult person may change from time to time.

3. Our own self-image, probably drawn from the previous two. Often this tends to
   be "good" or "bad", "successful" or "unsuccessful", "right" or "wrong". There are
   often no gray shades, but only sharp blacks and whites.

Therefore, the following brief self-inventory contains no right or wrong answers. This chapter will later ask you to complete an attitude test that may

|  |  | *Yes* | *No* |
|---|---|---|---|
| I. | *My Physical Self* |  |  |
| | A. I worry about my health and wonder, "What would happen if . . . ?" | ____ | ____ |
| | B. I try to keep healthy consciously by eating a balanced diet and getting plenty of sleep and exercise. | ____ | ____ |
| | C. I consider myself attractive to people of both sexes. | ____ | ____ |
| | D. My interests are varied: |  |  |
| |    1. I have good manual dexterity. | ____ | ____ |
| |    2. I dance well. | ____ | ____ |
| |    3. I like to fix things around the house. | ____ | ____ |
| |    4. I excel in at least one sport. | ____ | ____ |
| II. | *My Outer Self* |  |  |
| | A. My clothes communicate who I think I am. | ____ | ____ |
| | B. I wear what I am comfortable wearing and don't care what others think. | ____ | ____ |
| | C. Others compliment me on my clothes or my physique. | ____ | ____ |
| | D. I have heard a tape recording of my voice and I like it. | ____ | ____ |
| | E. People compliment me on my skills in |  |  |
| |    1. Mathematics. | ____ | ____ |
| |    2. English. | ____ | ____ |
| |    3. Typing. | ____ | ____ |
| |    4. Others (do not include sports). | ____ | ____ |
| III. | *My Social Self* |  |  |
| | A. I consider my family life satisfactory. | ____ | ____ |
| | B. My family disagrees often | ____ | ____ |
| |    1. When it's over, we laugh about it. | ____ | ____ |
| |    2. We mistrust one another. | ____ | ____ |
| |    3. They respect my opinions in general. | ____ | ____ |
| | C. I feel confident about myself. | ____ | ____ |
| | D. I consider myself easygoing and cheerful. | ____ | ____ |
| | E. When a stranger or foreign-looking person comes into my group (church, school, or business), I respond by |  |  |
| |    1. Waiting to see how that person is going to be accepted by the group. | ____ | ____ |

2. Immediately trying to be friendly
   to that person.                                    ____        ____
F. I am most comfortable with
   1. People of the opposite sex.                     ____        ____
   2. People of the same sex.                         ____        ____
G. I consider myself popular with both
   sexes.                                             ____        ____
H. I can *really* understand others' points
   of view.                                           ____        ____
I. My close friends number
   (Give the actual number.)      Female              ____
                                  Male                ____
J. In a competitive game:
   1. When I lose, I try to explain why
      I lost.                                         ____        ____
   2. When I win, I boast about it.                   ____        ____
K. I enjoy belonging to the following
   kinds of groups:
   1. Sports teams.                                   ____        ____
   2. Fraternal organizations.                        ____        ____
   3. Church groups.                                  ____        ____
L. I can accept criticism and be grateful
   to the person who gives it.                        ____        ____
M. When I receive criticism, it comes
   easier from
   1. A friend.                                       ____        ____
   2. A stranger.                                     ____        ____
   3. An enemy.                                       ____        ____

show you specific *areas* of communication you may need to work on more than others. Notice that in the following inventory there are only two choices, "yes" or "no." You will avoid "sometimes," "perhaps," and other equivocations.

There are many conditions attached to these statements, or implied by them. Having to give a "yes" or "no" response may force you to an awareness of three facets of yourself. Further research is being conducted into the correlation between how individuals evaluate themselves and how they communicate at the time of this writing.

The next sets of statements tend to move away from introspection and blend into interpersonal communication skills. Note that some of the statements themselves are negative and can be responded to with either a "yes" or "no". These statements are followed by a key so that you can score yourself. They are arranged in groups of five to make the scoring easier.

IV. *My Self as A Communicator*

| | Yes | No |
|---|---|---|

**GROUP ONE**

    A. I consider myself a good conversation-alist with all types of people. \_\_\_\_ \_\_\_\_

    B. I can talk easily to one or two persons but not to a large group of people. \_\_\_\_ \_\_\_\_

    C. I know *what* I want to say but not how to say it. \_\_\_\_ \_\_\_\_

    D. When I speak, even in a discussion group, people listen to me eagerly. \_\_\_\_ \_\_\_\_

    E. Often I don't listen to others because I'm preoccupied with my own ideas. \_\_\_\_ \_\_\_\_

**GROUP TWO**

    A. I never correct another person, even if I know he is wrong, for fear of an argument. \_\_\_\_ \_\_\_\_

    B. I feel tense and fearful at *all* times when I must stand up and speak to a group. \_\_\_\_ \_\_\_\_

    C. Others have told me that I express myself in a clear and well-organized manner. \_\_\_\_ \_\_\_\_

    D. I think that I have good voice and diction and that my vocabulary is satisfactory. \_\_\_\_ \_\_\_\_

    E. Even if I know I am apt to disagree with a person, I still listen closely to his ideas. \_\_\_\_ \_\_\_\_

**GROUP THREE**

    A. I enjoy sharing my ideas with others and am curious about their ideas. \_\_\_\_ \_\_\_\_

    B. I never know how others will respond or whether they will be hostile to my ideas. \_\_\_\_ \_\_\_\_

    C. It is hard for me to find examples that will illustrate what I want to say. \_\_\_\_ \_\_\_\_

    D. People often don't hear me or understand me clearly. \_\_\_\_ \_\_\_\_

    E. When other people talk, my mind wanders, or I am often distracted by things around me. \_\_\_\_ \_\_\_\_

**GROUP FOUR**

    A. I tend to judge others by their appearance; don't all of us do this? \_\_\_\_ \_\_\_\_

    B. When I speak to a group, I feel that they will criticize my clothes, or that I won't

remember what to say, and my hand
starts shaking.
C. I always "think through" a sentence before speaking.
D. In a group discussion, I hesitate to speak
because others seem to know so much
more about the subject than I do.
E. It is easy for me to summarize what a
speaker has said, or what a group has
discussed.

*GROUP FIVE*
A. I find it easy to change my language if
I feel that I'm not reaching people.
B. I have difficulty looking directly at an
entire audience, and usually look in one
spot.
C. Even when using the telephone, I usually organize what I'm going to say, and
sometimes even jot it down.
D. I am unsure of my grammar and pronunciation.
E. Unless individuals are rude, I can't tell
whether or not they are listening to me.

## Scoring Yourself As A Communicator

In all of the five foregoing groups, each letter of the alphabet concerns itself
with the same facet of communication. For instance:

All of the "A's" concerned themselves with small group (dyadic or triadic)
communication. If you had a preponderance of negative scores among the A's,
perhaps you should devote more study to conversation and interviews so that
you will be more at ease in small group situations.

The "B's" were statements concerning what is popularly called *stage fright*,
which is further discussed in this chapter.

The "C's" were statements regarding organizing and preparing your presentations. One statement in particular may surprise you, but a good business
man or woman even plans his or her telephone calls!

All of the "D's" concerned voice and diction. An authoritative voice and clear
speech are absolutely necessary for anyone in the business or professional
hierarchy.

If you had a high negative score on the "E's," it is a good indication that you
have not yet learned to concentrate on *listening*. You might go back to Chapter
Two and practice the suggestions given there for this most important function.

Don't be discouraged if you had low scores on more than one of the preceding groups. You wouldn't be reading this book if you were already skilled in communication.

## SPEECH ANXIETY—CAUSES AND CONTROL

This form of fear has a misleading name "stage fright," since it happens less often on the stage than it does in other real-life situations;[1] for instance

1. You must make a report to supervisors from other plants on handling staff personnel.
2. You ask the boss for what you consider a well-deserved pay raise.
3. You are called into the Dean's office for what you thought was a harmless prank, but which had serious consequences.
4. You have a new video tape recorder and you call in your neighbors who are eager to see a program that they have missed.

In all of the foregoing situations, you may have a little fear or stage fright but situation no. 4 is different from the others. After you become accustomed to adjusting the new video tape recorder, you lose your anxiety about it but you are likely *never* to lose your anxiety about the first three situations.

While mechanical appliances remain the same for the most part, you can't expect the same thing where people are concerned, because they are *never* quite the same from day to day. Even couples who have been married for twenty years, and who think they know each other's every mood, may be in for a surprise from their mates.

### Causes

Psychologists tell us that the *basic* fear is the fear of falling. You can induce fear in a two-day-old infant by holding it securely in your hands and then suddenly removing support and letting it fall a few inches before catching it again.[2] The infant will tense its muscles spasmodically, and then scream. (Don't try it; just take our word for it!) *Support,* to which the infant has *always* been accustomed—even within its mother's womb—has suddenly been removed and it is being plunged down to—where? "Man is always afraid of the *unknown.*" People are always an unknown quality.

There are two types of fear: (1) instantaneous fear and (2) conditioned fear. Instantaneous fear is the fear that one experiences when an elevator suddenly lurches downward without warning, or when one encounters any unknown situation. Conditioned fear is that which comes from a long experience with people who are untrustworthy or brutal (not necessarily physical brutality, but also psychic brutality). We react *in much the same way* to the two because our bodies cannot distinguish between them.

A set of glands just above the kidneys, called the adrenal glands, produce *adrenalin,* a powerful organic stimulant. When fear sets in, those adrenal glands shoot adrenalin into the liver, causing it to manufacture almost instantly a large amount of blood sugar, thereby providing an excessive amount of energy. These glands are one of nature's safeguards, to provide energy in an emergency. If you compared a blood sample of a person who has just dodged a dagger aimed at his head with that of a person who has a pathological dread of talking to a group of people, you would find the same excessive amount of blood sugar. It is difficult to work off that surplus energy when you are supposed to be standing calmly before a group of people. So, your blood rushes to your head, your mouth gets dry, you twist your fingers nervously, pace back and forth, or talk rapidly in a high-pitched voice. You're scared!

*Conditioned stage fright* is a different thing. There are people who have such a deep-seated feeling of inadequacy about speaking that it is painful physically for them to make a presentation. DeWitt and Lila Wallace, in their *Book of Lists*,[3] name public speaking as the *greatest* fear of the American public. This bit of research was written by a graduate student at New York University:

> In teaching adult education students in public speaking courses, I discovered many who were simply incapable of getting up before the class. I tried everything I knew to encourage them, but their "stage fright" was so deep that most of them dropped out of the course before it was over.
>
> After three years (six semesters) of such discouragement, I finally persuaded sixty of them, over the next five years, to visit the head of the Psychology Department, who was a practicing clinical psychologist. The psychologist found, without exception, that one or more of three things gave them a lingering feeling of inadequacy: (a) a social background that was judged "inferior" in early youth, (b) an irrational sense of guilt, and (c) a *minor* physical defect.
>
> Since we were unable to find enough suitable adult students to act as a "control group," the study was abandoned.[4]

## Controls

It is useless to try to dismiss stage fright as silly and unfounded; in some people it is *very* real. We, personally, have known two writers and a scientist who have been offered lucrative contracts by a lecture bureau, but who had stage fright to such a pathological degree that their physicians advised against it. However, it *can* be controlled.

*Instantaneous stage fright* is that which many of us get when faced with the unknown. Here are some suggestions for controlling it:

*First,* be prepared. If you know what you are going to say and have rehearsed it aloud *twice,* you are ready. Memorized presentations should be avoided, but if it will give you confidence, memorize the beginning and the end of your speech. Actually memorizing the *end* would seem more important: At the beginning there may be a special introduction that you will wish to acknowledge, or an event of current interest on which you wish to comment, making it awkward to use a "canned" opening. However, if you have memorized your closing statements you can manage to get to them somehow.

*Second,* control your breathing. Never let your breathing become rapid and shallow; you can actually induce fear *without cause* by doing so. A minute or so before you are to speak, take the deepest breath you can manage on a slow count of "four"; hold it for a slow count of "two," and then let it out on a slow count of "three." If necessary, put a note to yourself on the margin of your notepad: "Breathe slowly!"

*Third,* try to engage in some planned, controlled physical activity just before you start to speak: Erase the chalkboard vigorously; move the table or lectern slightly; grip the edge of the table three times firmly and let go. The keynote here is "planned and controlled"; it must not be random movement, or it will only increase your nervousness.

*Finally,* adopt a good attitude toward your listeners. They *don't want you to fail* in your presentation. They don't want to be bored. And, they are all thinking, "There, but for the grace of God, stand I!" There is a story (probably apocryphal) told about Olympic ice-skater, Sonja Henie: During an exhibition solo, she slipped and fell flat. The audience gasped. Miss Henie, not bothering to tidy her costume, continued the exhibition as if nothing had happened, to the wild applause of the spectators. The story goes that, after that, she always took one *deliberate* "fall." It endeared her to her audience; she made them realize that even the great Sonja Henie was capable of a mistake.

In working with blind people for more than twenty years, and in doing speech correction work among amputees for more than a year, I never encountered a single one who had any hesitation about making a public presentation. This was what puzzled me about Alan Price's study when he named only "minor" physical defects. These were defects such as being too skinny, being too fat, or having a poor complexion or poor teeth. Perhaps it is because those people with *major* physical defects have had to learn to live with them because they are irreversible. Apparently, it is "the *little* foxes that spoil the vines." (*The Bible,* "Song of Solomon" 2:15.)

Much the same can be said about a socially inferior background and a sense of guilt for what has happened in the past. A psychiatrist once remarked that one of the chief causes of people's unhappiness was their constant burden of guilt about something that happened so long ago that it should be forgotten, or about something they are not really responsible for in the present. You cannot change the past, and you can only change the present to a degree, but the pages of the future are clean; write on them with confidence!

A certain amount of stage fright can be good *if* you *control* it. Speakers who have no concern about how well their message is getting across to others, or whether it is received or rejected, will find that the listeners care as little about the speaker as the speaker does about them. If you don't feel some anxiety about how you and your message are going to be received, your listeners can *sense* that you don't care about them, and they will respond to that.

To summarize speech anxiety: (1) If you have it, you'll probably never get rid of it, but you'll be in good company; many famous people—theatrical performers as well as business and professional people—have it also. (2) It *can* be controlled if you make a conscious effort. (3) A certain amount of anxiety is good for your message; the receivers may realize that you *care* about them.

## SUGGESTED CLASSROOM EXERCISE

### Communicating to a Partner

Just before the end of a class period the instructor may pair off the students for a "buzz session." Even though the group may know one another's names, each student is to be known only as "Mr. A," "Miss B," and so forth. (If the class numbers more than twenty-six, the alphabet can be repeated with "Miss Double-A" . . . ) The paired-off students withdraw to various parts of the room or to the corridor.

The students are instructed to shake hands and introduce themselves by their fictitious names (A, B, C . . . ). Then individual students talk about the *skills* they possess, or hope to acquire, for not more than three minutes. The other students may take notes or ask questions if they wish.

At the following class meeting, all students will report on their partners as communicators, identifying their partner only by the alphabetical name, and answer the following questions:

1. Did the partner have a firm handshake? Loose? Limp?
2. Did the partner stand too far away? Too close?
3. Did the partner speak with enthusiasm about his/her skills (or hoped-for skills)?
4. Did the partner have any *pronounced* mannerisms, such as
    A. Playing with coins or keys in a pocket, or playing with a necklace or charm bracelet?
    B. Mouth distractions, such as chewing on a paper clip or pencil, chewing gum, biting fingernails, or chain smoking?
    C. Touching her/his hair too often?
    D. Scratching his/her body?
5. Did the partner show interest in your skill?

Each report should take only a minute or two. Class discussion is not suggested until all of the students have reported, for reasons of anonymity and brevity.

## FOOTNOTES FOR CHAPTER FIVE

[1]George Hill in *Time Magazine,* August 13, 1979, pp. 64–65.

[2]Arthur T. Jersild, Charles W. Telford, and James M. Sawrey, *Child Psychology* 7th ed. (Englewood Cliffs, N.J.: Prentice-Hall, 1975).

[3]DeWitt and Lila Wallace, *The People's Almanac Presents "The Book of Lists"* (New York: William Morrow, 1977).

[4]Alan Price, (unpublished term paper under the direction of Dr. Dorothy Mulgrave, 1955).

# VOCABULARY STUDY FOR CHAPTER SIX

Following are words used in this chapter with which you may not be familiar. Try to select the multiple-choice definition that fits the word. Answers are in Appendix C at the end of this book.

1. CONCOMITANT — A. Accompanies, or goes along with automatically B. Shipping charges   C. A military aide.

2. CONSONANTS — A. Members of a consortium   B. The noises in speech, made by breath or sound being inhibited by lips, tongue or teeth   C. Hired mourners at a funeral.

3. DICTION — A. Acceptable style and enunciation of a speaker B. Mandate   C. Opposite of friction.

4. EMULATE — A. Try to equal or excel   B. Arab State on the Persian Gulf   C. To fertilize.

5. GUTTURAL — A. A throaty sound like a growl   B. A "gut" feeling C. Breathing from stomach.

6. LUDICROUS — A. Describes a malignant growth   B. On a losing streak in gambling   C. Amusingly absurd or ridiculous; comical.

7. ORGANIC — A. Pertaining to the organs of a plant or animal B. Music from a wind instrument   C. Made from natural elements of plants or animals.

8. TONUS — A. Toxic   B. The pitch of a human voice   C. Normal state of continuous slight tension in muscle tissue, to facilitate response to stimuli.

9. VACILLATING — A. Lubricating   B. Injecting   C. Wavering in mind or opinion

10. VOWELS — A. The open, unobstructed sounds in speech   B. The pauses between consonants   C. The parts of speech that make us heard.

# 6 Voice and Diction

Actions lie louder than words.

Carolyn Wells (187?–1942)

Blanche Yurka,* the late international actress, once said, "Let me hear two sentences spoken spontaneously by a person, and I can tell you that person's cultural and educational background and something about that person's temperament." Most of us cannot claim such expertise, but we all know that a voice that is strident, hoarse, guttural, or nasal interferes with our receiving the message—or at least until we become accustomed to it. And some people have voices so unpleasant that we find it difficult to *ever* listen to what they say.

John Morley (1838–1923), the English editor and statesman, wrote, "Three things matter in speech: *Who* says it, *how* he says it, and *what* he says—and, of the three, the last matters the least." We don't subscribe to that altogether; it seems to us that *what* is said—the message—is more important than how it is said. Nevertheless, business and professional people do far more talking than writing; hence, it is valuable to devote at least some time and effort to developing a speaking voice that is firm, authoritative, and pleasant. Barring an organic speech defect, anyone can cultivate an effective speaking voice.

## Listen to Yourself

Use a tape recorder and listen to yourself. Do not read, but *talk* into the microphone. Perhaps you can get a friend to assist you: Tell the friend a story

*A close personal friend of the author for more than thirty years.

about something that happened to you, and talk for approximately three minutes. As you listen to the playback, ask yourself these questions:

1. Is the quality of my voice good? Is it too high-pitched? Do I have a nasal* "twang" or "whine"? Is it resonant? Is it "throaty" or hoarse?

2. Do I sound monotonous? There are two types of monotony: monotone and monorate. The first is when you drone along without varying the pitch of your voice; the second is when you talk at the same rate of speed for all sentences and phrases.

3. Do I emphasize the idea-carrying words and phrases? This chapter will discuss how to achieve emphasis in four ways.

4. Are the idea-carrying words and phrases spoken with clarity? Do I mumble? Do I leave out consonants (which give speech vigor), and do I distort vowels (which carry resonance)?

If you tape a sample of good speech from your radio or television set, you can work alone to improve your voice and diction, with surprisingly good results if you have a sensitive ear. Here is how it works:

1. Select someone who has won recognition by appearing on one of the national networks, but who is neither too dramatic or monotonous. If you are a man, record a man's voice; if you are a woman, use a woman commentator.

2. After you have made your recording, erase sentences #2, #4, and #6. (You will need some sort of marker in order to determine where the erasures start and end.)

3. Listen to sentence #1 several times and repeat it aloud. Then listen to it again and stop the recorder; switch from "listen" to "record" and make a recording of yourself saying that same sentence. Replay them and listen to the difference. Do this several times for each sentence.

There is no substitute for a good teacher who can detect *where* you distort certain sounds and *how* you can correct them. But if you work at it long enough, you can accomplish a lot. Try to select a different commentator each week. Your aim is not to *imitate* but to *emulate*.


## A GOOD SPEAKING VOICE

There are three requisites for obtaining a good speaking voice:

1. A steady column of *controlled* breath.
2. A relaxed throat and an "open" mouth.
3. An agile tongue and mobile lips.

*What the average layman calls "nasality" is actually the opposite, denasality; that is, there is not enough breath passing through the nasal passages to give resonance to the sounds of *m*, *n*, and *ng*.

These requirements are interdependent. Without controlled breath one cannot carry the sound waves into the resonating chambers and acquire a good tone and sufficient volume; without a relaxed throat and open mouth (plus clear nasal passages) one *has* no resonating chambers to control; without an agile tongue and mobile lips, one cannot make the consonant noises that are necessary to be understood by others; sufficient *breath* is also necessary for most of the consonants.

## Diaphragmatic Breathing

There is nothing mysterious about diaphragmatic breathing; we all breathe from the diaphragm while sleeping. Singers and speakers are urged to breathe this way *consciously* because (a) it is the *quickest* way to get air into the lower lungs, and (b) it allows the upper muscles of the chest and neck to relax, thereby providing more resonating space.

Charlatans have made extravagant claims for the "mysterious values of diaphragmatic breathing," often charging enormous sums for its "secret." They have been able to do so because the average layman does not know the actual physiology of breathing. Basically it can be summed up in one sentence: *You do not breathe in order to expand your chest cavity; instead, you expand your chest cavity in order to draw in breath.*

The lungs are like sponges, and when the chest cavity is expanded, the lungs expand and draw in breath. Most of us are familiar with the calisthenics teacher who told us in grade school, "Take a deep breath and expand your chest." But you can also expand the chest cavity by lowering the diaphragm, as shown in Figure 6-1. The diaphragm is a large muscle that separates the stomach cavity from the chest cavity; it forms the base of the pleural sac, which contains the lungs. Unless the muscles controlling it have been developed by specific exercises, nature uses it primarily to draw breath into our bodies while we are

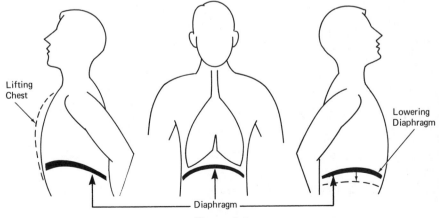

Figure 6-1

asleep. The upper part of the chest (bones, muscles, flesh) is heavy, and we would never get the required relaxation as we sleep if nature had to lift all of that weight. So, instead, only the *one* muscle is used to draw breath into the lungs. To summarize: You can get breath into the lungs (a) by expanding the chest, (b) by lowering the diaphragm, or (c) by using both.

*Exercises:*

1. With your arms extended in front of you at chin level, interlock your fingers, and turn your hands palms outward (that is, facing *away* from you). Take a very deep breath; you should feel your waistband become a bit tighter. Try pushing all of your breath out on a count of one ("Huh!"). Take another breath, and see how long you can count on the one breath.

2. Standing (preferably barefoot) about two feet from a vertical wall, extend your arms fully above your head, in vertical line with your ears. Fall forward, and let the weight of your body rest on the "heels" of your hands. *Keep your body in a straight line.* (See Figure 6-2.) Take a very deep breath and push it out on a count of one ("Huh!"). Take another breath and see how far you can count on the one breath.

These are only "crutches" for you to get the "feel" of diaphragmatic breathing. Try them several times a week, repeating each one half a dozen times. Two important points should be made:

1. You should feel breath coming into the bottom of your lungs *all around* your body—not just in front.

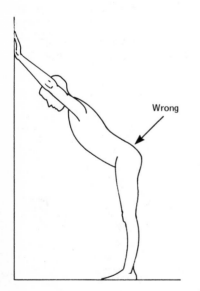
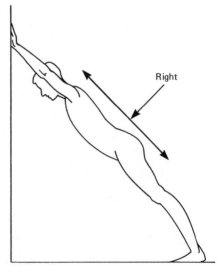

Figure 6-2

2. In *speaking*, you should never *exhaust* all of the breath in your lungs; at each pause in your presentation, take a "refill" of breath. The pauses in a good presentation should come *often*.

## Resonance

Here is why the second requisite of a good speaking voice is necessary: "A relaxed throat and an open mouth." Sound waves travel in concentric circles at approximately 1,000 ft. per second.* Air currents affect their direction of strongest impact, though not to a great degree. Turbulence in the air *does* disturb sound waves; thus, it is more difficult to hear a speaker in a small room with two electric fans blowing crosswise than it would be to hear the same speaker in a much larger room *without* the fans.

When encountering an obstacle, a sound wave is deflected and goes in the direction dictated by the largest flat surface of that obstacle. However, whenever a sound wave encounters a properly *curved* obstacle, it is reflected back to its source.

Examine Figure 6-3. A man is standing on a mountain top, with a cave in another mountain one-eighth of a mile away. He sounds the note "C" on a

*The speed varies slightly depending upon temperature, humidity, and barometric pressure. Thus, on a cold morning, on the surface of a quiet lake, one can hear the paddles of a rowboat for great distances.

Figure 6-3

bugle, and the sound waves are reflected off the cave walls and return to him as an echo. So he hears *two* distinct sounds: the original note "C" and an echo. Suppose the man climbs into the cave *entrance* and sounds the note "C" on his bugle. The same thing happens: The sound waves are reflected off the curved walls of the cave. But since they travel so fast (1,000 f.p.s.), the man no longer hears *two* distinct sounds but only *one* sound greatly amplified.

Resonance comes from the prefix *re* (meaning "again") and the infinitive *sonar* (meaning "to sound"), so it literally means "to sound again." Thus, our definition: *Resonance is the reflection of sound waves by the walls of a hollow chamber, preferably round.*

The sound of a human voice is actually *produced* by breath from the lungs vibrating the edges of the vocal folds in the *larynx* (voice box), which is located in the throat. The sound is flat and not very pleasant to listen to; it needs resonating. We have three resonators, which we can control in (a) the throat (the *pharynx*), (b) the mouth (oral cavity), and (c) the nose (nasal passages), used principally to resonate the sounds of *n*, *m*, and *ng*. This is why you should keep your nasal passages clear, your throat relaxed, and your mouth open wide (vertically) in order to obtain your maximum resonance.

Try this experiment for yourself: With your teeth clenched and lips slightly apart, make a humming sound. Continue the sound as you drop your jaw and round your lips until your mouth is open as far as possible and your lips are stretched over your teeth to form a perfect "O". You will hear an appreciable difference in tone and volume, even though you are using no more breath than when you started.

## Articulation and Enunciation

You cannot talk with an open mouth unless your lips are flexible enough to shape the vowel sounds, and your tongue is active enough to form the consonants. This is the third of the absolute requisites for a good speaking voice. The vowels are the "sounds" of speech, and the consonants are the "noises"; the vowels make us *heard,* and the consonants make us *understood.* Think about that statement, and then try these exercises for the lips and the tongue. It is VERY IMPORTANT that you use a mirror for *all* of these exercises so that you can see what you are doing.

*Exercises:*

1. Practice these individual sounds, observing the positions of the jaw and the shape of the lips.
   Now comes the difficult part! Try to *combine* these sounds in *one* steady flow of breath, aiming at these two objectives:
   A. Make each sound *distinctly different* from the ones which precede it and follow it.

| | Lips ROUND | Lips NEUTRAL | Lips WIDE |
|---|---|---|---|
| Jaw HIGH | (1) OO as in "food" | | (7) EE as in "see" |
| | | (5) UH as in "up" | |
| Jaw LOWER | (2) OH as in "low" | | (6) A as in "hay" |
| | | (4) AH as in "ha" | |
| Jaw VERY LOW | (3) AW as in "law" | | |

B. Aim for "continuous vocalization." That is, do not break the flow of breath as you go from one sound to the other. Use them in the order given on the chart in parentheses:

OO--OO---OH--OH---AW--AW---AH--AH---UH--UH---A--A---EE--EE.
   (1)          (2)          (3)          (4)          (5)          (6)          (7)

NOTE: This exercise is NOT EASY if done correctly; professional actors and singers work on it for *weeks*.

2. Place the tip of your tongue on the alveolar ridge (the wrinkled ridge just above your upper teeth) in the front of your mouth. Place it there lightly; do not press against it. Then, use either hand to pull down the jaw as *low* as it will go *without* pulling the tongue tip away from the gum ridge. Holding down the jaw, try making a dozen *each* of these sounds:

LA - LA - LA - LA . . . . .
NA - NA - NA - NA . . . . .
DA - DA - DA - DA . . . . .
TA - TA - TA - TA . . . . .

USE A MIRROR TO SEE THAT

A. The tongue tip does *not* touch the upper teeth; it should touch—lightly—*only* the gum ridge just above the teeth.

B. There is no "waste motion"; the tongue tip should touch the gum ridge lightly and then drop immediately to the "floor" of the mouth, without wavering between the teeth.

This exercise is also difficult to perform properly; it is important because almost one-half of the consonant sounds are made with the tongue elevated. Remember, the tongue is a mass of muscle controlled by other muscles, and it will not "elevate" properly unless it is in good muscular tonus.

3. With your teeth far enough apart for you to insert the width of your thumbnail, raise the back of the tongue to the position of "K". Switch the tip of the tongue to the position of "T" (touching the tongue tip lightly to the alveolar (gum) ridge). Practice saying, as rapidly as you can, these sounds:

GUH -DUH. . . . GUH-DUH. . . . GUH-DUH. . . . . .

Now, *very* rapidly, and without *any* sound except the sound of breath being exploded, practice these movements, rocking the tongue to and fro, from the back of the mouth to the front,

K-T . . . K-T . . . K-T . . . K-T . . . (Try it fifty times.)


## ACHIEVING VOCAL VARIETY

Listening to a young child is always interesting; the child may not have anything profound to say, but we listen just the same. This is because children—uninhibited as they are—always emphasize words and ideas that are important to them. They do not hesitate to voice emotions. Adults, however, have learned to hide emotions in order to avoid being hurt easily. When we create a "poker face," we also tend to create a "poker voice," and so we grow to sound monotonous.

The fault lies mainly in not placing proper emphasis upon idea-carrying words and phrases. There is no substitute for sincere emotion in a speech, but often our inhibitions prevent our using it. Following are a few suggestions that can help to relieve the monotony problem.


### Emphasis

Technically we achieve emphasis on idea-carrying words or phrases through using one of the following devices:

1. Change in *volume*
2. Change in *pitch*
3. Change in *intensity*
4. Change in *timing,* which involves
   A. Pauses, or phrasing
   B. Duration of sound.

Here are some sentences that illustrate how these devices might be used. Read the sentences as you normally would; then try to read them with emphasis on certain words or phrases, as indicated. Try them on your tape recorder.

*Volume* is increasing the loudness of your voice. It is not often used for emphasis, except for emergencies and in giving orders:

"The FIRE ALARM is not WORKING; this is an EMERGENCY!"

*Pitch* concerns the amount of treble or bass you use on certain words or phrases. In this next sentence use a higher pitch (more treble) on the words *above* the normal line of type, and a lower pitch (more bass) *below* the line of normal type:

```
              sale?                    how
"You made the        I don't know          you
                                        did it!"
```

*Intensity* means putting more energy (breath) on the word or phrase you intend to emphasize, without changing pitch or volume:

"Ladies, our *existence* as a business depends upon your help in this—our *actual existence*."

*Duration of sound* consists of lengthening the vowels within a word to give it emphasis:

"We decided on that policy a l-o-n-g time ago; it has worked for us for y-e-a-r-s."

None of these ways of acquiring emphasis is totally independent of the others; it is usually a *combination* of pitch and duration, volume and pitch, intensity and pitch, and so forth, that is used. We have used these illustrations simply to make you *aware* of the fact that vocal variety can be analyzed.

*Phrasing* is of paramount importance, both in the meaning and the effectiveness of your speaking voice. In the paragraph below we have indicated a short pause by one slant (/) and a longer pause by two slants (//).

"We have asked management to hear us; / they would not listen. // We have asked them to give reasons for the delay; / they would not talk. // Our threats / have been laughed at. // Our pleas / have been ignored. // There is nothing left now / but to strike. //"

Sometimes phrasing changes meaning to a ludicrous degree. Read aloud the following sentences, observing only the pauses, and see if you can figure out what the speaker meant.

1. What is that in the road / a head?
2. When we had eaten their daughter / the youngest child came to the table.

### Inflection, Steps, Intonation

In Figure 6-4, representing the lead sheet of a musical manuscript, you don't have to be a music student to know that the notes at the bottom of the five lines represent the bass (low-pitched) sounds, and that the notes at the top represent the treble (high-pitched) sounds. The average untrained voice is *capable* of producing one octave (eight notes) with ease. This is called one's *range*. However, too many of us stick to one or two notes on the musical scale, and it makes our voices deadly dull to listen to. Most of us could profit by increasing our overall range.

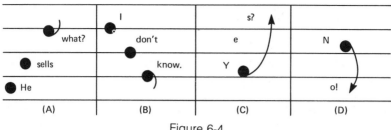

Figure 6-4

Here are some definitions from Figure 6-4.

*Steps:* Going from one pitch to another on *separate* words is called "steps" (Examples A & B).

*Inflection:* Gliding from one note to another *within a single word* is called "inflection" (Examples C & D). As shown, there are upward inflections and downward inflections and even circumflex inflections. Inflections are crucial in giving meanings to words.

A predominance of *upward* inflections makes a person sound uncertain, vacillating, and often weak. Sometimes this is used for a comic effect. On the other hand, a predominance of *downward* inflections makes a person sound dogmatic, inflexible, and overly demanding. Although they may not be conscious of inflection patterns as such, our listeners read these nonverbal clues in our speech and attribute a certain kind of personality to them.

*Intonation* is the overall pattern of speech. It is comprised of general tone, voice quality, range, pitch, phrasing, emphasis, and inflections. It is the tune or melody that distinguishes every individual from any other; it is our vocal identity. There are intonation patterns that are peculiar to different languages, to different localities among the same language, and sometimes to individual cities in those localities.

Your speaking voice is an indication of your personality to others, far more than your physical features or the way you dress. Any normal person who has an unpleasant voice *can* change it. It *may* require the help of a professional, and it *surely* will require hours of practice and critical listening. So, as Shakespeare said, "Mend your speech or you may mar your fortune."

## READING ALOUD

It is not often that a business or professional person is called upon to read aloud to a group. When it happens, it can be embarrassing because many people who read well do *not* read well *aloud*. Both communication experts Roger D'Aprix (Xerox Corp.) and Edward Hodnett (Dow Corning Corp.) emphasize the necessity of this skill.[1,2]

A business or professional person is actually called upon to read aloud on more *important* occasions than it would appear to a casual observer:

A businessman is required to read a report to a board meeting, or in a conference.

A professional woman is required to read a paper at a regional, state, or national convention.

Both business and professional persons may belong to a fraternal order where the ritual is required to be read aloud so that the wording is absolutely accurate.

No matter how seldom the occasion arises, the listeners of a business or professional person who is a poor reader equate poor reading ability with lack of intelligence or lack of efficiency. Reading aloud well is so simple that it behooves all professional and business people to master it.

The following exercise is designed to help you with two other means of improving your oral presentations: (a) to make it easier to establish eye contact with your listeners and (b) to obtain from your classmates an appraisal of your vocal delivery.

## Preparation

*First,* select a short piece of prose writing that you believe will be interesting to your classmates—a piece that can be read in three to five minutes. If the selection is longer, cut it to the time limit, but try to be sure that it is a complete episode within itself. It is fine to give a short introduction in order to explain it.

*Second,* read it aloud to be sure that you know the exact meaning of *every word* and the correct pronunciation of each word. Reading aloud something in which you do not know the meaning and pronunciation of each word is tantamount to speaking on a subject about which you know nothing.

*Third,* read the selection again silently, but try to imagine how your favorite news commentator or documentary narrator would say each sentence. You may need to do this several times. Then *mark* the selection for emphasis, pauses, and inflection, as shown in the early part of this chapter. Meaning is *everything,* so try to mark your selection so that (a) you will have contrasting pitch for contrasting ideas; (b) you will speed up on unimportant phrases and slow down for idea-carrying phrases; and (c) you will try to express the appropriate emotion* for each sentence, or each *group* of sentences that express the same emotion and mood—such as happiness, sadness, activity or passivity, anger, scorn, or sarcasm. You can see that preparation for even such a *minor* pres-

---

*This could lead us into "Oral Interpretation," which is based upon techniques beyond the scope of this text. However, your *awareness* is the main thing that is needed.

entation as reading aloud a prose selection requires *work* and *thought*.* However, we hope to put you into the position of an artist by the end of this course, and, as violinist Isaac Stern says, "An artist does not *beg* for attention; instead, he *demands* it!"[3]

## Practice . . . Practice . . . Practice . . .

Before you start to practice (in front of a mirror, of course), here are some mandatory directions:

1. If you are reading from a hard-cover book, *don't* hold it in a pinched-hand position at its binding; it will build up tensions that will affect your entire body. You will also probably tilt to one side or another, and this will cause your listeners to empathize uncomfortably because you are not on balance. Instead, hold the book in the palm of your hand and stand erect. You can then use the fingers of the *other* hand to follow your reading so that you will not lose your place.

2. If your selection is on a single sheet of paper, place it in a book or folder so that you can hold it as described under point No. 1. If you hold one sheet of paper between your thumb and forefinger, the paper may start to shake, giving you the appearance of nervousness.

3. Unless you are using a lectern, hold your reading material up high and out in front of you, at a distance allowing you to see it comfortably and to raise your eyes to your listeners without bobbing your head up and down. Any repetitive movement (such as the head bobbing up and down) is distracting. Also, moving your elbows away from your sides will help fill your lower lungs with more breath. We suggest *not* using a lectern because few of them adjust to your exact height.

4. This is the most important direction of the four. *Look at your listeners at least 50 percent of the time*—not just a quick, suspicious glance, but a full, direct look. There is a procedure which will make this easy: When you see the punctuation mark at the end of each sentence, deliver the final five words of that sentence looking at your listeners. If you can't do it with five words, try it with three words, and then increase your span to five or more. Don't worry about losing your place. (You are using the fingers of one hand to follow it—remember?) A word of warning: Do *not* try to look up in the middle of a phrase. It will make your delivery choppy. If you have an exceptionally long compound sentence, break it up into its clauses, mark each one, and look up for five words at the end of each clause.

As you reach the end of your selection, you should use shorter phrasing (that is, pause more often) and slow your rate of speaking; this gives your listeners a sense of finality, letting them know that the end is near.

If these details seem petty and tedious, remember that they mark the difference between the amateur and the professional; or, to quote Mark Twain, "the difference between lightning and the lightning bug."

*Note: It might help to type or write out your selection double-spaced or triple-spaced, so that the markings you make on it will not obscure the words.

## SUGGESTED CLASSROOM EXERCISE

Each student should prepare a short prose selection for reading aloud to the class, as suggested in this section. Other students may offer a critique on the reader's delivery, voice quality, and audience contact. If the equipment is available, the students' performances should be recorded on tape or, better still, videotaped.

## FOOTNOTES FOR CHAPTER SIX

[1]Roger M. D'Aprix, *How's That Again?* (Homewood, Ill.: Dow Jones-Irwin, Inc. 1971).
[2]Edward Hodnett, *Effective Presentations* (West Nyack, N.Y.: Parker Publishing Co., 1967).
[3]From an interview with Dick Cavett, PBS-TV, August 23, 1979.

# VOCABULARY STUDY FOR CHAPTER SEVEN

Below are some of the words that appear in this chapter with which you may not be familiar. They are offered here as a straight glossary.

1. ANALOGY:  A means of comparing things that are alike in many ways, but different in others. For example, "The flow of electricity through wire is like the flow of water through pipes."

2. BANTER  Usually an exchange of light, playful remarks; good-natured criticism of oneself or others.

3. CORRELATION:  The relation of one thing to another of a different nature; for example, the relation of progress over a period of time.

4. CUMBERSOME:  Weighty, heavy, awkward. Literally it means to hinder one's progress by imposing a heavy load.

5. EXIGENCY:  An unexpected happening, although not necessarily a dire emergency. One often speaks of being "ready for all exigencies and emergencies."

6. FLANNEL:  An inexpensive soft fabric of cotton, wool, rayon, or combinations of them, with a short woolly surface on one side (called the *nap* side).

7. PARAPHRASE:  To put into other words, usually to make the meaning clearer or the sentence shorter; sometimes it is a pun on words or on a *cliché* expression, as when Dorothy Parker said, "If all the girls who come to the spring prom at Yale were laid end to end—I wouldn't be a bit surprised!"

8. PATTER:  Amusing lines spoken by an entertainer or performer having no weighty meaning.

9. SHAMBLES:  Complete disarray; a collapsed building or enterprise.

10. TROUGH:  (Pronounced "troff") Originally, a long log, hollowed-out for the feeding of livestock; now, any holder of material, square-shaped with an open top.

11. VERBOSITY:  Unnecessary words; words used to pad material to make it seem important.

# 7 Visual Aids

Don't tell me that one picture is worth 10,000 words!
Sometimes it's not worth *one* word. If I'm drowning,
what do I do—hold up a picture? Hell, no; I yell
"Help!"

Irvin S. Cobb (1876–1944)

A chief petty officer was instructing other petty officers about the use of bulletin boards aboard naval stations. He held up a large calendar that displayed in full color the picture of a beautiful nude woman at the top. When the whistles and catcalls from the men had subsided, he put away the calendar.

"Okay. Now, which one of you guys can tell me which month of the year was shown on the calendar?" he demanded.

When not one of the men could answer, he remarked dryly, "Let that be a lesson to you. Don't let your visual aids distract from the message you're trying to get across."

Nevertheless visuals can be of great help in making almost any sort of presentation. The Socony-Mobil Oil Company conducted a survey that revealed how much we learn through using each of our senses. They found that we *learn* 1 percent through taste, 1.5 percent through touch, 3.5 percent through smell, 11 percent through hearing, and 83 percent through sight (including reading).[1] However, we *retain* 10 percent of what we read; 20 percent of what we hear; 30 percent of what we see; and a whopping 50 percent of what we both *hear and see!*

According to author Francis J. McHugh in his book *Graphic Presentation*,[2] one 160-page government report was condensed into six simple visuals and presented at *cabinet level* to a group of officers, and the "message was absorbed and approved in fifteen minutes." Considering the verbosity of most government reports, one should not be surprised if the report itself might not easily have been reduced to six simple paragraphs. Besides, Mr. McHugh's book was published by the Technifax Corporation, which *manufactures* visual aid materials. Some writers[3,4,5,6] claim that material which is *seen* is remembered 55 percent better than material that is only *heard*. The following paragraph paraphrases some of their findings on the subject, based on various experiments they claim to have performed:

> After three hours the people involved in the experiment remembered 70 percent of the material which was presented to them verbally, 72 percent of the material which was presented to them visually, and 85 percent of the material when it was presented to them *both* verbally and visually. After three days, the same people remembered only 10 percent of the material presented to them verbally only, 20 percent of the material presented to them visually only, and 65 percent of the material when it was presented both verbally *and* visually.

Please reread the foregoing paragraph. Now, read the following figures, arranged in tabular order, and determine for yourself which of the two is more easily comprehended:

*Percentage of people who retained material presented to them verbally, visually, and a combination of the two, after periods of three hours and three days.*

|  | After 3 hrs. | After 3 days |
|---|---|---|
| *Verbal only* | 70% | 10% |
| *Visual only* | 72 | 20 |
| *Both verbal and visual* | 85 | 65 |

You may have suspected that we are in the process of constructing a visual aid out of the foregoing information, and you were right. Look at Figure 7-1 and see how it conveys the same information, almost at a glance; use the same title as given in above table.

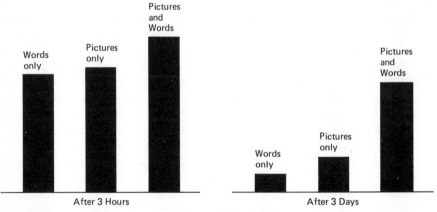

Figure 7-1

You can go further, and reduce the essential information into *two* bar-graphs, as shown in Figure 7-2. However, this is not quite so easily comprehended at a glance, and it violates one of the cardinal rules for all visual aids—simplicity.

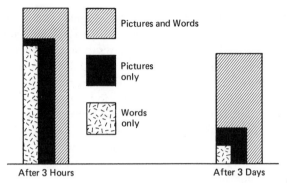

Figure 7-2

## VALUES

Visual aids *do* have many values, among them some which you may not have considered. Here are a few:

1. *They act as memory aids,* not only for your listeners, but for yourself as well. If you have a series of visuals and have them numbered in sequence, they will help jog your memory.

2. *They relieve tension.* We have observed for many years that one of the contributing causes of speakers' anxiety is not knowing what to do with their hands. Visual aids provide an assignment for the hands, thereby relieving some of the tension.

3. *They help hold attention,* especially if you have kept some of your visuals concealed and then exhibit them at various points in your presentation.

4. *They clarify and simplify.* They can help your listeners understand relationships at a glance. Often a relationship is too *vast* (outer space or the earth's oceans) or too *minute* (neutrons, atoms, viruses) for one to comprehend through words alone. How many of us can comprehend how small one two-hundred-thousandth of a millimeter is, or how long 18 million light years are? Using analogy, those things can be brought to a visual plane to help us comprehend them.

## THREE MANDATES

There are three absolute MUSTS required for an effective visual aid:

### A Visual Aid Should be VISIBLE

If this seems slightly ridiculous, you'd be surprised how many students attempt to use an ordinary snapshot (about two and one-half by four inches) as a visual in a classroom containing thirty or more people. "Of course, you can't see this very well, but here I am at the leaning tower of Pisa," is the lame excuse, while even the people on the front row are straining and squinting to view the tiny photograph. Never use a visual aid that is too small for everyone, even in the back row, to see comfortably.

"What about passing around the small photograph so that it can be examined at close range?" you may ask. When an object is passed from hand to hand, the person who is looking at it will not be listening to you; neither will those who are waiting for the object to be passed to them next. This means that they have lost your train of thought, and it may be difficult for them to pick it up again.

If you have complicated data, which needs to be examined by each member of the class, pass it out before you begin your presentation so that they may examine it and ask questions as you go along. It is even better to have the data accessible for the members of your audience to pick up after your presentation. If you have a chart or a picture to present, make sure that it is instantly visible to all members of your audience.

## A Visual Aid Should Be SIMPLE

Addison Steele wrote, "Simplicity of all things, is the hardest to be copied." If you are making a presentation showing how nylon thread is manufactured, it is not necessary to show all of the complicated machinery used in the process (the only one who would understand that might be the shop foreman or machinist); instead, use a simple flow chart, as indicated in Figure 7-3.

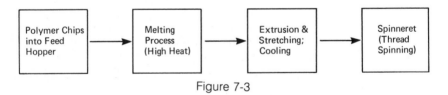

Figure 7-3

When a chart or other visual is necessarily complicated, break it down into two or more simple steps before showing the fully complicated final one.

*Too many* visuals can detract from your presentation rather than enhance it. Recently we encountered the sales manager for a large soap company who had been allowed fifty minutes to report on sales in his territory. He had prepared *forty* large, expensive flip charts to accompany his presentation. That's almost one per minute—enough to make his listeners dizzy. Many of the forty could have been incorporated into a single chart.

**Actual and factual visuals.**   When one thinks of using a visual aid, the first thing that comes to mind is, "Get the *real* thing." Aside from often being difficult to acquire, the "real thing" is not always the best visual you can use. For instance, the real article is often too small for an audience to see clearly. An oversize working model is better in such a case.

In industrial instrument plants and among aviation flight schools, huge "mock-ups" of the various small panel instruments are constructed. These are portable and lightweight; and they have all of the essential visible working parts. Such working models can be seen by a group of thirty or more people, depending upon the seating arrangement.

**Pictures—moving or still.**   Color motion pictures with sound have ranked high on the scale of effective visual aids; we are convinced that they have ranked higher than they deserve. For one thing, they are expensive to produce, and they do not allow for flexibility in the case of changes or mistakes. For another, unless they have been produced by highly skilled technicians, they are apt to have distracting artistic elements in them. They *do* have the advantage of being projected on a large variety of screen sizes, so that they are adaptable to large or small audiences.

Film strips and slides offer the same advantage with respect to audience sizes, and they are less costly to produce and to modify. Again, one must not allow the photographer's art to interfere with the main message.

**Graphs and charts.**   There are two main types of graphs, the bar-graph and the grid-graph. The bar-graph is the simplest but usually requires a separate set of bar-graphs to represent each change in time (See Figures 7-1 and 7-2). The grid-graph has the advantage of representing two correlations at once; it can portray as long a continuum of time as is desired. For example:

Rival's breakfast cereal exceeded our sales by a healthy margin, until we fortified our own breakfast cereal with extra vitamins and minerals, and carried on an active advertising campaign to announce the fact. The advertising campaign was slow in getting underway, probably because the general public was suspicious that our fortification of vitamins and minerals was merely a "gimmick." However, with testimonials from nutrition experts, the campaign showed definite results in sales, as the following graph will show.

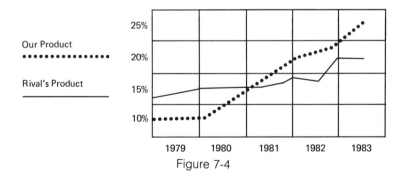

Figure 7-4

One should have no more than three (at the *most* four) plottings on a grid-graph; otherwise, it will look like a plate of spaghetti. Use two grids if necessary. Also, the plottings should have a distinctive type of line for each plotting:

————————, ....., — — — — —, *****. Color can be used for the various plottings, but beware of using yellow; it frequently washes out under artificial light.

To summarize, grid-graphs, or line-graphs, are generally used to plot data over a period of time. The pie graph or the pictograph is used to visualize *proportions*. For example:

Beauty products, such as creams, lotions, lipstick, and eye shadow cost relatively little to produce by comparison with what the buyer pays for them. The cost of the product represents only about eight cents out of each dollar spent. Research and development of new products account for about 10% of the dollar, warehousing and handling account for another 10%; packaging represents 20% of the total cost; while marketing (sales and advertising) are responsible for 52% of the cost per dollar.

The pie graph would look like Figure 7-5.

Your pie graph would look like this:

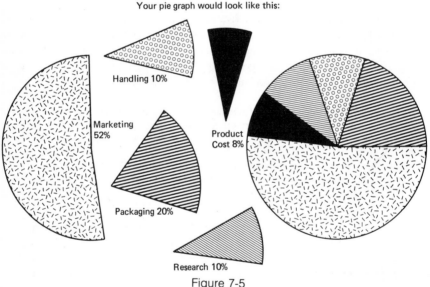

Figure 7-5

Pie graphs are ideally adapted for use on a flannel board. A flannel board is easily constructed by stretching a length of flannel cloth over a board (plywood or heavy cardboard) with the woolly side out. The pieces to be placed on the board are cut out of lightweight cardboard (if it is *too* light, the edges will curl) with extra flannel pasted on each, also with the woolly side out. Each piece will cling to the flannel board as it is placed on it. It makes for a more dramatic presentation if the individual pieces are placed on the flannel board one at a time, thereby producing a progressive visual aid. The individual segments should preferably be of different colors.

A pictograph represents in silhouette the actual article for those who must associate figures with literal objects. For example:

Should Graustark go to war with Ensylvania, the chances are that the conflict would be waged primarily by air, because of the mountainous terrain of both countries. At present, Graustark has two squadrons of fighter planes and bombers, while Ensylvania has at least one and one-half times that number. This would definitely give Ensylvania an edge over Graustark.

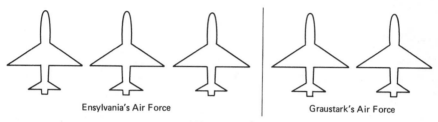

Ensylvania's Air Force                    Graustark's Air Force

Figure 7-6

## A Visual Aid Must Be HANDLED SKILLFULLY

This is where most beginners fail. The novice will attempt to hang his visual on the chalkboard (it falls down) or has used drawing paper, hoping it will stand in the trough of the chalkboard or against the lectern (it curls over). Since scotch tape will not adhere to a chalky surface, suspend your visual from the top framework of the chalkboard. Use masking tape instead of scotch tape; it will not damage the surface of the wood and is more easily removed.

Use visuals only as they are needed, or they can distract your audience. Keep them hidden until you need them; then, when you have finished with one, put it away unless you need it for future reference. Hide them behind the desk or drop them on the floor face down.

An ideal visual aid for a small room is an easel with flip cards fastened at the top and loose rings that allow the cards to be turned as needed. You can always use blank cards or paper when you have finished with one card and are not yet ready for the next card.

You may wish to use the chalkboard for your visual aid, which means that you do not need to carry around cumbersome equipment. If your drawing is complicated, you should gain access to the classroom and draw your visual ahead of time. Then, to keep it from distracting from your and other people's speeches, it should be covered (plain or newspaper will serve) until the time comes to use it.

If you must draw on the chalkboard *during* your speech, you should have a line of patter, or light banter, to accompany your drawing. Sometimes a brief skeleton drawing can be made, and the remaining lines can be filled in as you talk. This creates curiosity, which is good. Using chalk of different colors will give your drawing variety and interest.

If you are unable to get into the classroom beforehand to put your drawing on the chalkboard and the drawing is the least bit complicated, have an accurate copy on paper and *rehearse it at least twice* before class. It is annoying to an audience to watch a speaker engage in trial and error while attempting to use a chalkboard effectively.

Whatever type of visual aid you use, always stand to one side when presenting it to your audience. Do not block their sight lines. A pointer can be helpful in this respect.

## Projectors

There are many types of projectors that can be used for a presentation. This text will mention only four and give a few advantages and disadvantages of each.

1. The opaque projector allows you to clip a page from a magazine or even project a page from a book upon the screen without mutilating the book. At this writing the opaque projector has not progressed to the point where it is more than barely satisfactory. It requires *total* darkness to project the image distinctly. And the cooling fan is so noisy that people sitting near the projector may have difficulty hearing the speaker.

2. The overhead projector allows simple diagrams to be projected on a screen above the speaker's head. It has the specific advantage of allowing the speaker to draw additional lines on the transparency while speaking. Care must be taken to mark the transparencies carefully in order to avoid mixing them up. Better still, have the transparencies taped together in their proper sequence. While the overhead projector's use is limited to simple diagrams and cartoons, color can be used, not only in the transparencies that have been prepared beforehand, but also in the crayon with which the speaker draws upon the transparency.

3. Slide and filmstrip projectors. We group these together because, although the mechanical means of projection differ, they are essentially the same—one still picture being shown at a time. Check that you have put the slides in their proper order and right-side-up. Unless you have a remote control to run the projector, be sure to have a prearranged signal for the operator to know when to change the slide or go to the next frame of the filmstrip.

4. Motion picture projectors. The most important requisite is that you have an operator who thoroughly understands the machine. If possible, you should rehearse before using a motion picture projector, to allow for focusing and to arrange for the proper sound level. If the operator does not know how to thread the film properly or does not know what to do if the film breaks, your presentation can be a shambles.

Whenever using any type of projector, go back to our first mandate: "A visual aid should be *visible*." It is ideal to have a room where the seats are movable, as in Figure 7-7, Part I. However, in most instances the seats are *not* movable, and the projector often has to be placed in the middle of the room. In such an exigency, block off the seats where the screen cannot be seen, as in Figure 7-7, Part II.

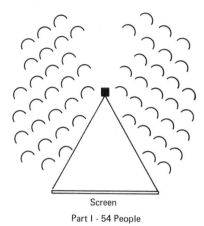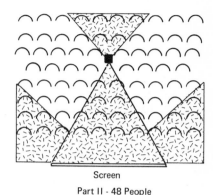

Screen                                    Screen

Part I - 54 People                     Part II - 48 People

Figure 7-7

Finally, try to be creative and use imagination in your visual aids. Don't rule out humor: If you use cartoons, you can show Danny Dimwit doing things the *wrong* way, and contrast him with Ernie Expert doing things the *right* way. However, never lose sight of the fact that a visual aid is *no more* than that—an *aid* to help you in your presentation.

This last point is one that we cannot overemphasize. If you rely completely upon your visual aids to convey your message, you run the risk of putting yourself in a treetop that woodsmen are cutting down. What do you do when you find yourself in Denver for a meeting, and the airlines have given your visual aids a free ride to Los Angeles?

You must be able to perform successfully without any props. You must be able to make your presentation by relying only on the spoken word.

It is wise to have a copy of all your charts and diagrams on paper in your briefcase (NEVER check your briefcase!). While these small copies may be of no use as visual aids—unless you can reproduce them on a chalkboard—they will help get you down from that treetop!

## SAMPLE SPEECH

The following speech was delivered in a speech class at Hillsborough Community College by a student, Octavia Rogers, in November, 1979, and is used with her permission.

(For visual aids, student used a portable sketching tripod, which she assembled before the class began, on which she rested four poster boards 20 × 30 inches; the poster board on the top was blank. She rested a small paper bag on the lectern with her notes.)

"The First Huckster"[1]

"Doing business without advertising is like winking at a girl in the dark. *You* know what you're doing but nobody else does."

So said Stewart H. Britt,[2] an advertising account executive with the firm of Batten, Barton, Durstine, and Osborne in New York City.

Do you know what the largest amount of money spent on television advertising is? (Pause) The first is foodstuffs of all sorts—including breakfast cereals, of course; the second largest amount spent is on advertising soap—cleansers, detergents, shaving needs, and so forth. According to The World Almanac of 1977,[3] 40 billion dollars of television advertising went to help keep us clean.

Before television became so widespread in this country, Tom Gilbert went into a small general store at a crossroads in the Georgia mountains. Tom was a salesman for General Foods, but he found that almost *every shelf* was filled with soap products; there were bath and beauty soaps, soap flakes and washing-machine powders, shaving soaps and dish detergents. Soap was everywhere.

Tom was amazed, and said to Emma Peplar the owner of the store, "Great day, Emma! You surely must sell a lot of soap in these mountains; there's not a store in Atlanta that carries such a large amount of soap products. How come people up here use so much soap?"

"Oh, they don't hardly use none at all," replied Emma, a sprightly widow of seventy-five years; "and them as does mostly makes their own from hog fat and lye. Nobody much shaves around here, and there ain't a washing machine within ten mile of here— "

Tom took in the shelves filled with soap products with a sweeping gesture. "But why—?"

Emma interrupted him. "Nope, I don't hardly sell more'n two bars of soap a week, but that George Grimshaw—that salesman from Lever Brothers—Boy! can *he* sell soap!"

The high-pressure soap salesman—whether on television or in person—probably started with this product.

[Student reaches into paper bag and takes out three bars of soap and lays two on table in front of class. Holds up the third.]

This is Pears' soap. As you can see, it is about the size of a cake of bath soap, it's sort of orange-colored and oval, and is translucent [Holds up cake of soap to light]; it has a very faint sweet scent. "Delicately perfumed with the flowers of an English garden," is the way its manufacturer advertises it. I'll leave these three cakes on the table, so you can smell them after class.

Andrew Pears set up shop in London in 1789, the year of the French Revolution, and became quite prosperous as a manufacturer of soap for the "better classes." But it was not until 76 years later that the product really "took off" when Thomas Barrat married Andrew Pears' great granddaughter and joined the firm. Barrat boasted that he was going to advertise as no other soapmaker had ever done before. Like the salesman from Lever Brothers in the story about Emma Peplar, Barrat could *sell soap!* He used most of the tricks in advertising that are used on television today and that was more than one hundred years ago—in 1865.

The first thing that Barrat did was to persuade the president of the Royal College of Surgeons to give him a testimonial stating that Pears' soap was "uncommonly safe and healthy," which he printed in the newspaper advertisements. But that wasn't enough; he needed some visual aids. So, he persuaded Lillie Langtry, one of the famous actresses of the day, to let him use her picture on sidewalk and newspaper advertisements, saying that she never used any other kind of soap. That was, as far as we know, the first celebrity to endorse a soap product.

Figure 7-8

[Student removes the cover from the poster board on the easel to show the first picture; a crude facsimile appears above.]

This created a sensation, because Lillie Langtry was not only a famous actress, but one of the most beautiful women of the era. Because she was born on the Isle of Jersey, she was known as "The Jersey Lily."

Thomas Barrat's next step was to set up a branch of the Pears Soap Company in America. On a trip to New York, he managed to get an appointment with Henry Ward Beecher, the city's most prominent clergyman, and got the Rev. Beecher to write an endorsement. Then Barrat did something that had never been done before: He bought the *entire front page* of the New York *Herald* and filled it with big, bold type carrying the words of the esteemed reverend:

[Student reads:]

"If Cleanliness is next to Godliness, soap must be considered as a 'means of Grace'—and a clergyman who recommends moral things should be willing to recommend soap. I am told that my recommendation of PEARS' SOAP some dozen years ago has assured for it a large sale in the U.S. I am willing to stand by any word in favor of it I ever uttered. A man must be fastidious indeed who is not satisfied with it."

Barrat had another enterprising scheme in mind that involved the English currency. In those days, as it is today—both here and in England—it was against the law to deface a coin. However, the French ten-centime piece was the same size as the English penny, and was usually accepted in England as being the same in value.

So, Barrat bought and imported 250,000 French ten-centime pieces, and had the word "Pears" stamped across the face of each coin. Then he put the pennies into circulation.

Figure 7-9

[Student removes the poster of Lillie Langtry from easel and sets on floor with its blank side showing, to reveal another picture showing enlarged pictures of French and English coins.]

The French coins were everywhere! Some of the members of the government were aghast at Barrat's audacity, and it took the passage of an Act of Parliament to get the French ten-centime pieces out of circulation! However, the British appreciate a good joke, and the sales of Pears' soap soared.

Barrat next entered the realm of art. In a Paris exhibition there was a painting depicting a family at home; in one corner was a baby in a tin bath, crying as he tried to reach a rubber toy on the floor just beyond his grasp. Barrat bought the right to reproduce just one corner of the painting, showing the baby in the bath reaching for the rubber toy. He substituted a bar of Pears' soap for the rubber toy, and captioned the picture, "He won't be happy till he gets it." The caption became immensely popular and was given a *double entendre* by many music-hall comics, cartoonists, and politicians. Once again, the sales of Pears' soap boomed.

During the first eighty years, Pears' soap spent only five hundred pounds sterling for advertising. Mind you, that is five hundred pounds for the entire eighty-year-period. Within ten years after Barrat came to the firm, the advertising budget was almost a hundred and twenty-five thousand pounds sterling *per year*.

[Student removes previous sketch from easel to show chart on page 83.]

That is 250 times the amount spent over a period of eighty years in just one year.

However, please note the increase in sales over the amount spent in advertising for the ten-year period.

[Points to chart]

I have translated British pounds sterling into American dollars for your better understanding. In 1865 the British pound was worth about $5.00 U.S.A. Five hundred pounds ($2,500) spread over eighty years amounts to just $31.25 per year. The sales on Pears' soap in 1865 amounted to $3,000 that year. In 1875, when Pears' soap spent $600,000 on advertising, the sales amounted to one hundred million dollars, as shown on the chart.

Apparently, Thomas Barrat decided that if art in advertising paid off, a little controversy might help—as well as a little free mention of Pears' soap in the very prestigious London *Times*. His next step was this:

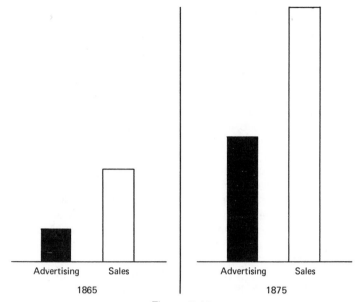

Figure 7-10

In 1886, Sir John Millais, an English portrait painter, portrayed his grandson watching a soap bubble which Sir John had blown from a clay pipe. The *Illustrated London News* owned the copyright, and Barrat paid them twenty-two hundred pounds (about $4,500) for it. Sir John had entitled the portrait of his grandson "Bubbles" and it became one of the most popular works of art in all England—with, of course, the name of Pears' soap associated with it. Again, sales of Pears' soap rose.

Figure 7-11

[Student removes diagram from easel and reveals replica of "Bubbles".]

Then, a peculiar thing happened. No one protested the "bastardization" of true art, as long as Sir John Millais remained alive. However, after his death in 1896—ten years later—a letter to the London *Times* was printed, deploring this commercial use of a highly respected English portrait painter's work. Some think that Thomas Barrat himself wrote the first letter, under an assumed name, in order to stir up controversy. Controversy there *was*, surely, and it went on for several weeks, while the sales of Pears' soap climbed to unprecedented heights.

Millais's grandson, the subject of the portrait, went on to become Admiral Sir William James, and lived for nearly ninety years, but his close friends never referred to him as anything except "Bubbles"!

It may be concluded that all one needs in order to conduct an advertising campaign is: (1) an endorsement from a doctor, (2) an endorsement from a celebrity—preferably a beautiful woman, (3) an endorsement from a prestigious minister, (4) a protest by the government involving money, (5) two works of art, and (6) a controversy in a major metropolitan newspaper. Thomas Barrat had all of those, and—while they took place about a hundred years ago —Thomas Barrat should certainly be ranked as the patron saint of all advertising men.

*Sources for speech:*

1Mary-Kay Wilmers, "Next to Godliness", *The New Yorker,* October 8, 1979, p. 179 ff.

2Dorothy Sarnoff, *Speech Can Change Your Life* (Garden City, N. Y.: Doubleday & Co., 1970), page 292.

3*World Almanac* (New York: Newspaper Enterprises Association, Inc.).

AUTHORS' NOTE: This is one of the better student speeches we have tape-recorded in the past few years because (1) Miss Rogers used a *variety* of visual aids—the actual article, pictures, and diagrams. (2) In reporting her sources, she used more than one format; students should be advised that there is no *one* rigid format in reporting sources, so long as the vital information is there. (3) *Most* importantly, her visual aids were *well handled;* she did not fumble around by trying to hang her visuals from the chalkboard, and she *limited* her visuals. A possible "extra" could have been the infant reaching for the bar of soap; instead, she omitted that temptation and went on to "Bubbles," which underscored the climax of her speech, with a rather amusing incident about the Admiral. Lesson: Avoid the temptation to use *too many* visual aids.

## Suggested Topics for Visual Aid Presentations

How to pose a subject for a photo

People get caught "off guard"

Where your tax dollar goes

Improving your tennis serve

Improving your golf swing

Genes and the color of your eyes

How radar works

Buying a used car

Our immigration quota

The proper way to walk

How to read hands (Chirography)

Our jury system

The basic structure of a business

The structure of our Federal government:

1. Executive
2. Judicial
3. Legislative

# A SELECTED BIBLIOGRAPHY

RUDOLF ARNHEIM, *Visual Thinking* (Berkeley, CA: University of California Press, 1969).

MICHAEL J. LANGFORD, *Visual Aids and Photography in Education* (New York: Hastings House Publishers, 1973).

W. A. MAMBERT, *Presenting Technical Ideas* (New York: John Wiley & Sons, Inc.), 1968.

W. A. WITTICH and C. F. SCHULLER, *Audio-Visual Materials: Their Nature and Use* (New York: Harper & Row, 1962).

## SUGGESTED CLASSROOM EXERCISES

1. Your instructor may divide the class into four or five groups, each group being assigned to present meaningful visual aids of various types. A general critique should follow.

2. Your instructor may assign several students to work on a presentation—from compiling the necessary research, to making the presentation with appropriate visual aid(s).

## FOOTNOTES FOR CHAPTER SEVEN

[1]B. Y. Auger, *How to Run More Effective Business Meetings* (New York: Grosset & Dunlap, 1964).

[2]Francis J. McHugh, *Graphic Presentation,* (Holyoke, Mass.: Technifax Corp., 1956).

[3]Rudolf Arnheim, *Visual Thinking,* (Berkeley, CA: University of California Press, 1969).

[4]Michael J. Langford, *Visual Aids and Photography in Education,* (New York: Hastings House PUblishers, 1973).

[5]W. A. Mambert, *Presenting Technical Ideas,* (New York: John Wiley & Sons, Inc., 1968).

[6]W. A. Wittich and C. F. Schuller, *Audio-Visual Materials: Their Nature and Use* (New York: Harper & Row, 1962).

# VOCABULARY STUDY FOR CHAPTER EIGHT

Following are some words used in this chapter with which you may not be familiar. We have given their definitions and in some instances their connotations.

1. BIGOTRY — Stubborn and complete intolerance of any belief, creed, or opinion that differs from one's own.

2. DEXTERITY — Skill or agility in using body or mind.

3. ESPRIT DE CORPS — (Pronounced "es-PREE d' core") The "spirit of the (military) corps;" high morale or team spirit.

4. EXTRACTION — To pull out, usually by force, as "extract a tooth"; deduce a meaning from an argument; take out a passage from a book.

5. FLAMBOYANT — "Showy"; conspicuously bold and brilliant; strikingly colorful.

6. NONCOMMITTAL — Not committing oneself to either side of an argument or a cause.

7. RAMROD — A rod for ramming down the powder and shot in a muzzle-loading firearm; absolutely straight and rigid.

8. REJOINDER — An answer to a reply; response.

9. SEPTUAGENARIAN — A person over seventy years of age. A sexagenarian is over sixty; an octogenarian, over eighty; a nonagenarian over ninety.

# 8 | The Employment Interview

The world is full of willing people; some willing to work and the rest willing to let them.

Robert Frost (1874–1963)

This chapter is not concerned with the temporary job you may take as a lifeguard or the retail salesclerk position you accept part time in order to supplement your college allowance. Instead, this chapter addresses the job interview that you hope will start you on your career—although sometimes summer or part-time jobs have resulted in doing that.

Chapter Seventeen is devoted entirely to employment resumés, application forms, and letters. This chapter will be confined to the physical aspects of the interview.

## THE INTERVIEWER

If you are interviewing a person for any reason (such as employment, appraisal, or correction) you represent not only your company but also yourself at your best. Be firm, but courteous and kind. The interviewer may come from behind the desk and sit comfortably in an easy chair along with the interviewee.

If the person being interviewed remarks on the surroundings, don't brush it off as a waste of time, but comment on it also so that the interviewee will not feel rushed. Take time to allow the person to feel at ease and that you are giving that individual your full attention.

This chapter contains some questions that seem to apply only to the person being interviewed, but they can also serve as a guide for obtaining the information you wish.

Even though an interview is not an adversary situation, the person being interviewed is in your territory. That gives you an advantage. Use it graciously.

## THE ACTUAL INTERVIEW

The following will examine some of the fears and anxieties many young people experience when they go for an important job interview.

"Am I too young? Am I too immature? Have I had the necessary experience for the job?" Remember, the employer who wanted an older person would have advertised for one. Many firms *prefer* younger people because they are more easily trained. However, it is helpful to have done *some* sort of work by the time you've reached college age, even mowing lawns or babysitting. As for maturity, most personnel directors understand young people if they have worked with them (and what are *you* doing in a job, if you're the first person under age sixty whom they've hired?). Potential employers don't expect you to act like a septuagenarian. Nevertheless, you want to present your best self, and nowhere is this more important than in your appearance.

### Clothes and Grooming

The style and nature of your clothing will depend upon the type of job you are applying for. If you are seeking a position in a brokerage firm or a law office, you will be expected to wear tailored clothing, such as a business suit. If you are applying for a job as a retail clerk, somewhat more casual clothing is acceptable. Don't be uncomfortably *over*dressed, but don't appear looking as if it were vacation time in the mountains or at the seashore. Avoid fads and the extreme "in" thing. More important than your clothes is your general personal grooming.

We have interviewed dozens of personnel directors and asked this question, "Aside from the overall appearance of a person, what is the one *detail* you examine first?"

Their answers didn't surprise us, but they may surprise you. "Hair!" they all said, although some of them added, "and fingernails." Paraphrased, most of the responses amounted to this: "I don't care how long or how short a person's hair is, if it isn't carefully combed and trimmed and doesn't give a neat appearance, I wouldn't hire that person because I know that I'd have a sloppy worker on my staff."

Here are some other tips we learned from our interviews.

For the female: Look *clean*. Don't wear extreme hair styles. Be moderate in your use of jewelry—costume or otherwise. Avoid strong perfume—some people actually have an allergy to it. Don't wear theatrical make-up; heavy eye shadow and mascara are for evening, and the same goes for flashy nail polish.

For the male: Don't appear in flamboyant clothing. Look *clean;* fingernails should be impeccably clean and trimmed short. Shined shoes without rundown heels are a *must;* never wear sneakers—even if you're applying for the position of athletic director. Avoid looking unshaven. If you sport a beard, it should be neatly trimmed and groomed.

## Deportment

Perhaps your deportment for an interview can be summed up in one sentence: "Be courteous, be friendly, be concerned, and be earnest in your pursuit of the *job you want!*" The next pages provide more detailed suggestions about the interview, from your first appearance to the end of the interview—and *beyond.* The "beyond" may make all the difference as to whether you get the job you want.

As you enter the officer of the interviewer, if the door is ajar, leave it that way unless asked to close it. If the door is closed, close it again after entering, unless told not to.

If the person interviewing you offers to shake hands, then do so firmly. When asked to be seated, do not move the chair; the interviewer may have placed it strategically. When you sit, don't assume a ramrod position on the edge of your chair, but don't slump. You should appear physically relaxed but mentally alert.

Never chew gum. It is a breach of etiquette in a formal situation; it is also an impediment to clear speech.

Do not place your purse, your briefcase, or any other other article that you are carrying on the desk of the person interviewing you. That is the interviewer's "territory" and the person may be subconsciously annoyed if you invade it.

If you're wearing an outside coat of any sort, remove it before entering the interviewer's office; otherwise you seem to imply, "Let's get this over in a hurry so I can get out of here!"

Some interviewers go abruptly to the business at hand; others prefer an icebreaker or warm-up period to put the applicant at ease. You should follow the interviewer's lead. For example:

INT: Did you have any difficulty in finding the address?
YOU: No, you (or the secretary) give very good directions.
INT: Is the name Janovic of Czechoslovakian extraction?
YOU: Yes, how clever of you to know. Your name, Ruda, is of German extraction. Right?
INT: Suprised you could get here so promptly in this heavy snowfall.
YOU: Oh, I heard the weather forecast and allowed myself a little extra time.

If the interviewer indicates that it is permissible to exchange pleasantries, try to do this. Most offices reflect something about the personality of their occupants. Look for some outstanding conversation piece and make a pointed remark about it.

For example:

The interviewer may have a huge sailfish mounted on the wall behind his desk. He's obviously proud of it, so comment on its size and beauty and ask where he caught it. (Even if you know nothing about fish, ask about it.)

The interviewer may have several potted plants in her office. Comment on how much plants brighten up an office.

Perhaps there are a number of bowling trophies in the office. You might ask if the firm has a bowling team, or if they were all won by the interviewer.

Don't talk on and on about the surroundings. Nevertheless, a pleasant comment about the interviewer's surroundings will show (a) that you are observant, and (b) that you appreciate the other person's taste or hobbies.

Do not smoke unless you are specifically invited to do so, and then never a pipe or cigar.

Keep your hands away from your face. This may seem peculiar advice for us to give when admonishing you to appear at ease. Desmond Morris in his book *Manwatching*[1] claims to have done research on "face feelers." While Dr. Morris does not state that face-feeling or nose-feeling is an actual indication of an outright *lie*, he suggests strongly that such a gesture *is* an indication of conflict between our *actual* thoughts and those which we expect others to believe. He also suggests that hair-stroking, seat-shifting, and a total *lack* of normal gestures can be signs of deceit. So, while you may have nothing to hide, some personnel directors may take Desmond Morris's book as Gospel.

In some large firms you may have to pass a polygraph (lie detector) test or a handwriting analysis (graphology). In these times of so many people who are functionally illiterate, you may even be required to write a paragraph or more in your own handwriting, as a check on your punctuation and spelling.

Should the interviewer be interrupted by a telephone call, try not to eavesdrop or show curiosity about the call. Use that interruption to look around the office for points of interest—trophies, awards, certificates—that may be displayed. You may then make a complimentary remark about them when the telephone call has been completed.

## Questions and Answers

Obviously you would not have been chosen for an interview if your resumé or application had not shown that you are capable of holding the job. Mere capability, however, is not enough. It is vital that an employer know two things that cannot very well be put on paper:

1. He needs to know that you have a complete understanding of what the job entails.
2. He must be assured that you have a positive attitude toward the job.

Let us assume that you are applying for a summer job as a tour guide. Let us further assume that all four of the triangles may be turned over to fit onto any other triangle (See Figure 8-1).

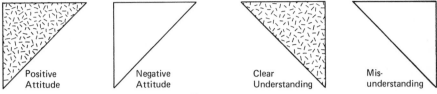

Figure 8-1

Here are some possible combinations:

1. "This job is going to be great! I'll stay in only the best hotels, eat anything I like on the menu, and get a laundry and dry cleaning allowance—all free. I'll also get a salary, plus tips from the passengers; and all I have to do is ride on the coach and point out the scenic and historical sites to the passengers. I also have all of my evenings free, once I get them into the hotel, just to have fun."

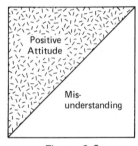

Figure 8-2

This is a positive attitude, but a misunderstanding of the job. There is more to being a tour guide than that. (Figure 8-2)

2. "I'd never take that job! First, you have to be on duty twenty-four hours a day, and you work without a single day off; as soon as you finish one tour, you start all over again. Then, there's all of that accounting to do; you have to keep books on every single penny that is spent. Besides, most of the people who go on bus tours are old, and I'd never have any fun, with all of these old grouches complaining about their food and their rooms, and so on."

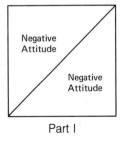

Part I

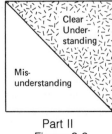

Part II

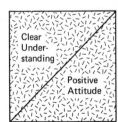

Part III

Figure 8-3

Here is both a negative attitude and a misunderstanding of what is required of a tour guide. (Figure 8-3, Part I)

3. "I'm not sure I'd like all that responsibility; you'd have to be on call during the night to find a doctor if someone got sick, even if you did have most evenings free. You'd also have to study too much to answer all of the people's questions. I don't really care too much about staying in luxury hotels and having all of that fine food to eat—I'd rather have the money—and I'm not sure about how much I'd get in tips."

The above is an understanding of the job, but a negative attitude toward it. (Figure 8-3, Part II)

4. "Yes, I know the job is a responsible one; that I'll have to check the luggage to see that none gets lost. But the tour company has worked out a system that makes it easy. Most people are reasonably healthy when they take a tour, so I don't anticipate too many emergencies. I've heard that the accommodations are first-rate, so I don't expect many complaints. I love showing folks a good time, I love meeting people, and I'll have a new group of tourists every two weeks. I've heard that the tips can often be as much as the salary."

Here, at last, is a realistic understanding of the job, along with a positive attitude. (Figure 8-3, Part III)

The interviewer will usually use both direct and indirect questions to obtain the information desired. The interviewer is apt to start with direct questions to which you are expected to give definite answers. Direct questions are often intended to channel the discussion to a specific point. From there the interviewer is likely to proceed to rejoinders or questions that create an open climate in which you are encouraged to talk freely about your attitudes and feelings. The following will examine in detail how some of these directive and nondirective techniques work, so that you will have some idea of what to expect.

## Directive Techniques

1. *The direct question.* There is probably only one possible answer that you can give, so make it short and to the point.

"How much college work have you had?"
"What do you plan for your major field?"

2. *The yes-no question.* There are only two possible answers—"yes" or "no."

"Did you participate in sports while in high school?"
"Are you an American citizen?"

3. *The leading question.* In itself it contains part of the answer. You may feel that this question is unfair since you know the answer that is expected of you; answer it honestly.

"Don't you think that it's important for a salesman to be willing to relocate if he works for a national company such as ours?"

"We have no policy of allowing vacation pay or days off to accumulate; they must be taken two weeks only at one time. Does that seem fair to you?"

4. *The testimonial question*. It asks you a third party's comments or ideas on a particular situation, rather than yours. It can be valuable in telling the interviewer what your feelings and attitudes really are, by reflecting the attitudes of those closest to you.

"What would your parents say about your working the graveyard shift?"

"What did your wife say when you told her you'd have to travel?"


## Nondirective Techniques

Personnel and other trained interviewers will almost never subject you to a barrage of questions, because they know that such a practice will cause you to withdraw from expressing your actual understanding and true attitudes. Direct questions can be threatening, yes-no questions can back you into a corner, and leading questions can be uncomfortable if you don't agree with the answer you know is expected of you. Even leading or testimonial questions can put you on the spot by forcing you to a certain topic.

The likelihood is that once an attempt has been made to put you at ease, the interviewer will use a *combination* of questions and nondirective responses. Here are some examples of what you might expect.

1. *The listening response*. This type of response is one in which the interviewer makes a completely neutral comment in a way calculated to keep you talking—such as "Uh huh," "I see," or "Tell me more." (The interviewer will probably *not* use an interjection such as "Ah hah!" or "Oh no!" lest you interpret it as being judgmental.) If you sense that the interviewer is not actually interested—if eye contact is not maintained, for example—then cut the talk short. In any case say what is necessary and then be quiet.

2. *The reflective response*. Basically this is when an interviewer will repeat, or *reflect back*, something which you have said. You will note that the interviewer does not add anything to your phrase or words, but it should give you a clue that something is not clear to the interviewer. For example:

YOU: I never cared much for advertising courses.

INT: Advertising courses?

YOU: Yes. . . What I mean is, I had a course in motivational research and . . ."

3. *The interpretive response*. Essentially this is another form of the reflective response; the difference is that the interviewer definitely *adds* something. The

interviewer is trying to interpret in the clearest way possible what you say. Give some help!

YOU:  I'm sure I'm qualified, but I'm a little concerned about the travel.

INT:  Let's see—as I understand you, you feel that you can handle the job, but you're concerned about how many nights you'd be away from home.

You will notice that the interviewer has added something you did not say; you made no mention of the number of nights you might be away from home. Be careful not to allow resentment at having "words put into your mouth." The interviewer is merely trying to understand you. If the interviewer has made a clear *mis*interpretation, you might make a courteous correction, but do it with a smile.

4. *The supportive response.* This is the type of response in which the interviewer goes beyond merely reflection or interpretation and voices support for your comments. You should be encouraged by this, because it indicates that the interviewer is trying to find some common ground with your own experiences. It might take this form:

YOU:  I never was able to find the time to get involved in intramural sports . . .

INT:  I know what you mean. Holding down a job and trying to make good grades kept me too busy for less important things.

YOU:  I'm glad you appreciate that, because I hated to miss out on the games. . . .

Sometimes—although not often—an interviewer will give a supportive response to try to find out what your prejudices are, or if you have strong ones. Be careful! However, most interviewers will not try to trick you into giving answers you might regret.

If the interviewer shows strong prejudices with which you do not agree (bigotry, racism, cruelty), you do not have to assent to them. You may pass off such remarks with a noncommital, "That's interesting," and be thankful that the person interviewing you will not be your immediate boss.

In answering questions, avoid prefacing them with such expressions as "to tell the truth," "frankly speaking," "candidly," or "to be honest with you." These phrases might be taken to mean that you are *not* honest and straightforward most of the time.

Above all, you must consider this: While you may *want* the job, and the personnel director wants someone to *fill* the job, the interviewer also wants someone who is genuinely interested in the company, the position itself, the other workers—and even in himself or herself. You must show enthusiasm in your interview, along with warmth and friendliness . . . and this cannot be faked.

Bernard Haldane Associates, the nation's largest job and counseling organization, points out that personnel directors rarely hire a person on the basis of that person's qualifications alone; much depends on the rapport established between the interviewee and the interviewer. This is logical: The personnel director has probably hired many (if not most) of the current working force and probably knows their temperament and the sort of *esprit de corps* they have. The personnel director is not likely to hire an individual who may not work well with others, one who may become dissatisfied, and who may even become a troublemaker.

## Now It's Your Turn

Unless you have been invited to ask questions during the course of the interview, the interviewer is likely to reserve the final portion of it for that purpose. It is impossible for us to anticipate the questions you might ask, since we do not know the nature of the job for which you are applying. However, try to anticipate the work you might be doing and make a mental note of the questions to be asked during this period. They may cover a wide range:

1. Working conditions (safety and occupational hazards)
2. Physical demands (long hours of standing? heavy lifting?)
3. Types of dexterity required
4. Supervisory responsibilities
5. Your place in the chain of command
6. Opportunities for promotion
7. Sick leave? Vacation leave?
8. Fringe benefits: Insurance? Health and disability insurance?

Some of these questions may be prepared in advance and listed on paper. Your interviewer might be impressed by your orderliness and sense of responsibility. On the other hand, the interviewer may think that you are nit-picking. You'll just have to take your chances!

## MORE INTERVIEWS

In some positions there will be more than one interview. Richard German, executive vice president of Bernard Haldane Associates, says that the primary objective of that first interview is to get the *second* interview, as well as all of the succeeding ones.

If you feel that you have established a friendly relationship with the interviewer, *ask* the interviewer for a second interview after all of the other applicants for the position have been interviewed. This assures him that you are confident that you can meet competition head-on.

MOST IMPORTANT: Write a short note, thanking the personnel director for seeing you. If you have additional information attesting to your competence, such as a letter of recommendation, include it. The note will serve to make the interviewer aware of you as a person, especially if there have been a large number of applicants. Haldane Associates says that most interviewers don't get many thank you notes.

Haldane Associates has also provided this chapter with a unique suggestion, and we are grateful for their permission to use it. They advise that if your interview has definitely been a failure on your part, you might telephone the interviewer for an appointment to *find out why* you failed. This is reasonable: All of us love to show our expertise, and personnel directors are no exceptions. You can learn something from them, even if you're not hired by the firm for which they are working.

## Your Voice and Diction

You can never *obtain* any responsible position—much less hope to grow in it and receive a promotion—unless you have an acceptable voice and good diction. It is the mark of an educated man or woman. Oren Arnold wrote in *The Kiwanis Magazine:*

> Watch your speech. A man's command of the language is most important. Next to kissing, it's the most exciting form of communication mankind has evolved.

If your voice and diction are poor, seek help. Many college courses are available, and you should take one or *more* if needed.

## SUGGESTED CLASSROOM EXERCISE

Stage an interview in class. Each student could prepare an advertisement that might appear in the classified section of a newspaper. The ads should be posted on the classroom bulletin board several days in advance. If there are not enough volunteers to answer every ad, the teacher may assign someone to be the "prospective employer."

## FOOTNOTES FOR CHAPTER EIGHT

[1]Desmond Morris, *Manwatching: A Field Guide to Human Behavior* (New York: Harry Abrams, 1979), p. 106.

# VOCABULARY STUDY FOR CHAPTER NINE

Following are some words used in this chapter with which you may not be familiar. Below are given their definitions and in some instances their connotations.

1. ARCHAEOLOGICAL — Pertaining to the scientific study of historic or prehistoric peoples and their cultures by analyzing their artifacts, monuments, inscriptions, and other such remains.

2. AMORTIZATION — The act of reducing a debt (or cost) by regular payments or by its savings in the cost of production.

3. CHARISMATIC — Having a special personal quality that gives an individual influence over a large number of people.

4. FALLIBLE — Likely to be mistaken; liable to err.

5. FUROR — A general burst of excitement, enthusiasm, controversy, or the like.

6. HELLION — A disorderly, troublesome, or rowdy person.

7. INEFFECTUAL — Not producing results; weak and unsatisfactory.

8. INGRATIATE — To establish oneself in the favor or good graces of others.

9. IRREPARABLE — Cannot be repaired; permanently damaged.

10. PERSPICACIOUS — Having keen mental perception; highly discerning.

11. PHILANTHROPIST — One who has an affection for mankind, especially insofar as donating money for the sick and needy, or for other worthwhile social purposes.

12. SUCCINCT — Expressed in few words; concise, terse.

13. VALIDITY — The state or quality of being well founded; sound; just.

# 9 | Other Dyads

Complaint is the largest tribute Heaven receives,
and the sincerest part of our devotion.

Jonathan Swift (1667–1745)

## HANDLING COMPLAINTS

The world is rife with complaints. A 10-volume encyclopedia could hardly begin to catalog them, to say nothing of telling you how they should be handled. In the business and professional world there are complaints about service, complaints about working conditions, complaints about pay, complaints about personnel, complaints about the weather, and complaints because some people want to find something to complain about. To paraphrase Beverley Nichols,[1] "The worst thing you can possibly do to such a person is to deprive a complainer of his complaints." This is why we have confined ourselves in this section to *customer* complaints. Having learned something about how to cope with this problem in communication, you should be well on your way to handling other complaints.

Only two considerations govern the handling of customer complaints in a legitimate business:

To *satisfy* the customer
To keep the business in operation and *showing a profit*.

This text is discussing customers who actually believe that they have a legitimate complaint, and not those who perpetrate "scams," such as one in which I once unwittingly participated:

> In 1967 I became acquainted with Aldo and Monette, a handsome couple who lived together without any visible means of support. Each had impeccable evening attire and costume jewelry which appeared elegant, and somehow they managed to circulate among the cities of New Orleans, New York, and San Francisco. It seemed that a friend had a vacant apartment ready for them whenever they chose to show up in those cities. They ate only at the most expensive restaurants, always with a reservation made under the name of minor royalty.
>
> After we had dined sumptuously at a fine Italian restaurant one evening, at a table reserved for the "Baron Strasburg," dessert was served, and Aldo had hardly dipped into his when he let out a cry of pain: There were slivers of glass in his Zabaglione! The waiter promptly summoned the maitre d'hotel, but before the headwaiter could appear, Aldo turned to a neighboring table, and held out his dessert for inspection.
>
> "You see? It is there—glass! Who knows how much of it I may have swallowed? Already I am feeling pains in my esophagus!"
>
> The slivers of glass were positively there: Aldo had made sure of that by inserting them into his Zabaglione. By the time the headwaiter appeared, Aldo had succeeded in creating such a furor that the headwaiter was glad to assure him that our check would be paid, and asked for his name and address, further assuring him that the restaurant would gladly pay any doctor or hospital bills if the "Baron" had any ill aftereffects.
>
> After we left indignantly and were half a block away from the restaurant, Aldo turned to me and chuckled. "You see, it works every time!"
>
> —Hugh P. Fellows

Most people are honest, and do not try such stunts as that just described. Many customers will put up with less-than-satisfactory goods and services, because it's too much trouble to complain. However, there are people who have legitimate complaints and the courage to voice them. How should they be treated?

## Two Sides to Consider

Customers who are dissatisfied with merchandise or a service they have purchased think of only two needs:

1. I'm hurting! Something is wrong!
2. What are you going to do about it?

Such needs are dealt with daily by physicians; this is why doctors are so careful in their diagnoses. Woe to the M.D. who mistakenly diagnoses a migraine headache when the patient has a brain tumor! There is a common belief that "Doctors don't ever tell you anything"; doctors don't tell you because they may not *know*—yet. Or, at least, they must be *sure* before they speak.

If businessmen and businesswomen were as careful in diagnosing customer complaints as doctors, there would be fewer dissatisfied customers. The business person must consider at least *three* things:

1. Something is obviously wrong (in the view of my customer) with my goods or services.
2. What caused the complaint? Who is at fault?
3. What can I do about the situation so that (a) I can keep the customer and the customer's good will, (b) at the least cost to my business?

Here are some case histories:

## Case A:

Your name is Vera Bingham, and you are the manager of Carson's, a large "exclusive" clothing store for men and women. A Mrs. Sawyer has asked to see you, telling you over the 'phone that she has been a customer of Carson's for ten years. You check the files and find that she has had a charge account for ten years, and that she has purchased a sizable amount of merchandise during that period, although you have never seen her before.

Mrs. Sawyer enters and places an open box of ladies' shoes on your desk. She is obviously upset.

"I bought these shoes here just two weeks ago. I didn't really like them, but Mr. Johnson talked me into taking them. He said that they were the latest style, and that the color would go well with any dressy outfit. At the time he fitted me, I said that I thought them too tight, but—no!—Johnson insisted that they were exactly my size. Well, I wore them for three days and nearly died from pain! I *knew* they weren't the right size!

"Well, when I tried to return them to Mr. Johnson in exchange for a pair of shoes I really liked, he was *very* rude to me. That man shouldn't be working at Carson's! He said I had worn them, and he couldn't exchange them. He also implied that I am one of those shoppers who buys something, wears it, decides she doesn't like it, and then tries to return it. That man ought to be fired! Now, what are you going to do about it?"

Well, what *would* you do? Here are several choices for you to consider (the shoes in question cost fifty dollars):

1. "Oh, Mrs. Sawyer, I'm sorry to hear that! Mr. Johnson has worked at Carson's for fourteen years, and we've *never* had a complaint about him. Why, women have been coming into Carson's for *years,* just to be fitted by Mr. Johnson. I can't understand what happened . . . "

2. "I am *terribly* sorry, Mrs. Sawyer! However, you must understand that the law forbids our taking back clothing or shoes that have already been worn. Now, we can stretch the shoes so that they will not hurt your feet; why don't you let us do that? After about two days on the stretcher, I'm sure that the shoes will fit you perfectly. How's that?"

3. "How dreadful of Mr. Johnson to treat you like that! I'm going to call him in and give him a good dressing down immediately. If he *ever* shows such discourtesy to another customer, he will be discharged on the spot. Meanwhile, we'll take the shoes and stretch them for you so that they will not hurt your feet."

4. None of the above. Specify how you would handle the complaint.

## Case B:

You are Carl Monks, the owner of The Sound Shop, which carries a large stock of radios, television sets, and stereos. Your supplier, Rogers Electronics, has offered several thousand Apex color TV sets at a greatly reduced price to its regular dealers. You order four dozen of the Apex TV sets, intending to use them as the "leader" item on a sale you are having. Rogers Electronics sends you photo-plates to be used for advertising in the local newspapers. Your sale has been announced for Wednesday; it is now Monday, and the TV sets have not arrived. You call Mr. Rogers, and he gives you one of the following reasons why you have not received shipment:

1. Your shipment of last month has not been fully paid for, and he will not ship you any more appliances until the account has been settled.

2. Rogers Electronics had a 5-day strike on the assembly line. Even though the strike has been settled, there are much larger orders ahead of you which must be filled before your order; you can't expect shipment for at least ten days from today.

3. Your shipment went out a week ago by Surex Trucking Company. You had better contact Surex to find out what happened to it.

4. None of the above. If you were *Mr. Rogers,* how would you handle the situation in order to satisfy Mr. Carl Monks?

## Case C:

You are James Danby, owner of Danby's Fine Furniture Store, located in downtown Minneapolis. Mr. and Mrs. Fred Riggs have recently built a home in Wayzata, Minn., a suburb of Minneapolis about thirty-five miles from your store, and have bought all of their furniture from Danby's—about $15,000 worth.

There was a problem with the dining room suite: Mrs. Riggs wanted a French Provincial suite, which was not in stock, so you ordered it from Naylor's Furniture Manufacturing Co., who promised delivery within four weeks. Naylor's also promised to deliver it directly to the Riggs home in Wayzata. Instead of a four weeks delivery, Naylor was delayed for two extra weeks, but a telephone call from the manufacturer announced that Mrs. Riggs would receive delivery today which is Saturday.

Your store closes at 5:00 P.M. on Saturdays. All of your employees have gone, and you are alone in the store at 5:30 P.M. when Mrs. Riggs telephones.

"Oh, Mr. Danby, the most terrible thing has happened to my dining room suite!" she says excitedly. "When the truckers uncrated it just about an hour ago, two of the chair backs are completely broken off, the leg of another one of the chairs is broken, and the buffet and the dining table both have huge scratches on them. It's just awful!"

"That's all right, Mrs. Riggs," you reassure her. "I'll put in a call to Naylor the minute I finish talking with you. Tell me again which pieces are damaged, and I'll call the factory; if anyone is still there at this hour, I'll have them put new duplicates of the damaged pieces on an express truck the first thing Monday morning, and you'll have replacements by Wednesday of next week."

"But you don't understand!" she wails. "The dining room suite was supposed to arrive *two weeks ago!* Just to allow for a delay, I didn't plan my party until tonight. I've got thirty people coming for a housewarming party *tonight* at eight o'clock, and I'm supposed to give them a buffet dinner. What in the world am I going to do?"

If you were James Danby, what would you do? Here are some possible ways of handling the complaint. Would you use any of them?

1. Tell Mrs. Riggs that there is nothing you can do except offer your sympathy until Monday. All of your trucks are in the garage miles away, and their drivers have gone home. Otherwise you might be able to lend her some dining room furniture from your store.

2. Tell her that you'll try to find a furniture repairman and get him out to patch up the damage as best he can. (Remember, it's Saturday, 5:30 P.M., and Mrs. Riggs is expecting her guests at 8:00 P.M.)

3. Suggest that she put the damaged furniture in the garage where it won't be seen; then go out and borrow folding chairs and card tables from the neighbors and set them up for her buffet dinner.

4. None of the above. How would you handle the situation?

## Case D:

You are the manager in the home appliance department of a large mail-order firm which has a retail store in Abilene, Kans. We'll call the store Bears. The store in Abilene is running a special sale on Zinger sewing machines. Jessica Klugman finds a sewing machine which is on sale for $122.00 and decides to take it. She is surprised that the cabinet for the sewing machine is not included in the price and protests to the salesman that, "The *sign* says $122.00, so one would naturally assume that the cabinet would be included." The salesman points out that the sign says "This 40-A Model Zinger, only $122.00." He also points to a tag which prices the cabinet at $80.00.

Ms. Klugman waits until she gets back to her office at the local community college, where she telephones you (the manager) and claims that you are guilty of misrepresentation in the price of the sewing machine; the machine is placed on *top* of the cabinet, which would lead everyone to believe that the cabinet is included in the price of the machine. When you explain that the cabinet is plainly marked $80.00, she counters with these statements:

"Anyone would *assume* that the cabinet is included in the price of the sewing machine. Now, I teach at the local community college, and I can easily tell all of my students that Bears is guilty of misleading buyers insofar as prices marked on merchandise is concerned. You should not have placed the sewing machine on top of the cabinet if the price didn't include both. I have a great many students, and they will tell their parents, and it could certainly make many buyers distrustful of Bears. Don't you agree?"

Here are some choices which you, as the store manager for Bears, might make:

1. You can tell Ms. Klugman that your manner of displaying prices *could* have been misleading and that Bears will be glad to include the $80.00 cabinet in the $122.00 cost of the sewing machine.

2. You can tell Ms. Klugman that, since she did not understand that the cost of the sewing machine did not include the cabinet, you will offer her the cabinet at half price.

3. You can tell Ms. Klugman that you don't think much of her as a college instructor if she is too stupid to inquire whether or not the cabinet was included with the machine. You can also tell her that, insofar as her trying to blackmail you into giving her the cabinet by telling her students that Bears is misleading their customers won't work. Bears is too well known for honesty to be intimidated by such tactics.

4. None of the above. How would you choose to handle the incident?*

## The Customer Is *Not* Always Right

If you are in a business firm, you cannot be subject to the whims of *every* cranky customer; if you do, you will not be in business for very long. However, most people are fair-minded, and you should do anything possible to serve them. Following are some precepts that tell you when to say "yes" and when to say "no."

I. *When your company is clearly at fault:*
   A. Say "yes" immediately; otherwise word-of-mouth reports can damage your business irreparably.
   B. Explain *why* the company made the mistake, so that the customer will know you have taken the trouble to investigate why the customer suffered an inconvenience.
   C. Let the customer know *definitely* the precautions you have taken to see that the customer (or any other customer) will not be inconvenienced again.
   D. Express confidence that the customer will understand your good will, and look forward to doing business with the customer in the future.

II. *When a third party is at fault:*
   A. Take the initiative in seeing that your customer is not inconvenienced further. You, and you alone, should get to the bottom of *why* the third party caused trouble to your customer.

*Your instructor has our suggested solution to these problems.

B. Explain what happened to the third party, and (a) assure your customer that you are no longer using the third party, or (b) be prepared to defend that third party to show that people are fallible. Cite the third party's record of long and faithful service to your customers.

C. Show concern for your customer, and assure him/her that you will do everything possible to prevent a similar inconvenience from arising in the future.

III. *When the customer is at fault—and you say "yes"*:

A. Explain carefully the policy of your firm and the quality of the merchandise, to be sure that neither was misrepresented.

B. Let the customer know—*tactfully*—that he/she is at fault.

C. Explain why you are making an exception in *this* instance, and granting the customer's request instead of denying it. (Length of patronage, honest mistake by customer, and so forth.)

D. Look forward to future happy relations and continued patronage.

Perhaps we are over-cynical, but we often think that saying "yes" to a customer (when the customer has been at fault) is more risky than saying "no." If a customer thinks he has "gotten away with something," he knows that the chances are not very good with his doing so another time, and you *may* lose his business. By *no* means should you make the customer feel unnecessary guilt about the transaction, or you will *surely* lose his business.

IV. *When the customer is at fault—and you say "no"*:

A. Explain that you have investigated the situation carefully, and that neither the service nor the quality of the merchandise was lacking.

B. Outline briefly the policy of your firm that prevents your granting the customer's request.

C. Appeal to the customer's sense of justice and fair play.

D. End by looking forward to future pleasant relations and continued patronage.

## Avoid Adversary Roles

Try to avoid putting yourself in the position of an adversary to the dissatisfied customer. Remember, your purpose is to solve a problem in a mutually beneficial way. Above all, never interrupt a complainant during a stream of angry talk, because you cannot reason with an angry person. When the complainant pauses for breath, you may interject a comment of a nondirective type, such as, "And that disappointed you, didn't it?" or "That really got you angry, huh?" Or, better still, "Yes, I can see why that would make you angry," or "Yes, I can certainly see your point of view."

After the first angry outburst has been exhausted, you can usually reason with a dissatisfied person. Only when the customer is more calm can you explain calmly that this is a *problem* which *both* of you can help solve. Examine the facts, as far as they can be determined, and then appeal to the customer's sense of fair play and ask for the customer's judgment under the circumstances. When people have *helped* in making a decision, they will usually abide by it.

Finally, do not allow yourself to be intimidated. Stand by your convictions, no matter how much bluster the other person uses. Eleanor Roosevelt once said, "No one can make you feel inferior without your consent."

## TELEPHONE COMMUNICATION

In this country there are telephones in most homes, offices, and other places of business. We feel a compulsion to answer the telephone when it rings, no matter what we may be doing. We also tend to *listen* to the voice on the other end of the wire, even though our minds may wander from time to time. It may surprise you that many people don't know how to *use* this common instrument of everyday life properly.

### Limitations and Use

Although the microphone in a telephone mouthpiece has improved vastly during the past few years, it is still not as sensitive as most mikes; it *couldn't* be, considering the amount of abuse it must take. So, the instrument should be held properly, with the mouthpiece directly in front of the mouth. Holding the microphone under the chin is particularly poor practice because our mouths are constructed so that most people have a slight overbite. This directs the stream of breath from our mouths downward at an angle of approximately forty-five degrees. Many of the consonant sounds in speech (T, D, K, G, P, B, CH, J) are plosives; that is, little puffs of breath held back by the lips or tongue and then released quickly. When these noises are "exploded" into a microphone, they can be distracting and destructive to other sounds. Thus, the noise/signal ratio is too high. Speech intelligibility, over a telephone mike, can be distorted by as much as 30 percent when held at chin level (see Figure 9-1).

Another reason for holding the mouthpiece directly in front of your lips is that some of the consonant cognates may be mistaken for one another. To be less technical, an *s*, which is an *unvoiced* sound, is often mistaken for a *z*, which is a *voiced* sound. To be even less technical, here are some words that are often mistaken for one another by the listener:

Sign—fine—vine—line—mine, buy—pie, bit—pit, ride—wide, whether—weather, shine—sign, mare—bare.

There are many others, but this gives you a pretty good sample.

There is another important limitation to the telephone that you should be warned about—especially in a business firm: It takes the listener at least three

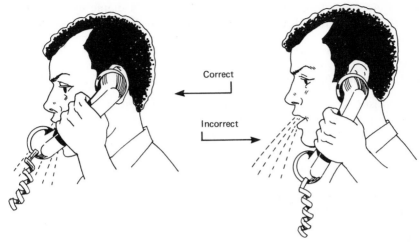

Figure 9-1

syllables before adjusting to the sound of your voice and enunciation. So, in answering a business call, you should always give your greeting ("Good morning/afternoon/evening") *before* you give the name of your business or company. Instead of answering the call with, "A. H. Moore Towmotors; good morning," reverse the greeting and the company name, and answer with, "Good morning; A. H. Moore Towmotors."

We ran this experiment at the Baruch School of Business in New York City: Twenty students were given five business firms in the city to call; they were given only the telephone number, not the name of the firm. As soon as the student received a response to the call, the student was to say, "Sorry, wrong number," and hang up. Then the student was asked to write down the name of the company—if the student could understand it. Out of the one hundred numbers dialed, in only *six* cases could the *name* of the business firm be understood. We repeated the experiment for four semesters, and the highest number of firms whose names could be understood was seven, while the lowest was only two out of one hundred.

Here is a suggestion to help you become more intelligible if you are talking above noise—the clatter of typewriters and business machines, or the steady roar of machinery. Talk slowly and in short phrases; in other words, pause between each group of four to six words. It may take all of the personality out of your voice, but it will aid you in being *heard* and *understood*. You should also try to *pitch* your voice to contrast with the prevailing noise. If the noise is high-pitched, speak in a lower pitch; if the noise is low-pitched, speak with as high a pitch as you can reach without strain.

Finally, when you have concluded your conversation, don't slam the receiver down onto its cradle (or hook) with a bang. The telephone microphone is definitely sensitive to percussion at close range. It's a simple matter to press down the buttons that disconnect the 'phone with your finger and then put down the receiver.

## The Telephone's Amazing Anonymity

It is surprising how drastically the personalities of some people change when they get on the telephone. The normally most courteous people become fire-breathing dragons, and bullies become as meek as mice with the cat near. The reason must be that the telephone has an anonymity that is not accorded us in any other form of equally familiar communication. Here is a case in point:

> I was engaged to teach an evening class at a large university. I met the dean and his assistant, and was told that a Miss Gray would take care of details such as duplicating, making appointments with students, getting necessary equipment for use in class, and so on. I did not meet Miss Gray for months, but talked with her several times weekly by telephone: She had a lovely bell-like tone, and a smile in her voice, with an extremely warm and friendly personality; she also had a breezy sense of humor that was delightful.
>
> After a few weeks, I had a complete mental image of Catherine Gray: She was tiny, pert, efficient without being hurried, and very feminine. She preferred tailored clothes—always with a colorful touch, such as a bright silk scarf or a corsage of flowers; she had soft, light brown hair with a windblown cut, and sparkling grey eyes.
>
> This vision of her was so entrenched in my mind that when I finally met her in person I was almost prostrate with the shock. She was a hippopotamus! Her weight was close to 300 pounds, and she had great, bulging black eyes with heavy, drooping lids. Her clothes were a disaster! But, what can you drape around 300 pounds of fat and make look neat?
>
> Soon afterwards, I was asked to take a daytime class which met in the lounge adjoining her office, and realized that Catherine Gray was petty, suspicious of everyone, incredibly selfish, and shockingly inconsiderate to her subordinates—a real Hellion!
>
> Yet, somehow, I never felt that Catherine was "two-faced." She had almost no contact with other people except by telephone (with the exception of the few people who were unlucky enough to work for her), and she *had* to be pleasant and personable in order to hold her job. But, when she had the upper hand in her own office, she didn't have to be anything except what she was.[2]

If there is a moral to this anecdote, it is, "Try to make your real personality match your telephone personality, depending on which one has a pleasanter attitude in dealing with people."

## Sending and Receiving

SECRETARY:   Good morning; this is Mr. Butler's office.

YOU:   Good morning. I'd like to speak with Mr. Butler. This is John Burnopp.

SEC:   May I ask what it is you wish to talk with Mr. Butler about, please?

[Or, "May I know the nature of your business, please, Mr. Bert—
Mr. . . . , sir?"]

It is hoped that the foregoing conversation makes you at least faintly angry. If Mr. Butler is busy, or in conference, let the secretary say so. If he isn't busy, he isn't saving himself any time by refusing to take the call without knowing what your business is about, and he is insulting you. Many business and professional people are dropping this procedure. Let's go back and see what might happen if Butler decided to talk with you without screening:

SEC:    Good morning; this is Mr. Butler's office.
YOU:    Good morning. I'd like to speak with Mr. Butler. This is John Burnopp.
SEC:    Yes, Mr. Burnopp. (Into intercom system) Mr. Burnopp is calling.
BUTLER:    This is Carl Butler.
YOU:    Mr. Butler, I know that you have always been very much of a philanthropist, and I wondered if you'd consider seeing me to talk about the wonderful opportunities to donate to our tax-exempt- - -
BUTLER:    No. Sorry, I'm not interested.

A waste of both of your times, isn't it? Let's try again from the third line of the original conversation:

SEC:    May I know the nature of your business, please?
YOU:    The nature of my business is that Mr. Butler's 16-year-old daughter is pregnant, and I am the man who is responsible; I'd like to talk with Mr. Butler on whether an abortion or marriage to me is preferable.
                         [You'll get to talk with Butler—quickly!]
    *or*

SEC:    May I inquire what it is that you want to talk with Mr. Butler about?
YOU:    It's personal.
SEC:    (After a short delay) I'm sorry, but any personal matters should be *written* to Mr. Butler privately, so that an appointment can be set up.
YOU:    There's no *time* to set up an appointment! I'm Butler's lawyer. His son has been apprehended by the police for a homosexual act in a public park, and I want to know if he wants me to make bail, or wait until the trial comes up!
                       [You'll get Butler on the line with this one, also!]

These are all ridiculous examples. It's much simpler to use the following:

SEC:    Good morning. This is Mr. Butler's office.
YOU:    Good morning. I'm John Burnopp. I'd like to speak with Mr. Butler about the option on the Terrell property.

You *should* state your business briefly, unless you are a close acquaintance of Butler. If you think you're going to sneak by his secretary by using some ruse such as "it's personal," it won't do you any good when you've reached the man.

The *purpose* of a business telephone call is

1. To get or give information.
2. To pose or solve a problem (See Chapters Eleven and Twelve).
3. To reach an agreement.

**When you are the sender.**   First, you should plan and organize your telephone calls as you would any other presentation. Jot down the points you wish to make in the order of their importance. Look them over and think about them for a few minutes so that you won't need to say, "Oh, I forgot one thing I meant to tell you!" It will only confuse the receiver if you are on point three and suddenly remember something about point one that should have been included.

Second, *date* the notes on your telephone call. You wouldn't send out a business letter without the date, would you?

Third, if there is an agreement to be reached, jot it down and read it to the other party for that individual's approval. The other party should do the same for you.

Finally, be brief.

**When you are the receiver.**   If the call promises to be important, jot down the date.

If the caller desires the solution of a problem, (a) listen for its general nature, and (b) write down specific details. Unless you can give a definite solution at once, ask for a *specific* length of time in which to arrive at a decision. Keep your promise to call back within the time limit.

If an agreement is to be reached, offer any countersuggestions you feel called upon to make, and help the caller to formulate the finished agreement. Then, write it down before you forget it.

If information is requested that is not immediately available, don't keep the caller waiting while you look for it. Call back later, and have the information well organized.

Be brief.

Speaking of the desirability of brevity in business calls, Mr. E. M. Rauschelback, former Director of Personnel for Union Carbide and Carbon Company's New York City office, offers this experience:

> Both the Finance Manager and I were appalled at our bills for long distance telephone calls to and from our New York office and other branches and plants throughout the country. A memorandum circulated throughout our office, asking that only essential calls should be made, did no good. We got permission from the telephone company to monitor and record all outgoing long distance calls. Our switchboard operator handled the tape recorder.

After one week's time had elapsed, the Office Manager, the Finance Manager and I listened to the tapes. It was quite a job! We finally found the culprit who was guilty of running up our bills. We spliced together a half dozen of the calls on tape, and called a meeting of all department heads. When we played the tape at the meeting, we all agreed that the trouble lay in this tape of a typical long distance call:

ALBANY, N. Y.:   Hello; this is Bill Shoupe speaking.

NEW YORK CITY:   Hi, Bill! This is Tully Freeman, down at the New York office.

ALBANY:   Surprised to hear from you, Tully; thought you were taking your vacation.

N. Y. CITY:   Nope, the wife and I plan to fly down to Mexico early in November, when her sister can come east to look after the youngsters. How're *your* family?

ALBANY:   Couldn't be better, thanks. Jonathon won the "Prize Pitcher Award" in the Little League, and he's decided that he's gonna be another Dizzy Dean. Mexico, eh? What part are you going to—Acapulco?

N. Y. CITY:   Nope; the wife's sort of an archaeological buff, you know, so we're going to spend a few days in Mexico City and then go on down to the Yucatan Peninsula, where all the Mayan ruins are . . . Bill, what I really called you about was to find out about those conveyor belts we ordered from that new supplier. . . .

It is commendable to be pleasant to those who work for the same company as you. It is friendly to inquire about their families, their golf games, and their laundry detergents—but *not* on the company's long distance telephone bill! A business telephone call should be (a) organized, (b) courteous, and (c) brief.

Let us reiterate that your telephone calls should be planned, and *add* to that by saying that you should even *rehearse* what you are going to say if you lack fluency in speech. This requires no more than a minute or two, because of the differential in the speeds of speech and thought. Nothing is more ineffectual than what is known as "vocalized pauses" in telephone speech. They sound like this:

"Well-*ah*, you see—*uh*—this man's credit is really good, but-*ah* he-*uh* sometimes is a little late in paying his bills. He . . . *ah* . . . is just as honest as he can be, but—*uh*—he seems to have more-*uh* problems than most people do-*ah* around the first of the month . . . *Mmm.* So-*uh* I can recommend him as a good credit risk, but-*uh* you'll have to put up with his-*ah* little peculiarities . . . *Hmm* . . . "

Edward Hodnett, in his fine book *Effective Presentations*[3] claims that telephone speech "may cause you to be more fluent because you aren't dependent on other faculties—such as unusual clarity and eloquence." This may very well be true—for *some* people—because of the magnificent anonymity of the telephone; however, if you're guilty of the vocalized pause in ordinary speech, you should have a tape recording made of one of your telephone conversations to see if it disappears.

## Telephone Selling

When Fellows wrote a book in 1964,[4] his editor insisted that he have a few words to say about telephone selling. He wrote:

> First, let me distinguish between telephone solicitation and telephone salesmanship. I am so firmly opposed to blank solicitation by telephone that I cannot be objective about it; to me it is not only an annoyance, but a criminal invasion of privacy.

Fifteen years later this author feels even *more* strongly about blank solicitation of residential telephones. Can you imagine what your home life would be like if everyone who has a product to sell rang your residence only *once every two years?* Yet, I got many letters of protest when the book was published, containing statements such as

> "I'm handicapped in a wheel chair; how do you expect me to earn a living except by using the telephone for selling?"
>
> *Reply:* "Learn to repair watches or something else that does not demand complete mobility."

In this author's opinion there is simply no excuse for this annoying invasion of privacy. Representative Les Aspin of Wisconsin has introduced a bill prohibiting unsolicited commercial telephone calls to persons who have indicated they don't want such calls.[5]

Telephoning a person's place of business is a different matter. The telephone may aid you in selling, with no loss of personal prestige, if you use it in the following ways:

1. You may telephone a prospect and ask for an appointment. The chances are you won't get it unless you refer to a friend or business associate who uses your product already.

2. After you have presented your product, you may call a day or two later to tell the prospect of an additional feature of your product, which you have neglected to mention (purposefully) in your first sales presentation; or, it might be a slight change in price, or a faster delivery than had been anticipated.

3. If you have *not* used the foregoing (No. 2) practice, you may call to ask if the prospect has made a decision. It is suggested that you not use *both* No. 2 and No. 3 because it might annoy the prospect. However, there are salespersons who have made their sales through sheer persistence. There is a third alternative for a follow-up call, which is

4. If you have sold your product to a friend of your present prospect, you might call and ask the friend to call your prospect and express his satisfaction. There is nothing so effective in making a sale as word-of-mouth recommendations.

## EMPLOYEE GRIEVANCES

This topic is mentioned only briefly here, since it belongs properly in the province of labor relations and is beyond the scope of this text. However, we offer a few suggestions to help you in presenting a grievance or in receiving one.

Employee grievances are usually concerned with one of three things: working conditions, personality conflicts, and lack of benefits or promotion opportunities. If you have been chosen as the spokesman to present the grievance, you should make sure that it is a *genuine* grievance, affecting a *significant number* of employees, and not the disgruntled complaints of only one or two workers.

Planning the presentation of the grievance is essential. The following is a suggested format:

1. Open your presentation with some *favorable* comments concerning the company and the general satisfaction with the way it treats its employees.

2. Limit your presentation to *one* grievance, and present it clearly and succinctly.

3. Show how the grievance, if left uncorrected, is likely to result in (a) lower morale among the employees, (b) decreased productivity, or both.

4. Suggest a possible solution to correct the source of the grievance. If the employees do not know what they *want,* it becomes merely an unfounded complaint.

5. Thank the personnel manager, or the labor relations officer, or whoever is receiving your grievance, for allowing you to present it.

If you are the person *receiving* the grievance, we suggest that you handle it in much the same way you would treat a customer complaint, detailed earlier in this chapter. There is one definite attitude that you should take, however: you should be profoundly grateful—and should show it—to the person presenting the grievance. Genuine grievances that are not reported can develop into passive hostility on the part of employees. If you do not show yourself ready to listen to grievances, when you *need* actual information from employees, you are apt to get only "defensive reporting"; that is, employees will report only what they think you want to hear, rather than the real truth on a matter.

## APPRAISAL INTERVIEWS

In a perspicacious business firm—one that scrutinizes carefully the contributions made by all employees in key positions—appraisals are made periodically by supervisors or their next highest executives. The time interval may be every year, every two years, or every six months. They are made for the purposes of (a) ascertaining satisfactory performance in the position the employee now holds, (b) evaluating whether pay raises are merited, and (c) determining if the employee can fill *another* position of equal or superior importance within the company. Such appraisals are usually made in writing by supervisors or executives, on a rating scale or a multiple-step questionnaire. However, in the event of an important promotion for the employee, interviews with that employee may be conducted by the next highest supervisor, the next highest executive, or the personnel officer.

## The Interviewee

It has been a popular misconception that the employee can do nothing concerning such appraisal interviews, since the employee's performance is on record and that is all that counts. Quite the contrary! File records do *not* show everything, and the employee who goes into the appraisal interview with a prepared presentation is at a tremendous advantage.

Here are four items to which an appraiser wants favorable responses; if you have thought about them, jotted them down, and can cite *specific examples* of how well you performed on these four requirements, you will probably do well in the appraisal interview.

1. Employee Performance—Was it merely satisfactory, or did the employee show an improvement in performance?

What about your suggestion that, instead of enclosing self-addressed envelopes in the monthly bills sent out to charge-account customers, a gummed seal bearing the company's address be substituted, requiring the customer to furnish his own envelope? The suggestion was put into practice and saved your firm a few hundred dollars.

2. Employee Development—Does the employee strive for self-improvement and thereby strengthen the entire organization?

Don't forget those night courses you've been taking at the local community college for your own improvement: courses in Spanish or Russian, courses in business English and speech, courses in economics. Even self-study courses, taken by correspondence, show a desire to enhance your abilities.

3. Supervisory Understanding—Does the employee have the ability to organize the work of subordinates so that the unit operates more efficiently?

Recall the distribution of interoffice mail when you first took over your job. One messenger was tied up all day, often delivering only one memo at a time. You instituted two distributions only during the day—at the time the outside mail arrived. Thus, you freed the messenger to do other things, such as keeping the stockroom in order and helping with the files.

4. Morale—Does the employee work cheerfully and well with peers and subordinates? Has the employee done anything to enhance the morale of either?

Here is an opportunity for you to tell something that your file will not show: You reorganized your unit so that people on routine jobs would rotate them with other people doing routine work, thus relieving boredom and also ensuring that one worker's job can be covered in the event of an absence. You may cite the fact that the turnover among employees has dropped since you took on your position.

These are items that should not be left to chance, hoping vaguely that they will be remembered when an appraisal interview comes up. It is suggested that you keep a weekly log (a daily one is too restricting for most people) and think back over each week as it ends; then, enter any contributions you may have made or any efforts you have made toward your personal growth. Before you can outgrow a position, you must first grow within it.

## The Interviewer

In an appraisal interview, remember that the employee is apt to be on the defensive. While you cannot always assume that the employee will change if you remove these defensive feelings, it does happen sometimes. So, while you as a supervisor are not expected to be sycophantic and bring yourself down to the backslapping level of a subordinate, neither should you position yourself as a forbidding judge.

In your first appraisal interview, you should devote much of the time to learning if the employee is comfortable with the work, with the surroundings or working conditions, and with the other employees. You can do this best by using some of the nondirective techniques described in the previous chapter. If there are any suggestions for change forthcoming from the employee, listen carefully. Defend the *status quo* only if there is no possibility of change, but explain patiently why things must continue as they are for awhile, and try to suggest ways in which the employee can adjust to them.

If the employee has shown particular aptitude and initiative in the job (after ample time has been allowed for the individual to do so), you might suggest ways by which he or she may grow with the company. A note should be made on the appraisal sheet if the employee evinces a particular interest in another area in the company.

In subsequent appraisal interviews, there is no denying the fact that you must judge the employee's performance since your last appraisal, but you can learn as much by letting the employee do most of the talking as by asking questions. Your technique should be that of listening, reflecting feelings of the employee, and summarizing.

The final category of appraisal interviews is worded somewhat euphemistically. Stated bluntly, it might be "Your work has not been satisfactory, and if it doesn't improve you will be fired." Considering the cost of hiring and training an employee for a responsible position in a company, a minimum of employee turnover is highly desirable; on the other hand, a maximum of efficiency is just as desirable.

If an employee's work is not satisfactory, it is the responsibility of the supervisor to find out *why*, to try to find ways of helping the employee, and—as a last resort—to issue a warning. An ultimatum should be avoided if at all possible.

The difficulty for the interviewer in such cases is not one of passing judgment, but in the proper approach. You should handle it as a problem to be solved. Try to lead the employee into reflective thinking: the cause of the problem, possible solutions to it, and choice of the best solution. Your role should be that of a helper, and your attitude should be such that the employee will confide freely in you by your assurance that his or her confidence will not be violated.

Aileen worked at *Yvette d'Paris*, a high fashion producer of hand-painted silk scarves and neckties. The designs were not actually painted on the expensive silk by hand, but the operation could be only partly automated because of the eccentric drying pattern of the dyes used. It required precise human judgment to know when to apply the next color (by lowering a lever) so that the overall effect was not spoiled. In training, Aileen was at the top of her group, but when she actually started work she spoiled almost every design she worked on. Working conditions could not be blamed because the trainees used the same equipment as the regular workers. Fellow workers scorned her because she wasted so much material. She was in tears at her first appraisal interview.

Her supervisor used reflective thinking. What were the causes of Aileen's failure? Was it a careless attitude? No, she had shown great care and dependability during training. She wore glasses; was her eyesight causing her failure? That was ruled out. Did she have personal problems that were spoiling her concentration? That was also ruled out. Was she taking drugs or excessive alcohol? No, Aileen was opposed to drugs or stimulants in any form. Finally, the supervisor asked, "Whose place did you take at the print table?"

"I think they said her name was Bertha," Aileen replied.

Bertha! The supervisor formed a hypothesis: Aileen was barely five feet tall, but Bertha had been six feet—so tall, in fact, that she had asked to have her seat at the print table lowered so that she could watch the drying dye from a better angle. The problem was solved simply by raising the seat of the chair Aileen occupied.

## Counseling Interviews

Personal problems of employees are not ordinarily handled by supervisors or personnel directors. However, a personal problem becomes a company problem when it prevents an employee from doing a job properly. Consider this case:

Albert has worked at the architectural firm of Medford and Associates for two and a half years. He is a fine draftsman, and is well liked by the other members of the firm for his sunny disposition and careful grooming. Earlier six-months appraisals of him indicate that he might be a good replacement for the chief draftsman, who will retire in two years.

During the past six months a change has come over Al. He often calls in sick, and is frequently late for work. His neat appearance has deteriorated; he is unshaven most of the time, and his shirts look as if he had worn them for days.

The chief draftsman has told the personnel director that Al makes many mistakes in his work, and is belligerent when the mistakes are called to his attention. The chief draftsman has smelled liquor on Al's breath and suspects that Al has a drinking problem.

The personnel director calls Al in for an appraisal interview at the regular six-months interval, and notes the changes in Al's appearance. After an exchange of pleasantries, Al blurts out that his wife has left him, taking their two-year-old child with her, and that he has been drinking heavily because of loneliness.

If you were the personnel director in the foregoing case, you should listen to Al with empathy, letting him know that you understand his feelings. Be non-judgmental, and non-directive in your approach. Point out the high potential he has (do not use the past tense!). Make it plain, in the kindest manner possible, that Al cannot continue to work for the firm in his present state. Leave the way open for Al to ask for your advice. When and if he does, you might offer to refer him to a marriage counselor, or to an agency for rehabilitation of alcohol abuse. A proficient personnel director should keep a referral file for employees who have personal problems such as these. Above all, be as supportive as you can, and express confidence that the problems can be solved.

## ORAL REPORTS

A part of your presentational speaking in business or the professional world will be in some form of report. Your audience may vary in size from more than a hundred (at a legal or medical convention, for instance) to a few people seated around a conference table, or even just one or two persons. Whatever the audience, it is an information-giving process that requires a more precise degree of organization than the ordinary speech to inform. Most reports are made before listeners who are already interested in the subject, so there is no need to ingratiate yourself or use attention-getting devices in order to capture their interest. This does not rule out a pleasant manner or a sense of humor.

Reports may be the result of research you have undertaken, or they may be the findings of a committee of several persons. The report may be given extemporaneously from notes, or written and read. Most reports contain some portions that *require* reading aloud because accuracy is mandatory; Chapter Six in this text discusses how to read aloud.

The keynotes in a report are *accuracy, brevity,* and *careful organization.* Business reports generally fall into one of three categories:

1. Reporting on a PROCESS or procedure
2. Reporting on a POLICY (a problem that has arisen, with its practical solutions, and usually with a recommendation for adopting a certain solution). In the section of this text on writing, this is referred to as the analytical report.
3. Reporting on PROGRESS, or the lack of it.

Here are some recommendations:

**Use essentials only.**    Most reports are made to executives, people in charge of running a business who don't have time to hear the methods you adopted in gathering the report, the details of "leads" that led nowhere, how much time you spent gathering information, or how much work it required. They only want to know the facts that will give them the basis for making a decision.

On the other hand, you should *have* all of those details, and have them arranged in an orderly manner. When one of the reportees asks how you obtained certain information or questions its validity, you should be able to put your fingers on such supportive materials in the briefest possible time. The reportees are interested only in the tip of the iceberg, but they are well aware of the vast portion of that iceberg that is submerged, and they may wish to know how solid it is and how deep it goes.

**Use visual aids.**    In no type of business speaking are visual aids more important. If you have worked out your visuals carefully, they can give your listeners a quick grasp of the essentials in a way that no amount of words can. Edward Hodnett devotes more than one third of his book on professional presentations to the subject of visual aids.[6]

## Policy Reports

Here is an example that might call for a report leading to policy formulation by the executives in a company.

Apko Frozen Foods is located in a small rural city of approximately 50,000. Mae Bevis, one of the supervisors on the staff, has been appointed to the school board, which means that she must take the afternoon off twice a month for the board's regular meeting, with a few hours outside work in the interim. When Mae asks permission to do this, the executive vice-president of Apko grants it gladly, saying that Apko must fulfill its duties to the community.

A few weeks later, Bill Scott, another supervisor in a different sector of the plant, is elected to the board of directors of the Chamber of Commerce. This necessitates Bill's leaving his work two hours early once a week so that he can attend their meetings. Once again, the executive vice-president gives his blessings in the name of "civic responsibility." Soon after, Mildred Britt is elected president of the P.T.A. and must take most of the mornings off from work twice monthly. Mildred is head of the stenographic pool at Apko, but the vice-president allows her this time off. Fred Olanski, a shop foreman in the plant, has been asked to coach Little League baseball, and needs to leave work at three every afternoon twice weekly during the Little League season. Olivia Burton has been appointed to the city planning commission and asks for permission to take the afternoon off from her job with Apko twice a month.

Apko is a fairly small food processing company and maintains a tight work schedule. The executives, fearing a trend that could seriously hamper Apko's production if allowed to continue, ask a committee to investigate and report on the situation.

To conduct an exhaustive investigation could consume a great amount of time and expense. It would involve examining several other plants about the same size as Apko, in towns about the size of the one where Apko is located, and asking what their policy is toward allowing time off from work for civic duties. The most important thing to be determined is whether or not there has been a significant drop in productivity in the departments where members have been allowed time off to engage in community affairs. It is possible that there has been an actual *increase* in productivity, because of morale factors.

The executives don't want the tedious details of the departments of Mae Bevis, Bill Scott, Mildred Britt, Fred Olanski, and Olivia Burton. It is up to *you* to strike an *average* of the productivity or nonproductivity of those five departments so that you can come up with something as simple as this in your report:

> "Productivity in departments where one employee is given time off for civic duties, averaging two hours per week, has not changed."

or

> "Productivity in departments where one employee is given an average of two hours per week free to engage in civic activities, has actually risen by 2 percent."

### Formulas for a Policy Report

A report intended to be the basis for policy making is generally accompanied by recommendations, but not always. The reporter may show the conditions and leave it up to the higher executives to decide what is to be done. Here are two formulas for making a report, which carry with them a recommendation:

### Formula "A"

1. State the problem as it exists
   a. If there is time, give the history of the problem
   b. State the severity or mildness of the problem, without exaggerating
2. Outline a number of possible solutions
3. Recommend one possible solution that is
   a. Practicable
   b. Desirable

### Formula "B"

1. (Follow step 1 in formula "A")
2. Recommend *one* solution only
3. Anticipate objections to that one solution and answer those objections *before* they are made
4. Show that the solution recommended is
   a. Practicable
   b. Desirable.

## Reporting on a Process

Reputable business executives are constantly seeking better ways of accomplishing things, whether it be in their offices, in their manufacturing plants, or in marketing methods. Before a change can be made from the old way of doing things, the executives must have a report on whether a new way will be better.

When you have done your research, the outline of your presentation to the executives of your company might look like this:

I. Current method of processing crops (Use visuals)
   A. Waste of manpower hours
   B. Loss of vitamins and taste in vegetables
II. New proposal for processing crops (Use visuals)
   A. Refrigerated trucks with electronic device:
       half-freezing and bacteria killing en route to plant
      a. Preserves taste and nutrients
      b. Eliminates scalding process
      c. Eliminates cooling period
   B. Attachment for packaging machine
      1. Increases capacity by one-half
      2. Decreases manpower hours by one-half
III. Summary of advantages of proposal
   A. New equipment's amortization
   B. Faster food processing
      1. Better taste and nutrients
      2. Greater profits.

## The Progress Report

Progress (or the lack of it) is the subject of annual or biannual reports to executives. The subject may be sales, absenteeism, accidents, or any other matter that is subject to fluctuation and is the concern of the company as a whole.

The progress report must contain a comparison. It might be a comparison of your company's sales with those of a competitor's over a period of time. It might be a comparison of the number of factory accidents which occurred during the first six months of this year with the number that occurred during the first six months of last year. You should not compare the first six months of this year with the last six months of last year, and you should not compare the month of May this year with the month of December last year. People respond to weather and holidays in much the same way from one year to the next, unless there is a catastrophe in one year and not the others.

## Use of Visuals

You would do well to review Chapter Seven in this text, on visual aids, before attempting to prepare a progress report, because visual aids are almost essential in making the report. The best type of visual for this type of report is the bar

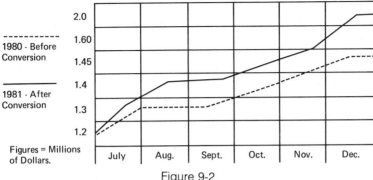

Figure 9-2

graph or the line (grid) graph; the line graph is the better because it offers two coordinates in logical progression—time and degree (or amount).

Figure 9-2 shows an example of how a progress report of a company's sales over two six-month periods, before and after converting to the new manner of processing, might look.

## The Big Why?

A progress report is useless unless one tries to find out *why* some thing (such as sales, absenteeism, accidents, attitudes) has progressed or regressed. Your report is of no service to your firm if you simply *report* trends without trying to find the underlying *reasons* for the facts that constitute such a trend.

The reasoning from cause to effect (or vice versa) is one of the most difficult types of reasoning to *prove*. However, in business a probable cause is about as close as you can come to answering the BIG WHY in a progress report. Be sure that you have exhausted all of your resources to get at the *actual* cause.

The BIG WHY is equally important in reports on sales, accidents, or absenteeism:

1. What caused sales to drop or to increase? Was it an advertising campaign of a particular kind? Was it new sales managers in certain areas where sales had gone poorly before? Perhaps it might have been greater incentives for the individual salesmen?
2. What *conditions* were changed that may have caused a decrease or increase in the number of accidents in the plant? Was it a safety campaign actively waged? Was it a drop in morale—if so, why? Was it added incentive?
3. What—if any—changes in procedure caused an increase or decrease in absenteeism? Was it threat or incentive? What changes in personnel have taken place that might have caused absenteeism to increase or drop?

In a business situation the progress report takes *time* to prepare. You can get the material for your visuals (statistics) from the sales manager, the safety engineer, or the personnel director. However, when you try to answer the BIG

WHY, you will need to do *field work*. In sales, you will need to contact regional or local sales managers, or individual salesmen, to learn what retail outlets are saying about the competition; in safety, you will need to know the history of conditions, and question the workers (discreetly) about their morale; in absenteeism, you may also have to question employees, and learn the history of changes made in the general procedure.

Once your research is completed, you must make your presentation using the best speech techniques you can.

## Formula for a Progress Report

  I. State the purpose of the report
 II. Cite your statistics (in rounded numbers, please!) Use charts—but not too many
III. Make your recommendations

In the discussion that inevitably follows a progress report, you can contribute to answers to the BIG WHY by using the results of (a) your research, (b) any changes in physical or psychological conditions that you have observed, or that have been reported to you, and (c) by the opinions of experts in the field. Be brief, but have your raw materials in perfect order.

## SUGGESTED CLASSROOM EXERCISES

Your instructor may give several students the same assignment; it will be interesting to compare their presentations.

1. Interview five instructors of relatively small classes (25-40 students), and ask whether or not students who sit in the front of the classroom make significantly better grades than those who sit toward the back. Prepare a visual of the results.

2. Take a poll of fifty students at random on campus to determine how many of them read what percentage of the campus newspaper: 90 percent? 70 percent? 50 percent? 25 percent? Chart your findings.

3. Interview ten instructors and inquire if there is a direct correlation between students who make poor grades and those who cut classes before and after holidays. Or, if your school does not have an overall "class cut" policy, take a poll of ten or more instructors to find out their individual policies on class cuts.

4. Take a poll of twenty or more students who read most of the student newspaper and find out what they believe should receive *less* coverage, and what should receive *more,* in the paper than is now allotted. Sports? Information on academic policies? Faculty personalities? Student government? Interviews with students? Fashion? Gossip?

5. Report on a book that you think would be of particular interest to your classmates. Or, the instructor may divide a book into three sections, and ask three students to report on one section each.

## Exercises for Telephone Use

*NOTE TO INSTRUCTOR:* For the following classroom exercises to be *ideally* performed, you should have two working telephones in adjoining rooms, with provisions for the conversation to be recorded. This is fairly simple. If this set-up is not feasible, an intercom between the classroom and another room is suggested. Failing that, a simple screen placed between the "caller" and the "receiver," so that they cannot see each other, will serve.

Each of the following exercises should be completed in five minutes or less. Real names, and locations other than those in the problems, may be used.

## The Conveyer Belt Problem

1) The Caller:

You are John Byer, of the Manifold Packing Company in Emporia, KS. You have ordered a conveyer belt from Pete Cellar of the Cellar Manufacturing Corporation in Kansas City, KS. Delivery was promised one week ago. Since you have had no invoice or other word from the Cellar Company, you call Pete Cellar. Specifications on the conveyer belt are as follows:

Standard type
60 feet long
2½ feet wide
3 inches thick (light duty)
Purpose: To carry medium-size boxes from the packing room to the loading platform.

2) The Receiver:

You are Pete Cellar, Cellar Manufacturing Corp., Kansas City. Your firm manufactures special equipment for various industries, and the Manifold Packaging Co. in Emporia has bought much of their total equipment from you. You receive a call from Manifold, asking about a conveyer belt, made to his specifications, which was supposed to be delivered a week ago. Upon checking orders from Manifold, you can find no record of any such order, but you *do* find record of a check Manifold has sent you to cover the cost of the conveyer. So that you can process the order, you try to get the specifications of the belt from Mr. Byer, *without* his knowing that the order has been lost. The specifications you need are:

Type of belt:
Length
Width
Thickness
Purpose for which it is to be used.

## B. The Faulty Roller Skates

1) The Caller:

You have bought your 9-year-old daughter Elena a pair of the *most expensive* roller skates available from Bick's Department Store. Elena has been skating since she was four and hopes to use the skates in competition. On the first day she tries out the new skates, Elena tumbles forward on the sidewalk and hits her skull on the pavement, receiving a skull concussion. Upon examining the skates, you discover the housing enclosing the ball-bearings was cracked open on the right-foot skate, losing the bearings, and pitching your daughter forward on her head. It was a near-fatal accident for Elena, and there is a doctor bill to be paid. You telephone the store manager at Bick's, Mr._____.

2) The Receiver:

You are the manager of Bick's Department Store and carry a line of first-rate roller skates in your sports department. You receive a call from the parent of a 9-year-old child, claiming that the housing enclosing the roller-bearings in a pair of your most expensive skates has cracked open, causing the child to fall and receive a skull concussion. There is a doctor bill to be paid and the possibility of a lawsuit. Nevertheless, the roller skate manufacturer has not provided you with a safety guarantee on the skates. How do you handle this?

## C. Speedy's Diner's Credit

1) The Caller:

You are the credit manager for ABC Restaurant Supplies. Speedy's Diner, owned by Mr./Ms. (use real name), has placed an order with your company, dated August 1, for $378.00. Speedy's Diner has always been a few days late in paying its bills, until the order *preceding* this one. The preceding order was for $252 and is 52 days overdue. Your terms are cash within 30 days of delivery. Now, you have been handed this new order for $378, and have been asked to authorize delivery. You call Mr./Ms. _____, owner of Speedy's, and discuss the problem.

*Note:* Is Speedy's Diner failing in business? Do you risk losing the unpaid $252, as well as the new order for $378—a total of $630—if you authorize shipment?

2) The Receiver:

You are the owner of Speedy's Diner and have been a customer of ABC Restaurant Supplies for nearly four years. On August 1st, you placed an order with ABC for $378 worth of supplies; it is now August 15th, and the supplies have not been delivered, although both ABC and your diner are located in the same city.

Your last order was approximately two months ago, and this sequence ensued:

June 30th - You received ABC's bill; you mailed a check on July 2nd.

July 10th - Your check was returned to you; the bill had been for $252, and you had mistakenly made out the check for $250. (Instead of crediting you with $250 and putting a debit on your account for the $2, ABC had returned the entire check!)

July 25th - You mailed another check for the *full* $252, which has not yet cleared through your bank.

There *are* other restaurant suppliers in the area.

## D. The Spoiled Fishing Trip

1) The Caller:

You bought a motorboat a week ago and immediately took off for a few days of fishing in Lake Winnetka, 50 miles away. You expected to return to the city completely refreshed, because you had an important job interview on the afternoon of your return. The fishing was great! Your wife has almost ten pounds of bass filets in your portable ice chest. As you started home early on the morning of your job appointment, one wheel came off the trailer carrying the boat, causing some damage to the boat and trailer. It was not serious, but the delay in getting home (six hours) caused you to miss your employment interview for the position of a lifetime. There were no telephones en route, so that you might call and ask for another appointment. You can certainly expect Aquafun, the firm from which you obtained the boat and trailer, to pay for repairs and towing charges, because the lugs on the wheel that came off were too small, so the holes on the wheel slipped right over them with a little wear. But what about the job appointment you missed?

2) The Receiver:

You are the owner/manager of Aquafun, a local company that sells pleasure boats and the trailers on which they are carried. The trailers you sell are purchased from Jessup Body Works in a city 100 miles away and arrive at your place of business fully assembled. During the five years you have done business with Jessup, you have had no complaints about their trailers, so you do not inspect thoroughly each individual trailer you receive from them.

## E. Fred's Parent-Teacher Association

1) The Caller:

You are the homeroom teacher of a fifth grade class. Fred, a 10-year-old boy, is one of the brightest pupils in the class but is a disquieting "smart Aleck." He talks with other students constantly, interrupting the math class that you teach; he refuses to sit quietly and study, but pokes at other students, drops things on the floor, gets up and down from his seat, and is a general nuisance. His disturbances have caused you to keep him after school several times as punishment. You receive a pleasant note from Fred's parent (mother or father) asking for an appointment to talk about Fred. You are busy with a school competition, it is final examination and report-card time, and you don't have much spare time. You telephone Fred's parent and suggest that you might solve your mutual problem by 'phone.

2) The Receiver:

You are the parent (male or female) of a 10-year-old boy who complains almost daily that his homeroom teacher picks on him. You know that your son places a great value on truthfulness, since he takes pride in his Cub Scout duties. His complaints and his vivid descriptions of his being singled out for ridicule and minor punishments prompt you to write his teacher a friendly note, asking if you may make an appointment to talk about Fred at school, or asking the teacher to drop by your home for coffee some afternoon after school. The teacher telephones in response to your note.

## FOOTNOTES FOR CHAPTER NINE

[1]Beverly Nichols (1899–    ), English wit and writer.

[2]Hugh Fellows, *The Art and Skill of Talking with People* (Englewood Cliffs, N.J.: Prentice-Hall, 1964).

[3]Edward Hodnett, *Effective Presentations* (West Nyack, N.Y.: Parker Publishing Co., 1967).

[4]Hugh Fellows, *The Art and Skill of Talking with People.*

[5]Reported in *Everybody's Money,* Summer, 1979, p. 23.

[6]Edward Hodnett, *Effective Presentations.*

# VOCABULARY STUDY FOR CHAPTER TEN

Following are some words used in this chapter with which you may not be thoroughly familiar. In order to reinforce your knowledge, it is suggested that you match correctly the word with its definition (for example, 1 - L). Answers are in Appendix C.

1. ALLEVIATE
2. CADAVEROUS

3. DISRUPT
4. EFFICACY

5. FIXATE
   (FIXATION)
6. GENEALOGY
7. MOOT POINT
8. PEDAGOGY

9. PRECEPT

10. SPECIOUS
11. STEREOTYPE
12. UNWIELDY

A. Subject to argument or discussions; debatable.
B. A record of the ancestry or descent of a person or groups of people.
C. The function or work of a teacher; teaching.
D. To suffer a partial arrest in one's emotional or physical development.

E. A directive given as a rule of action or conduct.
F. Capacity for producing results; efficiency.
G. Apparently right, but lacking merit; deceptive.
H. To cause disorder or turmoil, usually of a temporary nature.
I. A simplified and standardized image of a person, in which it is believed that the person is like all others of his class or occupation.
J. Of, or like, a corpse (cadaver); pale, haggard, thin.
K. Awkward; too large to handle well.
L. To make easier to endure; to lessen.

# 10 | Giving Instructions

An education is the only thing a college student will gladly pay for and not get.

Unknown

Bessinger's, a large, prestigious mail-order house founded near Atlanta, Ga., in 1869, opened a retail store in downtown Atlanta in 1946. As long as Bessinger's had been a mail-order house and the employees were never seen by the public, they wore clothes for comfort rather than appearance. In warm weather these usually consisted of T-shirts, slacks or shorts, and loafers. Since it was immediately apparent to Mr. Bessinger that such clothing would be highly unsuitable in fashionable downtown Atlanta, he summoned the heads of all departments to his office and asked for suggestions about a dress code for Bessinger's.

"Most of you own stock in Bessinger's and you run the store, so pick out something suitable for the entire staff," Arnold Bessinger directed.

At the next meeting, Mr. Brennan, who was head of the accounting department, and who had been a captain in the Marine Corps during the Vietnam War, presented his idea. "Since we have Fort McClellan and the Naval Air Station, I propose that we wear uniforms that are similar to those of the armed forces, even down to the stripes, epaulets, and collar insignia. It would not only be a patriotic gesture, but the customers would know whether they were dealing with a departmental head or a mere stock clerk."

Mr. Lowden (Men's Clothing) objected. "We've just come through the Vietnam War, and people are sick of uniforms."

Mrs. Slinsky (Ladies' Wear) proposed that they employ a leading fashion designer to design all of the clothes for the store's personnel. "Can you imagine how delightful it would be to have everything in the store color coordinated? For instance, if the woodwork in Ladies Wear were walnut, the saleswomen would wear autumn shades of taupe and rust and brown, with a touch of orange and red here and there. The walls of the Cosmetics Department could be painted lavendar and . . ."

One of her own saleswomen interrupted, "I refuse to stand on my feet all day, just to blend into the woodwork!"

Mr. Jimson (Sporting Goods) said, "Now I think our dress code should be something regional. We have a professional football team and several collegiate football teams in this area. What would be more suitable than wearing sportswear?"

"I'll be danged if I'm going to go running around in shoulder pads and knee breeches with my skinny legs!" snorted Mr. Gerard (Hardware) who was almost sixty.

All Arnold Bessinger wanted was to get rid of the shorts, sneakers, and T-shirts with holes under the arms!

This example is not atypical. Consider the Incas of South America, who built 10,000 miles of roads over and through the Andes Mountains; yet, in spite of the fact that round objects such as nuts and fruits were all around them, they never suceeded in constructing a wheel for the purpose of transportation. It is because *learning does not necessarily transfer* from one skill to another. Sometimes knowledge of one skill can actually be detrimental when learning another skill is required. This is one of the few "almost certainties" we know about learning.[1]

## SOME DISCOVERIES ABOUT LEARNING

During the past fifty years psychologists and educators have conducted many experiments into the learning and training processes, some of which are of particular interest to us as we discuss giving instructions. However, these observations may not be *absolutes*. Improved research facilities and improved methods of experimentation over the past decades have changed drastically our concepts of how to teach. The changes will probably continue. So, as you read these precepts, please transfer the verb "is" into the more cautious "appears to be." The following are a few of the instructional tools that have been developed.

1.  *The mind cannot be trained like a muscle*.[2] If your objective is to chin yourself on a gymnasium bar twenty times, then doing push-ups and calisthenics may help in developing your arm muscles in order to help you do so. However, it won't help you solve a problem in mathematics. When I was in grammar school, the standard answer of the teacher, when I complained about a subject I didn't like,

was, "It's good training for your brain." That was nonsense. Learning a foreign language is not going to help you with your physics course.

2. *Learning can be an uncomfortable effort*.[3] Learning anything new requires a disruption of something that we have already learned. We tend to continue doing things that are easy and pleasant for us, things we already know, and to avoid those that are difficult and uncomfortable.

3. *Interest and motivation are essential for effective learning*.[4] You must realize that when you are giving instructions, you must interest the person receiving the instructions in taking the next step toward achievement. You must first get that person's attention—interest alone is not sufficient motivation. Attention, interest, and the basic drives that motivate most people to act are more fully discussed in Chapter Thirteen (the chapter on public speaking).

4. *Learning is aided through the use of several senses*.[5] The class exercises at the end of Chapter Two demonstrated that the chances of information being passed from one person to another are enhanced if more than one medium is used; that is, talking, listening, showing, taking notes, good organization, and utilizing feedback. Chapter Seven, on visual aids, discussed how much more is retained by both hearing and seeing, rather than by hearing alone. In giving instructions, we must add another medium: *action*. Psychologists believe that learning is more effective and is retained longer when one actually puts that learning into practice. "Telling is not teaching," should be the motto of any first-class instructor.

5. *The learning pattern differs for each person*.[6] Although you may be giving instructions to a large group, the effectiveness of your instruction actually depends on the learning of individuals. A person with a special mechanical aptitude can perhaps learn quickly upon being *shown* how an intricate piece of machinery operates; the same person may have a low verbal aptitude and may derive little or nothing from being *told* how to operate that same piece of machinery.

You should also remember that learning is influenced by the trainee's past conditioning and what that individual has already learned. This is probably one of the reasons that men are often believed to have more mechanical intelligence than women, while women are supposed to be more sensitive to colors and scents than men. These stereotypes no doubt result partly from toys given them as children. Little boys hardly ever played with dolls and doll dresses, while little girls seldom played with firetrucks, guns, and chemistry sets. Truly fine instructors do not abandon the *essentials* of what they have to teach, but they must learn to adapt them to each of their students. This is the main difference between a speech to inform and a speech to instruct.

## SOME TECHNIQUES OF A GOOD INSTRUCTOR

There is a saying among educators that "A person who knows how to teach can teach anything." This is obviously a specious statement; however, it might be fair to say that a skillful instructor can learn new subject matter in a shorter period of time than a specialist can learn to instruct.[7]

Figure 10-1

Recently a large Naval Air Corps Training Station had need for a number of instructors to teach technical subjects. The engineering and technical colleges and universities were scouted, and their best graduate students were recruited, given Navy Reserve commissions of various ranks, and sent to teach at the Training Station. The move was an almost complete failure. There was no doubt that the experts were giving information concerning their subject matter (see Figure 10-1). However, one vital step in the *teaching* process had been overlooked. It is not enough for an expert to impart knowledge; experts who know their pedagogy must teach their knowledge to *people*. (See Figure 10-2). Witness this confession from a teacher of more than forty-five years, who has won "outstanding teacher" awards from three colleges and universities:

In going from the first grade to a Ph.D., I must confess that I have had only five—six, at the most—really excellent teachers. After 45 years, I still don't know how they *became* such good teachers. I have studied the matter at great length: I have read Gilbert Highet's fine book on *The Art of Teaching*[8]; I have taken several graduate courses in Education, which were *not worth the time* I spent on them (although *one* of those teachers ranked among the "greats" in my opinion); I have listened to the blatherskate among student teachers about how "dedicated" they were—mostly hogwash, I assure you! Now, at a very advanced age in life, I have yet to solve the mystery of why those five or six teachers were so *great*. They had the most diverse personalities and physical forms that anyone could imagine:

1. Miss Mallie Corbin, my second-grade teacher, was a "dried-up," elderly spinster. She was as thin as a pencil, had a sallow complexion, and wore metal-rimmed glasses. She was dictatorial, believed in absolute strict discipline, and she didn't have a single friend in the second grade. Yet, somehow she managed to get through to me that what she was teaching us was *important* and would last us for the rest of our lives.

2. Irene Kingery, in the fourth grade, was a little too plump, used a bit too much make-up (looking back on it now), and was fired from her job after one year, because she had earned the reputation of sleeping with most of the high school athletes. Even at that unappreciative age, I realized that she seemed to have no favorite subjects, among the four that she taught: English, history, arithmetic, and geography; she *loved* ALL of them, and taught them with equal enthusiasm. In fact, she loved a *lot* of things (including the high school athletes, if gossip is to be believed!). I can pin-point the reason Irene Kingery was a great teacher: She taught me an invaluable thing—*curiosity*.

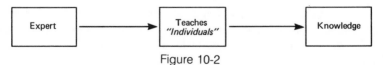

Figure 10-2

3. Martena McKim, my geometry teacher in high school, had a great personal challenge in me: I had *never* passed—except with the lowest *possible* grade—any mathematics class in my life. I was *terrified* with any course that had anything to do with exact figures. Martena seemed to sense my fear, and tried to give me confidence; knowing that I was artistically inclined, she showed me the *beauty* in geometry, and turned what had been a handicap to me into an asset.

4. Lew Sarett, truly one of the greatest teachers of all time, for those who were his students at Northwestern. A Russian immigrant, who sold newspapers as a boy in Chicago, he had spent one summer in the north woods of Canada, and took to nature like a forest creature. He knew and loved all wildlife, all plants, and was a fine poet and humanitarian. In a class of more than a hundred students, he knew all of us by name, and when he returned papers to us, each paper bore a personal comment. The remarkable thing about this master teacher was that he never demanded our taking notes in his class, and always talked as if he were saying things to us for the first time he had ever spoken them; yet, when I reviewed my notes at the end of any class, everything was perfectly organized.

5. Letitia Raubicheck, who spent her life doing speech correction work in the public schools of New York City. In a difficult course in speech therapy, she rarely used technical terms or academic jargon. What was more remarkable, I never heard her use the word "handicap"; instead, it was always "a person who needs some help." Fierce as a tiger where child abuse was concerned, she was nonetheless a person of infinite patience and ingenuity. "If something doesn't work the way 'the book' says it should, then try another method" was the great lesson I learned from her.

6. Adolf Meyer, a cadaverous old man, teaching a subject in which I had no interest whatsoever, "History of Education." What a surprise! Each class period sounded like a soap opera: There was a hasty synopsis of what he had said during the preceding period, and then his lectures on what could have been a dull subject, built up in suspense until a student could hardly wait for the next episode. His dry humor and caustic wit, as he applied it to "know-it-alls" and "great discoverers" in the field of education, made those extinct people come alive.

—Hugh P. Fellows

It would be marvelous if you could have all of the magnetic qualities detailed in the foregoing paragraphs, and perhaps you can develop them. For now, this discussion will examine some techniques that can help you become a better administrator, especially when you are giving instructions.

*First,* strive to have clear, understandable speech. Speak at a rate of speed that is not too fast to be readily comprehended, nor so slow as to be tiresome. Furthermore, you should know something about the technique of emphasizing the idea-carrying words and phrases in your instructions.

*Second,* organize your materials for instruction. They should be *carefully* organized but *flexibly* organized so that the materials can be altered to fit the learning capacities of your students. If you have more than one group to instruct on the same materials, you will find that the learning capacity of each group will differ slightly—if not *more* than slightly.

*Third,* learn to reinforce the key points of your presentation so that they will be remembered. You can do this by using case histories, specific examples, and visual aids.

*Fourth*, constantly evaluate the method of instruction to determine if it is effective. If you find that it is *not* effective, then change it. A good instructor is like a good cook, who is constantly tasting the food to see if the flavor is right. Testing, like tasting, must be a continuous part of good instruction. The *purpose* of testing should not be to pass or fail a student, but to evaluate the instructor's teaching methods.

*Fifth*, you should recognize each trainee's aptitude, ability, and achievement.[9]

Aptitude refers to what a student may eventually be able to do. There are numerous types of aptitude, such as artistic, mechanical, and verbal. If a student shows one kind of aptitude but is being trained for a totally different kind of performance, then you must recognize that the student is likely to be slower in learning the performance being trained for. However, do not rule out the possibility of the individual's *ever* achieving competence in that performance; most people can be trained to perform a reasonable task if the motivation is high enough. Among training directors in business, one of the first things to be stressed is that "All trainees do not learn at the same pace."

Ability refers to what a student can do after training. It will vary from person to person, but should never fall below the norm of competency. All men may be created equal *under the law*, but to claim that all men are created equal in ability to perform even a simple task is nonsense!

Achievement refers to the present—and the future. Many factors affect it: students' interest in the subject, whether or not they have had proper training, and their differences in health, stamina, and even background may affect their individual achievement.

## ANALYSIS AND ORGANIZATION[10]

The first task in giving instructions is to find out *what* you are going to teach—and how *much* of it. Analyze the entire job operation and break it down into teachable units. For example, teaching photography might involve all of this information—and more:

> History of photography
> The principle of how a camera works
> Composition and lighting
> Types of black-and-white film
>> Sensitivity and speed
>> Texture for enlarging
> Types of color film
>> A.S.A. rating
>> Faithfulness of color reproduction

Types and characteristics of printing
papers
Necessary equipment for developing
and printing
Safelights

Photographic optics
   Depth of focus and field
   Principle of light meters
   Adjusting lens opening and shutter
   speed
Photographic chemistry
   Developers and emulsions for black
   & white
   Developers and emulsions for color
   Fixatives
   Timing for each emulsion and fixa-
   tive
Enlargers
Mountings

The foregoing list could easily be doubled in length, and you can see that it is already unwieldy. However, instructing a person in only one step of the process becomes simpler. For example, here is the knowledge that might be required to give instructions for developing and printing a black-and-white film:

Necessary equipment for developing and printing
Knowledge of chemicals used, and their characteristics
Each step in the procedure, with cautionary measures.

It is important to divide each unit, for instructional purposes, into "knowing" steps and "doing" steps. Trainees need to know *why* they are performing certain steps, and *what* steps to take. Teaching material that is beyond the knowledge required for a particular task, can be confusing and a waste of time. Homer C. Rose, in his book, *The Development and Supervision of Training Programs*,[11] says:

Thousands of hours of valuable training time can be saved through the relatively simple process of teaching only theory that is clearly related and necessary to the best performance of required skills and procedures.

In other words, if you're going to instruct a student in how to prepare an omelet, you don't need to know the genealogy of the hen that laid the eggs, nor the chemical composition of the eggs themselves!

## Step by Step

When persons who are highly proficient in a skill or procedure give instructions, they are apt to overlook or leave out some steps that they, themselves, take for granted. Those steps become second nature to an expert. The expert who is teaching should check and recheck the steps carefully, If you are the instructor, perhaps you should make a written outline as follows:

1. List the specific steps to be taken, in their proper order. Be sure to include every significant and essential step, but *not* each movement.
   (If possible, perform the operation yourself and check each step against your list.)
2. Under each step list the key points and information that tells how to do the step. Emphasize these key points by demonstration or visual aids.
3. Underline in red those points that could be of potential danger to the student or the equipment. Use the word *caution* in your list to remind yourself of this.
4. If the list of steps is lengthy, revise the list so that some of the steps can be incorporated into others. Trainees can remember four MAIN steps with ten subordinate things to do under each step, better than they can remember forty individual steps.
   (Forty steps in *any* procedure is too many! Better divide your instruction into four periods if you have that many to handle.)

For more than forty years psychologists have known some basic factors about how people learn and remember (at least in this society).[12] These factors are impact, recentness, repetition, and association. At the bottom of the page is a little mnemonic device to help you remember them; we call it "Ira."

**Impact.**   If the impact (or impression) is *vivid* enough, then the fact or incident it portrays will be remembered. You probably will not remember for very long the text of a political speech you hear and see on television, but the face and body of a starving child in a war-torn country will leave an impression on you that you will not soon forget. Hence, visual aids, case histories, and training aids give impact to your important points in giving instructions.

**Repetition.**   Advertisers have known the value of repetition for years. Coca-Cola saturated the country with its signboards saying nothing more than, "Coca-

Figure 10-3

Cola, delicious and refreshing," for so many years that a person would automatically think of Coca-Cola when a soft drink was desired. There is one danger in using too much repetition in training: A phrase that is repeated *too* often can lose its meaning. The same is true for drill in performing a manual task; the drill should be accompanied by an explanation that does *not* repeat itself, each time a trainee is asked to go through the motions.

**Recentness.**  It is obvious that what happened to a person yesterday is better remembered than what happened last week. However, reviewing what happened last week will keep it fresh in the memory. This is why frequent reviews of past material are necessary. Frequent testing over past material is also desirable; each time students or trainees are required to recall something, the material becomes more deeply ingrained in their minds.

**Association.**  If trainees can link something new to something they already know, it will help them recall the new information. Also, associating a fact vividly with some object will help the student. Medical school students, when attempting to learn the names of all the body's muscles and bones, often associate them wih comical limericks, to make them more easily remembered. Most of the so-called "memory improvement" courses are based entirely on association. But learning should be based on *more* than mere association if it is to have meaning.

Before you set out to give instructions, you might wish to review the chapter on oral reports (Chapter Nine), and the chapter on visual aids (Chapter Seven). Each of those chapters contains additional information and reinforcements for giving information effectively.

## Formula for Giving Instructions

This formula is for manual tasks but applies to instructions involving procedure as well.

1. Motivate your students by appealing to one or more of their basic drives: desire for security, desire for companionship and close friendship, desire for recognition and approval of others, desire for feeling of accomplishment and success, and desire to help others.
2. State the *overall* objective of the task to be performed: "Here is where we are *now*; here is where we *should be* when we have finished."
3. Break down the overall objective into units. (Give plenty of time for trainees to make an outline, advising them to leave spaces for details.)
4. Explain step #1 of the task. Demonstrate, or use visual aids, for its key point.
5. Ask for questions. Don't hesitate to reexplain, or redemonstrate, any step which even one student finds unclear. FEEDBACK is crucial at this point!
6. Allow student(s) to demonstrate step #1, noting when something is done in-

correctly. It is a moot point whether or not you stop the student *immediately* upon making an incorrect move, or wait until the student has finished before calling attention to it. We prefer the latter, unless the mistake is critical, but it depends upon how much confidence the student already has. At any rate don't forget to praise students for what they have done *correctly* before criticizing their mistakes. Encouragement is *essential* for one learning a new task.

7. Proceed to step #2 of the task. Repeat the routine for step #1.

8. Follow the same procedure for the remaining steps. There is an advantage in allowing other students in the instruction group to observe. They learn from mistakes of others, and profit by repetition of a demonstration when something is done correctly.

9. Allow each trainee to perform each step in each unit. If this seems like an excessive amount of time spent in training a student for a certain task, consider how much money it may save your firm to have a thoroughly trained employee who is not apt to make expensive mistakes.

10. Encourage trainees to learn *more* about their present jobs and to acquire some knowledge about future advancement. This is as desirable as your basic training of them.

## Giving Critiques

Unfortunately, instructors often find it easy to criticize, but difficult to praise. They do this, even though they *know* that research and experiments have shown how important the reward of praise can be in teaching.[13] The actual *deep* satisfaction comes to students when they know they have done a good job, but it is the job of the instructor to give students encouragement in achieving this. Following are some precepts that you should follow when criticizing a trainee's performance:

1. Find something to praise (even if it is no more than the way he cuts his hair, or the attractive dress she is wearing) for each adverse criticism you give.
This is not needless flattery. Remember, the student may be fearful, or frustrated at not being able to perform well in front of the training group—things that will probably disappear when the job has been mastered.

2. Show the trainees how they have progressed so far toward attaining their goals. Knowledge of progress motivates students to do their best.

3. In training, *never* (well, almost never) encourage competition among trainees to see who can do the task best or fastest. That is tantamount to criticizing slow learners, who can easily be discouraged.

4. When a reprimand is necessary, a good instructor will
A. always talk with the trainee alone
B. criticize the *mistake*—not the trainee
C. never become angry; remain calm and use *facts*, not hearsay
D. suggest a more constructive course of action
E. include some encouragement, and praise work well done in the past, or praise the trainee's effort.

## Other Considerations

This brief chapter cannot begin to touch upon all of the aspects of pedagogy or psychology that enter into giving instructions. However, giving instructions is futile unless they are given in such a manner that the trainee will accept and follow them. Therefore, this chapter concludes with considerations which an instructor should take into account—some feelings that may make learning difficult for the student or trainee:

1. *Fear and worry.* A trainee may fear failure, or fear ridicule from other classmates or from the instructor. The trainee may have family and home problems, such as a family illness or financial worries. An instructor, although unable to *solve* such problems—and should not be expected to—can try to understand them. If you, as an instructor, are alert and sensitive enough, you can spot these problems by a student's behavior or the look in his eyes. Don't be taken in by malingerers, or by the student who offers a constant apology for shoddy work. A kind word to let the student know (in private) that you understand these problems will sometimes go a long way toward alleviating them. Make it plain, however, that you *cannot* be responsible for training employees who will be a liability to the employer.

2. *Discomfort.* Avoid demanding that the students stand too long, or become subject to eyestrain because of poor lighting or visuals that they cannot see well enough. Dirty working conditions, poor ventilation, and poor organization of your instructional material can be a real barrier to learning.

3. *Boredom.* Be thoroughly prepared. Avoid talking too long at a time, without giving the training group an opportunity to participate. Give trainees an opportunity to *use* the training equipment. Make the most use of training aids (visuals, demonstrations, and case histories or specific examples), so that the trainee will retain interest.

4. *Frustration.* Boredom can often lead to frustration, in which case a trainee may react in one of many ways. Here are several:

   A. The student may stop listening and fixate on information or behavior present at the time the student stopped being interested. In other words, students will repeat what they have learned up to a certain point, although they know it is getting them nowhere.

   B. The student may become overly aggressive in the training group. If the instructor is doing a competent (but not interesting) job, students cannot justifiably take out their aggressions on the teacher. So, they may bully, belittle, and generally disturb the other students.

   C. The students may become apathetic, listening halfheartedly and performing only when prodded. Or the student may actually try to escape, subconsciously, by inventing excuses for being tardy or absent.

When a trainee exhibits such behavior as the foregoing or shows other signs of frustration, you must talk privately with the trainee. If the trainee's frustration has reached the point of total disinterest in the training program, you should advise that individual to withdraw from the program. If you have done your job to the utmost of your ability, you should not feel guilt at this; you can't win 'em all!

A summary of this chapter is difficult, because some of the details it contains are almost as important as the main points. However, your efficacy as an instructor definitely depends upon (a) careful organization of your material, (b) the use of more than one medium, (c) feedback from the trainees, and (d) consideration of each trainee as an individual. The most important ingredients, however, are your enthusiasm for what you teach and a pride and delight in your trainees' learning.

## QUESTIONS FOR CLASS DISCUSSION

1. What are the most important differences between a presentation to inform and a presentation to instruct?
2. Cite a specific example from your own experience in which the quality of instruction was particularly good. What were the factors that made it successful?

## SUGGESTED CLASSROOM EXERCISE

Your instructor will assign you an instructional presentation. You may choose one or more of your classmates to use in this assignment, or you may instruct the entire class on knowledge or procedure. Allow eight minutes or less for the actual instruction and four minutes for feedback or testing.

## FOOTNOTES FOR CHAPTER TEN

[1] Henry C. Ellis, *The Transfer of Learning* (New York: Macmillan, 1965).

[2] Homer C. Rose, *The Development and Supervision of Training Programs* (Chicago: American Technical Society, 1966).

[3] Abraham Maslow, *The Farther Reaches of Human Nature* (New York: The Viking Press, 1971).

[4] John Jung, *Understanding Human Motivation* (New York: Macmillan, 1978).

[5] Avice Saint, *Learning at Work* (Chicago: Nelson-Hall Co., 1974).

[6] James E. Gardner, *Helping Employees Develop Job Skill* (Washington, D.C.: The Bureau of National Affairs, Inc., 1976).

[7] Homer C. Rose, *The Development and Supervision of Training Programs.*

[8] Gilbert Highet, *The Art of Teaching* (New York: Knopf, 1950).

[9] Alfred Adler, *Understanding Human Nature*, 10th Ed. (London: George Allen and Unwin, Ltd., 1974).

[10]Verne C. Fryklund, *Analysis Technique for Instructors* (Milwaukee, Wisc.: Bruce Publishing Co., 1956).

[11]Homer C. Rose, *The Development and Supervision of Training Programs*.

[12]Hugh P. Fellows, *The Art and Skill of Talking with People* (Englewood Cliffs, N.J.: Prentice-Hall, Inc., 1964).

[13]B.F. Skinner, *About Behaviorism* (New York: Knopf, 1974).

# VOCABULARY STUDY FOR CHAPTER ELEVEN

Following are some words used in this chapter, with which you may not be familiar. Try to select the correct meaning of each word from the multiple-choice definitions.

1. ADVERSARY    A. Unfortunate circumstances  B. A small religious sect  C. A situation where there are opposing sides.

2. AUTONOMY    A. Art of stuffing birds or animals  B. Independence, freedom; self-government  C. Knowledge of automobiles.

3. ESOTERIC    A. Understood by only a few  B. Violent behavior  C. Sexy.

4. EUPHORIA    A. Exotic plant  B. Feeling of well-being  C. Abnormal fear of height.

5. OGRE    A. One who predicts evil things to come  B. A monster or demon of terrifying proportions  C. A southern vegetable.

6. OSTENSIBLY    A. Frequently  B. Sensory  C. Professed, apparently.

7. PROPONENTS    A. Advocates, adherents  B. Parts of a whole  C. Antagonists.

8. REBUTTAL    A. Fortified military position  B. Refuting by evidence or argument  C. Debut.

9. SUBSERVIENT    A. Process of underground surveying  B. Servile; one who acts as a servant  C. Second or third in command.

10. THERAPEUTIC    A. Air pressure  B. Harmful, dangerous  C. Dealing with treatment or cure of disease.

11. VEHEMENT    A. Cannot be verified  B. Strong or violent expression  C. Boastful.

# 11 | Small Group Discussions

"Good talk" . . . is talk that does what it's supposed to do in a particular situation, assuming that the purpose of that situation is to serve rational and humane ends. "Bad talk" is talk that doesn't.

Neil Postman[1]

Some presentations in the business and professional world are delivered by several people. Among them, going from the least structured to those of a more rigid format, are discussions, brainstorming sessions, meetings, conferences, symposia, and debates. The symposium* and debate are not discussed in this chapter, because of their overlap with public speaking in this text. Some textbooks regard discussion as a means of problem solving, but that is only one of its purposes. This text considers problem-solving conferences in a separate chapter. In business a conference is usually reserved for decision making and is closed to the public. This chapter examines discussions, both private (the "team") and public (the panel or round table), and brainstorming sessions.

## Values of Discussion

The value of studying small group interaction is indicated by the fact that more and more businesses are forming teams within the organization as a whole, and

*A symposium consists of a group of talks on different facets of the same general subject.

especially within the boundaries of various departments—for example, sales, quality control, and product development. Discussion is the backbone of such teams. To participants it offers training in accurate listening, learning how to give and take criticism, the use of proper evidence and straight thinking, when and how to compromise, and an exchange of ideas and other points of view. All of these values rest on two premises: that the participant has come into the discussion group *prepared* and tolerant—ready to listen to others.

A productive discussion is a group of prepared people, under the guidance of a moderator, who are ready and willing to *investigate, explore* and *evaluate* some issue. Perhaps Thomas Babington Macauley (1800–1859) had this concept in mind when he wrote, "Men are never so likely to settle a question rightly, as when they discuss it fully."

## The Topic

In a debate or a persuasive speech one is said to have *won* the debate or *captured* the audience; those are sometimes adversary confrontations. Not so in a discussion: the participants may come up with two or more alternatives, any of which might be acceptable to the group as a whole. In an adversary situation the results are usually an "either/or" decision, whether the topic is one of fact, value, or policy. To illustrate:

Fact:   The United States of America has more natural resources than the Republic of Mexico.

Value:   Abraham Lincoln was a greater President than George Washington.

Policy:   The United States should cut off all foreign aid to nations who do not practice the doctrine of human rights.

In a discussion, the topic lends itself to issues of all three types; facts and values are the premises upon which policy is determined.

It is important to comment here briefly about some behavioral characteristics of individuals and their belonging to groups.

## INDIVIDUALS AND GROUPS

It is important for the leader (moderator) of a discussion group and the participants to consider three facts about an individual's rights:

1. The individual has a right to be recognized
2. The individual has a right to be heard
3. The individual has a right to stick out his neck without getting his head chopped off.

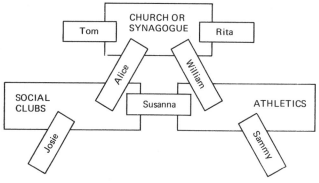

Figure 11-1

Americans tend to join organizations—for example, bowling teams, sororities or fraternities, churches or synagogues, and service clubs. Nearly all of these groups have some common tendencies: they insist on certain cultural and social values; they insist on conformity to their rules; they tend to resist change; and they tend to be dynamic rather than static. They also have certain prejudices and prestige.[2] However, each individual may belong to overlapping groups, as shown in Figure 11-1. The individuals also have parts of themselves that are not subservient to any group. So, it is important in a group discussion to be discreet about attacking or criticizing lawful group organizations. You have a right to your opinions; however, you must also ask yourself how much the groups to which *you* belong have influenced your own thinking and attitudes.

Also, consider the individual backgrounds of the members of the discussion group: their social, economic, ethnic, and religious influences. Participation in small groups can be destructive as well as therapeutic. A group can attack an individual with savage animal behavior, and that individual will feel it much more deeply than when in a larger group; that individual will retreat from being an active participant in the group. On the other hand, the same group can act as a buffer by responding favorably to that person and thereby help to relieve that individual of anxiety.[3] Be aware that every group member plays a different role in relation to every other member, as well as to the group. This is why the *first and foremost* rule is COURTESY, from both the leader and the participants.

## Characteristics of Small Groups

Through research and observation much has been learned about small group discussions.

When a person with a higher position (such as a major in the military in the company of noncommissioned personnel) or an obviously popular person (one to whom the other members of the group speak familiarly and admiringly), that person's opinions tend to be valued more highly than others, even though others in the group may disagree.[4]

A group of college students was shown a series of three lines, all clearly of different lengths, and a fourth line that was the same length as one of the other three. Each member of the group was then asked to decide which of the first three lines matched the length of the fourth line and to announce a decision. The task would normally have been an easy one, but all but one member of the group had previously been instructed to select the wrong line. *The result was that fully one-third of the time the one uninstructed group member was willing to forsake his own clear sense perception in order to be in agreement with the majority.* This was true even in groups as small as four people, where the odds were only three against one.[5]

These examples would lead us to believe that some people go along with the small group despite their own convictions. In making that decision, a member must sacrifice a portion of his autonomy perhaps, but that member is rewarded by a feeling of being a harmonious part of a group.[6]

### Requirements for Participants

Far too much has been written about the leader (moderator) of a discussion group, and not nearly enough about the members themselves. Here are a few suggestions for the participants, which can contribute toward a successful discussion.

1. Be prepared. You must be better informed about the topic than the general public. Read about the topic from several sources, and take notes if necessary. Your opinion—however strongly you may feel about it from your own background—should be an *informed* opinion.

2. Use reflective thinking (explore, investigate, evaluate) about your own ideas and those of others. Before you offer a criticism of another panel member's opinion or proposed solution, turn it over carefully in your own mind.

3. Work to acquire skill in cooperative group thinking. This comes with time and experience—often after you have taken a beating on some of your pet ideas—but you can practice it daily. Whenever a group of friends gets into a heated discussion, try to exercise reflective thinking.

4. Be *more* than courteous. When you notice a member of the group who is not contributing, ask that person's opinion, or invite comment from that person. This is usually the discussion leader's duty, but there is no reason why you should not undertake it on your own.

5. Try to keep an open mind. For example, if one member takes a portion of your suggestion and adds something to it, perhaps it is more *acceptable* that way. THINK before you say, "No! It's my *whole* idea or nothing!" Thank another member who has made an improvement on your idea.

The requirements for moderating a small group discussion in a private group are much the same as those for conducting a small group discussion before an audience—usually referred to as a panel. Consequently, we have placed these requirements for moderators at the end of the next section.

## WHEN THE SMALL GROUP DISCUSSION HAS AN AUDIENCE

The value of public discussion about current issues extends both to the participant and to the listeners in the audience, who are sometimes asked to participate toward the end of the discussion. It can sometimes change the attitudes of listeners toward an issue; it can help listeners make decisions; it can expose them to new points of view. It can also offer occasional entertainment for them, when an issue is hotly debated.

When an audience is listening, speak especially clearly. Usually the seating will be arranged as shown in Figure 11-2 so that the panel members can see one another and can also be seen by the audience. Remember that we tend to adjust our volume to the person being spoken to directly, but if you don't speak a trifle louder than that, the audience will miss most of what you have to say.

The following questions examine some proporties of a good topic for discussion staged before an audience:

1. Is the topic of equal interest to listeners and participants?
2. Does the topic lend itself to investigation, exploration, and evaluation?
3. Can supportive material be found easily—on more than one point of view?
4. Is the topic suitable to the group who is participating? The case histories at the end of this chapter are not all strictly business situations. However, they are suitable for most college students, and it is the *technique* of discussion that this text is concerned with.

### Size and Structure

You will notice that Figure 11-2 shows only four participants and one moderator. The number of participants may run as large as six, but this is not advised.

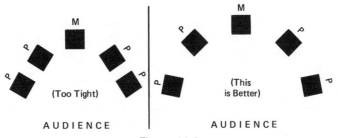

Figure 11-2

With too many participants, it will be difficult to conduct the discussion within a reasonable time limit.

The structure should be that of free and spontaneous speech among the participants. No participant should need the moderator's permission to speak; however, if two people start talking at once, the moderator gives a turn to each speaker.

## Requirements for the Moderator

While the part played in the discussion by the moderator may seem minor, that person's actual duties and responsibilities are enormous. Ostensibly, this is all the moderator does:

1. Welcomes the audience and announces the topic for discussion.
2. Introduces the members of the panel.
3. Asks for volunteers on the topic and calls on a specific panel member if there are no volunteers. Theoretically the panel members will take over from there, until it is time to close; then the moderator thanks the panel and calls for questions from the audience.

But there is much more to handling a discussion group than that. Although the members of the panel take the spotlight, the moderator is the one who guides the light. Here are some of the things that you as a moderator should prepare for:

1. Do your homework and know the subject *thoroughly*. If the subject is controversial, know the evidence for and against the topic.
2. Although knowing both sides of the issue, you must be absolutely impartial. Even if a member of the panel states something that you believe to be untrue, wait for *another member* of the panel to correct the panel member—do not do it yourself.
3. Never interrupt a speaker, except on two possible occasions: (1) when you believe that there is a semantic difference in terms that may be clarified; (2) when the panel is straying from the subject. A certain amount of levity is allowable among the panelists—and can be amusing to the listeners—but the panelists should for the most part stick to the subject.
4. In the event that the panel members reach a pause in the discussion, you should always have a few questions to ask them; the questions should be prepared *beforehand*. Two suggestions about these questions follow:
    A. Don't ask questions that can be answered with a simple "yes" or "no."
    B. Here are some sample questions which cannot be answered with a monosyllable:
       (1) Can you give us some examples of what you said earlier?
       (2) What have been your experiences with. . . . ?
       (3) Can you suggest some other possibilities for (doing something or other)?
       (4) Do you mind if I ask why you think as you do?

5. There are exceptions to all suggestions, and this one applies to "letting the members of the panel take the lead." If the moderator knows that there is vehement disagreement among some of the members on a certain issue, the moderator should take control *at the beginning*, skirting that particular area. This is *not* because the moderator is trying to *evade* the area of disagreement; instead, it is to allow the panel a few minutes to build rapport among themselves.

The moderator must be a person of considerable tact.

## Handling Questions From the Audience

It seems that in every gathering where the audience is allowed to ask questions, some member of the audience stands up and airs his or her own views *at length*. Here is a typical example:

*Man from Audience* (MFA):   Now, I've had 33 years of experience as a supervisor in a variety store; I have worked for Woolworth, Kresge, Golden Triangle, and several others. Now, we found that the best way to prevent shoplifting--

*Moderator* (MOD):   Please, sir; we appreciate your experience, but what is the question?

MFA:   I'm coming to that later, but I want to say that we hired plainclothesmen, put in convex mirrors, and even tried television cameras, but the best way we found--

MOD:   Please, sir, I must have your question!

The moderator isn't going to *hear* the question until the man from the audience has had his say. The audience did not come to hear the man from the audience, but to hear the panel of experts, so it's a waste of their time to let the man go on. The moderator may leave him talking and go to the next person who has a question, but there is a better way of handling the situation.

Before allowing any of the audience to speak, the moderator can politely impose restrictions on them by announcing: "We would now like to open this discussion to questions from the audience. We have only thirty minutes for this [or whatever time is allotted], so we *must* ask you to word your question so that it will take no more than thirty seconds. Now, if you cannot possibly word your question in thirty seconds or less, please *write* to the panel and we will be glad to answer it."

If some audience member still insists upon exceeding thirty seconds, allow another ten seconds *after asking* for the question, and then go *immediately* to the next questioner, calling in a loud voice, "Next!" This may be discourteous to the questioner, but it *is being courteous* to your listeners as a *whole*.

*Topic:* After the accident at the Three Mile Island (Pennsylvania) nuclear plant, should the U.S.A. continue to build more nuclear plants to supply us with energy?

*Before* the discussion I felt this way:

☐ FOR      ☐ AGAINST

Very
strongly

Strongly

Some reser-
vations

*After* the discussion I felt this way:

☐ FOR      ☐ AGAINST

Very
strongly

Strongly

Some reser-
vations

*Comments:* _____

_____

_____

_____

Figure 11-3

## Evaluation of a Discussion

Of all speech activities, a discussion is the most difficult to evaluate. It is difficult to come up with any sort of fair grading system that will work with the *individuals* in a group except "satisfactory" and "unsatisfactory." Judging the success of the discussion *as a whole* is another matter.[7]

First, a reminder of some things that a discussion is NOT supposed to do:

1. The members of the panel are *not* necessarily supposed to be in complete agreement at the end of it.
2. The discussion does *not* need to settle something. Often it is most successful

when it unsettles the minds of the participants and the audience by casting doubts in their minds about their previous ideas.
3. The audience does *not* necessarily need to ask many questions. Listening is an active process, and the audience often participates *without* asking questions.

The following are some criteria to help indicate whether or not the discussion has been a success.

1. Polling the members of the discussion group and the audience before and after the actual discussion is often useful. Figure 11-3 shows a sample ballot. If *any* members of the panel itself, and even a *few* members of the audience, show that their opinion has shifted in the slightest, the discussion has been successful.
2. If the members of the panel stay around and want to talk about the subject further, you can bet it was successful.
3. If members of the audience ask for further discussions of the same topic, it's a sure sign that your discussion has succeeded.

"I hold to the belief that if folks get around a table and talk things through, they usually can come to the right and fair answer."
—Supreme Court Justice Harold H. Burton (1888–1964)

## BRAINSTORMING SESSIONS

These sessions were a fad in the 1950s and 1960s, when some proponents hailed them as great incubators of ideas. The format consists of a moderator, or chairman; a recorder, or secretary; and almost any number of participants, from five to upwards of twenty.

The basic idea is for any participant to express any idea that he/she considers to be for the good of the organization. Participants are encouraged to toss out ideas, no matter how wild or inconsequential, while the secretary makes notes of them. The theory is that, no matter how far-fetched an idea might be, it might trigger a response for a practical contribution by some other member. There are only two rules:

1. An overall time limit is set—usually from ten minutes to one hour. Sometimes a time limit is set for each participant (two or three minutes), until all other members have had an opportunity to participate.
2. Absolutely *no* evaluation, criticism, or any form of judgment (good or bad) is allowed until the session is over.

The secretary then reads back all of the contributions from the group, and they are evaluated.

In 1969 we took an informal survey of twenty business firms who had used brainstorming to get ideas and found the results discouraging, but some organizations still use this device.

# SUGGESTED CLASSROOM EXERCISES

Assuming that there is time enough for the class to spend three or more periods on this chapter and the one following it, your instructor may divide you into four groups, in order for you to have some practice and observation of the four types of presentation discussed in this chapter. The following are suggested:

1. Two groups of five persons each for two discussions, or one group for discussion and the other for brainstorming. Each group should elect a moderator, and each should discuss (or brainstorm) a separate topic. The time allotted to each will be thirty minutes (twenty minutes, if class periods are limited to one hour). Six people are acceptable if this helps balance the number of students in a class.
2. One group of five persons to produce a symposium on some current problem. The time limits may be shortened to four or five minutes for each speaker in order to allow time for a question and answer period.
3. One group of four persons to debate a currently controversial topic. The time allotted may be changed: five minutes for constructive speeches and three minutes for rebuttal speeches. The instructor may select three judges from the class, who have already made their presentations.

## Case Histories for Discussion

Although discussions are not generally for the purpose of problem solving, they can offer a consensus, among members of the group making the presentation as well as among members of the audience. The following case histories have been tested in classrooms for several years and have generated a great deal of interest. Although none of them is esoteric enough to require technical knowledge in a specific area of business or the professions, all of them necessitate preparation and limited research.

## CASE HISTORIES—I

### The Pitman Copyright Case

Lecturers or writers may secure copyright protection for their literary efforts, provided they have not already dedicated the specified work to the public, or given it to the public gratuitously.

Nicols, an author and lecturer upon various scientific subjects, was hired by the Workingmen's College to give a lecture on "The Dog as a Friend of Man." The audience was admitted by free tickets that the college issued. Nicols read from his own manuscript, which was not copyrighted.

Pitman, the author of a system of shorthand writing, attended the lecture and took it down in shorthand; afterward, he published the lecture *in shorthand* (almost in its entirety) in a manual that was sold to students. He gave Nicols credit for the lecture, just as he gave credit to other lecturers whose material he used.

Nicols sued Pitman to recover damages for the publication of his lecture.

QUESTION: Should Nicols win the lawsuit?

## CASE HISTORIES—II

### Ethical Problem

Professor Dearborn teaches at a large state university that does not use the honor system. Examinations are closely proctored, and other precautions are taken to prevent cheating. Professor Dearborn does not enforce the proctoring regulation; he believes in the integrity of the individual. A student was absent from Dearborn's midterm examination and had to make up the examination. Dearborn gave the student several essay questions, provided him with a chair and table in his office, and left for the library, telling the student to leave his examination paper on the table when he had finished.

Dearborn returned after two hours to find the student gone and the student's paper on the table. On reading the paper, he found that the answers it contained had obviously been copied from several books on his office bookshelves.

Dearborn had authority to give the student an "E" on the paper, to give him an "E" or "F" in the course, or even to report the student to the dean for disciplinary action. "However," he reflected, "I knew that this student was averaging only a "D" in the course when I left him alone in my office. Did I not put temptation in his path? Am I, rather than the student, mainly responsible for his dishonesty?"

QUESTIONS: (a) Is Dearborn chiefly responsible for the student's action? (b) What should be Dearborn's course of action?

## CASE HISTORIES—III

### The Berea College Case

Berea College, a private institution under the aegis of a Protestant church, is almost completely self-supporting; that is, its students farm, do mechanical and electrical work, and provide other services to maintain the physical plant, in exchange for their tuition. Berea is coeducational and is located in a Kentucky town of approximately 5,000 inhabitants.

One of Berea's rules prohibits students from "entering eating houses and places of amusement not controlled by the college." The penalty for disobeying this rule is dismissal from the college, which has an enrollment of approximately 1,000 students. Berea receives no state or federal government subsidy.

Mike Graham owned a restaurant in the town of Berea. He claimed that the enforcement of the rule about not entering eating places not controlled by the college seriously injured his business. Accordingly he sued the college to restrain it from enforcing the rule. He was abetted in his case by the parents of a student who was taken to Graham's restaurant during spring vacation. Graham stated that the college had no right to take away the privilege of free citizens and that restaurants and the movie theatre were being boycotted by the college, since students were free to trade in clothing stores, drug stores, and other such places of business.

It is a well-known fact that during the Prohibition Era Mike Graham was convicted of bootlegging alcoholic spirits and has served a term in prison for this crime.

QUESTION: What should be the decision of the court?

## CASE HISTORIES—IV

### The College Fraternity Case

Purdue University is at least in part supported by the State of Indiana. The university's Trustees adopted a rule that no student would be permitted to join a Greek-letter or any other secret society. Penalty for disobedience was expulsion from the university.

Jim Hawley, a student, left the university in April, not expecting to return. While out of school, he joined a Greek-letter social fraternity, whose initiation ceremonies and councils were secret from the public. Later he sought to return to Purdue, but the president of the university demanded that he sign a pledge to the effect that Hawley had not been a member of a secret fraternity at the time he left in April, and that he would disconnect himself (resign from) the fraternity Lambda Delta Sigma, which he had joined while out of school. Hawley refused to sign the pledge and brought action in the courts to compel the university to readmit him without requiring him to resign from the fraternity that he had joined.

QUESTION: Should Hawley win the lawsuit?

## CASE HISTORIES—V

### A Loyalty Problem

You are a freshman in college. Your roommate, a junior who has been warm and understanding, is extremely well liked on campus and is a leader in several organizations and in student government. Furthermore, the roommate has helped you in mathematics, tutoring you patiently and without pay; otherwise, you would surely have flunked the course.

Only in the past few weeks did you discover that your "roomie" has a hypodermic syringe and needle and gives himself/herself injections. The roommate explains that he/she is a diabetic and takes regular injections of insulin.

Lately you have noticed that the roommate experiences a "high" after taking the insulin, becomes positively euphoric and indulges in all sorts of fantasies. The roommate only takes the injections at night and is perfectly normal the next day.

Your suspicions grow. Finally, you steal one of the white pills from your roommate's supply and take it to a private M. D. (not the campus doctor). He confirms your suspicion; it is morphine, a habit-forming drug.

The college you attend forbids the use of any habit-forming drugs and permits no one except the college physician to administer injections. The penalty for infracting this rule is immediate expulsion.

QUESTION: What should your course of action be?

## CASE HISTORIES—VI

### The Louvre Museum Case

You are a *night* guard in the Louvre Museum in Paris. At 2:00 A.M. you discover a man hiding there and recognize him as a vicious criminal and murderer who has escaped from prison. He attacks you and you knock him out with your club. At that moment you discover that the building is on fire. You turn in a fire alarm and close all of the fireproof doors to keep the flames from spreading, but the smoke is over-whelming you. You must get to fresh air in a hurry.

The unconscious criminal is lying just below the immortal painting, *Mona Lisa,* by Leonardo da Vinci. You have the choice of dragging the criminal to safety or saving the *Mona Lisa;* you *cannot* do *both.*

Question: What would your decision be—and *why?*

### Student Critiques

The instructor might appoint three students to give a critique of each discussion group. The critique guide that follows will help the student critic to briefly and precisely evaluate the discussion.

### Critique For Discussion

This is a brief—and broad—critique sheet; it covers only the essentials. However, it can be used for both discussions and conferences.

| | Participant's Number | | | | | |
|---|---|---|---|---|---|---|
| *Participants:* | 1 | 2 | 3 | 4 | 5 | 6 |
| 1. Showed evidence of preparation by quoting authority or using facts or statistics from a reliable source. | | | | | | |
| 2. Showed interaction with other members by addressing them directly. | | | | | | |
| 3. Interrupted other members and tended to monopolize the discussion. | | | | | | |
| 4. Did not participate enough. | | | | | | |

| *Moderator* | *Yes* | *No* |
|---|---|---|
| 1. Did moderator encourage *each* member of the group to participate? | _____ | _____ |
| 2. Did moderator clearly show preparation and knowledge of the subject? | _____ | _____ |
| 3. Did moderator insist (gently) that the members keep to the issue and not digress from it? | _____ | _____ |
| 4. Did moderator attempt to get members to agree with one another, by showing that differences were often semantic rather than real? | _____ | _____ |
| 5. Did moderator get a consensus of the members before and after the discussion? | _____ | _____ |
| (For Conference) | | |
| 6. Did moderator attempt to obtain an agreement at (a) each step of the conference and (b) at the end of the conference? | _____ | _____ |
| 7. Did moderator put the members' decision into words that were satisfactory to each member? | _____ | _____ |

## FOOTNOTES FOR CHAPTER ELEVEN

[1]Neil Postman, *Crazy Talk, Stupid Talk* (New York: Delacorte Press, 1976).

[2]Gerald M. Phillips and Eugene C. Erickson, *Interpersonal Dynamics in the Small Group* (New York: Random House, 1970). p. 170.

[3]Ibid. p. 218.

[4]Lowell W. Gerson, "Punishment and Position: The Sanctioning of Deviants in Small Groups," *Case Western Reserve Journal of Sociology,* Vol I (1967) pp. 54–62.

[5]Cal W. Downs, David M. Berg, and Wil A. Linkugel, *The Organizational Communicator* (New York: Harper & Row, 1977) p. 131.

[6]J. W. Keltner, *Interpersonal Speech Communication* (Belmont, Calif.: Wadsworth, 1970), p. 68.

[7]Gerald M. Phillips and Eugene C. Erickson, *Interpersonal Dynamics,* p. 219.

## SUGGESTIONS FOR FURTHER READING

S. E. ASCH, "Effects of Group Pressure upon the Modification and Distortion of Judgments" in *Groups, Leadership and Men,* H. Guetzkow, Ed. (Pittsburgh: Carnegie Press, 1951).

Paul V. Crosbie, Ed., *Interaction in Small Groups* (New York: Macmillan Publishing Co., 1975).

Gerard Egan, Ed., *Encounter Groups: Basic Readings* (Belmont, Calif.: Wadsworth, 1971).

Richard J. Ofshe, Ed., *Interpersonal Behavior in Small Groups* (Englewood Cliffs, N.J.: Prentice-Hall, 1973).

J. Wofferd, E. Gerloff and R. Cummins, *Organizational Communication: The Keystone to Managerial Effectiveness* (New York: McGraw-Hill, 1977).

# VOCABULARY STUDY FOR CHAPTER TWELVE

The vocabulary study for this chapter consists of a crossword puzzle. The clues and puzzle are below, and the answers on page 354.

*Across*

1. Frozen water
5. Third person singular of the verb "to be"
8. Knowing everything on earth and in heaven
11. International Garment Union
12. A hollow tubing for conveying air or liquid
13. Second or third person of verb "to be"
14. 3.1416
15. Acting without thinking; impulsive
18. Lack of harmony; needing completion or satisfaction
22. To swerve to one side
23. To shear or reduce
24. A long-standing grudge or quarrel, for which revenge must be taken
27. A circle with a very wide empty center

*Down*

2. An adjective that describes perception, or knowing
3. Large flightless Australian bird
4. A young goat
5. Interstate Commerce Commission
6. To half recline
7. Cracks asunder, or replies irritably
9. An Islamic ruler
10. Prefix meaning "three"
16. To assume a posture (p.t.)
17. To possess
19. To transmit (p.t.)
20. One object of mining
21. A reflected sound wave
25. Scottish for "thanks"
26. "____ ha!"

Figure 12-1

# 12 Problem-Solving Conferences

The third-rate mind is only happy when it is thinking with the majority; the second-rate mind is only happy when it is thinking with the minority; and the first-rate mind is only happy when it is thinking.

A. A. Milne (1882–1956)

The word "conference" has almost as many meanings as it has designated purposes. Mr. Bixby's secretary reports that he is "in conference" when he is in fact discussing his golf game in his office. Sometimes delegates from dozens of organizations meet to confer on other delegates' opinions or progress, and it is called a conference. Conventions often have many "conferences" to share information without regard to its immediate use. Some mutual interest groups—lawyers, doctors, bankers—meet to formulate courses of action or to settle disputes, and it is called a conference. There are even "training conferences," where foremen, supervisors, and management are used to pass on information to lower echelons; those last described are considered highly productive so long as the leaders speak the language of the general group and are not regarded as high-minded and impractical.

This chapter will focus on a problem-solving conference within one organization or business firm. The purpose of a problem-solving conference is not so much to talk as it is to *think*. This may involve formulating policy, determining future action, organizing or distributing authority or responsibility, or extricating one's business firm from a difficult position; its purpose is still the solution of a problem.

## VALUE

Fred Allen (1894–1956) took the pessimistic view when he remarked, "A conference is a gathering of important people who singly can do nothing, but together decide that nothing can be done." Nothing could be further from the truth if one *listens* and *thinks*. While it is true that one person may not be able to solve the problem at hand, another person's ideas may trigger a response in the first person's thought that will provide a solution. A group of minds who are working intelligently and without bias can solve almost any problem.

We believe firmly in our jury system. While it is often wasteful and expensive, when the prosecution and defense have had equal opportunity to examine the prospective jurors, it is rare that a jury will convict an innocent man or allow a culprit to go free. An analogy might be drawn between a jury and a problem-solving conference; if the personnel are selected carefully, the problem will usually be solved.

> ". . . members perceive several alternatives for accomplishing their tasks. As discussions progress, these alternatives are debated, refined, accepted, changed, rejected, etc., until the final task product evolves from their deliberations—largely through a 'method of residues' or elimination of available alternatives."[1]

So the members of a problem-solving conference search for answers in precedents, in the ways competitors have solved similar problems, in the light of recent and current research, and in ideas gathered by field representatives. Problem-solving conferences use the process of reflective thinking:

A. What is the problem, its probable causes, and the degree of its seriousness?
B. What are the possible solutions?
    1. Their short-term advantages or disadvantages?
    2. Their long-term advantages or disadvantages?
C. What, finally, seems to be the *best* solution?
D. How can this solution be put into operation in a way that is both
    1. Practical?
    2. Practicable?

Unless *all* participants approach the problem-solving conference with these things in mind, there is no conference. In fact, one of the chief values of a conference is training people to think in this way.

Another value of the problem-solving conference is that people learn to work with one another: to listen actively, to be willing to compromise when a better solution than one's own is offered, and to work toward a common cause.

Two additional values have been enumerated by Bert S. Cross, former President of the 3M Company, from the standpoint of management: (a) their value as a training aid and (b) their use as an appraisal tool. Cross states that people whose training has been in specialized fields, such as engineers, accountants, or scientists, become cognizant of the problems of sales, research, and production, when they are called upon to solve business problems. He goes on to say that no better appraisal can be made of an individual's potential than in the individual's presentation of material, the individual's responses, and the individual's attitude toward others, as a member of a conference team.[2]

In the area of decision-making, mention should be made of Leon Festinger's *A Theory of Cognitive Dissonance*.[3] Briefly, Festinger states that cognitive dissonance occurs when there is a need to choose between two alternatives without clear and compelling support for either of them. In another work,[4] Festinger states that "Outside support may be necessary to help the person continue to believe what he wants to believe." Jung[5] and others treat dissonance theories lightly, suggesting that further *enlightenment* on the alternatives will resolve that dissonance. Practical business men and women make decisions on the bases of the available information, and do not hesitate to change those decisions when other information becomes available.

A final value: in no other form of group speaking do *observers* seem to learn more than they learn from a conference. In one class after another, we have organized several conferences on various subjects, always observing the strict format which will follow. Usually, the first conference is not too good; the second is better, the third is good, and the fourth is usually excellent. We have not seen this among other presentations, no matter how many of them the non-participants may have witnessed.


## THE FORMAT

In their *Handbook of Group Discussion*,[6] Wagner and Arnold state, "It is almost impossible to describe a 'best' conference procedure." Drawing from the experience of business executives over a period of more than twenty years, this author has found one that most of them would agree is about as good as is possible.

First, some semblance of parliamentary procedure must be followed. The purpose of such procedure is to guard against hasty—and often poorly considered—action, to give each member an equal opportunity to speak, to protect the minority, and to determine the will of the majority.

The first order is to choose a leader and a secretary. The leader does not necessarily have to be the most important person in the business firm. Witness this testimonial from an Air Force Colonel:

All of my command's problems are solved by the conference method. These include solving technical problems, disseminating information, explaining directives, clearing up misunderstandings, and training recruits. What is more, those problems are solved by lower echelon and noncommissioned officers, without deference to rank more than any adult should pay to any other adult who is working with him on a problem.

When my men come in for a conference, I tell them, 'Gentlemen, these eagles on my shoulders do *not* denote intelligence—only responsibility. *You* have the intelligence about this problem because you're closer to the men than I am. So, if you'll solve the problem, I'll take the responsibility.' It works every time.[7]

If there are to be two or more conferences, it might be tactful to select a different leader for each one so that no one will feel that the group has a "favorite." However, if the conferences are sequential, the secretary should remain the same in order to provide continuity. The leader should be carefully selected, as will be discussed later.

A format that has worked well in many business conferences consists of four stages. To make them easier to remember, they have been dubbed "The Four D's."

## Disclosure

This is the only stage where the conference leader does a large amount of talking—and even that can be averted by adopting some of the suggestions that follow. The conference leader thanks the participants for taking part and gives the background of the problem. Here the leader may call upon some of the other members to give probable causes of the problem; the leader may also call upon other participants to indicate the gravity of the problem and its need to be solved immediately or in the near future. At this stage the leader may also call upon other members for special reports that they have been asked to prepare beforehand, such as sales figures, accident reports, floor space requirements, and cost accounts for various purposes. It is preferable for the leader to call upon other members to give this information, in order to get the conference off to a "participatory" start. The leader should also define all terms used in the problem and call for agreement on those terms, so that there will be no semantic difficulties.

After this introduction to the problem and the seriousness of it the conference leader should participate only when necessary, as defined in the next three stages. The leader who does his job well will be too busy *listening, taking notes,* and *spotting areas of agreement* to do much else.

## Discourse

This is the bulk of the conference, where the members make suggestions for solving the problem. The individual's suggestion may be amended, or an alternate suggestion might be offered. While it is natural for everyone to defend their decisions, no one should resent an amendment or an alternative solution. Even if your suggestion is totally rejected, you have at least done your best by contributing. Your "rejected" contribution may have sparked the suggestion of another member who had theretofore *nothing* to contribute. Share! It's team work.

A conference is a *joint* effort and must be treated so. After all, the result can help determine the failure or success of the business firm for which you are working.

Don't sulk if your suggestion is amended, changed, and finally thrown out, and try not to be suspicious of the other members: "Herman is the shop foreman, and he is making that suggestion to get better working conditions for his shop!" or "Sam is trying to shift more responsibility onto the superintendent so that management will have more time to play tennis!" A business firm cannot live by its shop alone, nor by its marketing program, nor by its top management alone; it takes a conglomerate of all factors to produce a business. So, when a problem arises, think of the *whole* rather than the part you play in it.

The discourse period should be one during which each member is free to question, to doubt, to deny, to make alternate suggestions, and to ask, "Where are we going?"—All based on the parliamentary procedure of noninterruption.

While this is essentially the function of the leader of the conference, any member may join in—after receiving recognition from the leader—if the group seems near an agreement. Often, amid the wealth of ideas being considered, members overlook how near they have come to an agreement. The leader should be especially perceptive about this, but it is not out of order for some other member to call attention to it instead. At each step of recognition of agreement the secretary should be instructed to write it down as a *separate* part of the notes.

## Decision

As the group progresses toward a solution to the problem—or alternate solutions to it—the leader again steps in. The leader words the solution in a manner that is satisfactory to all members and, if a chalkboard is handy, writes it out in detail. If there are alternate decisions, the leader appoints committees to study the alternatives and report at a later conference. The group should be willing to accept any viable alternate as being advantageous to the business, even though some favor one over another. There should be no feeling of dissonance here, only receptivity to additional information.

## Decorum

Once a decision, or alternate decisions, have been reached, the leader plays an important part. The leader who has done a good job has kept track of the proposals made by each member and thanks them individually. The leader who is a genius *names* those contributions and shows how they led on to a solution of the problem. This doesn't take much time, and all members know that they have contributed. If all members are thanked, they will be more than willing to participate at the next conference.

It is difficult to separate a conference itself from the people who comprise it. The following describes the qualifications of its participants.

## THE CONFERENCE LEADER

Often a conference originates in the president's office or in the office of the executive next in charge. One of them will say, "Call a conference to settle the Blaisdell affair, and have Gordon, Charles, and Frank there." If present, the highest-ranking officer will not always take charge—although don't bet on it! Ideally the conference leader and secretary should be elected.

The cautious, overdeliberative thinker does not make the best conference leader; neither does the impetuous, dynamic person who is in too big a hurry to get things done. It is unfortunate—though almost inevitable—that the conference leader is the highest ranking official present. This often causes the conferees to hesitate about disagreeing or speaking out.

The ideal conference leader is one

1. Who can listen with patience
2. Who can think objectively
3. Who is an *expert* at jotting down pertinent facts
4. Who can prevent useless digressions when necessary
5. Who has enough of a sense of urgency to press gently for a decision.

As is mentioned above, the conference leader tries to prevent *useless* digressions. But, the leader who is tactful may recognize that a digression from the main subject can be useful. When two or more of the conferees get into a heated argument that is becoming a matter of personal ego, it is useless to say, "Now, calm down, you two!" Instead, the conference leader introduces a topic that is totally irrelevant, such as, "Joe, I forgot to ask you about that expensive bet you placed on Bellarmine in the sixth race last Saturday; did it pay off?" When the conference has gone on for a *long time* (and more than one hour is a long time), the leader may interject a bit of humor or some other irrelevant matter. This gives the conferees a rest period so that they can approach the problem in a fresh manner. The leader may even call a recess for the same purpose.

### Encouraging Reticent Speakers

Part of the leader's duty is to give all members a fair share of the time in the conference. There are shy people who would much rather let other people do *all* of the talking, and they are frequently worth listening to. The leader may try a question such as "Let's get John's reaction to that proposal." If the leader knows *beforehand* that John is a nontalker, the leader can resort to a clever strategy: immediately after the introduction is given, the leader should call on John to contribute *first*. Shy people tend to recede more and more into the background as others carry the ball; however, once John has made a contribution, he has an *investment* in that conference and will continue to *protect* that investment by speaking up.

## Discouraging Loquacity

On most occasions the overtalkative person who threatens to monopolize the conference can be subdued by saying something as simple as, "That's a good idea, Pete, but I wonder if we may know what the others think? What about you, Tom?" Now and then you may get persons who believe themselves omniscient and that nobody else's ideas are worth anything. The English language can be used cleverly in these situations. First, you interrupt the all-knowing one by asking the person to clear up a certain term he or she has used. Then, while the person is clarifying that term, you interrupt again—always politely and apologetically—by asking for clarification of a term used in the clarification. If absolutely necessary, ask for clarification of something in the clarification of the original clarification! Chances are, the person will become absolutely dazed and sorry for having ever started talking. However, be kind to the person and ask a question that the person can answer with a simple "yes" or "no."

People are *not* stereotypes, and no way of dealing with them will *always* work. However, the following are suggestions that may be of value to the conference leader.

TO JERRY, who talks too much: "That was a good point that Jerry raised. What do the *rest* of you think about it?"
"Jerry has been carrying the ball long enough; how about a suggestion from somebody else?"

TO SUSAN, who knows all the answers: (Turn away from Susan) "Did you want to say something, Max?"
"Great idea, Susan, but let's see what Mary or Sam think about it."

TO FELIX, [Tricky, because people will be *dominated* by him.] "Now, Felix, that's just one person's viewpoint; how do the rest of you feel about it?"
"Felix, that's good, but we want *everyone's* opinion. Do you mind holding onto that idea until we've heard from someone else?"

TO MARY, who is a rambler and never comes to the point: "Just a minute, Mary; I want to be sure to get all of these points down. [Use chalkboard] Now, your first point was . . . ? Add your second point . . . ?"

TO LUKE,   who is reticent: "Luke, you're new to the group. Give us your slant."
            "You're probably as close to the problem as anyone else. Why not
            give us your reaction?"

TO DICK,   who is totally disinterested: "Dick *says* very little, but when he says
            something, it's worth listening to. What do you say, Dick?"
            "I know we'll want to get Dick's opinion on this, before we go on."
            [We must go on record here as saying that we are against such blatant
            flattery; if Dick is disinterested, his opinion is not worth much!]

TO ANNE,   who is antagonistic and pessimistic: "Anne, this conference was called
            for the *solution* of. . . ."
            "Anne, you know the purpose of this conference: can you solve it more
            efficiently than the others? If so, we'll be glad to hear from you."

## Recording Progress

Although there is a secretary present (perhaps two—one elected by the group,
plus a professional stenographer), it is wise for the conference leader to make
notes of pertinent points. Both the elected secretary and the professional stenographer are so busy listening for words that they have little time left to listen
for *meaning*; and there are a great many useless words bandied about in a
conference. Notes taken intelligently by the conference leader can be more
concise than those taken by either secretary—although both are useful.

The following is a suggested plan for taking notes. The conference leader
prepares ahead of time a number of large sheets of paper, numbered consecutively and divided into equal spaces for each conferee's name (See Figure 12-
2). Because of the differential between the speed of thought and the speed of
speaking,* the conference leader can condense any one member's sentence
into a few words and write it in the square bearing that member's name.
Suppose Al makes a proposal and Sid objects to that proposal; the proposal and
the objection are both written in condensed language in the space bearing their
names—and numbered. Then, Tom makes a proposal, Sid makes a counter-
proposal, and Joe offers an amendment to that proposal; these, too, are written
in their proper spaces, along with a number "two." Now, you can see that, after
awhile, that sheet of paper is going to look like a mass of tangled string, so the
leader goes on to the next sheet of paper. When the conference is over, the
leader has a complete condensation of all the major contributions to it and can
repeat them in sequence, without wading through all the verbiage of the secretary. This procedure requires a little practice, but it is well worth the effort

---

*The speed of speech is only about 150 words per minute, while the speed of thought
ranges upward from 300–800 words per minute.

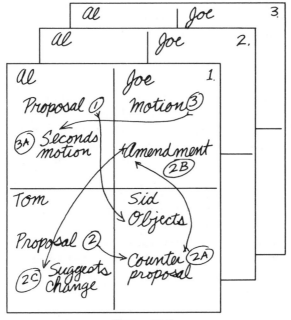

Figure 12-2

in the long run, and it enables the conference leader to thank each conferee by name for his/her contribution.


## THE CONFERENCE PARTICIPANTS

Far too much has been written about conference leadership and not nearly enough about the participants. After all, *you* are the ones who are solving the problem—if your leader will allow it!


### Preparation

If your conference leader or committee has asked you to furnish a certain report, you should do it. You should also think through what the conference may be about and have some definite ideas about how the problems under consideration might be solved. Go back to the discussion about "reflective thinking" and consider all of the alternatives. But don't fall in love with your own solution to the point where you become *blind* to a *better* solution! After gathering materials that have been requested, look for any *other* materials that you believe pertinent and label them clearly.

## Attitude

Try not to practice one-upmanship. If Fred has a good idea, *commend* him for it. Remember, it's *your* business firm, and the most important consideration is that it survives and flourishes, no matter who gets credit for the most brilliant ideas. If you want to get down to basic self-interests, if Fred has the most brilliant idea and you commend him for it, he isn't likely to forget that you *supported* him!

This is not to suggest that you support every idea offered in a conference. You have a right to disagree with *anyone,* particularly if you have facts that show a decision will be detrimental to management and personnel, to customers and stockholders, and to legal operations. However, have your *facts,* with some authority to support them, and present them courteously and concisely.

## Discipline

Contribute to the discussion whenever you have something definite to say, but don't monopolize it because others seem less inclined to contribute. Resolve to stick to the issue and to help the leader by asking opinions of others.

Observe parliamentary procedure strictly. A brief guide to it appears in Appendix B.

One final word: becoming proficient in solving problems with a group requires experience. You can derive much value from observing conferences as they are held by other people, whether they are good or poor; however, one of the most valuable experiences is to note how a skillful leader handles other people.

## WHY SOME CONFERENCES FAIL

This portion of the chapter is reserved for last in order to emphasize the positive aspect of conferences.

**"Passing the buck."**   This is probably the most prevalent excuse for a weak administration, and one that will not admit its weakness. When an administrator is weak and feels inadequate to make decisions that belong rightfully to him or her, a conference is called to either share the blame for failure or to take the credit for success. Under these circumstances you can stand up for your principles of being responsible to the stockholders—and possibly look for another job.

**Predetermined decisions.**   Often a decision has already been made by the top administrators, and the conference is only an attempt to coerce other executives into concurring with those decisions. The top executives believe that the lesser executives can be persuaded to go along with their decisions, or that the conference might make it *appear* that those decisions have been decided by all. Under these circumstances you can object *strongly* to those decisions—and almost *surely* look for another job. . . . unless you possess persuasive powers that will turn the situation around.

**Size.**   Perhaps twelve or fifteen people can think together toward solving a problem, but it seems highly unlikely. Keep conferences *small*—six or eight people if possible. There may be as many as eighteen people who are vitally involved in a certain decision that is to be made; in that case divide your group into three groups of six each. You should also ask those groups to select two members to serve on a final conference and to agree to abide by the decision of that final group. The remaining twelve may act as audience; they may even be allowed to voice their opinions *after* the final conference and to vote on the final issues. You will find that you can accomplish more by holding three preliminary conferences of thirty or forty-five minutes each than you can in three hours if there are eighteen people voicing their opinions. Also, the individual members will often speak up for their convictions more readily in a small group than in a larger group.

**Poor timing.**   This contains two aspects: the advance notice given to the conferees and the actual amount of time the conference is supposed to consume. If a conference is announced two weeks ahead of time, individual conferees will make a note of it on their calendars and *may* turn the page the day before, but can easily forget the conference until the very day that it is to be held. If the conference is important, there should be a sense of urgency about notifying those involved. On the other hand, too short a notice can be just as much of a mistake; it allows no time for preparation. The conferee may need to collect facts and figures, and to put them in order, and to prepare visual aids in order to make a more effective presentation. Give conferees two or three days to obtain data and do some thinking about the subject—unless the problem is a dire emergency.

The time *length* of the conference is also important. If a specified length of time is set aside for the conference, it should be held to that limit. If the conference fails to solve the problem within the time limit, then call another conference at a later date—barring an emergency. If Bill Speck's wife is waiting downstairs, and he has told her that he will be there at a certain time, Bill is not going to be thinking about any problem except how angry his wife may be if he's late. Try *not* to let your conference run overtime!

**Lack of preparation.**   The greatest single cause of conference failure is lack of preparation—on the part of both the leader and the participants. Of course, if the leader is elected on the day of the conference, he or she has had no time for preparation *as a leader;* nevertheless, that individual should have done some homework as a conferee. Answers given by business people as to why conferences fail are invariably, "No agenda." Therefore, the conference leader should prepare in advance a list of the problems to be considered in order of their importance.

**Setting.**    A number of business people say that the setting for a conference should not be too comfortable: no plush, overstuffed chairs and clubroom atmosphere. Instead, it should be strictly a working atmosphere. We were amused several years ago when the shape of the table almost caused a breakdown between two enemy countries at a Paris conference. They finally decided on a round table so that no one nation could be at the head of the table. When sensitive parties are involved, Auer and Ewbank have a couple of suggestions:

> Begin the conference with a luncheon or dinner. Arrange place cards so delegates from [the same] organization will not sit together. People find it harder to hate each other after they have eaten together.
>
> Arrange the conference room so hostile groups do not sit on opposite sides facing each other. If the group can be seated at a round table, no one can complain that he is seated at the foot and his favorite enemy at the head.[8]

## SUGGESTED CLASSROOM EXERCISES

1. Many problems plague business and industry constantly: Absenteeism, Alcoholism, Failure to Use Safety Devices, Disgruntled Workers, Over-Lengthy Coffee Breaks, and so forth. You may wish to select one such problem and advance ideas for solving it.

2. You may wish to select a problem nearer home—on the college campus, for instance: The Catering Service in the Dining Rooms, The Class-Cut System, Editorial Policy of the College Newspaper, Student Rating of Professors, More Flexible Library Hours, The Cost/Economy of Coed Dormitories, and so forth. The *problem* to be handled in these class exercises is not as important as the *procedure:* Once you understand successful conference procedure, it is apt to remain with you.
   Don't forget the "Four D's"!

## FOOTNOTES FOR CHAPTER TWELVE

[1]B. Aubrey Fisher, "The Process of Decision Modification in Small Group Discussion Groups," *The Journal of Communication,* 20 (March, 1970), pp. 51–64.

[2]B. Y. Auger, *How to Run More Effective Business Meetings* (Foreword) (New York: Grosset & Dunlap, 1964).

[3]Leon Festinger, *A Theory of Cognitive Dissonance* (Stanford, Calif.: Stanford University Press, 1962).

[4]Leon Festinger and others, *Conflict, Decision and Dissonance* (Stanford, Calif.: Stanford University Press, 1964).

[5]John Jung, *Understanding Human Motivation* (New York: Macmillan Publishing Co., 1978).

[6]Russell H. Wagner and Carroll C. Arnold, *Handbook of Group Discussion,* 2nd Ed., (Boston: Houghton Mifflin Co., 1965), p. 162.

[7]Hugh Fellows, *The Art and Skill of Talking with People* (Englewood Cliffs, N. J.: Prentice-Hall, 1964).

[8]Jeffrey Auer and Wayne Ewbank, *Handbook for Discussion Leaders,* Rev. Ed., (New York: Harper & Brothers, 1954).

# VOCABULARY STUDY FOR CHAPTER THIRTEEN

Following are some words with which you may not be familiar; they are all used in this chapter. Try to select the correct meaning of each word from the multiple-choice definitions. It is suggested that after you have checked the answers, you *underline* the *correct* one for future reference.

1. ACRONYM     A. Opposite in meaning   B. Word formed from first letters of entire title   C. Sarcasm.

2. ASSIDUOUSLY     A. Constantly, persevering   B. Sinfully   C. Opposite of evergreen.

3. CONCUBINE     A. Blue flower   B. Woman living with a man to whom she is not married   C. Mechanical wheat reaper.

4. ENCAPSULATE     A. Insult in a mild way   B. Place in a capsule   C. Detonate.

5. ENIGMATIC     A. Inserting soapy water into rectum   B. Energizing   C. Perplexing, mysterious.

6. ICONOCLAST     A. Person who attacks cherished beliefs   B. Charge of dynamite   C. Snobbish person.

7. IMPETUS     A. Hasty, rash   B. Skin disease   C. Moving force, stimulus.

8. PALATABILITY     A. Expertise in dental work   B. Pleasing to the taste   C. Artistic work done with palette knife.

9. PECCADILLO     A. Burrowing animal covered by bony plates   B. Petty sin or offense   C. Strolling guitarist.

10. POTENTATE     A. A strong magic drink   B. A native of Polynesia   C. Sovereign, monarch.

11. PRECEDENT     A. Preceding action which may later serve as an example   B. Chief executive of company, elected office   C. Act of ceding territory to another nation.

12. SPATE     A. Sudden outpouring, flood   B. Garden implement   C. Neuter an animal.

13. SUBLIMATE     A. Sugar substitute   B. Underground passage   C. Divert energy from immediate goal to one of a higher nature.

14. SYMMETRY     A. Enclosure set aside for graves of deceased   B. Quality of being harmoniously proportioned   C. Metric measurement.

15. VERBATIM     A. Flowering plant   B. Verbal contest   C. Word for word.

# 13 | Public Speaking

There are many excellent books on public speaking; a few of which are listed at the end of this chapter, selected primarily for their appeal to the practical business and professional people who are too busy to delve into the exhaustive theory behind rhetoric and public address. In this chapter the authors have attempted to encapsulate their research, observations, and practical experience of several decades.

## Purpose

All public presentations can be generally classified as having one of three purposes:

1. To inform
2. To persuade
3. To entertain.

One may ask, "What about commencement addresses, funeral orations, presentation of awards, sermons given by the clergy?" They are chiefly for entertainment, although they have often been *used* for other purposes. For example, the funeral oration delivered by Mark Antony in Shakespeare's *Julius Caesar* was given partly to eulogize Caesar but primarily to incite the citizens of Rome to riot in protest over his assassination. Many sermons are for the purpose of *persuading* their hearers to lead a better life or for *instructing* them about man's relationship with God, quite apart from their inspirational value. The verb *to entertain* originally meant "to hold the attention of, in an agreeable manner" and had little connotation of amusement.

## Delivery

Perhaps you think it is putting the cart before the horse to write about delivery before writing about preparation, but the manner in which you intend to deliver your presentation will affect your preparation of it. Do you intend to write out your entire presentation and read it? Do you intend to write it out and then commit it to memory? Do you intend to speak extemporaneously with only an outline to guide you? Or, are you going to do your entire presentation impromptu? Each of the first three methods offer some advantages and disadvantages. The fourth doesn't actually exist.

**The written-read method.**   This method allows you to (a) polish your presentation so that every word and phrase conveys the exact shade of meaning you intend; (b) make sure that your timing is exactly right—very important for radio and television; and (c) mark the presentation for pauses, emphasis, and inflection.

It has the disadvantages of (a) sounding formal and stilted, since the language of spontaneous speech differs from the language of writing; and (b) potentially losing contact with your listeners. If you *must* write out your presentation and read it, you can follow the suggestions presented in Chapter Six, in the section on reading aloud.

At times it is imperative that a presentation be written and read aloud. The following provides two examples:

1. When you are speaking on a highly controversial topic to a hostile audience—if someone in the audience tries to distort what you have said, you can always refer to your manuscript, with the remark, "I beg to differ with you; here are the exact words I used."

2. If you are the chief of state—such as a king, a president, or a premier—the presentation is usually written and read for two reasons: (A) A slip of the tongue might cause an international incident, or cause the stock market to take a dive. (B) Such important addresses are usually given to the press in advance so that they can have their newspapers or broadcasts ready almost the moment the speech is given. It has always amused us, when a broadcaster announces a Presidential speech, to hear him say, "The President is *expected* to say so-and-so." Hell! That announcer *knows* what the President is going to say, because he has already read the speech! For an announcer or newscaster to try to "scoop" a Presidential speech seems a trifle unethical to us; we're waiting for the time to come when a President *changes* his speech at the last moment. However, those "eager-beavers" always protect themselves with that phrase, "*expected* to say."

**The written-memorized method.**   This has all of the disadvantages of the written-read presentation, *plus* the added peril of forgetting what you intended to say. It is dangerous, and—besides—it's *too much work!*

**The extemporaneous method.**   Some people believe that an extemporaneous speech is one that is made on the spur of the moment with little or no preparation. Quite the contrary! Material is gathered and organized, and it should be rehearsed several times. It has few disadvantages and has the advantages of (a) appearing spontaneous, (b) being flexible with regard to time, and (c) being adaptable to most audiences.

**The impromptu method.**   As mentioned previously, there is no such thing as an actual impromptu speech. Whenever you say *anything*, it is the result of some sort of life experience and, therefore, some preparation. Mark Twain once remarked that it took him about two weeks to prepare a good impromptu speech. The late Winston Churchill was known for his ability to speak eloquently on almost any subject at a moment's notice; recently, a close friend of Churchill claimed that Churchill spent many hours preparing those brief "impromptu" speeches. They were ready when the time came!

## PREPARATION

Psychologists tell us that most of us do not take full advantage of our subconscious thinking process.[1] Many scientists report that they have wrestled with a particularly knotty problem to the point of exhaustion; then, having gone to bed and slept soundly for a few hours, have awakened with the solution quite clear in their minds. So, take advantage of your subconscious power of thought, and don't try to plan your presentation all at once. If you estimate that your speech can be planned within two hours' time, divide that time into six periods of twenty minutes each, spread over several days. Try the "Six Day Plan":[2]

*First day:* This assumes that you have already selected your subject and have decided upon its purpose. In this first time period simply think about it. Put aside some time for thinking, not random thinking but concentration and creative thinking. Robinson[3] claims that our thoughts break down as follows, when we are not actively engaged in a job that requires concentration:

75% is spent in daydreaming or aimless reverie.

10% is spent in making routine decisions, such as "Should I take the car, or ride the bus?", or "Should I eat at Greasy Joe's Diner, or should I eat at The Famous Kitchen?"

10% is spent in either *justifying* those routine decisions or *blaming* ourselves for them, *e.g.* "I'm *glad* I ate at The Famous Kitchen; it gave me a lift, and I feel I can cope with that difficult business deal I have to take care of this afternoon." Or, "I *knew* I should have taken the car, instead of trying to save a few pennies by riding the bus; it's started to rain now, and my new suit will be ruined."

5% is spent in creative thinking.

Does that sound unfair to you? Try to analyze your thinking for just one day, and you may find that Dr. Robinson is not too far wrong.

On this first day (or period) try also to *talk* about your subject with someone. Select someone who does not always agree with you; in this way you can accomplish two things: (a) It will give you a better focus on your own thinking. (b) If the person you have selected disagrees with you, it will cause you to defend your conviction, thereby strengthening it.

*Second day:* During this period you should write down what you actually *know* about your subject. It doesn't have to be in any orderly fashion, and it doesn't have to be in complete sentences. This will accomplish two purposes: (a) It will help clarify your thinking. (b) It will show you where the gaps are in your knowledge of the subject and what you need to find out while doing your research.

*Third day:* Research does not necessarily mean plowing through dusty volumes in the public library; it may mean picking up your telephone and making inquiries. However, if you *do* go to the library, begin by checking *The Reader's Guide to Periodical Literature*. It is much more *current* than the card catalog, and all of its items are listed by subjects. You don't need to read the *entire* article, once you have found the periodical in which it appears, but you should scan it, following this procedure:

1. Read the opening. You may need to read two or three paragraphs to find out if the article contains the information you require.
2. Read the close of the article. Chances are that the author has given a recap of the article's main points.
   Following these two procedures (that is, reading the opening and the closing of the article) can usually tell you whether or not you need to search further for material within the article itself. Either discard the article or take the next step:
3. Scan the article, paragraph by paragraph, searching for *italics*, Names of people or places, and numbers. In a factual article these are the ways a skillful writer tells you what he deems important.
4. Write down the material you intend to use. This is best done on 4 × 6 cards, one item on each card, as they can then be shuffled to various points in your presentation. You may copy portions of the article verbatim, or you may paraphrase them. In making your notes, here are two absolute "musts":
   A. Never take a sentence out of context. That is, make sure that the portion you copy or paraphrase expresses the author's *true meaning* for the paragraph or entire article.
   B. *Always* copy the source: Author, title of article, periodical in which it appears, its date, and the page number. Taking time to do this may save you much searching at a later date if you need to refer to the article again.

If you practice the skill of scanning, you can soon learn to pull the main points from a 10,000-word article in about ten minutes. However, you must avoid the temptation to read material that you know is going to be of no use to you.

*Fourth day:* Prepare your outline. This is of primary importance; for that reason this text devotes an entire section to it.

*Fifth day:* Rehearse your presentation ALOUD and moving about. This is the step that many beginning speakers refuse to take. Practice moving about because (a) motor activity stimulates mental activity, and (b) if you forget what comes next in your actual presentation, just a step or two may help you to recall it. William Norward Brigance believed firmly in "muscle memory" in advising all speakers to rehearse standing up; he also advocated from five to ten rehearsals of *any* presentation.[4]

*Sixth day:* Rehearse your presentation ALOUD again; however, after having rehearsed it several times moving about, this time rehearse it sitting or reclining. Thus, you will not become too dependent upon movement. An important factor in this rehearsal is *not to try to recall the exact words* you used in your previous rehearsals. Follow your outline rigidly, but use your own words as they come to you. If you have access to a tape recorder, by all means record the presentation; erase and record it several times if you have a tendency to use a lot of vocalized pauses.

You may need to spend *more* time on some of the steps we have prescribed than on others, but try to space out your preparation time over several days.

## THE OUTLINE

In making an oral presentation your skill as a speaker matters more than your skill as a writer. You will have living people in front of you, and they cannot go back and reread your meaning if they lose a portion of it as you speak. For this reason it is preferable to adjust the traditional outline of introduction, body, and conclusion, to an outline that will consider your listeners at every step. A good presentation is one that will satisfy the demands of your audience. Those demands are that (a) you get their *attention*, (b) you generate their *interest* in your subject, (c) you *develop* your subject logically, still holding their attention, and that (d) you *summarize* your subject to their satisfaction. To help you remember these important demands, one can use the acronym AIDS, representing

Attention
Interest
Development
Summary.

### Attention

Attention and interest are essentially different, although there is a relationship between them. Attention is a *momentary* response of our senses; interest is a *continuum* in our brain. Attention can be roused by a sudden loud noise, or by someone wearing outlandish clothes; such attention is useless in an oral presentation. For a presentation to be effective, the listeners' attention should be focused on your subject matter, in order to get a response from them. There are many trite devices for gaining a listener's attention, and some of them still work very well. Here are a few:

1. *Tell a story*—funny or otherwise. This is a good attention-getter, ONLY if the story is relevant to your subject. It works because stories contain people, and people are always interested in other people. However, if the story is not related to your subject, it can be detrimental; you may start your listeners' minds wandering in a different direction from the one in which you want them to go.

2. *Ask a question*, or a barrage of questions. Most of us think that a question deserves an answer, so we almost automatically pay attention to the question. Go through the table of contents of almost any popular magazine, and you will notice that many of the titles are phrased as questions. If you use a question for an opener, try to use one that will be answered in the affirmative, and make sure that it is relevant to your subject.

3. *Create curiosity* by making an enigmatic statement or by bringing on at the beginning of your presentation a veiled visual aid. In using such a masked visual, try not to prolong the curiosity too long, or your listeners will stop listening and start wondering about what is under the mask.

George Fletcher was an instructor in sales and marketing at the Baruch School of Business in New York City. George was also a professional magician. He was often called on by business groups to be their luncheon or dinner speaker, and he made good use of his magic tricks as an opener.

The first time I heard George was at a Sales Executive Club luncheon. His opening remark was, "People are always suspicious of a salesman." He took from the righthand pocket of his jacket a string of brightly-colored silk handkerchiefs, with a white handkerchief at each end of the string. "Even you who are in this room are suspicious when I tell you that I can make this string of handkerchiefs disappear into thin air." Whereupon, he began to stuff the string of silk handkerchiefs into the fist of his right hand, as he went on, "Sometimes we have a right to be suspicious, but we shouldn't be so suspicious that it spoils our enjoyment of people, and makes us distrust *all* salesmen." He opened the fist of his right hand, and the handkerchiefs which he had stuffed into it had disappeared. Then he turned to the left and walked a few steps away from the lectern, talking all the while, but nobody listened to a word he said! For there, protruding from his righthand pocket, plain enough for everyone to see, was one of the white handkerchiefs that had been on the ends of the string of colored ones. Still standing to the left of the lectern, he talked on for a few seconds, and nobody listened; we were all thinking, "What a lousy magician this guy Fletcher is! All he did was to stuff the handkerchiefs back into his pocket." Then he took off his spectacles, reached into his righthand pocket and took out the white linen handkerchief that was there, and used it to wipe his glasses.

"You see," he continued, "we fail to *listen* when we are suspicious, and that causes us to make a lot of errors in judgment. From the time you saw this handkerchief sticking out of my pocket until right now, I could have told you that I had just murdered my father, and you wouldn't have heard it."

—Recounted by Alan Price

4. *Make a startling statement*, but be very careful about it! Some startling statements can offend some of your listeners. Know you audience *well* if you're going to use this device, and stay away from derogatory statements about individuals.

I was a senior at a small college operated by a Christian church, when Dr. M_____ visited us for a series of five daily convocations. Dr. M_____ was an orthodox Christian minister, and a magnificent speaker. He had a great sense of humor, he was a master of dramatic oratory, and he obviously had a genuine affection for young people. We loved him! and attendance at convocation had never been so large within my memory. That is, until the fifth day.

Dr. M_____ came to the lectern and opened his sermon with, "Thomas A. Edison is in hell to-day!" We were not startled; we were insulted! Whatever Dr. M_____'s beliefs, how did he know what was between God and this great benefactor of mankind? Dr. M_____ might as well have stopped right there; we had no more use for him.

—Hugh P. Fellows

5. *Use an apt quotation,* particularly from a famous person. If you use this device, the quotation must be appropriate for your subject. Ideally the quotation should be dramatic or witty as well. There are many source books for finding such quotations, and we have listed a few of them at the end of this chapter.

## Interest

We wrote earlier that attention is often a momentary phenomenon, while interest is a long-lasting one. However, one cannot generate interest in a subject without first getting attention. Now let us explore *who* interests people, and *what* they are generally interested in.

**The "who."** People are interested in themselves, of course. After that, in descending order, they are interested in their family, their friends, their community, their state—or the section of the country where they live, their country, and sometimes in the world around them. However, most of them don't really *care* about what goes on in the rest of the world unless what is happening there is going to affect their country, their community, their friends, their family, or themselves.

You share a car pool to work with three other people in your neighborhood. As you wait for Suzy Costello to pick you up, you glance through the morning newspaper, and note that its front page headlines are: "Chinese earthquake kills 20,000," but you hardly glance at it in your eagerness to get to the sports page or the stock market report. Suddenly a *very* small item at the bottom of the column catches your attention:

"County Judge John Peters and his companion Miss Ellen McKay were arrested this morning and charged with drunkenness and indecent exposure. The Judge and Miss McKay, a strip-tease artist, were found bathing in the fountain on the courthouse square in the nude. Miss McKay was also charged with foul, abusive language and resisting arrest."

When Suzy drives up, you can't wait to show her the item. After the two other members of the car pool are in the car, the four of you talk about nothing else all the way into work. Why? Because Judge Peters is one of your county's judges and lives in your neighborhood, although none of you in the car pool actually know him. Yet there are 20,000 people dead on the front page, and they are never mentioned. The judge's little peccadillo is more important to the four of you than 20,000 Chinese deaths because he is *closer* to you than they are.

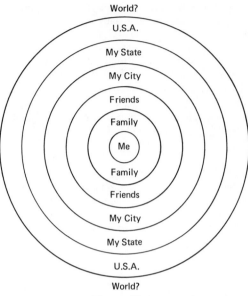

World?
U.S.A.
My State
My City
Friends
Family
Me
Family
Friends
My City
My State
U.S.A.
World?

Figure 13-1

So, if you can aim for the center of the target (see Figure 13-1) you will help satisfy the audience demands of *who* people are interested in:

**The "what."** Psychologists tell us that more than thirty motivating forces cause people to act as they do. However, the most vital ones—those that interest people *most*—are these six:

Self-Preservation
Sex
Ego
Altruism
Desire for Change
Desire to Maintain the *Status Quo*.

Pick up any popular magazine that carries a number of articles on a variety of subjects and you will find that the preponderance of articles deal with sex, self-help, and inspiration (altruism).

*Self-preservation* is the strongest and most primitive drive in the Occidental world. It is concerned with food, clothing, shelter, and protection from our enemies. You can sell the average American man or woman anything that promises to help that individual be healthier and live longer. So, if you can show your listeners that what you have to say concerns their health and well-being, they will be interested.

The first four drives that we listed are connected to one another. Self-preservation gives an added impetus to the sex drive because people believe that they will never be completely dead if they have left behind something that they have created: a child, a masterful piece of architecture, a painting, or a book bearing their name.

*The sex drive* is tied to the drive for self-preservation and is our creative urge. Sublimated, it is responsible for our masterpieces of painting, sculpture, music, architecture, and even philanthropy. Even standing alone, it is a powerful drive, and you can sell normal Americans almost anything if they think it will make them more attractive to the opposite sex. So, if you can show your listeners that what you have to say will satisfy their emotional or creative needs, they will surely show some interest in your presentation.

*Ego* is a powerful force among all mankind. It has its roots in the mythology of most nations, and in some parts of the Orient it is even stronger than the desire for self-preservation. People want to be respected among their peers; they want to *excel* over their peers if they can. The surest way for you to make an enemy for life is to make a person appear ridiculous in front of that individual's colleagues. Ego is closely allied to the fourth basic drive, altruism; it flatters our ego when we do something generous for another person. So, try to show your listeners that what you have to say in your presentation will increase their status, and you will succeed in interesting most of them.

*Altruism,* or the desire to promote the welfare of others, is not a basic primitive drive; it has been acquired over the centuries by what we call civilized man. In fact, some psychologists deny that it exists; they claim that the only reason we care about others is that we fear for our own safety, or that we seek to boost our ego, or a combination of the two. This author chooses to believe that man does care for other men and animals, as witness our rage when we see an adult mistreat a child or a pet that cannot defend itself. Show your listeners that what you are going to say will affect their humanity, and you will interest at least *some* of your audience.

Each of these four drives affects at least one of the others (see Figure 13-2); usually a combination of two of them will interest most people. There are two other drives that motivate people's interest, but they are of interest primarily to the younger or the elderly people in our society:

*The desire for change* appeals primarily to younger people. Anything new or different catches their interest, whether or not it has value. This is the spirit of adventure.

*The desire to maintain the status quo,* on the other hand, appeals mainly to elderly people. "Don't rock the boat" is often their slogan. Their tendency is to leave things as they are, for fear they will get worse; so, appeal to change does not interest them, unless a situation is unendurable.

From one of the foregoing motivations, or a combination of them, you should find a way of generating interest in your presentation.

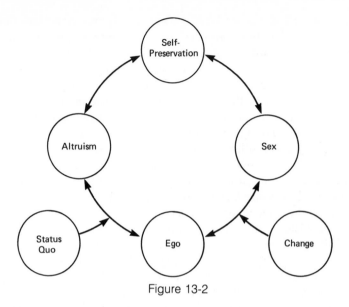

Figure 13-2

## Development

This is the main body of your presentation, but it is no more important than
the preceding steps. Unless you have gained your listeners' attention; unless
you have shown them why your subject is important to *them*, they will simply
turn you off before you get to the main part of your presentation. There are
three things that you should remember in the body of your presentation:

1. You should have some sort of *structure*
2. You should *support* each point you make with examples that have immediacy
   for your listeners
3. You should *limit* the number of points in your presentation.

**Structure.**   People remember things better if they have some structure.
Chapter Four, under the heading, "Listening for Structure," detailed some of
the structures that presentations ordinarily take. They are reviewed here.

1. Simple enumeration
2. Cause and effect, or vice versa
3. Problem/solution*
4. Chronological order
5. Geographical or spatial order.

*Analysis and synthesis follow somewhat the same order as the problem/solution
structure.

**Support.**   People do not think in abstract terms until after they have learned by logic to make generalizations that are valid. That is a lengthy process, and it is touched upon under the heading, "Persuasive Presentations," in this chapter. For the moment consider a few abstract terms: Justice, Commerce, Trade, Philanthropy, Pleasure, Good, or Evil. Can you picture any of those abstractions without picturing *somebody doing something?* Or, at least, a *concrete work* of some sort? If you can, you are a genius, and it is doubtful that you will have an audience of geniuses. So, use *specific examples:* people, places, concrete objects, someone *doing* something, someone *saying* something. Jesus Christ, whom some people believe was one of the greatest teachers of all time, espoused his abstract philosophy entirely by parables, that is, stories of people doing things, or acting in a certain way, toward other people.

Never try to make an important point without *supporting* it with at least one of these (two are better):

1. Case histories (Someone who is doing something)
2. Authority (Someone speaking, for whom your listeners have respect)
3. Visual aids (So that your listeners can *see* something concrete)
4. Statistics (Also having authority because of their integrity, and—preferably— raised to a visual point)
5. Comparison or contrast (Again, where someone is *acting* in a manner that is advisable or inadvisable)

It is not enough to support your point in a presentation by using the foregoing. The examples you choose must also have relevance (immediacy) for your listeners. It is futile to use as an example a Middle Eastern Potentate who had his nine concubines put to death because they lied about his three wives. You will be talking to men who have only *one* wife and *no* concubines.

Any point you wish to make will be lost if you don't support it. You can use one support only, if it is *strong* enough; two supports are better; three are often unnecessary, but may add symmetry (see Figure 13-3); more than three types of support can clutter the point and may even smother it.

**Limitation.**   Abraham Lincoln was once asked how long a man's legs should be. With characteristic logic for such a foolish question, Lincoln replied, "Just long enough to reach the ground." The same question might be asked about the length of an oral presentation, and the answer is, "Just long enough to accomplish your purpose."

Just as you should limit the number of supports you use for a point, so should you also limit the number of *points* you make in a presentation. If a listener can remember *two* points you make in a 10-minute speech, that speech has been successful. If the listener can remember *three* points from a 15-minute presentation, that is a good batting average. This is not to say that you should make a point every five minutes; often it can be made in two or three minutes.

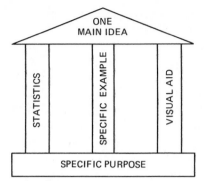

A. **Good.** Excellent support with symmetry (style).

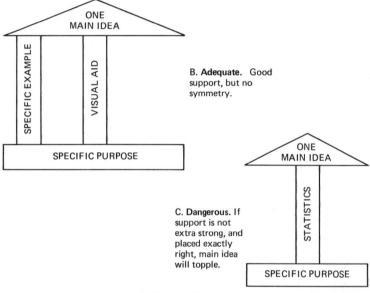

B. **Adequate.** Good support, but no symmetry.

C. **Dangerous.** If support is not extra strong, and placed exactly right, main idea will topple.

Figure 13-3

However, if you try to make five points in a 30-minute presentation, the chances of a listener's remembering more than three of them are slim.

You are in the market for a new automobile, and do not have a trade-in. You have two friends who are automobile salesmen; Sam sells Stalwart and Don sells Dasher. Both the Dasher and the Stalwart are in the same price and performance class. Which should you buy? You tell your friends, "Look, fellows, both of you are my friends, and I think that the Dasher and the Stalwart are about evenly matched. I'm going to buy from one of you no later than tomorrow, and I'll give each of you fifteen minutes to make a final pitch this afternoon. No matter which car I buy, there'll be no hard feelings among the three of us. Okay?"

The factory advertising department has furnished Don with *twenty* reasons why Dasher is the best automobile in its price class, including road tests, statistics, colorful visuals, and testimonials from distinguished owners. He smothers you with such powerful evidence that you are sure you are going to buy a Dasher at the end of Don's allotted fifteen minutes. However, you have promised to at least give Sam a chance, and Don knows it. You part amicably.

Sam's advertising department has also furnished him with twenty reasons why Stalwart is superior to any other car in its price range, but he doesn't *use* all of them. He knows three things about you (Don also knows these things): (a) He knows that you have been a mechanical engineer in your early career. (b) He knows that you are a "speed-demon," eager to get places once you start going. (c) He knows that your wife is a social climber, acutely conscious of her prestige among other society matrons. So, during the fifteen minutes allotted to him, Sam may *mention* the twenty reasons why Stalwart is better than any other car in its price class, but he *dwells* on only three:

1. He talks about the marvelous precision of the engine design, and shows you diagrams of how the Stalwart has fewer parts to go wrong.
2. He shows you how the ignition and combustion systems combine so as to accelerate the Stalwart from a standstill to 55 miles per hour within 10 seconds; he also mentions the Stalwart's safety at high speeds.
3. He shows you photographs of Mrs. Astorbilt, Mrs. Richbitch, and the Baroness Bushwa, all of them testifying to the beauty of design in the Stalwart, and proclaiming it the "in" car to have.[5]

—Hugh P. Fellows

Which automobile are you most apt to buy? All precedent shows that you will pick the Stalwart because (a) you have only *three* points to remember, rather than twenty; and (b) the salesman has given you three points that are of *immediate* interest to you and your family. The length of a presentation should be like the length of an alluring garment: long enough to cover the vital points, but short enough to make you want to see more.

## Summary

The ending of your presentation will differ considerably, depending upon whether the purpose has been to inform or to persuade. (The next part of this chapter discusses persuasive presentations.) Your summary will also depend upon the type of structure you have used in the main body of your speech. For example:

1. If you have used simple enumeration, review the main points, preferably re-wording them so that your listeners will receive a repetition of the *ideas* without getting a repetition of the same words.
2. If you have used a cause-to-effect structure, emphasize that the cause (or causes) have been the *primary* cause of the effect.
3. If your material calls for a problem/solution structure, show that your solution will be (or has been) the most practicable and desirable solution to the problem. Don't use the word *only;* there may be a solution as yet unknown to you.

4. If you use chronological order for your structure, recapitulate only three or four of the early developments leading up to the main event, and do not go into details.

5. If you have used spatial or geographical order, you have undoubtedly gone into some detail concerning the separate parts (or areas) of the territory. Now is the time to review the outstanding characteristic of each area and show how they constitute a whole.

## PERSUASIVE PRESENTATIONS

There is a popular misconception that any type of persuasion is an underhanded method of playing upon our emotions. Rubbish! Despite the spate of television commercials for headache remedies and stomach ailments, persuasion is a highly respectable technique, and one that intelligent business and professional people admire.

Far from being wildly emotional or impersonally logical, the technique of persuasion maintains a delicate balance between the two (see Figure 13-4). The objective of ethical persuasion is to cause your listeners to alter their thinking about some particular matter, or to cause them to act in a certain manner which you honestly believe to be to their advantage. In business this is usually concerned with (a) *judgment* or *value*, followed by (b) *policy* or *action*.

Some examples of judgment are

1. The advantages of one process over another, as shown in Chapter Eleven, in the matter of the food processing company.
2. The advantage of reorganizing personnel in one department so as to utilize manpower hours more efficiently.
3. A comparison of a business firm similar to your own, and the results of an active safety campaign there.

Some examples of policy are:

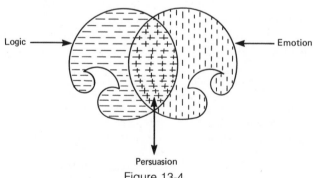

Figure 13-4

1. Establishing a "work hours bank," to allow employees to take time off when the work is slack and work overtime when the burden is heavy, without penalty for time off and without pay for working overtime.
2. Staggering workers' hours so that all workers, in their turn, have a couple of weeks for arriving at work after the traffic rush hours.
3. Employing a part-time psychological counselor on alcohol abuse among the workers.

Aristotle (384–322 B. C.) maintained that a speaker was truly convincing only if that speaker evidenced a rational balance among (a) appeal to reason *(logos)*, (b) appeal to the emotions common to most men *(pathos)*, and (c) personal integrity *(ethos)*.

Throughout this text we have advocated your personal integrity. In the foregoing section we have demonstrated the basic drives that constitute emotional appeals to most persons (self-preservation, sex, ego, altruism, desire for change, and the desire to maintain the *status quo*). Chapter Eighteen discusses some of the ways people reason logically (by analogy, cause and effect, authority, instances—signs and evidence—and association). However, we now wish to consider the process of logic by which most people make decisions: inductive and deductive reasoning.

## Inductive Reasoning

Inductive reasoning involves moving from specific examples to a general statement, or generalization. For example, if you touch a lighted match to a piece of ordinary paper, it will burn it; if you drop a lighted cigarette onto the upholstery of a couch, it will burn it; if you leave a steak for too long over a hot charcoal grill, it will burn beyond palatability. So, by these experiences and many others like them you arrive at the generalization that fire burns everything. Obviously such a generalization is not valid; ordinary fire will not burn metal—but the fire from a blowtorch will. Therefore, one must qualify the generalization and say, "fire burns (but not everything)". It is doubtful that a *perfect* generalization could ever be found, because there are always unusual exceptions; but the generalization, "fire burns," comes close. (See Figure 13-5.)

## Deductive Reasoning

Deductive reasoning moves from the general to the specific. If we begin with the generalization, "fire burns," then we assume that if fire *burns,* it will burn wood, which is a flammable object. But wood that has been treated with certain chemicals will *not* burn, except at extremely high temperatures. This begins to look as if *nothing* is *certain,* and truly it is *not.* However, adult reasoning consists of assumptions based upon a high degree of probability.

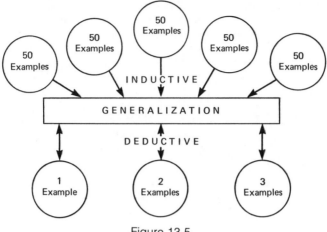

Figure 13-5

**Tests for inductive reasoning.** Following are two criteria to help in determining the validity of inductive reasoning.

1. There must be a *sufficient number* of individual cases in order to form a valid generalization. You will note that, in Figure 13-5, we have used 250 individual cases. Furthermore, each of the cases (specific examples) must have the same thing in common; for example, "something that fire will burn."

2. Each specific example must be typical, or representative of an entire class or species. For example, Mrs. Jones, your next door neighbor, abuses her small child, and you have certain knowledge of this. Mrs. Smith, who lives across the street from you, also abuses her small child, and you have proof of it. You could not use either Mrs. Smith or Mrs. Jones to form a generalization that "mothers abuse their children," because it is an accepted truth that most mothers do *not* abuse their offspring, and neither Mrs. Smith nor Mrs. Jones is typical of the class of mothers. (What kind of neighborhood do you live in?)

**Tests for deductive reasoning.** Following are two criteria to help determine the validity of deductive reasoning.

1. Make sure that the specific example you draw from a generalization *belongs* in that generalization.

2. Make sure that the specific example is not an exception to that generalization. For example, if we take the generalization that "The Roman Catholic Church is against abortion"—it does not necessarily follow that, because Mr. Bello belongs to the Roman Catholic Church, Mr. Bello is against abortion. He may be an exception.

Aristotle developed a system of deductive reasoning that he called the *syllogism*. It consisted of three statements: a major premise, a minor premise, and a conclusion. This text has oversimplified the syllogism to show how deductive reasoning can be tested. The classic example Aristotle used was as follows:

Major premise: All men are mortal
Minor premise: Socrates was a man
Conclusion: Therefore, Socrates was mortal.
Now, consider this syllogism:
Major premise: All dogs eat meat
Minor premise: My brother eats meat
Conclusion: Therefore, my brother is a dog.

Obviously, the second syllogism is ridiculous. Without going into all the terms of Aristotelian logic we need make only one simple rule, which can be tested by a series of concentric circles: *The specific example must fit into the minor premise, and the minor premise must fit into the major premise,* as in Figure 13-6(A).

Thus, while "dogs" and "my brother" both fit into the circle of "meat eaters," "my brother" does not fit into the circle of dogs. Such advertising statements as "Four out of five dentists recommend Taffy Toothpaste" can be shown up for the absurdities they are, if put into the form of a syllogism as in 13-6(B).

## Audience Analysis

Chapter Eleven emphasized the importance of knowing something about the background of participants in a discussion. In making a persuasive presentation, knowing your listeners is just as important. In a large group you cannot be expected to know every individual; however, you can learn something about the group as a whole by inquiring ahead of time as to:

1. The average age of the group
2. The predominant sex of the group: mostly men? mostly women?
3. The socioeconomic status of the group; blue-collar workers? executives?
4. Any strong affiliations of the group with organizations such as churches or fraternal organizations

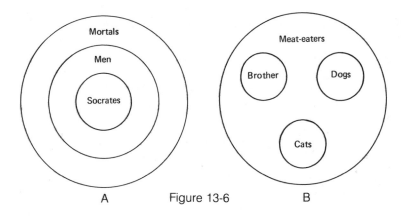

Figure 13-6

These things will help you to prepare your emotional and logical appeals to the group. Know your audience!

## Formula for a Persuasive Presentation

Use AIDS!

1. Get the attention of your listeners.
2. Show them how the situation affects them.
3. Detail the need for a change, and use strong support for the need.
4. Propose a change, and show that it is
   A. practicable
   B. desirable
5. Describe some of the benefits that will accrue to the listeners if the proposed change is put into effect (sometimes called "the dawn of a new day" step).
6. Appeal for action.

## Dealing with Strong Antagonism

When you are dealing with listeners who are strongly antagonistic to your ideas, or to the change you propose, do not expect them to do an about-face as the result of one persuasive presentation—although it has been known to happen. Most of us do not give up our convictions easily, and it almost always requires a neutralizing step before we are ready to exchange our old convictions for new ones (see Figure 13-7). What can you do to neutralize antagonism and thereby get a fair hearing for the ideas you propose?

*First,* show that you are a person of integrity, and not an iconoclast who wishes to tear down all of their beliefs.

*Second,* try to identify yourself with their interests. Let them know that you are working for the common good of all.

*Third,* show that some of the people they respect most have the same ideals that you do; that those whom they respect are in favor of the change you propose. *This is your strongest point*, and the one on which you will need to do the most research.

*Fourth,* cite examples of other organizations or groups who have made the change you propose, and show how well it is working there. Get testimonials from those in the other organizations.

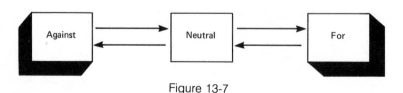

Figure 13-7

*Finally*, do *not* appeal for action in this presentation. Give them time to think about it. If what you have said has been accurate and honest, they will give it fair consideration.

## BODY LANGUAGE

Although the terms *body language* and *nonverbal communication* are relatively new, people have known since the dawn of history that they could tell other people things by using their bodies. Perhaps it began when Aku tried to show and tell to his other tribesmen just how he killed a wild boar; perhaps some of the other tribesmen joined in, showing how they assisted Aku in the kill by beating the bushes to frighten the boar and to bring him into range of Aku's primitive spear. This noise and action were pleasing to the eyes and ears of other tribesmen; so it evolved into a dance, and then into drama. We know that formal drama began in Egypt at least 3,200 years B.C., and history records that a group of *mimes*—people who told a story *only* through body movement— found their way from the Doric peninsula in Greece to Italy and Egypt in about 600 B.C.[6]

The appeal of these *mimes* was chiefly that their audiences were able to identify and empathize with them. The term *empathy* is used to convey several shades of meaning, but we use it in a specialized sense: *Empathy is the tendency of the large skeletal muscles of the body to imitate anything which the eye beholds.*

Imagine that a large (six feet in diameter) white balloon with a spotlight shining on it is placed in the front of your classroom. Aside from the spotlight the room is dark. You and your classmates are asked to observe the large balloon. Then the balloon is slowly and silently deflated to a fraction of its original size. You and your classmates will almost surely slump forward; your shoulders will droop and your heads will lower. You are empathizing with this inanimate object. (Inanimate in the broadest sense of the word—actually it moves.)

Or, imagine that you are at a wrestling match, and one of the wrestlers hooks his thumb into his opponent's buccal cavity.* It seems as though he is going to rip apart the right side of his opponent's mouth. Look around you; you will observe that many of the spectators are tightening the right side of their mouths, as if the aggressive wrestler had his thumb in *their* mouths! They are empathizing with the unfortunate opponent.

When you make a presentation, your listeners empathize with the way you walk, your posture, your gestures, and even your body muscles' tensions and relaxations. If you slump, they tend to slump; if you fidget, they tend to do the

---

*The slight cavity between the teeth and the side of the jaw.

same. If you appear uncomfortable and your speech seems to have difficulty in getting out of your mouth, they are frustrated. In a sense it is a case of "monkey see, monkey do."

## Walking, Posture, Gestures

Your presentation begins *before* you open your mouth to speak; it begins when you rise from the conference table and take the position from which you are to make the presentation, or when you *start* walking to the front of the class-room. In those few seconds those in the room with you decide, "She's going to be dull or interesting," "He's a good guy or a scoundrel," or "She's stupid or smart."

When you move, don't pussyfoot; don't shuffle or drag your feet; don't strut. Take Orson Welles' advice, "Walk as if you are going someplace and are glad that you're going there."

We are always impatient with an instructor who tells a student, "Relax and be natural." Nonsense! If you are totally relaxed, you are asleep—and you may take your listeners with you. If you were being natural, you wouldn't be in the unnatural position of making a presentation; you'd be outside fishing or playing golf. Yes, you should *appear* natural, but you should also appear *alive*, with a certain amount of muscular *tonus* that is not easily discernible by an untrained observer.

## Supraliminal and Subliminal Stimuli

When you see a person whose eyebrows are drawn together in a frown, whose eyes are dilated, and whose teeth are clenched with the mouth slightly open and the lips drawn down at the corners, you say, "That person appears angry." That person has given you an overt semblance of anger, and you have responded to the stimulus.

If you are outdoors standing upright with your feet chained to the ground and your hands tied behind you, and someone throws a baseball that is aimed precisely at your nose, you duck your head or fall to the ground to dodge the ball and avert a bloody nose. The person throwing the ball has committed an overt act, and you have responded to it overtly.

We also respond to stimuli that we cannot detect easily—or covert actions. There is an imaginary line, called the *limen*, which separates those stimuli which are easily discerned, from those which are almost impossible for any but a trained eye to see. Many of us are familiar with the experiment carried out by a marketing researcher named James Vicary in a Fort Lee, N.J. moviehouse[7]: During the run of the regular feature, the words "HUNGRY? EAT POPCORN" were flashed on the screen at 1/100ths of a second at regular intervals. The audience was so engrossed in the feature that they were unconscious of the intrusion, but popcorn sales jumped upwards by almost 100 percent during

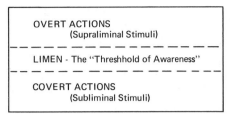

| OVER T ACTIONS <br> (Supraliminal Stimuli) |
| LIMEN - The "Threshhold of Awareness" |
| COVERT ACTIONS <br> (Subliminal Stimuli) |

Figure 13-8

intermission. The same thing was tried with Coca Cola, with the same results. The audience was the victim of subliminal stimuli. (Figure 13-8)

In the movie *The Exorcist*, a death mask was flashed on the screen at intervals to give the audience an extra scare. Warner Brothers was sued by a teenager from Indiana who fainted during the movie and broke his jaw and several teeth; his lawyer contended that this subliminal stimulus was one of the major issues.

Psychologists tell us that no matter how strong the subliminal stimulus may be, we will not do anything that is completely *foreign* to our nature. For example, we will not go to our bank and draw out the savings we have accumulated for the down payment on a home to buy a diamond necklace, no matter how many times the words "BUY A DIAMOND NECKLACE" are flashed on a movie screen . . . or, so we are told.

Nevertheless, the Federal Communications Commission is taking no chances where weak-willed citizens are concerned. *Time* magazine[8] informs us that "A television commercial for children's toys included the subliminal message 'GET IT!' until the FCC issued a warning against further TV or radio sublimations."

The same is true of posthypnotic suggestion. Until more conclusive research is done, we cannot be sure how strong the effect of it may be, or how long it lasts on *each* person. The movies and television shows have overdramatized the cases of meek, mild persons turning into raging beasts under hypnosis, but hypnotherapists[9,10] claim that this is impossible.

There is no doubt that a tremendous amount of nonverbal communication occurs all around us. Meharabian[11] claims that we depend upon words to convey only 7 percent of our meaning; vocal cues take care of 38 percent, and facial expressions and other muscular movement complete the 55 percent needed for complete meaning. Scheflen[12] says that there are total sets of body movements in any communication with others. For example, a major shift in posture may mean that one speaker wishes to withdraw from the communication; certain movements of the head, neck, and eyes indicate the end of a "structural unit"— presumably a transitional point; a cough can be taken as a warning [Of what sort, we wonder?]; clearing the throat can mean that the subject is taboo.

This is interesting, but body language has its hazards, the chief one being that of interpretation or *mis*interpretation. Though words may be fraught with semantic difficulties, they are as precise as a razor when compared with body language. As Desmond Morris points out in his comprehensive book on the subject, *Manwatching*,[13] a gesture of affection in one culture may be an insult in another. We know that body language exists and that it affects many people, but *how* and to *what* extent we are not sure. Until more research has been conducted on the subject, body language remains inexact and undependable. Further research can explore such statements as, "The face may be the most expressive . . . but it is also the best liar. The hands and feet do not 'talk' as much. But they tell the truth."[14]

## Gestures

Francois Delsarte, a French musician and teacher, tried back in 1811 to catalog *all* gestures and expressive body movements and interpret them. It was known as the "Delsarte System of Expression" and was taught widely until it reached its zenith in the silent movie. Even so, the silent movies found that words were necessary in the subtitles. When the "talkies" came along, the technique of the silent movie became slightly ridiculous because of its overexaggeration. On the other hand, many silent film kings of *great* magnitude found themselves toppled from their thrones because they were unable to use anything *other* than their mimetic qualities. Their voices were too high-pitched, their dialect was too regional, or their speaking was utterly devoid of the nonverbal qualities of emotion.

Let us reiterate that gestures seem to be useful in helping one to express one's self. Too often, however, they become nervous habits with little or no expressive content except to say, "I'm fearful before my listeners." Here are some precepts that should help you in the use of gestures:

1. *A gesture must be meaningful.* It should appear to rise spontaneously from the words themselves, along with the meaning and emotion you wish to convey. In light of the precepts that follow, there is no reason why a gesture should not be rehearsed, as you should rehearse any presentation, but its *origin* should be in the context of the idea you hope to express. It is thus not likely to be misinterpreted.
2. *A gesture should be well-timed.* It should accent precisely the word or phrase for which it is intended. You can demonstrate this for yourself. Standing before a mirror, repeat the sentence, "This is the largest factory in the whole wide world!" and accompany it with a sweeping gesture, as if to take in the entire world. Now, repeat the sentence and make the gesture *after* you have finished the words. Ridiculous, eh? It will be even more ludicrous if you try the gesture *before* the sentence.
3. *A gesture should be unrestrained.* It should be free, and not cramped and "stingy." Try the "whole wide world" gesture with your elbow pressed against your side, and you will see what this means. Your entire body should enter into the gesture. Here is where you can use covert action and subliminal stimuli; use the muscles of almost the entire body—even though those muscles cannot be seen because of clothing—to make one gesture. It's worth the effort.[15]

## Eye Contact

"Eyes speak a universal language," says Bill Orr, the portrait painter. In more than a score of nations we have visited, we have found this to be true. The averted eye seems always to signify shyness, sorrow, or guilt. Even with a language barrier, people's eyes can express trust, anger, shrewdness—and love. In a business presentation there is no substitute for direct eye contact with each one of your listeners; it is a weapon as well as a tool. Here is an example:

> For two years I was sent out to various club meetings in our state to make a pitch for the college where I was teaching. Most of the groups were service clubs—Rotary, Kiwanis, Lions—who held their meetings over a midday meal. They were the most inattentive audiences I have ever known—and for good reasons. First, most of the members didn't really *care* about their clubs, but it was "good business" to belong to one. Second, they were not accustomed to eating a heavy lunch, and that made them drowsy. Third, after they had put in an appearance and shaken hands with everybody, they wanted to get back to their businesses, but the program chairman had arranged for a speaker. So they sat there, unwilling captives, but they didn't have to *listen;* instead, they lit up their cigars and started thinking how they were going to skin a few bucks out of Joe Doe & Sons.
>
> Whenever I saw one of those guys staring into space or out of the window, I would look and talk directly to *him.* He would react as if he had been stuck by a pin! He would start, turn toward me, and pretend to listen. Then I would move on to the next stray sheep and round him up. That was when I realized what a powerful tool I had in being physically direct and using eye contact.
>
> —Recounted by Prof. Alan Price

Not only should you look directly at your listeners when making a presentation, but you should also use a "searchlight" technique, taking in each person to whom you're talking. Some people find this difficult to do, but it becomes easier with practice.

### HOW PERCEPTIVE ARE YOU?

I. Following are statements that contain basic drives common to most people (Many of them are paraphrases of current television commercials). Using the abbreviations that precede the episodes or statements, identify the motivations that are implied or stated.

SP = self-preservation
SX = sex
E = ego
AL = altruism
CH = desire for change
SQ = desire to maintain the *status quo*

_____ 1. Fasten your seat belts.

_____ 2. This perfume *La Nuit d'Amour* will entice the man of your dreams.

_____ 3. Pete Rose, the baseball player, says that he wants an after-shave lotion that makes him smell like a man!

_____ 4. If you don't take your medication for your own sake, do it for your family.

_____ 5. Won't you be a foster parent for an orphaned child in a foreign land?

_____ 6. *Women's voices:* Aldo! Aldo! Oh, Aldo!
Announcer: Aldo is not pretty; he is not rich; but Aldo *knows* what women want—Chill a Cella!

_____ 7. This year, join the ranks of the world's most important people with a Boyota.

_____ 8. Wear the pantyhose that are invisible—everywhere but in the stores!

_____ 9. It makes you feel so *good* when you give to the United Fund!

_____ 10. Don't get into a rut; take a vacation that is totally *different* from anything you've ever known.

_____ 11. People will *know* it when you wear the finest that money can buy—Harris tweeds. Like nothing else on earth!

_____ 12. We have given protection to millions of people for more than a hundred years; our insurance has withstood the test of time.

_____ 13. Play golf along with the *executives* at the Caribe Bilton!

_____ 14. Instant Made Orange Juice has no additives, no special preservatives—just the finest *natural* juice you ever tasted!

_____ 15. It's new! It's different! Enjoy a fresh taste sensation with Granolade.

_____ 16. Poor Juana never had a chance; she died of malnutrition at the age of three, and she was the only child her parents could ever have. Could Juana have been *your* child? No way, you say! Save another Juana by giving to the Overseas Children's Relief Fund.

_____ 17. Are you afraid of every shadow lurking in the streets? You don't need to be, with Wilcox-Grey's purse alarm. This miniature siren summons the police in a matter of seconds.

_____ 18. Make your own decorative wall plaques, for the beauty of your home and for gifts to friends. Seventeen colorful designs to choose from, and you save many dollars by doing them yourself.

_____ 19. You can't improve upon the way Grandma used to cook! Here is an old-fashioned recipe for chicken pot pie that has all the flavor of Grandma's tastiest dish.

_____ 20. Why were the Roman Gladiators so virile? Why were they adored by all of the Empire's maids and matrons alike? Scientists have recently discovered that the Gladiators drank Papula Juice to keep them in perfect health and give them strength. Papula Juice has been a fine nutrient for two thousand years and yet its taste is completely new. No need to fear old age or gray hairs if you drink Papula Juice. It will give you that extra "something" that makes you outstanding among other people. But don't keep our secret from your friends; buy it for them to become healthy, also.

(Answers are in Appendix C.)

II. Some of the following sentences and paragraphs carry overtones other than purely inductive and deductive reasoning; however, you are to rate them *only* on the bases of those two types of reasoning.

I = inductive reasoning   D = deductive reasoning

_____ 1. No, thank you! I've tried several kinds of plums before, and I just know that I won't like this one.

_____ 2. If he's an Irishman, that's all I need to know; he's bound to be a drunk.

_____ 3. If the Harrisons use Glyco Cleaning Fluid, it *must* be good, because they are wealthy enough to afford only the very best.

_____ 4. Don't introduce me to him if he's a Lithuanian. I lived next door to a family of Lithuanians for five years, and they were absolutely crazy—and so were their friends.

_____ 5. If it's a Digby machine, and you can get it at a good price, then buy it! Digby makes the finest business machines on the market.

_____ 6. I've tried a can of Blipton's cream of chicken soup, and a package of Blipton's minestrone, and both were disappointing. Blipton simply does not make good soups.

_____ 7. "God made him; therefore let him pass for a man."
—Shakespeare

_____ 8. Third grade pupil to his teacher: "Miz Morgan, they fooled me about Santa Claus, and they fooled me about the Easter Bunny; now, when I get a little older, I'm going to investigate this Jesus Christ business."*

_____ 9. Chief Flight Instructor's memorandum to other flight instructors in the old Army Air Corps: "Be especially careful of cadets with light blue, watery eyes; they are not likely to become reliable pilots."*

_____ 10. "You're asking me to go on a blind date with Barbara? You told me that she is a redhead and a Scorpio. Not a chance of my dating *her*! I went with Sylvia for four years and she cheated on me all that time; she was a Scorpio. I went with Shirley for two years and found out she was married all the time and never told me; Shirley was a redhead."

## SUGGESTED CLASSROOM ASSIGNMENT

Your instructor may assign you to make a presentation to the class of (a) an informative nature, (b) a persuasive nature, or (c) one of each, if time permits.

## ANNOTATED BIBLIOGRAPHY

RICHARD C. BORDEN, *Public Speaking As Listeners Like It* (New York: Harper & Bros., 1935).
A "golden oldie" but one of the best for a busy person. Public speaking textbooks

*These were actual incidents. Names withheld.

have plagiarized it for forty years, but Borden still says it more concisely than any of them.

WILLIAM NORWOOD BRIGANCE, *Speech—Its Techniques and Disciplines in a Free Society,* 2nd ed., (New York: Appleton-Century-Crofts, 1961).

Another "oldie", but the Bible of all speech texts. Brigance was known in speech circles as "the grand old man of speech" and was one of the few people at Speech Communication Association Conventions who scorned "reading papers," but gave his learned lectures extemporaneously.

ROGER M. D'APRIX, *How's That Again?* (Homewood, Ill.: Dow Jones—Irwin, Inc., 1971).

Written by former English teacher who is at present a communication expert with Xerox Corporation, this title is included for those who want to improve their style. Clear, exciting prose, but not a "how-to-do" book.

EDWARD HODNETT, *Effective Presentations* (West Nyack, N. Y.: Parker Publishing Co., 1967).

A former dean and college president, Hodnett is at present Assistant to the President, Dow Corning Corporation. Excellent book on no-nonsense presentations, with emphasis on logic and visual aids.

LOREN REID, *Speaking Well,* 3rd ed., (New York: McGraw-Hill, 1977).

Academic, but thorough and authoritative. Its author is one of the most highly respected scholars in the field of speech.

W.P. SANDFORD and W.H. YEAGER, *Effective Business Speech,* 4th ed., (New York: McGraw-Hill, 1960).

Good information on the basics of communication and presentations. Carefully written by men who have been in the field for many years.

## SUGGESTED SOURCES FOR SPEECH MATERIALS

### For Anecdotes, Quotations and Specific Examples:

CARROLL C. ARNOLD, *et al., The Speaker's Resource Book* (Chicago: Scott Foresman Co., 1961).

GURNEY W. BENHAM, *Putnam's Complete Book of Quotations* (Boston: Little, Brown & Co., 1948).

HERBERT V. PROCHNOW, *The Public Speaker's Treasure Chest* (New York: Harper & Row, 1964).

RALPH L. WOODS, *The Business Man's Book of Quotations* (New York: The Macmillan Co., 1971).

### For Facts and Statistics (These are Annual Publications):

*The Statesman's Yearbook* (New York: St. Martin's Press).

*The World Almanac* (New York: Newspaper Enterprises Association, Inc.).

*Reader's Digest Almanac and Yearbook* (Pleasantville, NY: The Reader's Digest Association, Inc.).

*The Statistical Abstract of the U. S. A.* (Washington, DC: Dept. of Commerce).

*Facts on File* (New York: Facts on File, Inc.).*

Most encyclopedias, such as *Americana, Collier's,* and *The New Funk & Wagnalls,* publish yearbooks.

## FOOTNOTES FOR CHAPTER THIRTEEN

[1]James Harvey Robinson, *The Mind in the Making* (New York: Harper & Brothers, 1969).

[2]Hugh Fellows, *Speech: Sense and Nonsense* (To be published).

[3]James Harvey Robinson, *The Mind in the Making.*

[4]W. N. Brigance, *Speech: Its Techniques and Disciplines in a Free Society* (New York: Appleton-Century-Crofts, Inc., 1961).

[5]Hugh Fellows, *Speech: Sense and Nonsense.*

[6]G. Freedley and J. Reeves, *A History of the Theatre* (New York: Crown Publishers, 1941), p. 33–34.

[7]Reported in *Time* magazine, September 10, 1979, p. 71.

[8]Ibid.

[9]Emily d'Aulaire and Per Ola, "When Hypnosis Casts Its Spell," *Reader's Digest,* January, 1980, p. 102.

[10]Interviews with Dr. Leo Wool and Dr. Harry Rockberger, hypnotherapists.

[11]Albert Meharabian, *Silent Messages* (Belmont, Calif.: Wadsworth Publishing Co., Inc., 1971), pp. 42–47.

[12]Albert E. Scheflen, *Body Language and the Social Order* (Englewood Cliffs, N.J.: Prentice-Hall, 1972).

[13]Desmond Morris, *Manwatching: A Field Guide to Human Behavior* (New York: Harry N. Abrams, 1978).

[14] Randall D. Harrison, *Beyond Words* (Englewood Cliffs, N.J.: Prentice-Hall, 1974), p. 137.

[15]For much of the material in this section, the authors are indebted to the late Professor Lew Sarett of Northwestern University, and the late Professor Frank Rarig of the University of Minnesota, from notes taken in their classes.

*A world news digest with index.

# VOCABULARY STUDY FOR CHAPTER FOURTEEN

Below are some of the words that are used in this chapter, with which you may not be familiar. They are offered as a straight glossary.

1. ALTRUISM     Devotion to the welfare of others.
2. CONVOCATION     Assembly, especially a group of people summoned for some purpose.
3. LEVITY     Flippancy, frivolity, lightness.
4. MANDATORY     Containing a command.
5. MAXIM     An expression of a general truth or principle.
6. PHENOMENAL     Extraordinary; prodigious.
7. PROTOCOL     Customs and regulations concerning official etiquette.
8. RIBALDRY     Vulgarity or coarseness in speech, language.
9. SATIRIZE     To attack with ridicule.
10. SQUALOR     The state of being neglected and filthy.

# 14 | Special Occasions

The best way to improve an after-dinner speech
is to shorten it.

Mark Twain (1835–1910)

Every business and professional person should have a repertory of short speeches for special occasions. They should be researched, outlined, and rehearsed carefully at least twice, before putting them away in a safe place to be pulled out whenever you need them. As a matter of practice, you probably *won't* build up such a repertory; instead, you will probably wait until you are actually asked to speak, and then you will scurry about frantically trying to find something to say and how to say it. This chapter will not supply you with *what* to say, but it outlines a format of *how* to say it on some of those occasions when you are called upon to speak.

You *can* and *should* make some preparation for the time when you are called upon to talk impromptu. Collect the following information, and you will find that you can always mold it into an impromptu speech—if not all of it, then at least most of it:

1. A funny story about your occupation or profession. It should be brief.
2. One statistic—or a set of statistics—about your business or career. This information should, preferably, be facts which are unfamiliar to the general public. (For example, did you know that the large mail-order houses try to avoid having their semiannual catalogs weighed for postal rates in rainy weather? The paper absorbs enough of the moisture in the air to make them heavier.)

3. A quotation from a well-known person about your business or profession. (For example, a manufacturer of safety pins quoted Bob Hope as saying, "All of the electricity in the world can't keep your drawers from falling down—but a safety pin can.")

With a little adaptability to the specific audience you are addressing, the foregoing three elements can be woven into a respectable impromptu speech.

## INTRODUCING A SPEAKER

The speech of introduction is a courtesy accorded to most speakers, and it seems to be expected in our social system. You can almost surely make a successful speech of introduction if you confine yourself to this three-part question and little else:

"Why this *speaker*, on this *topic*, for this *audience*?"

### The Audience

Before a speaker is approached to talk on a particular topic, your first concern should be your audience's interests. A convention of bankers may have, as individuals, a variety of interests: one may be interested in golf, another in fishing and hunting, still others in aviation, oil painting, or health foods. However, you know that *all* of them are interested in banking, or they would not be attending that convention. So it would be hazardous to select a speaker who is an authority on needlepoint to speak on that topic. Suppose you have an audience composed of lawyers, physicians, clergymen, plumbers, officers in the armed forces, stockbrokers, and leaders of the Woman's Liberation movement? Then you should select a speaker who has something to say about the basic drives that motivate most people: self-preservation, sex, ego satisfaction, or altruism. Or, you may have discovered that your audience are *all* interested in civic clubs or are all members of one church congregation, in which case you may select a speaker on one of those topics. Your audience's interests must take priority over everything else, or you will be doing an injustice to that audience—and to the speaker as well.

### The Topic

Although the subject must be something of interest to each member of your audience, it should not be trite or something your audience already knows—unless presented in a particularly attractive or amusing manner. Almost all adults felt that they knew whatever there was to know about sex, yet the book *Everything You Always Wanted to Know about Sex but Were Afraid to Ask* became a best seller a few years ago. So, the topic should have some novelty or at least some additional information.

## The Speaker

The first three commandments in introducing a speaker are: (1) Be brief, (2) be brief, and (3) be brief! Nothing is so exasperating as a long-winded introduction. Here is a formula for a speech of introduction:

1. Remind your audience of their interest in the subject on which your speaker will talk. (Sometimes even this can be dispensed with.)
2. Give, briefly, your speaker's qualifications for talking on that subject.
3. Announce the speaker's name and the speaker's topic.

There are more *don'ts* than *dos* when introducing a speaker. Here are some things to avoid:

1. *Don't talk about yourself* or your interest in the topic. The audience is interested in hearing the *speaker*, not you.

2. *Don't give a biography* of the speaker—not even a short one. The audience's only concern is, "What makes this speaker qualified to talk on this subject?" Other details can be distracting: If your speaker is talking about the relationship between interest rates and inflation, and you have mentioned that the speaker has just returned from two months in Florida, some members in the audience are bound to wonder where that Florida suntan is!

3. *Don't tell your audience how GOOD the speaker is.* This imposes an obligation upon the speaker that *no* person should be expected to live up to. Let the audience find out for themselves how good the speaker is! If you tell them that the speaker is "marvelous," and the speaker turns out to be a bore, then that is a reflection on *your* judgment.

4. *Don't withhold the speaker's name* in order to build a false climax. Most of the audience will *know* who the speaker is, or they probably wouldn't be there in the first place. To attempt to surprise the audience is false theatricality.

5. *Don't use a nightclub introduction*, such as, "And now, ladies and gentlemen, I give you ISAAC O'TOOLE!" or "Now, without further ado, here is the one and only Mario Pulaski!" Have you ever considered how meaningless that latter phrase is? Of course, he's the "one and only" Mario Pulaski! Who else would it be?

6. *Don't try to be a stand-up comic.* Humor can be a real asset in a speech of introduction, but don't tell a funny story just to get a laugh. If you know of a *true* humorous anecdote involving the speaker, you may tell it—but only with the speaker's permission. Never, never tell a funny story that has appeared in print and name the speaker as one of the characters appearing in the story; it may be offensive to the speaker. Besides, someone else in the audience may have read the story, and you lose credibility for both yourself and the speaker.

## Questions and Answers

The following questions reflect aspects of introductory speeches that are often of concern.

1. *Question*:

We are a statewide organization of business people. Each year we hold a state convention and invite a prominent person to address us at our final meeting. It is customary to have our state president, our state vice-president, and our state secretary-treasurer on the platform with this speaker. The secretary introduces the vice-president, who makes a short speech and introduces the president; the president, in turn, makes a short speech and then introduces the main speaker. It seems to me that this takes an awfully long time, but our membership insists that we should extend recognition to our state officers.

*Answer*:

You are not only boring your membership by using this procedure, but you are also detracting from your main speaker. No doubt your state officers enjoy basking in reflected glory of the main speaker, but it is wholly unnecessary. If there are prominent people (including your state officers) present at your final meeting, keep them in the audience. Before the main speaker begins, they may be asked to stand and be recognized, asking that applause be withheld until all are introduced. Of course, if the state president wishes to introduce the main speaker, that's the president's privilege, although it is usually delegated to someone else.

2. *Question:*

Suppose there are two or more speakers on the program. Is each speaker introduced by a separate person?

*Answer:*

No. A single chairman, or toastmaster, should introduce each speaker.

3. *Question:*

If the speaker is a person whose accomplishments are known to everyone in the audience, is there any need for the speaker to be introduced?

*Answer:*

No, there is no real need for an introduction; it is only a matter of courtesy. A short, humorous anecdote—used with the speaker's permission—is all that is necessary. Observe the way in which the President of the United States is usually introduced: "It is my high privilege and great pleasure to introduce the President of the United States of America," or simply, "Ladies and gentlemen, the President of the United States."

## Classroom Exercise

Because the introductory speech has been abused so often, this text devotes a comparatively large amount of space to it. Following is the somewhat detailed biography of a real person, although the name is fictitious. Study the details carefully, and then plan an introduction of John Schonfelt to the various groups that are listed after the biographical sketch.

John Schonfelt (J.S.) was the eldest of five children born on a farm about forty miles from Indianapolis, Indiana. John's parents owned 300 acres of land, on which livestock and poultry were raised, and which grew wheat and corn, as well as fruits and vegetables for the family's use. John had every intention of becoming a farmer because he loved the farm animals, the growing of crops, and the outdoors in general. Then, in grammar school, he learned to draw and paint, and he was sure that an artist's life had to be his. He entered several art competitions and took prizes with his paintings of nature—plants and animals alike.

The Great Depression of the thirties struck, and the farm was lost to its creditors. An uncle found work for John's father in a factory that manufactured farm equipment, so the family moved to Cicero, Illinois, a suburb of Chicago. They lived in a slum district, and John was appalled by the filth and the crime in the ghetto where they lived. In defiance of Child Labor Law, John worked part time alongside his father, but he attended school with a dogged determination to get an education; he believed that the loss of the farm in Indiana had been because of his father's lack of education and, consequently, poor management. Memories of the outdoor life gradually dwindled, and the squalor of his daily living conditions displaced them. By his tenth grade year in high school, John was determined to become either a sociologist or a criminologist, in order to improve life in the slums.

His mother died before his senior year in high school, and John had to stay at home and clean house, cook, and launder for his younger brothers and sisters while his father worked. His cooking was a disaster at first, but he found some old cookbooks and studied them until he became an expert. "It's only a matter of chemistry and good taste," he often said in later years. By scheduling his time carefully, he found that he had time to go to night school and even to do odd jobs during the day when the other children were in school. There was a dishwashing job at a neighborhood restaurant, and an occasional commercial sign to paint for local merchants.

John was ready for college, and his sister, who was two years younger than he, could look after the other children, but there was no money. He obtained a work scholarship at North Park College as assistant caretaker for the campus and was once again working with his beloved plants. To supplement his income, there was an occasional job with a caterer near the campus. After one year at North Park, he won a competitive scholarship to Cornell University, where he could major in criminology and minor in agriculture, so he moved to Ithaca, New York. He and two other male students rented an old farmhouse, which was infested with rats and mice. There had been a similar problem in the slums of Cicero, but the method of getting rid of Illinois rats did not seem to work with New York rats, so he studied rodent extermination in his spare time.

John's scholastic grades were barely good enough for him to maintain his academic scholarship, but he held down two part-time jobs: one as an assistant deputy policeman on weekends in Ithaca, and another as a helper in a fine nursery and landscaping establishment. At Cornell he met Anita, the girl he wanted to marry. She was a music major with a minor in literature, and she decided that his cultural education had been sadly neglected; she taught him to play the piano, at which he proved quite adept, and forced him to read Shakespeare (which he loved) and Dickens (which he hated).

Before John Schonfelt could enter his senior year in college, World War II broke out. He had always been curious about aviation but had neither the time nor money to pursue it, so he joined the Naval Air Corps, became a pilot, was in the Pacific theatre of war flying fighter planes off the aircraft carrier *Saratoga*, and was awarded the Distinguished Flying Cross. He and Anita had been married when he received his commission as Ensign in the U.S. Naval Reserve, shortly before going overseas. After more than three years of serving in the Pacific, John returned to Ithaca to Anita and his three-year-old son, whom he had never seen.

J.S. finished his degree in criminology and found a job that seemed made-to-order for him. He became a warden on Riker's Island, a short-term prison located in the middle of the East River in the Bronx. It was more than a mere warden's job: Riker's Island has about twenty acres of rich soil, and on it are raised all of the chickens, turkeys, and eggs for all of New York City's hospitals and jails, as well as all of the trees and shrubs for the city's streets. Aside from the prison cells, there are only two residences on the island—that of the Prison Chaplain, and that of John Schonfelt—so that John's two younger children could actually claim that they had been born in prison! At age 26 J.S. had found his life's work.

Once again, rodents were a problem. For the thirty-five years of Riker's Island Prison's existence, no warden had been able to rid the island of them; they swam ashore from the ships and barges that passed on either side of the river. Schonfelt used his expertise and was able to rid the island completely of these pests. The New York City newspapers ran the story, and soon people all over the United States and many foreign countries were begging the "rat expert" to rid them of similar infestations. *The New Yorker* magazine wrote a lengthy profile of John Schonfelt and his ability to rid almost any location in the world of rats and rodents.*

John Schonfelt is the author of two books, *Rehabilitation Through Labor* and *My Family's Life in Prison*.

NOTE: Each of the following exercises should be strictly limited to three minutes, spoken at the rate of about 125 words per minute. This translates into two and one-half pages of typed manuscript, double-spaced, with one-inch margins and twenty-eight lines per page, on 11 × 8 1/2-inch paper. Try to find a quotation that is appropriate for each introductory speech.

1. Introduce John Schonfelt to a group of high school seniors or college freshmen (both sexes). His topic is to be, "Decisions that affect one's life work."

2. Introduce J.S. to a group of sociologists or social workers. His topic is to be, "What kinds of people go to prison?"

3. Introduce J.S. to a luncheon service club, such as Rotary, Kiwanis, Lions, or Exchange. His topic is to be, "Relieving tension through your hobby."

4. Introduce J.S. to a chamber of commerce (both sexes). His topic is to be, "How we can replan our city," or, "What can be done about urban blight?"

5. Introduce J.S. to a group of business people (primarily manufacturers and supervisors). His topic is to be, "How much rats cost industry."

6. Select a group of your choice and decide what topics John Schonfelt might be able to talk upon that would be interesting to them. Make your introduction and assign a topic to Schonfelt.

*Among countries who have enlisted his services in this respect are India, France, Italy, and Brazil.

## PRESENTING AN AWARD

America is a nation of prizewinners. In the domain of literature alone there are twenty Pulitzer Prizes; in the entertainment world there are the Academy Awards, the Tony Awards, the Emmy Awards, and the Grammy Awards. Among colleges and universities the list of awards is so long that, in many schools, a special convocation service is set aside solely for their presentation: best all-around athlete, best scholar, greatest contribution to student government, outstanding teacher, and campus security guard and janitor for "services above and beyond the call of duty." Even our domesticated animals qualify for awards at county fairs: best of breed in the dog show, and prize bull in the livestock entries. So, the chances are that you will be called upon at one time or another to present an award.

Broadly speaking there are two types of awards: 1. Those given to the winner of a specific competition. 2. Those given for individual achievement, usually over a longer period of time than the one first named. The formulas for the two do not differ *except in the final step*. Here are precepts which we offer to help you in these types of presentations:

1. *Be brief*, but not so brief as to slight the purpose of the award, or belittle its recipient. Remember, most awards are given for the purpose of stimulating others to a higher standard of achievement.
2. *Tell why the award was established.* For example:
   a) To promote sales with an annual contest
   b) To encourage morale by "best suggestion of the year"
   c) To improve customer relations by recognizing outstanding acts
   d) To recognize long-term service or achievement
3. *Give the donor's name*, and the amount of the prize money or a brief description of the trophy.
4. *Give qualifications that are necessary to win the award.* Is it by virtue of a specific contest? Is it the result of a vote? If so, tell how the voting members were selected.
5. *Don't neglect the losers.* If the award is the result of a contest, some recognition should be given to others in the contest. Be careful not to embarrass them; for instance, if there are only four people in a contest, don't name the third and second place contestants and leave out the fourth. Instead, name only the person who took second place and the prizewinner. When there are five or more persons in competition, it is customary to recognize the third place contestant, then the second, and finally the prizewinner. If there is no clearly defined first, second, or third place, as there is in a contest, it is acceptable—but not mandatory—to name others in line for the award as "nominees." In the Motion Picture Academy Awards this is done, and it is considered an honor to be nominated. On the other hand, the Nobel Prizes do not mention others who were being considered for the award, as it would detract from the achievements of the recipient.

**6.** *Use humor sparingly*, as dictated by the occasion. In awarding the Nobel Prizes, humor is never used; the ceremony is much too serious and dignified. In awarding the winner of a sales contest, it is often used, even to the point of ribaldry.

## Sample Speeches

Following are two sample speeches, illustrating the presentation of awards. One is the result of a long period of effort by its recipient; the other is the result of a contest. Note that both speeches follow the precepts given in the foregoing paragraphs, except for points 5 and 6. At those points each speech differs.

I. For most of his adult life, George Light was impressed by the fact that there was a tremendous waste of human potential in persons who were mentally retarded. They could feed and dress themselves; many of them were strong and had no physical handicap. Why couldn't they be trained to do simple but useful jobs? Why *shouldn't* they have the satisfaction of achievement?

When George Light's son, Mark, died of muscular dystrophy at age sixteen, Mr. Light became more dedicated than ever to the plight of the handicapped. He became Chairman of the World Committee for Employment of the Handicapped, and established the Mark Light Award in commemoration of his late son. Since the award was established, ten years ago, no person has qualified for it — until now.

The stipulations were simple:

A. There were no restrictions as to nationalities or countries. The award was open to employers and educators of all nations.

B. Any employer or educator must have shown his/her good faith by having worked with training or employing the handicapped for a period of at least three years.

Arvel Morgan has been the Principal of Dade County's School for Exceptional Children for five years. During that time he has helped train some three hundred young people and place them in jobs where they could be self-supporting.

It was not easy. First, Arvel Morgan had to *plan* a program that would be practical in training the mentally retarded to cope with elementary and secondary work tasks. Second, jobs had to be found. That meant telephoning dozens of prospective employers, and many hours of scanning the "Help Wanted" advertisements in the county newspapers. Third, each employer had to be persuaded as to the ability of each mentally retarded man or woman he hired. But Arvel Morgan did not stop there: he made a practice of spending a portion of each week going around to the places of employment and checking on how well his protégés were doing their jobs, talking with their employers, and often showing one of his former pupils how he could do his job better.

It is significant that, when Arvel was informed that he had won the Mark Light Award, he asked, "Who is Mark Light, and what's the award for?" It is also significant that the trophy [Speaker produces the trophy, which until now has been covered] is in the form of a human pyramid, implying that the man at the top is dependent upon other men in the organization—even the mentally retarded workers.

It is a great pleasure for me to award Arvel Morgan this trophy and a check for

$1,000.00, because he, too, adopted the slogan, "Not charity, but conservation."
Congratulations, Arvel!
— Speech delivered by Joseph Hall, President of the Dade County Classroom
Teachers' Association, at their annual banquet in Miami, 1958.


II. The *very first* year after I became a salesman for Megathon Soap Products, I
won the award as best salesman. I had no idea of why or how I sold, so when they
told me that I had to demonstrate my selling technique to the President of Megathon
in front of all of the sales convention, I was petrified.

You see, they had this desk set up on the stage in a large auditorium, and old
Mr. Grisham—the President of Megathon—was seated at it; I was supposed to go
on the stage in front of hundreds of other salesmen and demonstrate my technique
of selling. Well, here is what happened:

I came up to the desk and asked Mr. Grisham, "Do you want to buy some
toothpaste?"

Mr. Grisham growled, "No, I do *not* want to buy any toothpaste! Now, get out of
here!"

I said, "But mister, we've got a special offer. If you will just *try* one of our products,
we'll give you—this is *free*—a video tape recorder worth one thousand dollars."

At that, old man Grisham's ears pricked up. What damn fool salesman was going
to give away the company's money, just to get a prospect to try one of the company's
products?

I went on and said, "Now look, mister, I've got a fresh toothbrush here that you
can use, and I've got a preparation for you to use in brushing your teeth, and I've
got a glass of water and a basin you can use. Just try brushing your teeth with this
preparation, and see if you don't want to buy some of my toothpaste."

Well, Mr. Grisham did as he was told, because he had never been approached
with that kind of offer by any other salesman. After he had put the preparation into
his mouth, he spat it into the basin and yelled, "Holy mackerel! That stuff smells like
cow-dung!"

I said, "That's *exactly* what it *is*! *Now*, do you want to buy some toothpaste?"

I'm sure that our winning salesmen here to-night have not had to go to that extreme
to collect sales, but they must have some new approaches that the rest of us don't
know, and which they'll tell us.

Seriously, Mr. Matthew Grisham established this contest for the best three salesmen in Megathon Soap Products before his retirement as President. For the first five
years after his retirement, he presented the awards himself. We regret that he is not
here to-night, but we believe that he would be happy with the winners. They are:

Joel Trask, for having increased his sales by 20% over a period of one year. Joel
gets a trophy and $1,000 in cash.

Lee Salisbury, for having increased *his* sales by 25% over the past year. Lee gets
a trophy and $1,500 in cash.

And, finally, Myra Cohen—the champion—who increased her sales by 35% in
one year. Myra gets the championship trophy and a cash prize of $2,500.

Congratulations to all three winners!
— This speech is fictitious. It is a composite of such speeches which the authors
have observed over more than twenty years of attending awards banquets in
business.

AUTHOR'S NOTE: Neither of the foregoing speeches is *better* than the other. They are cited as examples of adaptability to one's audience. In the first there is a mood of seriousness; in the second, a mood of levity prevails. There is no reason why humor should not be introduced in either type of presentation, but it should be done with caution.

## RECEIVING AN AWARD

In accepting an award such as those given for the sales contest, no speech of acceptance is necessary; a simple "thank you" will suffice. However, even "thank you" should be said graciously. A few years ago a young actress received the most coveted prize in the legitimate theatre, the Antoinette Perry Award, nicknamed the "Tony." The trophy was a simple sterling silver bowl. She rose to accept it, turned it over curiously, shrugged a shoulder, lifted an eyebrow, and said, "Well, I don't know what it's supposed to be—but thanks, anyway." She was *not* a comedienne, and her nonverbal communication conveyed the idea that the trophy was worthless. The personages in the audience were faintly insulted, and there was dead silence until the master of ceremonies announced the next award.

If you are the sole recipient of an award, or one of a *very* few, protocol indicates a short speech. This depends upon the reason for the award. The speech could include one of more of the following points:

1. Praise the donors of the award. They have spent time and money on it, and the spirit in which it is given should be recognized.
2. If the award involves money, you may tell how it is to be used, although this is not mandatory. For example, the winner of the 1979 Nobel Peace Prize, Sister Teresa of Calcutta, indicated that the money would go toward alleviating suffering in India.
3. Recognize others and the part they played in helping you win the award. Many awards are the result of team effort, and you should share the honors. Do not overdo this, or claim that "*others* did it all."
4. Be as brief as possible. Miss Grace Haight, a lady who volunteered her teaching services to Bob Jones College for many years, was awarded an honorary doctorate by the college, and responded simply by saying,

   "Shakespeare wrote that 'Some are born great, some achieve greatness, and some have greatness thrust upon them.' I thank you deeply for this greatness you have thrust upon me."

### Sample Speech

Following is the response Arvel Morgan gave upon receiving the Mark Light Award.

In the name of Mark Light's philosophy, we thank you. I said "we" because at the Dade County School for Exceptional Children, we work as a team. When I became their principal, it was Martha Strayhorn who suggested that we train the young for useful vocations, rather than simply keep them busy. The other members of the faculty quickly agreed, and our program has never faltered.

Our special thanks go to John Paul Richardson, our physical education director and therapist. It was he who made a study of hundreds of jobs in industry which our pupils might fill. Then he went to work to give each pupil the physical coordination to fit him or her for the jobs.

One of our chief obstacles at first was the lack of tools and machinery, and there was no budget for them. Lila Jenkins, one of our faculty, approached Mr. Carl Lindquist, head of the McCormick-Deering Corporation in Miami, and that company furnished us with a fine workshop. We are deeply grateful to them. Incidentally, the cash award will go to purchase a new woodworking lathe, which we have needed for a long time.

Finally, all of us should be grateful to George Light, who helped relieve society of the burden of the mentally handicapped, and who had the foresight to realize that our greatest resource in this country is human resource, and for his determination not to see that resource wasted. We thank him deeply.

## AFTER-DINNER SPEAKING

After-dinner speaking may have several purposes. It may be an occasion to welcome a new member of an organization, or an occasion to cheer a retiring or departing member. It may be for the purpose of honoring a member of an organization with a series of toasts (or "roasts"). It may be for the purpose of hearing an important person in the business or professional world deliver a speech of special significance, although this purpose is not advised; both the listeners and the speaker are handicapped somewhat after a full meal, amid the clutter of cutlery and china. Nevertheless, it is often done, and the success or failure of the speech can be attributed largely to the chairman who is in charge of the event.

### The Chairman

If you are in charge of arrangements for a dinner where there is to be an after-dinner speaker (or speakers), there are some things that you should not leave to chance—or to someone else. Check them carefully.

1. Make sure that all speakers know the occasion for the dinner, the topics on which they are to speak, and the time limits for their talks.
2. Check carefully the room where the dinner is to be held. If the dinner is to be held in a catering establishment where there is more than one dining room, ask the manager who has reserved the dining room next to the one you are using. Make sure that there is not a loud sound movie being held there (sound movies penetrate even thick partitions), and that the people next door aren't going to throw a boisterous party.

    If a public address system is to be used, make sure that it is in working order, and learn the volume adjustments it requires. This should be checked again, just prior to the dinner.

Check on the furniture and lighting. Make sure that the speaker is provided with a lectern with sufficient lighting. One author of this text attended a banquet recently where a speaker had traveled across the continent, to find there was no source of light except candles on the dining table, and he needed to read from his notes some highly technical material. To make matters worse, the speaker's stand was placed in one corner where no more than half the guests could see him. Abominable!

3. Check the seating arrangements. Usually there is a special table, reserved for VIP's, at one end of the room or in the center of one wall, with tables grouped around it in a semicircle. The chairman, or president, should be seated in the middle of the table, the guest speaker should be on the president's right, and on the president's left should be seated the next most honored guest, or the next highest ranking officer in the organization. At the guest speaker's right should be the third most important person. Guests should be seated to either side of the center in order of importance.

4. Make it clearly understood that the meal must be finished and the tables cleared before the speaker begins. We have known several speakers who were scheduled to speak *during* dinner, and have flatly refused; no one should blame them.

## The Speaker

If you are the speaker in an after-dinner speech situation, here is a list of things that you should ascertain before you begin preparing your speech.

1. Is it a routine meeting, such as Kiwanis, or Rotary, where the speaker is generally the only "program"? Is it a banquet to celebrate an achievement, a retirement, or some other special occasion?

2. Who comprises the audience? Regular members? Mixed sexes? All male? All female? What is the average age group?

3. Will there be other speakers? If so, what will be their topics?

4. What is the time allotted to the speech? Ten to fifteen minutes is long enough, provided there are no other speakers. Twenty minutes is too long for an after-dinner speech, unless you are a real spellbinder.

5. What is the physical set-up? Will there be a public address system? If so, will you be allowed to check it beforehand? Will there be a lectern or table? If you are to use notes, will there be plenty of light? Request that any routine announcements and introductions be made while the waiters and busboys are clearing the tables; you should not be asked to talk above the clatter of china and silverware.

## The Speech

The ideal after-dinner speech is a wise maxim, a grain of truth, or a morsel of instruction, fleshed out with wit and humor. People don't like serious subjects on a full stomach. Somerset Maugham wrote that, "At a dinner party, we should eat wisely, but not too well, and talk well, but not too wisely."

You may resort to telling outrageous stories built around a theme and make them appear to have happened to you; you may "roast" (gently) a member— or several members—of the organization; you may satirize a political or social situation. Whatever topic you choose, the after-dinner speech is primarily a speech to entertain and amuse.

In one sense the after-dinner speech is the most difficult of all speeches to make completely successful. First, because *fresh* humorous material is difficult to find; and second, because the average person cannot tell a funny story effectively. This is why we have spent a great many words in this chapter on the subject.

The late Paul Seaman, Vice-President of Sales for *Encyclopedia Britannica*, gained a great reputation as an after-dinner speaker, and he claimed that it came to him easily only after many years of collecting materials.

"You see," he said, "nobody ever expects me to talk on any subject except sales and marketing. So, over many years, I have collected humorous stories on those subjects. I search for them in such magazines as *Printer's Ink* and other trade publications not generally known to the reading public. If I find that the story has been duplicated in a magazine with a wide reading public, I discard it. Then I type the stories on 4 × 6 inch cards and file them under various topics that relate to sales and marketing, such as "prospects," "closing," and so forth. When I'm called on to speak, I simply pull out enough cards under a certain topic to fill eight or ten minutes of time. There's one other step that I take to keep from repeating myself to the same group of people: on the back of each card, I write *where* and *when* I've used that particular story; for instance, 'Advertising Club, May, 1976' or 'Sales Executive Club, October, 1977.' People often ask me, 'How can you remember all of those stories?' or 'How can you always find the exact anecdote you need to support a certain point?' The fact is I *can't*; I've got them written down and filed away methodically. It's only businesslike. Oh, yes, there's one other thing: some people simply aren't able to tell certain types of stories; I don't know why it is, but maybe it's because they can't relate to the characters in the story. When I try to tell a certain story and it doesn't 'go over' twice in succession, I toss it out. Why risk failure a third time?"

So, if you are hoping to become a seasoned after-dinner speaker, there's no better advice than that from Paul Seaman: You've got to work at it!

## HOW TO TELL A FUNNY STORY

While the funny story is the mainstay of after-dinner speaking, many people say, "I simply cannot tell a funny story without botching it up." What they really mean is that they have never learned the technique of telling *any* kind of story.

It is valuable to look at some of the bases of humor. Humor is essentially a human quality; animals don't laugh. Broadly speaking, most humor is based on politics, sex, and digestion; most wit is based on human manners and customs—specifically those which require some manipulation of the language. It's rare that one can combine many of the elements that make up humor into a single statement, as in the case of the teacher who asked her students to write a story that would deal with the topics of religion, royalty, sex, and surprise. Mary McArdle wrote for only one minute and turned in her paper. The teacher, who thought that the assignment would keep the class busy for at least an hour, changed her mind when she read:

" 'Good Lord!' said the pretty princess. 'I think I'm pregnant.' "

Here are some of the techniques for telling a funny story successfully. They require practice. Try to recall the funniest story you've ever heard and see if you've slighted some of these precepts. It might be a good idea to write out the story to see if you can eliminate certain details, or add details to make it funnier.

*First,* be sure that you have included all the necessary details for the setting. A story is like a play: one needs the setting and the cast of characters before one can advance the plot. Don't be guilty of saying, "Oh, I forgot to tell you that the man was a midget," or "I meant to tell you that this takes place in the deep South." On the other hand, don't give tedious details unless they are necessary for the development of the plot. If a "fat, middle-aged man" is sufficient, don't go into details, such as, "he was so fat that his belt was under his belly instead of around his waist, and his shirttail seemed always about to fall out. He wore no necktie, and he had a perpetual greasy ring around his collar . . ." These details are fine for a novelist, but not for an after-dinner speaker.

If the story is very long (and it *shouldn't* be!) you can brighten it up with some humorous details along the way:

> "The worst orchestra I ever heard sounded like two skeletons dancing on a tin roof and a pregnant bullfrog singing jazz."

Don't give too many of these humorous details, or they will only serve to lengthen an already overlong story.

*Second,* name your characters. Never talk about "this young man" or "an elderly lady." Instead, give them names—preferably slightly ridiculous ones: "Ura Sapp, a young man," or "Ima Holdout, an elderly lady."

> Three Texans were talking about their property.
>
> Mr. Bragg A. Lott remarked, "I got about 2,000 acres down in the valley, with about 1,000 head of Aberdeen Angus cattle on it, and I call it 'Peso Grande'."

Mr. Newley Rich responded, "Well, I got about fo' thousand acres up in the panhandle, with close to 1,500 whitefaced Hereford on it. I call it 'Mesa Moneda'."

Mr. I. D. Clare said modestly, "Well, all I got is fo'ty acres."

Mr. Lott and Mr. Rich were astounded. "Forty acres! Is that *all*? Whatcha call it?"

Mr. Clare answered calmly, "Well, some people refer to it as 'downtown Dallas'."

*Third,* use the first person, if possible. Even though you may have clipped the story from a periodical, or have been told it by a friend, try to tell it as if it had happened to you. If you take the story from a newspaper or magazine, you should take it from one that does not have a wide circulation or from very *old* periodicals. Stories tend to run their course and then are forgotten, so that they become fresh again. From my old copies of *Reader's Digest* I have saved for more than twenty years all of its sections on "Campus Comedy," "Humor in Uniform," "Laughter, the Best Medicine," and "Personal Glimpses." They are invaluable as source materials for a speech. Trade journals, such as *Printer's Ink* and others, are also good sources.

When you use a first person story, always make yourself the butt of the joke—always the "dope" and never the superior person.

In Fez, Morocco, there is a fine restaurant called La Legion. I appeared there for dinner one evening, to find that every table was taken. However, Pierre the maître d'hôtel said to me, "Eef you would not mind sharing a table weez a very nice man, I sink he would welcome you."

"Of course I wouldn't mind. In fact, I'd like some company."

Pierre led me through the maze of tables to where a seedy-looking little Frenchman was dining alone. As we approached the table, the Frenchman jumped to his feet, clicked his heels, bowed, held out his hand, and exclaimed, "Bon appetit!" I, not knowing one word of French, shook hands with him and gave him my name, "Fellows."

The Frenchman helped me order my meal. When I pointed to something on the French menu, he would either say, "Non, non," shaking his head disapprovingly, or respond with, "Oui! Bon, bon," nodding his head. We had a pleasant meal.

The following evening I spotted the Frenchman from the doorway. He waved for me to join him, and once again he jumped to his feet, clicked his heels sharply, bowed, held out his hand, and said, "Bon appetit!" I once again responded with "Fellows."

I was away for two weeks. When I returned to Fez, I went to La Legion and was disappointed to find the Frenchman nowhere in sight, so I asked the *maître d'hôtel,* "Where is Monsieur Bon Appetit?"

"*Quand?*" He looked puzzled; then he remembered. "Ah! You mean zee gentleman you had dinner wiz. But, M'sieu, zat was not hees *name*; hees name ees Jean

Chandonnet. He was simply weeshing you 'Good appetite.' He ees here and I will find him for you."

He guided me through the crowded restaurant until we came upon the Frenchman. This time I was determined to beat him to the punch, so I clicked my heels, bowed from the waist, and extended my hand, wishing him, "Bon appetit!"

As he took my hand, he responded with, "Fellows!"

*Fourth*, "place" your characters, and give them *individual speech* characteristics. Most funny stories involve more than one person speaking. You don't have to resort to the tedious practice of, "John said . . . Then Mary said . . . and Peter added . . ." In "placing" your characters, you should turn your head and body slightly to the *left* for *one* character's speech, then turn your head and body slightly to the *right* for *another* character's speech. You can even add a third person by varying the angle of turning. (See Figure 14-1.)

You can also indicate the relative *height* of two speakers. When the "tall man" is speaking to the "little girl," he lowers his gaze; when the "little girl" is speaking to the "tall man," she looks up. When there is no dialogue, you—as the narrator—look directly at your audience. Note the detailed instruction in the story below:

James Castellano, on his very first day at school, was greeted by a cute, curvacious young woman, who asked him,

"What's your name, young man?" [Head turned slightly to *left*; eyes lowered]

"My name ith James, but everybody callth me Jimmy, and it maketh me tho damn mad I could thpit," he lisped. [Head turned slightly to *right*; eyes looking up]

The teacher perceived immediately that she had two jobs to do: she had to give the youngster a sense of decorum, and she had to try to correct his lisp.

"How old are you, James?" [Head left, eyes lowered]

"I'm thix, but everybody thinkth I'm five, and that maketh me tho damn mad I could thpit."

[Head right; eyes looking up]

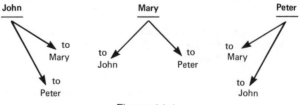

Figure 14-1

At that point the teacher decided that she'd better do something about this little hellion before he contaminated all of the other children, so she said,

"Now James, after school is over, and all of the other little boys and girls have gone home, you and I are going to stay right here by ourselves and have a nice, long private consultation." [Head left; eyes lowered]

He looked up at her with a wicked gleam in his eye. "Oh, noo-o we're not. I'm too young for that thort of thing, and *that* makth me tho damn mad I could thpit!"

In "placing" the characters in your story, you should give each one a distinctly different tone of voice. You don't need to be a stand-up comedian or have the vocal range of an opera singer to do this. Give one character a nasal whine, another a deep gruff voice, still another a southern accent, and so on. When the characters in your story are a man and a woman, remember that a man generally speaks slower and at a lower pitch than a woman; a woman usually speaks slightly faster, and at a higher pitch, than a man. If you're a man, don't overdo the higher pitch when a woman speaks, or you'll end up with a falsetto—which is perfectly all right if you want the woman in your story to appear ridiculous but unrealistic.

*Fifth*, know where the climax is and "point it up." In most funny stories the climax comes in the final sentence, commonly known as the "punch line," unless there is an admonition or a moral to the story. Be sure that you deliver it distinctly, and perhaps a little bit slower and louder than the rest of the story. Above all, don't spoil the punch line by laughing at it, thereby making it difficult for your listeners to understand.

The climax is often preceded by repetition of something that the listeners do not understand until the final revelation. Note in the following story how the young boy's grunts are repeated (only *twice*, or the story will be too long!), and how emphasis on the grunts *must* be given vocally, to show that the grunts have some *meaning*:

Donavon and Pulaski were ice fishing on Lake Champlain without any success. Not more than twenty feet from them was a lad of about nine years; he was having phenomenal luck. Each time the youngster lowered his line through the hole he had made in the ice, he waited only a minute or two before he pulled in a fine bass.

"This doesn't make sense," said Donavon. "I'm going over and find out how he does it."

"Hi, young fella," he said as he approached the boy. "That's a mighty fine string of fish you've got there. My friend and I haven't had any luck at all. What's your secret?"

The boy looked up and replied in a series of unintelligible grunts, "Muum *aam* tnn hmeep mumm *maam* wmm!"

"Sorry," Donavon said, "but I couldn't understand what you said. Mind telling me again?"

Once again the lad issued a series of meaningless grunts, but with great emphasis: "Hmm *unt* hmm *meep* hmm *mammt* wmm!"

"Hey, what's the matter with you? Can't you talk?"

"Sure I can," said the youngster, as he spat out a mouthful of earthworms into his hand. "I was trying to tell you that you *have* to keep your *bait* warm!"

*Sixth*, don't hesitate to use dialect. It enriches your story. There are some people—and groups—who object to stories that use dialect, on the grounds that they tend to ridicule minority groups. If the story is offensive to *any* group, it should not be used. However, if you're not good at dialect, don't attempt it. Find a first-generation American and note which sounds the person distorts. For example:

Frenchmen have difficulty with the "th" sound, so that the sentence, "This is the worst thing," sounds like, "Zees ees zee worst sing."

Italians have a tendency to add an extra syllable to some words, so that the sentence, "He is a good man" sounds like this: "He eez a gooda mana."

Both languages have difficulty with the American sound of "i" as in "it" or "bring." It's apt to become "eet" or "breeng."

Germans also have difficulty with the "th" sound, but it is more likely to sound like a "d," so that the sentence, "That is the most bothersome," comes out, "Dat iss dee most boddersome."

If you are good at *one* dialect, you can usually adapt the story to that dialect. *Last*, there are some things that you should *never* do in telling a funny story.

1. Never tell your listeners *how* funny it is. When you say "You'll *die* laughing at this one," they may simply die.
2. Never laugh at your own story. You should have an amused or pleasant expression, but don't cackle with laughter—especially on the punch line.
3. Never *explain* the point of a story. If your listeners don't laugh at it, maybe they didn't think it funny; to go back and explain it is tedious and even less funny.
4. Don't tell a questionable story to a strange group. If there is any doubt in your mind as to whether it might offend an ethnic group, a religious group—or even a fraternal order—don't tell it!

Remember, a person with a song or a good story is *always* welcome in *any* social group. So, bring out your best stories and try to improve them. They can be improved by observing the precepts in this article, but it takes practice, practice, practice!

## SUGGESTED CLASSROOM EXERCISE

Ideally the site for this assignment should not be in the classroom, but in a student dining room on the campus, a clubroom where there are food preparation services or in a restaurant with a private dining room. Its nature is that of an "end of the class" celebration. Students make all of the arrangements and may exercise all of the sections dwelt upon in this chapter: introducing a speaker, presenting an award, receiving an award, "roasting" the instructor; in addition, each student not involved in other activities must tell a funny story.

# VOCABULARY STUDY FOR CHAPTER FIFTEEN

The following words are used in Chapter Fifteen. Their definitions are included here. You may wish to look up the *pronunciations* of some of these words.

| | | |
|---|---|---|
| 1. | AGATE | Variegated marble, showing curved, colored bands or other patterns. |
| 2. | ALLEVIATE | To ease pain; soothe. |
| 3. | APHORISM | A terse saying, embodying a general truth, such as "Art is long but life is short." |
| 4. | BAKER'S DOZEN | Thirteen instead of twelve; originated when penalties were severe for any tradesman giving "short" weight. |
| 5. | BORDELLO | A whorehouse. |
| 6. | CONNIVING | Scheming, ignoring something that is important; conspiring deliberately. |
| 7. | CUDGEL | A club or stick for beating; used as a verb or noun, for example, "Cudgel your dull brain no further." |
| 8. | ECLECTIC | Choosing from several sources, and selecting the best; capable of seeing more than one point of view; sophisticated. |
| 9. | ERUDITE | Learned or scholarly. |
| 10. | GUMPTION | Common sense; initiative, resourcefulness, courage (informal or colloquial language). |
| 11. | LECHER | One who has excessive sexual drives. |
| 12. | OLD CHESTNUT | An old or stale saying or joke. |
| 13. | ORMOLU | An alloy of copper and zinc that gives the appearance of gold; cheap, but giving the impression of richness, usually because of an ornate design. |
| 14. | PITHY | Terse and full of substance or meaning. |
| 15. | SABOTAGE | Any underhanded interference with production; attempting to wreck deliberately. |
| 16. | SCINTILLATING | Brilliant; emitting sparks of light; charismatic. |
| 17. | SYCOPHANTIC | Insincerely flattering; "apple-polishing." |
| 18. | VERNACULAR | Expressions of the common man; not literary, but expressive. |
| 19. | WISTFUL | Melancholy; a longing or yearning expression; wishful. |
| 20. | WOEBEGONE | Indicating woe, or sorrow, in appearance; a hopeless facial expression. |

# 15 | Conversation

Educated people talk about ideas; semi-educated people talk about events; uneducated people talk about people.

Jacques Barzun (1907– )

Whether or not it's true that more business deals are made over the 3-martini lunch or in the golf or tennis clubs than behind office walls, the fact remains that most business people are woefully lacking in social conversation. This was even truer twenty or thirty years ago, when it was taken for granted that socially prominent or wealthy families would marry into equally socially prominent or wealthy families, and thereby inherit the position of business executives. At that time there was little written on the subject. The following is an account by Alan Price:

In the nineteen fifties, I was teaching courses in the Baruch School of Business in New York City. I had countless students come up to me after class (The question was never brought up *in* class—as if they were ashamed to admit it!) and ask, "Doc, how does one carry on 'small-talk' or 'chit-chat,' or just talk to people socially? Now, I can make a sale, I can lay out an advertising campaign, and all that, but I'm lost when I'm in a purely social situation."

Frankly, I had never thought about it. I had traveled a lot, and had been thrown together with people ranging from backwoods coon hunters, throughout a gamut of military officers and enlisted men, musicians, artists, actors, and college professors; I had no difficulty exchanging pleasant talk with any of them, but had never stopped to wonder how it was done.

Being a college professor, I went first to the library—the world's largest reference library—and found very little. Oh, yes, there was Dale Carnegie's book on *How to Win Friends and Influence People* (a bit too puerile and sycophantic for my taste—although don't sell it short!), but almost nothing else. Some of the speech texts mentioned talking about the latest football game and student body activities, as a means of finding common ground to talk about, but there was little or nothing for an adult business man or woman that was of lasting value. So, I started doing some inquiries of my friends, and learned quite a bit.[1]

We shall come back to some of the things Professor Price learned. Ralph Nichols and Leonard Stevens in their book, *Are You Listening?*[2] say that conversation often follows a format:

1. A verification of the *status quo*
2. A verification of problems ahead
3. A verification of who will be affected
4. Discussion of personalities.

This *could* boil down to the following conversation:

JO:   Hello! How are you?

JEAN:   I'm fine. How are you?

JO:   Are you ready for that history test this afternoon?

JEAN:   No, I'm going to the library to study for it right now. What about you?

JO:   Shucks, yes! Tom and Suzy and Francis and I studied until three this morning, and we've really got it licked.

JEAN:   Well, I saw poor Ellen a while ago. She went home this weekend, and forgot to take her history text, and she's frantic.

JO:   Yeah, Ed's in the same fix; he got an "F" at mid-term, and he had to go on that basketball trip to Chicago, and the plane was hours late, and didn't get here until. . . .

This is hardly the sort of conversation that would appeal to a large television audience on any of the current talk shows. Nevertheless, a successful social conversation *can* be planned, as some of those talk shows have shown us. And you don't need a celebrity who has starred in five Academy Award-winning movies to promote her latest movie, nor an author who has written a best seller book as your guests. You—even you!—surrounded by everyday people, can be an interesting conversationalist if you're willing to work *long* and *hard* at it. There's no magic key. Those talk show hosts who rank the highest will tell you truthfully that an entire team of research people, technical people, and even they themselves do an immense amount of preparation for the few minutes they are on camera. So, this is not an instant success chapter on how to become a poised personality and a scintillating speaker.

## YOUR PERSONAL EQUIPMENT

First, it should have started with your parents. The father who says of his 3-year-old son, "Look at him! He's just a born engineer. See how he's torn apart that kiddie car and put it back together again?" The mother who says of her 4-year-old daughter, "Why, she could read simple music when she was three years old! Isn't that marvelous? That's why we bought her a special piano with a keyboard that would fit her hands." Dad, who continues to buy his son mechanical toys, and Mom, who continues to take an interest in her daughter's musical "career," to the *exclusion* of everything else, are risking making dull conversationalists of their children.

"My son be in a school play the fourth grade is giving? Hell, no! He has to finish that rocket plane he's building in the back yard. School play indeed—that's sissy stuff!"

"My daughter become a girl scout and go on a camping trip? Of course not! She may burn her fingers, and that would keep her from practicing her piano. And camping out—eating that food? She has to have her own special diet."

Most parents these days are less restrictive. But the point here is that you should create a variety of interests if you are to be an interesting person, and you can't be an interesting conversationalist, even among *other* interesting people, unless you are an interesting person.

Robert Hutchins[3] once said that youngsters growing up in this country should have about six interests that they are seriously considering pursuing up until the age sixteen; by the time the youngster is twenty years old, those interests should have narrowed to about four—but four that one could go into seriously; between ages twenty and twenty-five, those interests should narrow to two, at which time one chooses a career—and knows *why* that career has been chosen. Hutchins explained, however, that such a range of choices is not likely to occur—and may even be impossible—in our economic circumstances. Eclectic interests are just as much a part of your education as your degree in physics or business administration. We cite two cases:

Jack Hirschhorn (actual name) was an official on Riker's Island, the short-term prison for New York City. He was a graduate of Cornell University in horticulture and poultry husbandry. Jack was in charge of growing, with prison labor, all of the trees and shrubs for most of the boroughs of Manhattan, and also for furnishing all eggs, chickens, and turkeys used in hospitals and jails of the city. He was a fine photographer and had a darkroom equipped with professional equipment in his basement. He played the piano and organ—not well, but enough for his own amusement and for group singing. He was renowned as a rat exterminator and traveled to many countries where rodents had become a national menace. He had studied penal behavior from his long experience in working with criminals, and was in much demand as a speaker. He also had great personal charm.

Harry Sydow (fictitious name, but real person) was a successful banker from the southwest. Since Harry was not particularly interested in the theatre, music, or museums, I took him up to Riker's Island to have lunch with Jack Hirschhorn. Harry was fascinated by Jack's personality and versatility. The two men were the same age—in their early sixties. Harry had the personality of a wet dishcloth.

Several weeks later Harry Sydow's sister visited me, and remarked wistfully that she didn't know what on earth the family would do with Harry when he retired, because he had no interest whatsoever in anything but the bank.

"You mean he doesn't play golf, or garden, or fish, or like to travel—or even gamble?" I asked.

"Nothing like that. He even goes to the bank on Saturdays when it is closed," she replied.

Jack's wife had died shortly before he turned sixty. At age sixty-two he married again. When he retired at sixty-five, he and his wife bought a thoroughbred horse farm in New Jersey; at this writing, he is still going strong. Almost immediately after Harry retired, he began to develop all sorts of ailments, literally became a vegetable, and was dead within three years.

—Hugh P. Fellows

Everyone should store up as many inner resources as possible for use in conversation. Those resources will also serve as happy memories as you grow older. Recently there has been a great upsurge of older people who are coming back to college to take classes—not out of boredom but out of curiosity. God bless them!

In her book, *Speech Can Change Your Life*,[4] Dorothy Sarnoff recounts this story: Senator Eugene McCarthy walked into a room of admirers, presumably for the purpose of talking politics, but spotted an agate marble lying on a table. He supposedly gave his fellow politicians a half-hour speech on the subject of marbles, which they claimed fascinated them and took their minds off politics and the war in Vietnam. This showed McCarthy to be an acute observer with something on his mind besides politics.

Almost any interesting experience that has happened to you—or, for that matter, almost any experience you have in common with someone else—can help you become a better conversationalist. But, don't overdo it and talk a subject to death. Take Mark Twain's advice: "A good memory and a tongue tied in the middle is a combination which gives immortality to conversation."

## ACTIVE PREPARATION

Recently we conducted an experiment that had unexpected but gratifying results. We asked students from three classes of approximately twenty-five members each to turn in the name, or names, along with the telephone numbers, of friends or acquaintances whom they felt were *especially* good conversationalists. No specified number of names was given, because we asked them not to list a name unless they considered that person particularly adept in all social situations. No student turned in more than five, and many turned in only one name. Then, we asked *other* students, who had no way of knowing the names that were turned in, to call those people, announce that they were doing a survey for H_____ College, and request the respondent to answer two short questions. The questions were

A. When you invite a guest to your home for a *small* gathering (no more than six people), do you inform that possible guest who *else* is going to be at the gathering and tell them a bit about the other guests?

B. When you are *invited* to a small gathering, do you make a discreet inquiry as to who else might be there, so that you can think of some possible topics of conversation?

Without reading further, answer those questions for yourself. Be honest about it!

Before giving you the results of the survey, we asked some of our colleagues (mostly in the academic field) the same questions and got many of these responses:

"Of course not! That would take all the joy—all of the spontaneity—out of conversation."

"I think that would be rude; my host or hostess has the privilege of inviting whomever he or she pleases, and it's none of my business!"

Later, we asked some very distinguished personages those same questions. However, let's take a look at the student survey first.

The students made a total of 120 telephone calls, all to strangers whom other students had considered exceptional personalities in a social situation:

Sixty percent (60%) answered "Yes" to both questions

Twenty percent (20%) answered "Yes" to Question "A," but "No" to Question "B"

Ten percent (10%) replied, "I don't know; I suppose I *do* sometimes." [We wondered if that 10% wanted to avoid a cast-off lover, or an embarrassing situation of a similar nature!]

Ten percent (10%) replied, "I've never thought about it. I mean, do I or don't I?"

The point is that *nobody* among those 120 "good talkers" replied to either of the questions with a flat "No!"

Let's look at some of the responses from "personages" to whom we put the same questions. Names have been withheld because *one* of the group forbade the use of his identity:

A. From the owner of a chain of beauty salons and a highly successful manufacturer of cosmetics:

"Of course I tell my guests who else is going to be there; oil and water don't mix, so I give them the privilege of refusing my invitation if they're going to be uncomfortable. After that awful picture of me in one of the national magazines, if a member of the press is going to be present, the guests are always served only *domestic* wines and champagne!"

B. From the widow of an Ex-President of the United States:

"I don't make out a list of topics I can talk about as if I'm making out a shopping list! But if a physician is to be present, I go over my back issues of the news magazines, just to see what has been going on in the field of medicine."

C. From a woman who was once the highest paid woman fiction writer in the world:

"When I invite guests into my home, I make it a point to tell them who else is going to be there, so that they can surmise what turn the talk will take. It is only common courtesy."

D. From the chairman of the board of governors of a stock exchange:

"My talk week in and week out is stocks and bonds, but when we invite guests for dinner or drinks, I spend the midnight oil going over what has happened in the rest of the world. I don't know who said it, but I don't want to be placed in the position of the guy about whom someone wrote, 'Your ignorance cramps my conversation.' "[5]

E. From the president of one of the largest electronic companies in the world:

"I'm a snob, and proud of it, because I worked my way up from a day-laborer in this company to president! You're damn right, I insist on knowing who's going to be there before I attend any sort of function. I'm not impressed by so-called 'important people,' because I can hold my own there; but I go out in the evenings for recreation, and I don't want to be bored by a bunch of silly pretenders and apple-polishers [*Not* the word he used!]. I want to get home early, reasonably sober, and look back over the evening thinking, 'Those were fun-people; let's have them over some night.' "

## Don't Bluff—Learn, Instead!

One cannot be an authority on every subject in the world. How dreary to have the reputation of a walking encyclopedia, whom no one could dispute! However, it is well to know at least one subject thoroughly and to be interested in several others. "It is a great misfortune neither to have enough wit to talk well, nor enough judgment to keep silent."[6]

In 1971 and 1972 two volumes appeared in print that appeared to give "instant erudition" on a variety of topics. Rumor has it that the books were regarded as *totally* ridiculous—which they *weren't* altogether—so the publishers decided to treat them as a great spoof on learning, and called them *The Bluffer's Guide*.[7] David Frost was hired to write a preface for each of the sections, which were about subjects such as football, antiques, gourmet cooking, interior decorating, travel, and the theatre, by such authors as Joe and June Singer, André Launay, Sandy Glass, Dixie Trainer, and Michael Turner. Unfortunately the books turned out to be neither fish, flesh, nor fowl. Although some of the articles have genuinely valuable information in them, one was never sure whether or not one would be a laughingstock if one took the information seriously. "Name dropping" will get you nowhere—except in trouble.

The same is not true of Barbara Walters' book, whose extravagant title, *How to Talk with Anybody About Practically Anything,*[8] is intended primarily for entertainment, with her anecdotes concerning celebrities she has interviewed on the TV program, *Today.* Nevertheless, the book contains some practical information about how to cope with difficult people, and this chapter draws heavily from that volume (with Miss Walters' permission, of course).

So, don't bluff, but try to create a variety of interests for yourself, and try to take a genuine interest in other people. "Being interested is what makes one interesting,"[9] as Dr. Erich Fromm has observed. You have nothing to lose by trying to create a pleasant relationship with other people; if you haven't had one in the first place, give it a trial!

## THE OPENING

One of the greatest difficulties in social conversation seems to be getting started. Assume that you are visiting a friend, and a stranger is present. The friend leaves the two of you alone while she goes to fix coffee. The stranger (male or female) does not seem inclined to talk. How do you open the conversation? Before reading any farther, jot down in the spaces below how you might attempt to get started:

1. _____
2. _____
3. _____

Before we evaluate your own methods for starting a conversation with a reticent stranger, here are a couple of samples for you to pass judgment upon:

YOU: Where are you from?

HE: Paterson, New Jersey.

YOU: Now where, exactly, is Paterson?

HE: It's on the Garden State Parkway, about twelve miles west of the George Washington Bridge.

YOU: Sounds like an interesting town.* How big is it?

HE: Oh, I think the population is about 200,000.

YOU: Gee! I had no idea it was so large.

HE: Yes, it's a good-sized town.

*(Long silence; you try again)*

YOU: What sort of work do you do?

HE: I'm in insurance.

YOU: That's interesting. What sort of insurance? And, do you sell it, or what?**

*You're lying! You don't even know where the town is!
**How do you know it's interesting?

Is this a conversation? No!
Now, consider this one:

YOU:   Boy! That snow is really coming down—big, wet flakes.

HE:   Yes, it has been a severe winter.

YOU:   Not as tough as the winter of 1978; it got murderously cold then.

HE:   I don't remember. But—in the long run—I prefer winter to summer, don't you?

YOU:   Yes, I suppose so. That summer of 1967 really *got* me. All the electrical power in New York City went dead because so many people were using their air conditioners. Remember?

HE:   No, I don't. You see, I don't live here; I'm only visiting.

YOU:   Oh? Where do you live?

HE:   Paterson, New Jersey.

YOU:   Now where, exactly, is Paterson?

And you are again on the Garden State Parkway, but are you *getting* anywhere conversationally? A conversation is somewhat like an airplane flight; one of the danger points is the takeoff,[10] but you can't get anywhere without it.

## "Don'ts"

Here are some of the ways NOT to try to start conversing with a stranger—or anyone else, for that matter.

1. Don't try to start a conversation by talking about the weather, because it can't lead anywhere. It can only be wet or dry, windy or calm, hot or cold—and rarely, if ever, two of them at the same time! Besides, aren't you being subtly offensive to the other person by implying that the person can't tell the difference between hot and cold? There is a reason why people start conversations about the weather: if they want to be friendly, they try to find something in common, and all of us have the weather in common. Ken Hubbard says, "Don't knock the weather; nine-tenths of the people couldn't start a conversation if it didn't change once in a while."[11] So, unless fire is falling from the sky, try not to use the weather as an opener.

2. Don't start with a *cliché*, such as the traffic problem, the energy crisis, the difficulty of getting good domestic help, or the headlines in the current newspapers. Assume that the other person has read today's newspapers, and let it go at that, *unless* you can make it a challenge (more about that later). Once you have launched the conversation, any of these *clichés* may be mentioned, but they are not very imaginative as an opener.

3. Don't open a conversation with a stranger by complimenting his or her apparel. This is not only considered a breach of etiquette in some circles, but it is poor psychologically; people select clothes to make *themselves* attractive, not to show off the clothes. Women are said to be particularly sensitive about this. On the other hand, after you have become acquainted with a person, or upon meeting an old friend, it is perfectly proper to offer a compliment on his or her clothing.

However, you should word it carefully. Instead of saying to a woman, "What a pretty dress that is!" say, instead, "My! How pretty you look in that dress!" The same is true for a man; instead of telling him how handsome his outfit is, tell him how handsome he looks in it.

4. This really falls into the same category as number three: Don't—*please* don't!—tell a stranger that he or she reminds you of somebody else. It doesn't matter if you compare him or her to the most handsome man or the most beautiful woman in the world. People like to think of themselves as individuals and not as a "runner-up" to someone else.

My friend Elizabeth was the "spit image" of a famous television singer whom I shall call Aggie Lee. Elizabeth *detested* Aggie Lee, but she was mistaken for her wherever she went. The situation was made worse because Elizabeth's brother was a television announcer in one of the network studios in Burbank, California, and she often visited him.

> "I could have ruined the reputation of Miss Lee by being *real nasty* to all of those little brats who were constantly clamoring for autographs when I came into the building where my brother's studio was, but I can't bear to hurt a child." "What *did* you do?" I asked.
> "I finally gave up. I just scrawled, 'Your friend, Aggie Lee' across all of their autograph books. It didn't hurt me any, and it made them happy."
>
> —Hugh P. Fellows

5. Try not to start with a question. The word *try* is used here because at times there is no other recourse. Use a question only as a last resource. You have read in the dialogues presented earlier in this chapter how unproductive they can be; sometimes they can even be embarrassing because they give the impression that you are prying into the other person's private affairs. However, if you must open with a question, try *never* to let it be more than two in succession. If, after two questions, the other person doesn't respond, or you cannot find something on which to expand, sneak into another room and start talking with yourself.

## "Dos"

Having ruled out some of the most common ways to start a conversation, you may wonder if there are any left; of course there are! Following are some suggestions for opening a conversation, which you may find helpful. They are listed in the order the authors consider to be the weakest to the strongest, because the stronger ones require real courage. However, "nothing ventured, nothing gained."

1. You can always talk about your host or hostess; "Where did you meet Peter?" or "How long have you known Josie?" These are questions and are weak unless you can follow them up with an amusing account of your own first encounter with the host or hostess; it doesn't matter if you have to confess the truth, such as "Oh, Josie was playing the piano in a bordello in Kansas City when I met her," or "Pete and I were in jail together in a Mexican prison for smuggling."
2. Open with an observation about your surroundings. All living rooms—and most

offices and restaurants—contain objects that can be used as conversation pieces. The success of this approach depends upon your being able to make a definite, intelligent observation; it should never be vague, such as, "The color scheme in this room is nice, isn't it?" (That says nothing and leads nowhere.) Try to be specific:

> A. "What beautiful lines that Queen Anne sofa has! Do you like traditional furniture, Mr. Dinkeldorf?"
> Mr. Dinkeldorf may reply that he knows nothing whatsoever about furniture styles, but don't be discouraged. You have eliminated one fruitless subject of conversation. What is more important, you have revealed yourself as a perceptive person—someone who is always respected.
>
> B. "Is that Mozart playing on the stereo?"
> Be sure that the music isn't "Beat Me, Daddy, Eight to the Bar." Otherwise, you're safe. At some point, almost any classical composer sounds like Mozart!
>
> C. "Why on earth does Marie have that horror of an ormolu clock on her mantle?"
> When we suggested a pointed observation, we did not mean a *barbed* one. The person you're addressing probably *gave* Marie the ormolu clock; that's why it's there tonight! So, be careful . . .

3. Use a courtesy gesture: "Please, take this comfortable chair by the fire," "May I offer you a cigarette?" or, "Would you like me to hang your coat?" Do not overdo this; give the other person credit for being able to get around without crutches, and avoid fussing over that person unnecessarily.

   You can use the courtesy gesture in reverse by asking a slight favor of the stranger: "I'm sorry, but I seem to have left my cigarette lighter at home; may I have a light?" or, "I've never smoked Slaloms; may I have one of yours to see what they're like?" It should be a trivial favor that you ask; don't expect conversation to get off to a smooth start by trying to borrow twenty dollars from a new acquaintance! Here is a true experience that falls into this category of asking a slight favor:

   > Once I shared an apartment with an advertising man who was invited to many parties; often, I was included. He always wore interesting cuff links (made from the decorations from a Samurai sword belt, from ancient Greek coins, or designed by Peruvian goldsmiths, and so on), and on our way to a gathering I would observe him slyly unfasten one of his links. Soon after he had been introduced to a lady at the gathering, he would "discover" that his cuff was undone and politely ask the lady to fasten it for him. This trick apparently brought out the mother instinct in the lady, and the unusual nature of the cuff link always acted as a conversation piece. Whatever it was, that guy "made out" socially as no one else I have ever known! It was such a transparent, juvenile trick that I never dared use it, but *it worked!*

   —Hugh P. Fellows

4. Toss out a challenging statement. Earlier, we warned against using current newspaper headlines for opening a conversation, but that should be qualified. If you have a fresh point of view on a current topic, this can stimulate good talk. Try not to be vague ("What do you think about so-and-so?"); instead, state your point of view:

   > A. I've been following the Heatherington case, and I'm sure that he is innocent, in spite of all the circumstantial evidence. What are your views on the subject?

B. I'm concerned by the Government's announcement of [some policy]. What motivation do you suppose is behind that announcement?

In using a challenging statement as a conversation starter, it is important to remember that you are *not* doing it to start an argument. Nobody ever wins an argument. In sales jargon there is a truism, "Win an argument and lose a customer." On the other hand, you need not "pussyfoot" or "bootlick." Some of the most scintillating conversations we have ever heard have transpired among people who disagreed totally, but who respected the views of others.

Let us say that you express an opinion boldly, and Tim O'Connor retorts, "Oh, you're dead wrong! These are the facts in the matter . . ." and proceeds to enlighten you. What do you do?

You take Courage by one hand and Discretion by the other, and reply, "I've always thought differently because . . ." Be sure that you are *able* to state your views logically.

Mr. O'Connor is not likely to let you off the hook so easily; he will probably say that you are even *more* dead wrong and promptly tell you why. This is the boiling point—but keep your "cool." Remember, you are not Abraham Lincoln, locked in deadly debate with Stephen Douglas; you are a pleasant person, trying to make social conversation with a person who may be a slob. Ease out of the situation gracefully by murmuring, "It's an interesting point of view." Then, smiling, go and help yourself to some refreshment. There are more than two hundred million people in the U.S.A., and you do not have to get along with *all* of them!

5. The important thing in opening a conversation is that you hit upon a definite topic *early*. Barbara Walters[12] has a few suggestions that she regards as "sure fire" starters for a conversation. It's true that most of them are in the form of a question, but each question has a definite *topic* within it:

A. If you were hospitalized for three months but not really too sick, whom, and it can't be a relative, would you want in the bed next to you?

B. If you were not doing the work you are now doing, what would you most like to be doing?

C. If you could live any time in history, when would you wish to have lived?

D. If you could be any person in history, whom would you like to have been?

E. If you were suddenly given a million dollars and told that you had to spend it just on yourself, what is the first thing you would buy?

F. If your house were on fire, what *one* possession would you grab on your way out?

6. Open "cold" with a humorous story. This requires a high degree of intestinal fortitude,* but it is such a useful way of opening other people's fund of ideas that it is worth trying. Your story should be brief, amusing, and in good taste; above all, it should not be one that is "making the rounds" and that everyone has already heard. It does not have to be a joke that has appeared in print or on radio or television; actually, it is more effective to use a personal anecdote. Use something that has happened to you at work or on vacation.

Why is this such a valuable device? If you will think back to the last time you heard a good story, you will recall that it reminded you of (a) *another* story or

*In the vernacular, "guts."

(b) something that happened to you or your friends or family. This gets you and your conversation partner onto a definite topic, which is the gold nugget in a stream of good talk.

I have used this story-telling device for many years, but—being at heart a timid person—I confess that I introduce it with a little white lie. I usually preface it by saying, "On my way over here, the taxicab driver told me a story I hadn't heard before . . ." Or, I may start with, "Funny thing happened at work this afternoon . . ." The white lie is that I have *not* taken a taxicab to get where I am, and that the incident I relate may have happened months ago. My conscience does not bother me too much, because it almost always opens an animated conversation.

I must say "almost always," because I was once introduced to two beautiful women at a party and went immediately into what I considered a brilliant, brief and pithy anecdote. I was certain that it would convulse them with laughter. Neither of them so much as grinned; instead, the baby-blue eyes of one of the ladies turned to ice, and her voice was knife-like as she turned away with the comment, "I see you're one of those revolting little men who tell funny stories!" However, the law of averages will be with you, rather than against you, if you use this device.

—Hugh P. Fellows

Most of the foregoing suggestions have been mere devices. They are for the person who feels especially inadequate in social conversation. However, don't hesitate to use them if you need to. Don't be deterred by the fact that they have been printed in this book; everyone will not have read it. If you are detected using them by someone who *has* read the book, you can still have something in common, and have a glorious time throwing verbal brickbats at it! Remember, also, that no device will substitute for polite listening, having worthwhile ideas, and expressing those ideas with courtesy and consideration for your conversation partner.

## YOU'RE OFF!

Once you have survived the takeoff of our figurative airplane, how can you assure yourself and your companions of a smooth flight? The late Mrs. Ramsey Hunt, one of New York City's most charming and successful hostesses, gave this advice:

Conversation should not be like a golf game, where each player hits the same ball again and again (if he can find it), while another player hits another ball time and again (if *he* can find it!). It should be more like a tennis match, where the same ball is volleyed back and forth between the two players, or among four players, until a point is made. Who makes the point is not really important; the sport—and the fun—of the game is in giving everyone his chance at the ball.

### Take Your Responsibility

The old chestnut, "A good listener is a good conversationalist" is only half true. You may listen with bated breath and shining eyes while others talk for hours; then, when you say goodbye, the only impression you leave will be on the chair cushion where you sat. You should take part at least by asking questions (talkers dearly love questions!), or by expressing agreement or disagreement with the ideas voiced by others. However, you should have some ideas of your own, and should not hesitate in expressing them.

Think of conversation as a barrel of apples; you are invited to take as many as you can carry. However, after taking an apple, do not take another until someone else has had a chance at the barrel. Participate, but do not monopolize.

A reader who signed the letter "An Educational Therapist" wrote to Ann Landers protesting the fact that a gentleman who droned on and on in conversation, connecting each run-on sentence with "and–uh–", was the victim of a "verbal expression disability." This "enlightened educator" expressed disappointment that Landers had not been more compassionate.

Ann Landers replied: "I may be inadequate in some areas but lacking in compassion I am not. Sorry, dear, but there are more crashing bores around than people with 'verbal expression disabilities.' "

The column was headed "Non-Stop Talker is Still a Crashing Bore."(The Tampa Tribune, Feb. 6, 1977. Field Newspaper Syndicate. Used by permission.)

## Think!

While you are listening, try to think of a story or comment that will fit exactly the topic being discussed. This is fairly easy to do, since we *speak* at a rate of approximately 150 words per minute, while we *think* at rates of between 300 and 800 w.p.m. Use this differential to search your mind for some contribution. A "contribution," when the topic of conversation is outer space, should be something more important than the way you space the baby's feeding formula, or how your husband got "spaced-out" from booze at the country club last Saturday night. If you do not feel qualified to talk on such subjects as international politics, Existentialism, or nuclear physics, don't try to bluff; however, you can at least encourage others—if only with your body language—and you can ask questions if you've read a few current news magazines.

## Suspend Criticism

In previous chapters we have encouraged you to listen with a critical ear, especially in speeches of persuasion. In conversation you should be much more tolerant. In 1973 Gerard Nierenberg and Henry Calero wrote a book entitled *Meta-Talk: Guide to Hidden Meanings in Conversations*,[13] in which they labeled practically everybody with names such as *strokers, continuers, softeners, foreboders, convincers, pleaders, concealed aggressors,* and *downers,* purely because of words or phrases those people might use. More than 200 phrases are listed at the end of that book, which are supposed to contain hidden meanings— phrases as innocuous as, "dinner is almost ready," "from my point of view," "by the way," "how much will it cost me?" "just a minute," "May I ask a question?" "There are several approaches . . ." and even "You're welcome." Admittedly, many of those phrases are trite and can even be used sarcastically (what phrases *can't* be used thus?), but most of them are a part of our American idioms, and it seems unduly critical to try to find hidden meanings in them. In social conversation don't worry about a few trite expressions or a few wasted words at the expense of being suspicious of everyone you meet. It's like the old story of the two psychiatrists who got into an elevator at the same time. One said, "Good morning," and the other thought, "Now, what did he mean by that?"

Given enough exposure, the conniver, the special-interest pleader, and the old lecher will soon make themselves evident, but to prejudge a person because that individual uses one or more trite phrases is unjust and will succeed only in making you uncomfortable. Conversation should be *fun*.

## Keep Up with the Topic

Never try to exhaust a topic. Conversation is not a problem-solving conference, a seminar, or a workshop. When you observe one member of the group looking away furtively as if bored, or when you have to cudgel your brain to find something else to say on the topic, it is time for a change.

Speaking of changing the topic, one calamity is almost sure to befall you if you have many conversations with versatile people. Assume that you are in the midst of an animated conversation on the subject of jealousy. Suddenly you think of an aphorism so pithy that it is certain to make you the hit of the evening. You withhold this little gem until you can polish it to a superb brilliance. Then, just as you are ready to let go with, "Jealousy is always *born* with love, but it does not always *die* with it," you realize that some lowdown, conniving, son-of-a-pig has sabotaged you by changing the subject! The group is now talking about the old Mississippi River steamboats!

Do you remark, "Going back to the subject of jealousy, I'd like to . . ."? You do *not*. Just forget your[14] little gem for the time being. There will always be another occasion when you can use it. Grover C. Hall, the Pulitzer Prizewinning newspaperman, once said, "No good idea is lost forever." So, *don't try to revive a dead topic* in conversation.

On the other hand, *do* hold onto a topic if you see that some other member of the group is utterly engrossed in it. Suppose there are five of you discussing Extra-Sensory Perception (mental telepathy). Three of the others switch to a discussion of Federal banking laws, and you can tell that the fourth person is disappointed. Then, by all means, break away from the others and continue to talk with this fourth person about telepathy. In short, do not try to revive your *own* pet topic, but be on the alert for others who wish to continue a topic they were enjoying.

Groups of five or more people tend to break into smaller groups in conversation. Groups of three do not break up, because courteous people hesitate to exclude the third person. When groups of four break into two tête-à-têtes, they soon become self-conscious about their neglect of the other two and rejoin them. When a group exceeds four, however, the old bromide of "safety in numbers" no longer applies, and the group breaks up. This breakup often affords you an opportunity for a courtesy gesture—turn to the person who has not contributed at all to the larger group, and try to engage that person in conversation. If that individual's reticence to join the larger group has been his or her shyness, he or she will appreciate your concern.

## Encourage Others

George Gordon, Lord Byron (1788-1824) wrote:

> "Society is now one polished horde.
> Formed of two mighty tribes, the Bores and Bored."

Give "Lonely Lillian" a lift. In a lively conversation there is almost always one meek little mousy person who sits in a corner and says nothing. Do not wait until that person's silence becomes depressing; you can include him or her with no more effort than the question, "What's your opinion on this?" or, "Do you approve of John's solution?" Good conversation need not go at machine gun speed—silences are often golden and relaxing—but all of those present should be encouraged to join in. Strictly speaking, this is the duty of your host or hostess, but it's your responsibility also.

If "Lonely Lillian" appears so dull and unattractive that you hesitate to talk with her, reason with yourself: "If she has lived long enough to grow up without being drowned in the bathtub or run down by a taxicab, she must have a *little* gumption, so I'll give it a try." You may be pleasantly surprised.

Barbara Walters in her book[15] writes admiringly of the writer, Truman Capote, and the manner in which he handles bores:

> One of the reasons that Truman is always interested in people is that he won't allow himself to be bored . . .
>
> He catalogues thoughtfully the bore's face, his hair style, his mannerisms, his speech patterns. He tries to imagine how the bore feels about himself, what kind of a wife he might have, what he likes and dislikes. To get the answers, he starts to ask some of these questions aloud. In short, Truman gets so absorbed in finding out why he is bored that he is no longer bored at all.

You need not *over*burden yourself with responsibility for others. Observe people at the next large gathering you attend. You are certain to see one or two standing alone, holding a glass or a cup and looking utterly miserable, or wearing a frozen smile but making no human contact, and making no attempt at alleviating the loneliness of others. Sometimes their isolation is largely the result of self-centeredness.

> At a recent holiday party, given by an actress, I observed a young woman sitting by a doorway, clutching an empty glass with a woebegone expression on her face. After nearly half an hour, I dutifully sauntered over.

"May I get you a fresh drink?" I asked.

"No," she replied, with no "thank you" following.

"My name is Hugh Fellows. What's yours?

"Ellen."

"Are you in the theatre, Ellen?"

"Why do you want to know?" she countered sullenly.

"I *don't*, really. I don't give a damn!" I replied, as I moved over to a congenial group nearby.

—Hugh P. Fellows

Some people should never be allowed out of their kennels. But, people like this are the *exceptions*, rather than the rule.

### It's Your Move

When you have left a group of strangers, they should know more about you than the mere fact that you were *there*. You can interject yourself and your interests into a conversation without being pushy or overly aggressive. Suppose you have just asked a stranger about his or her profession or occupation (Remember, no more than two questions!); after he or she has responded, you need only to remark, "That's quite different from my work," or, "In a way that's similar to my occupation." If the stranger isn't a blithering idiot, he or she will ask you to tell more. You can also take advantage of a lull in the conversation by relating a curiosity-provoking incident connected with your occupation. From there you can move on to any topic on which you feel knowledgeable. Beware, however, of "taking too many apples." We can forgive others who bore us, but we can never forgive others who show that we bore them. (La Rochefoucauld)

## SOME PARTING SHOTS

Following are some random thoughts that are only indirectly related to the art and skill of conversation, but which seemed appropriate for this chapter.

### Remembering Names

When you are introduced to someone, why don't you remember his or her name? The reason is probably threefold: (a) The name is mumbled unintelligibly by the person introducing the two of you, (b) you are so occupied with looking over the stranger and "sizing up" him or her that you don't catch the name, or (c) you just don't care!

If you don't catch a stranger's name when being introduced, ask him or her to repeat it. This is far less embarrassing than calling the person "Er–uh" all evening. Once you are sure you have caught the name, spell it out mentally, and then take another look at the person to associate the name with the person.

*Use* the person's name the first two or three times you address that individual: "Mr. Supinsky, did you attend the community concert this afternoon?" Or, "No, Miss Burlington, I rather enjoyed his playing." If you do this, you will find that you can remember twenty or more names at any social gathering. Peculiarly enough, polysyllabic names, such as Ostrowsky and Berensen, are easier to remember than those containing a single syllable, such as Judd or Brown.

## Introductions

You know, of course, that the gentleman is always presented to the lady, and that a young person is always presented to an older one, except when the young person is of rare distinction. This, however, is not enough. If you can do it gracefully, you should give each person a little of the other's background:

> "Phyllis Randolph, this is Pat Houston [Or, 'Miss Randolph, may I present Mr. Houston?'] . . . Phyllis is food editor for *McSwain's Magazine*, Pat. Phyllis, Pat is an attorney who specializes in patents and copyrights."

If you are hesitant about giving their backgrounds in the presence of your two guests, you can brief each of them on others who will be present at the time you invite them. If your guest list is large, this may lead to confusion, so save this device for small gatherings.

If your gathering consists of more than a dozen people, do not introduce a newcomer to everyone at once. Instead, present him or her to two or three people, and leave the guest with them to chat for a few minutes. Then, ask the guest to meet a few more people. You do not need to be constantly pushing or shoving your guests from one group to another, but *you* should take the initiative in seeing that they mix with one another. If a stranger meets half a dozen people during the course of a large party, that is sufficient. Knowing whom you have invited and their interests, you should be able to associate the ones most likely to be congenial with one another.

## Large Parties

If you are giving a large party, do not line up chairs in a circle or square around the walls of the room. This is deadly for your guests, since it allows them no mobility. Instead, arrange your seating spaces in clusters of three or four.

If you do not have the space to do it *properly,* then do not give large parties. This means entertaining more often than if you try to repay all of your social obligations at once, but it also means more comfort and enjoyment for your guests.

One woman who gives successful parties invites people for dinner at least twice a week. She usually invites five people, three of whom already know one another; the other two are strangers to the first three. In this way she accomplishes two things: (a) The strangers find an atmosphere of friendly warmth already engendered by three friends who are completely at ease with one another, and (b) the three friends are provided with the stimulus of meeting someone new. This particular hostess declares that no intelligent dinner party should include more than ten guests. After all, if it's crowds you seek, you can always go to a baseball game—or take a bus during the rush hour!

## FOR YOUR FURTHER DEVELOPMENT

### The Seven-Day Plan

You certainly cannot change your personality or your ability to converse easily overnight. However, you can make some changes in your behavior over a period of time.

Try to check one of the following points each day for one week; if you find that your attitude is on the negative side, try to change *just one thing at a time* for *one day*, and see if you can maintain that one change for one week. At the end of the week, when you're trying to observe all seven points at once, you will begin to like yourself better. You have nothing to lose by doing this, and you may *gain* greatly!

### Negative Fact

1. I'm a poor conversationalist because I never bother to find anything new or interesting to say.

2. I can't be bothered with other people's problems. I know what *I'm* interested in, and that's all that matters.

3. What's there to laugh about in this rotten world? Telling jokes is for silly-minded people.

4. What other people say is not important to me; I don't have time to listen to their silly chatter.

5. I wear what I like; if others don't like it, that's *their* problem! These dirty old sneakers with holes in them are comfortable; that's all that matters.

6. What right has he or she to criticize me? What I do or say is none of their business.

7. I'm never wrong because I don't "shoot off my mouth" about things I don't *know*. I can always *prove* that I'm right!

### Positive Action

1. Spend at least thirty minutes daily reading one of the weekly news magazines from cover to cover.

2. Ask at least two people each day about their hobbies; listen to one person's troubles each day.

3. Try, just once a day, to make someone smile or laugh. Read the humor columns.

4. Just for one day, try to *listen* to others TWICE as long as you talk. *Time* yourself!

5. Check yourself in the mirror before going to the supermarket: Is your hair neat? Clothes clean?

6. Take just one criticism each day gracefully; try to *believe* that it's for your own good.

7. Try, once each day, to say, "Yes, you're right." Be quick to admit your own errors.

## SUGGESTED CLASSROOM EXERCISE

Divide the students into groups of five and have them simulate a social conversation. One or two students should be "host and hostess," and other roles may be assigned; or, the students may play their own roles. Allow ten minutes for each group to get into a conversation. The author has used this assignment with great success when an outsider is invited into the classroom.

## FOOTNOTES FOR CHAPTER FIFTEEN

[1] Alan Price, in a personal letter written to the author, April 25, 1963.

[2] Ralph Nichols and Leonard Stevens, *Are You Listening?* (New York: McGraw-Hill, 1957), p. 74.

[3] Robert Hutchins (1899-1978), educator and philanthropist; youngest president in history of University of Chicago; active in Ford Foundation; founder and president of Center Democratic Institutions.

[4] Dorothy Sarnoff, *Speech Can Change Your Life* (New York: Dell, 1970), p. 113.

[5] The person who wrote it was Anthony Hope (1863-1933), pen name of Anthony Hope Hawkins, English novelist and dramatist.

[6] Jean de La Bruyere (1645-1695).

[7] *The Bluffer's Guide* (New York: Crown, 1971).

[8] Barbara Walters, *How to Talk with Anybody about Practically Anything* (Garden City, N.Y.: Doubleday, 1970).

[9] Ibid.

[10] Hugh Fellows, *The Art and Skill of Talking with People* (Englewood Cliffs, N.J.: Prentice-Hall, 1964).

[11] Frank McKinley Hubbard (1868-1930), American humorist and cartoonist.

[12] Barbara Walters, *How to Talk with Anybody*, pp. 190–192.

[13] Gerard Nierenberg and Henry Calero, *Meta-Talk: Guide to Hidden Meanings in Conversation* (New York: Trident Press, 1973).

[14] Quote is from La Rochefoucauld (1613-1680), French moralist and composer of maxims and epigrams.

[15] Barbara Walters, *How to Talk with Anybody*.

# II | BUSINESS WRITING

# 16 | Business Writing —Basic Principles

When one writes poetry, much is left to the imagination; when one writes fiction, too many details are often included. In business writing, the reader wants *all* the facts but *only* the facts.
H.P.F

Peter Ustinov, the British writer, actor, and director, once said,[1] "There is no writing—even news reporting—that is not *slanted* in some way. The news reporter, even though he tries to be completely objective, slants his reports by what he omits or adds, or by his like or dislike of the people or issues involved. Even news photography is slanted to some degree . . . I once wrote a play about it."

It is true that journalists or fiction writers try to appeal to as broad a readership as possible. Their purpose may be merely to entertain, to provoke attention in order to popularize a cause, or to inform in a general way. They are judged by their ability to describe settings and characters vividly, to dramatize, and to manipulate the language into memorable phrases and quotable sentences.

On the other hand, business writers must write for *specific* and *limited* readers (often only one or two), and their purpose is to persuade their readers to accept a point of view, to help solve a problem, or to guide readers into certain courses of action. Whether or not the business writer succeeds or fails is judged by the *impact* and *usefulness* of the writing, and by the strategy of persuasion the writer employs.

240

So, while business writing is much more restricting and *demanding* than journalism (and, certainly equally difficult), it is no less *creative;* for example, copy written for an advertisement that sells millions of bottles of perfume, or the strategy that leads a manufacturer into taking on a product that may make millions of dollars for that firm.

The purpose of this chapter is to examine the basic principles that govern business writing. To help you remember them easily, they have been grouped under the acronym PACE, with the individual letters in the acronym representing Purpose, Accuracy, Clarity, and Expression. The last-named concerns your individual manner of expressing yourself—in short, your style of writing.

## PURPOSE

In public speaking we stress the importance of audience analysis; in discussions and conferences we stress knowing something about the group and who the individuals in that group represent. In writing—at least, most of the time— you are concerned with only one reader; the *individual* readers must grasp what is in your mind and what you want them to do about it. In *business* writing you must assume that you are communicating with a busy person; often that is the *only* assumption you can make safely. So, tell that person what your *purpose* is at the beginning of your communication.

In general, the purposes of business writing are for (a) getting or giving information, and (b) recommending, requesting, or ordering a course of action. There must be some reasons, or support, for each of those purposes. Early in your opening you should state your purpose; then in the paragraphs that follow, you may amplify the support for your purpose. By doing this, you help the busy reader to detect the purpose immediately, and to know what to look for in the body of your communication.

The company which manufactures Powerall, a dry cell battery of low voltage, has recently sent all of its retail outlets an attractive store display, showing the many and varied uses of Powerall. The displays are relatively expensive, and the Advertising Manager of Powerall has asked its salesmen/distributors to find out if the retailers are using the display; if not, why not? Figures 16-1 and 16-2 show two letters that the busy Advertising Manager received.

In Figure 16-1 you will note that the recommendation is buried in next to the final paragraph. In Figure 16-2 the recommendation is made in the very first sentence, and the reasons given later. The final paragraph is reserved for paying a compliment to the advertising department. A pat on the back for a job well done doesn't hurt!

There is a maxim among old-fashioned businessmen that no written communication should contain more than one item to be acted upon. This obviously cannot be the case when a memorandum contains several directions leading to a total result. It is acceptable to use the sentence, "My purpose in writing this is twofold", so long as whatever is twofold works for the *same purpose*. Beware, however, of cross-purposes; they can only cause confusion.

---

Dear Mr. Broomall:

You requested that, while making the rounds of the dealers in my territory, I get the reactions to the new advertising display which was shipped to them recently, and to inform you how many of the stores are actually using it. I am happy to comply.

Most of the retailers liked the picture of the assembled display, showing all of the different uses the Powerall Battery could be put to, but felt that it would take up too much space in their stores. You see, in the picture of the assembled display no measurements were given.

Some of the dealers thought that the directions for assembly were not clear, and that it would take too much time to assemble it. One particular complaint was that the picture of the display was too small for them to see how the batteries should be attached to it.

All of the stores I called on agreed that it was an attractive display, and would undoubtedly increase their sales of Powerall Batteries. Several of them commented that even *they* had not known before how many ways the Powerall Battery could be used. However, I found only two stores out of the fifty I visited who were actually using the display.

I understand that each of these displays costs the company about $50.00. If the stores are not going to use them, that means a lot of money wasted. If you shipped the advertising displays directly to the salesmen in each territory, and asked the salesmen to assemble them for the stores, I am sure that more stores would use them. The salesmen could also find a strategic spot for them. After all, it takes only 20 minutes to set up the display, and it covers only three feet of counter space.

If this suggestion is followed, I am sure it would work better than shipping the advertising display directly to the dealers.

Yours very truly,
Benjamin Dismukes

---

Figure 16-1

Dear Mr. Broomall:

I recommend strongly that you ship the new advertising display for Powerall Batteries directly to the salesman in each territory, and ask that the salesmen themselves assemble the display and set it up in stores which will accept it. The salesman should emphasize that the display uses only three feet of counter space, and can be set up on a small table at the end of an aisle in many stores.

Only two of the fifty stores in my territory were using the display, although every retailer admitted that it was attractive and believed that it would increase their sale of Powerall Batteries.

The reasons for not using it were:

1. The picture of the assembled display looked as if it might take up too much space.

2. The directions for assembly were too long and not very clear; they were sure that it would take too much of their time to set it up.

I took the time to study the assembly directions, and they are *not* very clear; however, after I got the hang of it, I found that I could assemble the display and attach the batteries to it in 15–20 minutes. While it may not be worth that amount of time to a retailer, it is certainly worth that small investment to a Powerall salesman.

It is an attractive display, and the designer of it should be congratulated!

Sincerely,
Curtis Gilgash

Figure 16-2

## ACCURACY

A written business communication must be accurate—not only in the facts it contains, but down to finest detail of format, grammar, spelling, and punctuation.

"I have a professional secretary, and she takes care of all the details such as grammar, spelling, and punctuation," business people sometimes say. Not truly *effective* business people! If you don't know more than your secretary, how can you tell when that secretary makes a mistake? Often the mere punctuation of a sentence can change its meaning.

> Example: When they had eaten another child, the youngest came over to the table.*
>
> Example: While you were out, your wife called. Your secretary said she would be in town shopping all afternoon, and that you should meet her for dinner at Chasen's.**

Archer and Ames[2] point out that an incorrect letter is actually discourteous; if you cannot take the trouble to be accurate, it is faintly insulting to the reader. The reader feels you might have gone to more trouble if you were writing to a more important person.

In the interest of accuracy, here are some practices to avoid:

**1.** Do not use words or phrases that are prejudiced:

"The irresponsible *Daily News*"
"The temperamental Miss Bangs"

**2.** Do not make concealed assumptions, such as, "If we cut prices, we can increase sales." In fact, be careful of all sentences that assume there is only one cause for a certain effect. (See the section in Chapter 18 on "Report Writing.")

**3.** Do not be illogical, particularly in using generalities, or placing individuals or facts within those generalities.

"This is a Roman Catholic firm, so they are apt to be against our manufacture of contraceptives."

"We have had unfortunate experiences with Ph.D.'s in the past, because they seem unwilling to accept a task that they feel is obviously beneath them."

"This prospective employee comes from an ultraconservative company in the midwest and is a member of the John Birch Society, so we should not expect innovative ideas from him."

You can test such illogicalities by referring to the sections of this text on inductive and deductive reasoning, and particularly by the use of the syllogism (see Chapter Thirteen).

As a college student, if you have deficiencies in grammar, punctuation, and spelling, this text will not help you. At the end of this chapter is a list of reference books that *will* help you in such matters.

---

*When they had eaten, another child—the youngest—came over to the table.

**While you were out, your wife called your secretary; said she would be in town shopping. . . . meet her for dinner at Chasen's.

## CLARITY

Carl Goeller[3] writes: "When someone asks you what time it is, don't tell him how your watch was made." We are tempted to equate clarity with brevity, but that is not logical; there are some ideas that require many words for clarification, and other ideas that are smothered under blankets of too many words.

"Make it *easy* for a reader to respond; make it *hard* for a reader to misunderstand."[4] This is the essence of all written (and spoken) business communication, but HOW CAN YOU DO IT?

*First,* define your *purpose* in writing and state it in the easiest and simplest words you can manage.

*Second,* jot down all of the support for your purpose that you can think of.

*Third,* examine all of your support sentences to see if (a) two or more of them can be condensed into one sentence, or (b) two or more of them can act as subtopics for another support sentence. You are now beginning the process of organization and condensation.

*Fourth,* examine *all* sentences to see if (a) you can shorten them, and (b) if you can substitute a simpler word for one that is more complex.

*Finally,* organize each paragraph around a topic sentence.

### The Topic Sentence

The topic sentence is the backbone of the paragraph, and a paragraph can have only one backbone. In its simplest form it is placed either at the beginning or the end of the paragraph.*

When placed at the beginning of a paragraph, the topic sentence tells the reader what is to follow. The remaining sentences give details.

When placed at the end of the paragraph, the topic sentence summarizes what the other sentences have said, often with a recommended course of action.

Simple, isn't it?

It is not so simple in practice. After many years of familiarity with business communications, the authors have found that the chief barrier to understanding is lack of organization and obscure wording. If you will refer to the letters concerning Powerall Batteries, presented earlier in this chapter, you will find that the first letter has almost no organization, while the second is fairly well organized. Examine them closely for the sentences that have been added or omitted in the two letters. Although the recommendation is the same in each letter, the *attitudes* of the two salesmen are different. For example, in the second letter Gilgash doesn't give a hang about how much money the company

---

*In some sophisticated writing, the topic sentence may be placed in the middle of the paragraph, with information leading up to it, and further information coming out of it, as in the process of inductive and deductive reasoning.

wastes on the advertising display; he is more interested in increasing his own sales and is willing to invest some time in doing so. He also praises the company for helping him.

Following are two rather simple paragraphs, demonstrating how the topic sentence can be used at either the beginning or the end. You will note that when it is placed at the end, a short transitional phrase is needed.

1. Bicarbonate of soda (plain baking soda) has more home uses than any other substance we can think of. Aside from cooking, have you ever tried sprinkling it on your carpets before vacuuming, to remove odors? It works just as well as the more expensive, perfumed powders. An opened box of it, placed in your refrigerator or home freezer, will absorb odors for several weeks and can then be poured down the sink drains to "sweeten" them. When used for washing cooking utensils, it has no aftermath of detergent taste and is especially useful in removing the oils and acids that accumulate inside a coffee pot that is used every day. Baking soda will remove coffee or tea stains from the finest china cups without damaging their surface. While on the subject of stains, baking soda will remove surface stains from teeth and dentures. For people who are allergic to commercial underarm deodorants, baking soda—used sparingly—works very efficiently. For minor insect bites (ants, mosquitoes, bees, and wasps), a paste made of baking soda and water will relieve the stinging sensation almost immediately. What is even more appealing, it is one of the few items on the shelves of supermarkets that has not skyrocketed in price during this time of inflation.

2. Bicarbonate of soda (plain baking soda) is one of the few items on the shelves of supermarkets that has not skyrocketed in price during this time of inflation. Aside from cooking, have you ever tried sprinkling it. . . .

[The rest of the sentences in the paragraph remain the same. We have eliminated "What is even more appealing" from the final sentence, now at the top of the paragraph, and have added only two words to the topic sentence at the end.]

In short, bicarbonate of soda (plain baking soda), has more home uses than any other substance we can think of.

All topic sentences are not as easily displaced at the beginnings and ends of paragraphs as the one illustrated here. However, we have tried to show you how logical, factual writing proceeds.

## Word Fodder

Fodder is used in feeding farm animals (cows and horses). It has little nutritive value, but it fills the bellies of large animals and gives them a sense of well-being. However, it has no place on the pages of business writing; everything there should have meaning (nutrition). Many of us are guilty of using "word fodder" now and then, and it is one of the chief enemies of clarity in writing.

For instance, why write, "a substantial segment of the population," when "many people" says the same thing? Or, why say, "I have duly noted the contents of your letter," when "I have read your letter" will serve? As a matter of fact, if you are replying to someone's letter, you have obviously read it! Why do so many business people insist on writing, "in the normal course of our procedure," when "normally" expresses the same meaning?

Here are a few more expressions that contain "word fodder," alongside shorter expressions which say the same thing; there are others at the end of this chapter:

| *Why use this . . . . . . . . when this will do?* | |
| --- | --- |
| At your earliest convenience | As soon as you can |
| I enclose my check in the amount of | I enclose my check for |
| In the event that | If |
| Pursuant to your request | As you requested |
| Permit me to take this opportunity | I want to |

Many expressions containing "word fodder" are actually ungrammatical or poor usage. Here are a few examples:

| *Poor* | *Better* |
| --- | --- |
| Consensus of opinion | Consensus (means the *same* as both of |
| General consensus | the others) |
| Adequate enough | Adequate |
| Disappear from sight | Disappear |
| In close proximity | Near |
| Penetrate into | Penetrate |
| Protrude out of | Protrude |
| Very unique | Unique (If something is unique, it can't be "very," any more than a woman can be just a "little bit" pregnant!) |

## Simple versus Complex Words

Words are marvelous! In the English language they can express the finest shade of meaning where emotions, actions, or conditions are concerned. In journalism and in fictional writing the author is dependent upon the *connotation* of a word almost as much as upon its *denotation*. This is also true in business writing, but not to such a degree; *clarity* is the most important ingredient. So, in the following list of words, it is suggested that you use the words in the *right-hand* column, instead of those in the left-hand column. There are others at the end of this chapter.

| *Instead of this word, . . . use this word* | |
| --- | --- |
| Abrasion | Scratch |
| Acquiesce | Agree |
| Ambiguous | Not clear |
| Augmentation | Increase |
| Commodious | Roomy |
| Debilitate | Weaken |
| Disentangle | Free |
| Edifice | Building |

*Instead of this word, . . . use this word*

| | |
|---|---|
| Elucidate | Explain |
| Fallacious | Misleading |
| Impecunious | Poor |
| Indigent | Needy |
| Jocular | Funny |
| Lugubrious | Sad |
| Masticate | Chew |
| Mendacious | Lying / false |
| Nutriment | Food |
| Obdurate | Stubborn |
| Orifice | Opening / hole |
| Parsimonious | Stingy |
| Polemic | Argument against |
| Promulgate | Promote |
| Pusillanimous | Changeable / cowardly |
| Ruminate | Ponder |
| Sagacious | Wise |
| Sinecure | Easy job |
| Tertiary | Third |
| Vitreous | Glassy |

## Number or Label Specific Details

In business writing it is important that your readers know what is expected of them; therefore, you should always enumerate or caption items, if there are more than two or three. Following is a paragraph from a sales manager to a new salesman on the road:

> You're doing a fine job, Claude, but you must remember to indicate which of the States you made calls in; there are towns in Nebraska, Iowa, and Kansas, all with the names of "Elgin." Don't forget the zip codes of each. When you are calling on dealers, it's a good idea to look up their record of payments in the report that is sent to you each month. Old man Billings' account is two months past due, yet you took his order for $2,000 worth of additional merchandise. He's a fine old man, but he does forget to pay his bills on time. Be tactful about it, but it won't hurt to remind him. The same thing is true of Mrs. Mulgrave in Joshua County. I love that territory you now have, because that's where I started out. I particularly like Judson Wilkerson (Have you ever seen a neater store?), but I've just received a letter complaining that his shipment arrived four days late. We sent out a letter to all of our customers that the *guaranteed* date of delivery is now ten days instead of one week, but maybe you'd better remind them of the change. Don't forget to give my special regards to Ms. Grace Kynes the next time you call on her. Now, *that's* one spunky lady!*

While one may admire the fine spirit of camaraderie between the sales manager and his salesmen on the road, Claude will have to read the letter

*Used by permission; all true identities have been withheld.

carefully again to find the three things he is supposed to do. A business letter can be friendly without so much chit-chat. Notice how much clearer—and shorter—the following paragraph is:

> You're doing a fine job, Claude, but there are many details to it. Here are three you have overlooked occasionally:
>
> 1. Since there are towns in all three states with the same name, "Elgin," it is important that you indicate the state and the zip code on all of your orders.
>
> 2. A list of our customers who are delinquent in payment is sent to you each month. Check the list before calling on your clients. Most of them have good credit ratings, but a gentle reminder in person will help. If you can do it tactfully, get their past-due checks at the time you take their order for new merchandise.
>
> 3. Although we sent out letters to all of our customers explaining that *guaranteed* delivery is now ten days instead of one week, some of them have forgotten it. Please remind them of this until new order forms can be printed.
>
> Your territory is where I first started with the company, and I love the people there. Please give my warm regards to those who remember me.

As for labeling, you need only turn through the preceding pages in this chapter to realize that all major topics are headed with a label. This is often necessary in lengthy writing; it helps your reader find things quickly for reference.

## EXPRESSION (STYLE)

Style is the way you express yourself, as opposed to the way others express themselves. It is an elusive quality and can be acquired only after examining the writings of others and working on your own writing to see how it can be improved. Although style is difficult to define, there are techniques that can be examined and learned for improvement.

Reexamine the foregoing paragraph. It is almost totally lacking in style. Why? Because all of the sentences are long, and they are all about the same length. Try to vary your sentences—not only in length, but also in structure. Here are two more paragraphs for you to examine:

> A. In talking with a prospect, try to project yourself into his position so that you will understand him more completely. If you can obtain some knowledge of his situation, insofar as his problems and ambitions are concerned, you may be able to establish *rapport* with him. Most people have a considerable number of things in common, and this communality can operate favorably for you, if given the opportunity.
>
> B. In talking with a prospect, put yourself in his place. What are his present problems? What are his ambitions? Most of us have at least a few things in common. Try to find out what interests you and your prospect share; this will give you a sense of *rapport*, and will work in your favor.

Is there any doubt as to which of the foregoing paragraphs reads better? In paragraph "A" you will certainly discover some "word fodder" that could be eliminated. So, to review the first point of developing your style, we have come up with:

I. *Vary the length of your sentences and also their structure.*

[Notice that we have placed our "topic sentence" at the *end*, rather than at the beginning.]

II. *Use synonyms in a sentence,* to avoid monotony, provided they have exactly the same meaning.

The English language has such a rich variety of synonyms that varying your choice of words is no problem. All you need is a paperback thesaurus.

In the following paragraph do you get the idea that the writer was in love with the word *present* in several forms?

> Those present at the Sales Convention of Forewax enjoyed several pleasures which were missed by those not present. One of the highlights came when the Four Aces presented some songs from their latest album, which represented their third Gold Record. Another highlight came with our president's presenting an award of distinguished service to Al Kurtz, representing twenty years of outstanding sales on Kurtz's part. In presenting the award, President Albee said, "This represents not only a sales record, but also a fine presentation of the Forewax Company's image."

The combination of the letters *p-r-e-s-e-n-t* was used nine times in five sentences. Let us try a rewrite, avoiding that combination of letters altogether:

> Those attending the Sales Convention of Forewax enjoyed several treats. Among them were the Four Aces, who sang numbers from their third Gold Record album. Another highlight came when President Albee awarded Al Kurtz a trophy for twenty years of outstanding sales. In making the award, President Albee said, "Not only has Al Kurtz been our top salesman for twenty years; he has also upheld constantly the high image of the Forewax Company."

The second paragraph is sixteen words shorter. It also avoids an absurd bit of "word fodder" in the clause "which were missed by those not present." (Of course they missed the "pleasures" if they were not present!)

III. *Write actively, not passively.* Somehow, long ago, someone in authority confused the meanings of the words "objectivity" and "impersonality"; so, people in business and government have been writing *inhumanely* ever since! Most business writing *should* be objective and impartial, but not necessarily impersonal. In all writing, we are communicating with *people,* not objects. It sometimes seems that the cowardly, irresponsible person hides behind passive writing, such as, "the contents of your letter have been duly studied." By whom? Why not be brave and write, "I have studied the contents of your letter"?

Here are more examples of passive writing that would be more effective if written in the active voice:

|          *Passive*          |          *Active*          |
|-----------------------------|----------------------------|
| Experience has indicated that . . . | We learned that . . . |
| A statement of the financial condition of the company should be set forth by the treasurer. | The treasurer should make a statement on the financial condition of the company. |
| This meets with our approval. | We approve of this. |
| Avoidance of the problem should be sought by us. | We should avoid the problem. |
| An apple was eaten and the newspaper was read while I waited. | I ate an apple and read the newspaper while I waited. |

Those final examples are no more ridiculous than some encountered in serious business and governmental writing. So, don't hide behind a wall of passively written words. As the Scriptures suggest, "let your yea be yea, and your nay, nay."

(James 5:12)

IV. *Try it on yourself.* When you have written something, look it over and ask yourself, "What would my reactions be if I received this writing from somebody else?" Is its purpose clear? Is it accurate? Can I understand it? Does it sound as if some person wrote it to some other person? Or, does it sound as if it were manufactured by a machine, for consumption by another machine?

Many professors and textbooks on writing advise trying to write as one talks. The authors do not subscribe to this: First, because some people talk in a rambling, disjointed, and boring way. Second, because scholars have pointed out that there is a definite difference between the style of writing and the style of speaking.[5] Yet the "write-as-you-talk" advocates have some evidence in their favor.

For decades government agencies (including the armed forces) have been derided for written communications that were filled with verbosity, pomposity, and obscurity. Credit must be given to the heads of those same agencies for their valiant attempt at persuading their subordinates of the value of writing clearly and without pretentiousness. More than twenty years ago the General Services Administration of the Federal Government issued a handbook with a section on "Plain Letters," which deplored pompous writing. From the Bureau of Naval Weapons, one of the most bureaucratic of all agencies, comes this statement from its October, 1962, *Bulletin:*

Our biggest problem in communications is that you're there and we're here! We'd have no problem if we could all get together and talk whenever we wanted to. But we can't do that so we have to resort to writing to "talk" to each other.

At best, writing is a poor substitute for talking. But the closer our writing comes to conversation, the better our exchange of ideas will be. And when you think how 99% of the Bureau's business is conducted by the written word you realize how important it is to write as simply, clearly, and directly as you can. We have a job to do, and we have an obligation to be intelligible to each other.

Clear writing doesn't just happen; it takes practice to say exactly what you mean in the fewest possible words. But you owe it to your readers to make the effort . . . So, when you write to us, don't hesitate to say "you" and refer to yourself as "we." You don't need to tell us that you are "the station" and we are "the Bureau." The shorter word is always the better one. It's easier to read and sounds more natural than the longer one.

Oh, we know your first reaction to this: "Look who's talking about direct, conversational correspondence!" But just because we bureaucrats have always been accused of gobbledygook doesn't mean that we couldn't change with the right encouragement. "Talk" to us in your letters. Who knows? We may even "talk" back!

If we were stricter English pedagogs, we could probably find several things to criticize about the foregoing passage, such as fragmentary sentences and starting a sentence with a conjunction, but it *says* something, and says it with style.

V. *Avoid using clichés when possible*. This is almost in the nature of a footnote, because this text does not attach as much importance to it as many books and teachers of writing do. Of course you should avoid trite expressions and tired figures of speech when you can, but who can always invent a pithy bit of wisdom and wit on the spur of the moment? Marvin G. Gregory, the former editor of *The Economic Press Magazine,* has this to say about clichés:

Some people are quick to condemn clichés, but what is a cliché? It is a truth that has retained its validity through time. Mankind would lose half its hard-earned wisdom, built up patiently over the ages, if it ever lost its clichés.[6]

Our primary concern is that you do not use *too many* of these tried and true [Oops!] expressions, because such practice shows that you are not thinking of your reader—or are not thinking at all—but are simply stringing words together.

Here are some of the threadbare expressions that are common in business writing. Avoid them when you can:

| | |
|---|---|
| According to our records | Keep our options open |
| Allow me to state | This letter is for the purpose . . . |
| Attached please find | Under separate cover |
| Dictated but not read (This is insulting!) | We would ask that |
| | We wish to advise |
| Esteemed favor | Words are inadequate |
| In due course | Worse for wear |

To close this chapter, we can think of no finer advice than that offered by Alfred E. Kahn, when he was appointed as Chairman of the Civil Aeronautics Board:

*MEMORANDUM*

TO:    Bureau and Office Heads
Division and Section Chiefs

CC:    Board Members

FROM:    Chairman Alfred E. Kahn

SUBJECT:    The Style of Board Orders and Chairman's Letters

One of my peculiarities, which I must beg you to indulge if I am to retain my sanity (possibly at the expense of yours!) is an abhorrence of the artificial and hyper-legal language that is sometimes known as bureaucratese or gobbledygook.

The disease is almost universal, and the fight against it is endless. But it is a fight worth making, and I ask your help in this struggle.

May I ask you, please, to try very hard to write Board orders and, even more so, drafts of letters for my signature, in straightforward, quasi-conversational, humane prose—as though you are talking to or communicating with real people. I once asked a young lawyer who wanted us to say "we deem it appropriate" to try that kind of language out on his children—and if they did not drive him out of the room with their derisive laughter, to disown them.

I suggest the test is a good one: try reading some of the language you use aloud, and ask yourself how your friends would be likely to react. (And then decide, on the basis of their reactions, whether you still want them as friends.)

I cannot possibly in a single communication give you more than a small fraction of the kinds of usages I have in mind. Here are just a few:

1. One of our recent show-cause orders contained this language: "all interested persons <u>be and they hereby</u> are directed to show cause..." The underlined words are obviously redundant, as well as archaic.

2. Every time you are tempted to use "herein," "hereinabove," "hereinunder," or similarly, "therein" and its corresponding variants, try "here" or "there" or "above" or "below" and see if it doesn't make just as much sense.

3. The passive voice is wildly overused in government writing. Typically, its purpose is to conceal information: one is less likely to be jailed if one says "he was hit by a stone," than "I hit him with a stone." The active voice is far more forthright, direct, and human. (There are, of course, some circumstances in which the use of the passive is unavoidable; please try to confine it to those situations.)

4. This one is, I recognize, a matter of taste: some people believe in maintaining standards of the language and others (like the late but unlamented editor of Webster's *Third International*) do not. But unless you feel strongly, would you please try to remember that "data" was for more than two thousand years and is still regarded by most literate people as plural (the singular is "datum"), and that (this one goes back even longer) the singular is "criterion," and "criteria" is plural. Also, that for at least from the 17th through most of the 20th century, "presently" meant "soon" or "immediately" and not "now." The use of "presently" in the latter context is another pomposity: why not "now?" Or, if necessary, "currently?"

5. Could you possibly try to make the introduction of letters somewhat less pompous than "this is in reference to your letter dated May 42, 1993, regarding (or concerning, or in regard to, or with reference to)..." That just doesn't sound as though it is coming from a human being. Why not, for example, "The practice of which you complain in your letter of May 42 is one that has troubled me for a long time." Or "I have looked into the question you raise in your letter of October 14, and am happy to report.." Or something like that?

6. Why use "regarding" or "concerning" or "with regard to," when the simple word "about" would do just as well? Unless you're trying to impress someone: but are you sure you *want* to impress anyone who would be impressed by such circumlocutions? There is a similar pompous tendency to use "prior to," when what you really mean is "before." "Prior to" should be used only when in fact the thing that comes before is, in a sense, a condition of what follows, as in the expression "a prior condition."

I know "requesting," is considered more genteel than "asking," but "asking" is more forthright. Which do you want to be?

7. One of my pet peeves is the rampant misuse of "hopefully." That word is an adverb, and makes sense only as it modifies a verb, and

means "with hope." It is not possible to walk hopefully into a room, if one is going into the room with the hope of finding (or *not* finding) something there. It is not intelligent to say "hopefully the criminal will make his identity known," because the meaning is not that he will do so with hope in *his* heart, and *he* is the subject of the verb "make."

8. My last imposition on you for today is the excessive use of "appropriate" or "inappropriate," when what the writer really means is either "legal" or "illegal," "proper" or "improper," "desirable" or "undesirable," "fitting" or "not fitting," or simply "this is what I want (or do not want) to do."

9. A final example of pomposity, probably, is this memorandum itself.

I have heard it said that style is not substance, but without style what is substance?

## SUPPLEMENT A—"WORD FODDER"

In the left-hand column below are a number of expressions which can be shortened by using the word(s) in the right-hand column:

*Why use this, . . . . . when this will serve?*

| | |
|---|---|
| Accompanied by | With |
| Afford an opportunity | Allow |
| After very careful consideration | After considering |
| Apropos of the above | Regarding / concerning |
| At this point in time | At the moment / now |
| At the present writing | "     "     "     " |
| Due to the fact that | Because |
| If doubt is entertained | If doubtful |
| In a most careful manner | Carefully |
| It is often the case that | Often |
| Make an adjustment in | Adjust     (The expressions |
| Make an approximation of | Estimate     on the left |
| Make an examination of | Examine     are like weeds |
| Make mention of | Mention     in a garden! |
| Make the acquaintance of | Meet     Poor usage!) |
| Minimize as far as possible | Minimize |
| Never before in the past | Never before |
| Of the order of magnitude | About     (We, the authors love these |
| Of considerable magnitude | Large     pomposities!) |

| | |
|---|---|
| Prior to | Before |
| Pursuant to your request | As you requested |
| Take into consideration | Consider |
| Taking this factor into consideration, it is apparent that . . . | Therefore, it seems . . . |
| Within the realm of possibility | Possibly |

## SUPPLEMENT B—LONG WORDS VERSUS SHORT WORDS

Unless you have a specific connotation which you wish your words to convey, you will find that the short word (right-hand column) will do the job—and be clearer to your readers—than the long one (left-hand column).

| | |
|---|---|
| Actuate | Move / put into action |
| Altercation | Dispute |
| Approbation | Praise / approval |
| Bellicose | Warlike |
| Cessation | Stop / pause |
| Contusion | Bruise |
| Defunct | Dead |
| Engender | Breed / cause |
| Imbue | Fill |
| Ingenious | Clever ⎫ Often confused in usage and |
| Ingenuous | Innocent / frank ⎬ spelling |
| Internecine | In-fighting / conflict within a group |
| Malevolence | Spite |
| Meritorious | Worthy |
| Obsequious | Boot-licking / fawning |
| Pariah | Outcast |
| Parlance | Talk |
| Primordial | Primitive |
| Propitiate | Appease |
| Quadrilateral | Four-sided |
| Recondite | Obscure |
| Supercilious | Proud |
| Tripartite | Three-part |
| Vacuous | Empty |

## SUGGESTED CLASSROOM EXERCISES

1. Your instructor may ask you to write a paragraph (approximately 100–150 words) on some activity in which you have participated, or some observation you have made, during the past twenty-four hours. He will collect the paragraphs but will not correct them. After one week he will return the papers to you and ask you

to judge your own paper in the light of what you have learned about writing. This can be of great value in your training as a writer.

2. You may be asked to develop, outside of class, two paragraphs on any subject you choose; (a) one in which the logical place for the topic sentence is at the beginning of the paragraph, and (b) the other in which the logical place for the topic sentence is at the end.

## BIBLIOGRAPHY FOR THE *MECHANICS* OF BUSINESS WRITING

ANNA ECKERSLEY-JOHNSON and ANNE H. SOUKHANOV, eds., *Webster's Secretarial Handbook* (Springfield, Mass: G. and C. Merriam Co., 1976).

MARJANE CLOKE and ROBERT WALLACE, *The Modern Business Letter Writer's Manual* (Garden City, N. Y.: Doubleday, 1969).

JULIUS ELFENBEIN, *Handbook of Business Form Letters and Forms* (New York: Simon and Schuster, 1972).

WILLIAM F. IRMSCHER, *The Holt Guide to English* (New York: Holt Rinehart and Winston, 1976).

GREVILLE E. JANNER, *The Business Man's Guide to Letter Writing and to the Law on Letters* (Boston: Cahners Books, 1970).

PORTER G. PERRIN and JIM W. CORDER, *Handbook of Current English* (Glenview, IL: Scott, Foresman and Co., 1975).

MARIE M. STEWART, and others, *College English and Communication* (New York: McGraw-Hill, 1975).

See also the pages indicated in the following books, which have sections on formats, punctuation, grammar, spelling, and usage.

ROBERT M. ARCHER and RUTH P. AMES, *Basic Business Communications* (Englewood Cliffs, N. J.: Prentice-Hall, 1971), pp. 173–230.

WILLIAM H. BONNER, *Better Business Writing* (Homewood, Ill.: Richard D. Irwin, Inc., 1974), pp. 393–461.

LELAND BROWN, *Effective Business Report Writing,* 3rd. ed. (Englewood Cliffs, N. J.: Prentice-Hall, 1973), pp. 411–433.

## FOOTNOTES FOR CHAPTER SIXTEEN

[1]From personal interview conducted by author at the Haymarket Theatre, Chicago, June 2, 1975. The play referred to is *A Portrait of King Lear.*

[2]Robert M. Archer and Ruth P. Ames, *Basic Business Communications* (Englewood Cliffs, N. J.: Prentice-Hall, 1971), p. 21.

[3]Carl Goeller, *Writing to Communicate* (Garden City, N. Y.: Doubleday, 1974), p. 94.

[4]Norman G. Shidle, *The Art of Successful Communication* (New York: McGraw-Hill, 1965) p. 104.

[5]Gladys Borchers, in her doctoral dissertation at the University of Wisconsin, described eighteen of these differences as far back as 1932. Other scholars since then have substantiated her descriptions.

[6]Marvin P. Gregory, from *The Economics Press Magazine,* "Bits and Pieces," quoted in *Reader's Digest,* July, 1980, 117: 699, p. 170. Used by permission.

# 17 | Job Applications, Resumés, and References

Experience is not what happens to a man. It is what a man does with what happens to him.

Aldous Huxley (1894–1963)

For purposes of continuity, this chapter assumes that you are not yet ready to handle internal or external correspondence for your business firm, but are first interested in *getting* the job. This text is concerned with your *career* job rather than a temporary one. For such a purpose, a certain amount of writing must be done: an application for an interview, a resumé, and references. Your resumé is a history of your education or training, and your past employment record. Other items may be included, as you will see on reading further.

Some job seekers duplicate their resumés and send them out to a large number of firms in which they are interested, on the blind chance that their resumé will be impressive enough to obtain an interview for them. Others send out short letters of application, with just enough information about themselves to warrant getting an application from a company. If the company is interested, it may ask for a more complete resumé and mail the sender an application form to complete; or, it may send only the application form and ask that it be returned before granting an interview. In the latter case the applicant would take along at least two copies of his or her resumé when the interview is granted.

Authorities disagree[1] on whether a short letter or a complete resumé should be sent, but the authors of this text advise sending a short letter first. The application letter should be brief, but should include the following:

1. Special qualifications that may be useful to your prospective employer,
2. Some *particular* skill or accomplishment that shows initiative or ingenuity, and
3. A request for an interview.

You should know, at least, what department or division you wish to work in (such as sales, production, or office work). The message is essentially the same (see Figure 17–1).

If you are applying for a position that you know is definitely open, you should tell how you learned about the opening and give a few more personal details (see Figure 17–2).

---

(Your address
and the date)

(Name and address of the firm)

Dear Personnel Director:

Do you anticipate an opening in the Production Division of your company in the near future? If so, I should like to apply for it.

I shall receive my B.S. degree in Industrial Engineering from the University of South Florida in June.

My work experience, which has been part time during the academic year and full time during the summers, has been as follows:

1974–1976: Bottling-machine operator and "trouble-shooter," Coca-Cola Bottling Plant, Chamblee, Ga.
1976–1978: Assistant supervisor, labeling and shipping departments, Continental Can Company, Tampa, Fla.
1978–Present: Assistant to Quality Control Director, Mr. Herman Schmidt, Anchuser-Bush Brewery, Tampa, Fla.
In January, 1979, I devised a system whereby the mash-cooling process could be shortened by twelve hours, a system that is still being used by Anchuser-Bush.

I shall telephone to ask for an interview on May 5th. [Two days after the letter is mailed.]

Sincerely,

---

Figure 17–1

Dear Mr. _____: [You should *know the name!*]

My current supervisor, Mr. Herman Schmidt, has told me that Anchuser-Bush is opening a new plant in Wilmington, Delaware, and has suggested that I apply for the position of Production Supervisor in your brewery.

I shall receive my B. S. Degree in Industrial Management from the University of South Florida in June. During the summers I have worked full time for Anchuser-Bush, and part time during the academic years, from 1978 to the present.

In January, 1979, I observed that twelve hours could be saved in Anchuser-Bush's mash cooling process (a result of my time-motion studies at the University). I suggested this to Mr. Schmidt, and it was put into effect and is still being used, at a considerable saving to the brewery.

My previous work experience has always been part time during the school year and full time in the summer months, since my second year in high school, and is as follows:

1974–1976: Bottling-machine operator at Coca-Cola Bottling Plant, Chamblee, Georgia. Later I was assigned as a "troubleshooter" because of my knowledge of machine operations.

1976–1978: My family moved to Tampa, and I worked at Continental Can Company in the labeling department. It was unskilled labor, and I asked for a transfer to the shipping department, where I had heard there were problems. I learned a great deal about handling personnel from my supervisor, Mr. Speakerman, and am very grateful for the things he taught me. I left Continental Can and found a job with Anchuser-Bush only because it was so much nearer my home and the University. I had no idea I would like it so well!

I am a hard worker, not afraid to get my hands dirty, and have a deep loyalty toward Anchuser-Bush. I have talked this over with Mr. Schmidt, and he says I am now ready for a position as Production Supervisor, and will recommend me for the position in Wilmington.

I shall telephone to ask for an interview on May 5th.

Sincerely,

Figure 17–2

Suppose you do not have an "in" with a company supervisor such as Herman Schmidt? The training director of one of America's largest conglomerates has kindly furnished us with this letter of application and brief resumé (see Figure 17–3), which impressed the parent company so favorably that the applicant was granted an interview and hired:*

You will note that this young lady is not overly modest. Nor should *you* be, if you can back up your claim. You will note that the letter, as well as the brief resumé that accompanied it (see Figure 17–4), are not targeted *specifically* at Larrapee, Inc. They could serve equally well for *any* other firm where Tracy Budd wanted to apply for a position as management trainee. Indeed, she probably sent out at least a dozen of both the letter and the *resumé* to various

---

Ms. Tracy Budd
24 South St.
Palo, Texas, 77429
(573) 777-9275

May 10, 198–

Mr. Jack Nostaw
Larrapee, Inc.
400 Pecos Street
Houston, Texas

Dear Mr. Nostaw:

PLEASE DON'T FILE ME AWAY! I am a recent Honors graduate of Teco University, seeking a position as a management trainee where my creativity, problem-solving and organizational abilities can be developed and applied. I would appreciate your reviewing my résumé and taking note of my accomplishments (which include research for a published survey).

I believe that with the talents I offer, I can be an asset to your organization.

I look forward to meeting you in person to discuss the possibility of my employment with your firm.

Yours truly,

Tracy Budd

---

Figure 17–3

*All names have been changed, but the texts are an exact copy.

Ms. Tracy Budd
24 South St.
Palo, Texas, 77429
(573) 777-9275

POSITION DESIRED: Management trainee

EDUCATION: Received B. A. degree with Honors in Psychology from Teco University, Palo, Texas, in June, 1980. Taught introductory psychology to lower classmen in my senior year.

JOB EXPERIENCE:

10/78–    Contributed to the efficient management of student loans
6/80      at the financial aid office of Teco University.

9/77–    Gained experience in sales and customer relations as
10/78    salesperson in Durkee's Plaza Department Store in Palo. Shoppers can be fun!

6/76–    Utilized my various talents to help other young people
9/76     learn to read, write and participate in activities of daily living as a volunteer at LBJ Psychiatric Center in Palo.

6/74–    Skills including operating a PBX switchboard and other
6/78     telephone equipment, typing, operating adding machines and other general office equipment were acquired by working at various part-time jobs throughout my academic career.

HOBBIES AND MISCELLANEOUS ASSETS:

Drawing, driving, reading and music.
Patient, persistent, responsible, understanding and able to get things done quickly, smoothly and efficiently.

REFERENCES FURNISHED UPON REQUEST.

Figure 17–4

companies in the Houston area alone. However, the fact that she obtained the *name* of the personnel director or the training director makes it seem personalized for a particular firm.

The authors of this text would be a little skeptical about Ms. Tracy Budd, because she uses weighted words and phrases in her resumé—such as "contributed to the efficient management," "customer relations," and "utilized my various talents,"—and we would rather read about the qualities she claims for herself ("patient, persistent, responsible, understanding, and able to get things done smoothly and efficiently") from her *references,* rather than from herself. Nevertheless, she attempts to make the most of what she has, and we would reserve judgment about her ego until after an actual interview.

## MORE ABOUT RESUMÉS

First, you do not have to call your personal data sheet a *resumé.* You may title it *Personal Data, Data Sheet, Qualifications Record, Personal Record,* or simply *Vita.*

Second, it has more uses than simply getting a job.[2] If it is kept up to date, it can be used periodically to evaluate you for salary raises, promotions, or other jobs within the company. It is also useful for public relations purposes—both for internal newsletters or house organs and for use by the public news media. Third, it usually follows a set form:

1. *Education and training.* Include military service, if any.
2. *Honors and extracurricular activities.* Don't neglect sports, forensics, work on student newspaper or magazine, and social organizations.
3. *Student government activities.* We put this in a special heading because you should be extremely modest about it. While leadership is admired greatly on the campus, you should keep a low profile about it when applying for a job, lest management think you might want to take over the firm.
4. *Work experience.* This can go back to high school or beyond. Most prospective employers admire work and initiative at whatever age. D. H. Lawrence once wrote, "I am a great believer in luck, and I find the harder I work the more luck I have."
5. *Personal traits.* This is difficult for young people to write, since their personalities have not evolved to the point of maturity. However, a statement that can have an effect may be in order, such as:

A. "I'm not afraid to get my hands dirty. I shoveled manure for one summer on a large farm, and I can think of no work dirtier."
B. "I think I'm a good organizer. I came into the social fraternity, 'I Felta Thi,' when it was chaotic, and no one knew what responsibilities were delegated to him. By the end of two weeks I had organized the fraternity so that each member knew what his duties were."

    C. "People laugh at me, and I don't mind. I've found that laughter, in whatever form, relieves tension."

    D. "I am normal in that I hate carrots, and abnormal in that I like spinach."

That final one may be a little cute, but you should try to inject some personality into your resumé. Try to avoid extreme attitudes such as, "Everything is right with God's world, and I love it!" or, "Everything is rotten, and I'm determined to set it right!"

## Selectivity

Prospective employers and personnel directors look for many traits in an applicant. Here are a few:

1. Actual skill or experience, or willingness to learn
2. A well-rounded education, and willingness to work
3. Ability to learn and think, to create ideas, and to solve problems
4. Common sense, intelligence, and integrity
5. Ability to express one's self in writing and speaking
6. Evidence of social development
7. Ability to get along well with others, particularly those in the company in question
8. Modesty, sincerity, and emotional stability.

It is impractical to try to demonstrate all of the above qualities in one resumé. So, if you follow the format suggested earlier, you can save the others for the actual interview. Projecting a sense of humor into your personal data sheet is good, but please avoid gimmicks such as these:

"Ten reasons why you don't dare overlook Hosea Moses as one of your salesmen."

"You will live to regret it if you don't make Meegan Moran the Head of your Stenographic Pool!"

## Photographs

Not so many years ago, it was illegal in several states for an employer to require a photograph if a person was applying for a position in the public school system or as a civil servant; now, applications for almost all of those same positions ask whether an applicant is white, black, Hispanic, or Eurasian. Therefore the authors are not sure who was being discriminated against *then* and *now*. It is advisable to attach a small recent photograph to the resumé.[3]

Despite human rights codes a *prejudiced* employer is not going to change overnight, so you can save yourself the time it takes for a personal interview with him or her. No matter what color or race you may be, most prospective employers want to know what you look like, and they don't want to spend time for a personal interview to find out. They tend to judge alertness and good grooming by a good recent photograph. So, take your chances.

## THE APPLICATION FORM

The first rule is take care. Personnel directors tell us that almost *one-half* of all job applicants neglect to fill in *all* of the blanks on an application form, including the date and their signature.

Second, be neat. Type the application if possible. If not, print it neatly; most longhand is too large to fit into the blank spaces allotted for information.

Third, don't lie or exaggerate. If your previous job has been that of a janitor, don't try to make it sound important by calling it a "sanitation engineer." (Note "customer relations" in Figure 17–4, implying that it was more than a salesperson.)

Fourth, do not be negative—especially about your last place of employment. When you are asked your reason for leaving it, don't reply that your boss was a dirty old lecher who chased you around his desk. Try to say something good about your last job, even if you must be evasive and call it a "learning experience."

Finally, if references are required, be sure that you have asked *permission* of the persons whose names you give. This cannot be too strongly emphasized. Most applications ask for references, so go to the interview with the addresses and telephone numbers of your references written down. It doesn't speak well for you if you claim to know someone so well that he or she is willing to act as a reference, while you must ask for a telephone directory to look up that person's home or business address.

## REFERENCES AND RECOMMENDATIONS

Many applications ask for references that fit into special categories; for example,

1. List two references under whose supervision you have worked during the past four years.
2. List two persons (not family) who have known you for at least five years.
3. List two persons who have worked under your supervision for three weeks or longer. (For a student this may be difficult, but you can use summer jobs, or classmates who have worked under you on a school project.)

Asking permission of anyone you are planning to use as a reference is not only the courteous thing to do, but it can also help avoid mistaken identity. For example, suppose your name is Stevens and you are planning to list your supervisor from a former job as a reference. The supervisor may have had another employee whose name was also Stevens, who was an unreliable character and who was fired. Unfortunately, the supervisor is more apt to remember *that* employee (because of the trouble) than you. It doesn't happen often, but it *could*.

"To Whom It May Concern" recommendations are good to have, if they are written by an important person who cannot be reached easily as a reference; however, prospective employers usually want more specific information than that conveyed by this type of recommendation.

## The Follow-Up Letters

After the interview is over, you should always write a short note to the person who interviewed you, thanking the person for seeing you (see Figure 17–5). This note will reinforce your interview by recalling you to the personnel director or whomever you contacted. Richard German, Executive Vice-President of Bernard Haldane Associates,[4] emphasizes this strongly and says that most interviewers don't get many thank you notes.

---

(Address and date)

(Internal address)

Dear Mr. Nastow:

Thank you for seeing me yesterday, concerning a position as Management Trainee for Larrapee, Inc. You made the interview easy and comfortable for me.

I was glad to meet some of the other employees of Larrapee; they impressed me as being highly competent and happy in their jobs. I believe I could work well with them.

I am enclosing a general recommendation from my former employer at Durkee's Department Store, and I am looking forward to a second interview with Larrapee.

Sincerely,

Ms. Tracy Budd

---

Figure 17–5

*Here* is where your "To Whom It May Concern" recommendation can serve admirably. Enclose it. Since most such letters are of a general nature, they can be used here to advantage. Don't suggest that you overlooked or forgot you had it in your possession; just mention that you are enclosing it. It is good "reserve ammunition."

Suppose that the interviewer has indicated that a second interview is required, but you find another position in the meantime. Should you ignore that particular interviewer? Please do not! Write and let that prospective employer know that you are no longer interested. This may seem to you like unnecessary correspondence, but we know from experience how much personnel directors appreciate it. It need be only a brief statement, such as, "Thank you for your interview, but I am obligated to tell you that I am no longer an applicant for the position of _____ ." The author once took that extra effort, but with more detail, and—when the alternate job "went sour"—applied to the firm he had turned down, and was hired. The reasons given for hiring him, after he had turned them down, were "courtesy and consideration."

## Writing A Recommendation

First, if you are asked to recommend another person—either as a reference, or by writing a letter—you should *refuse* if there is any doubt in your mind as to that person's qualifications. The Academic Dean of Bernhardt College of Business,* who also taught some courses in the college, would recommend any graduate of the college, effusively and enthusiastically, whether he *knew* that graduate or not. It was not long until that particular dean's recommendations became worthless.

However, if you can honestly recommend the person, here are some precepts to follow:

1.  Be brief
2.  Give the circumstances under which you were associated with the person, and the length of time
3.  Never overpraise a referral; you may write enthusiastically, but never flatteringly
4.  Try to cite one specific example in which the referral has performed outstandingly, or in a manner that is better than average
5.  When asked about one specific quality in a referral, that is *all that is required;* however, you may close with, "Any other information will be given gladly."

Figures 17–6 and 17–7 show two letters of recommendation. In each case the Student Aid Director at Teco University has been asked to evaluate Ms. Tracy Budd's performance in the Student Aid Office.

*Name of college has been changed.

```
                        TECO UNIVERSITY
                        Palo, Texas, 77429

                        Student Aid Office
                                                        May 17, 198—
    Mr. Jack Nastow
    Larrapee, Inc.
    400 Pecos Street
    Houston, Texas, 77581

    Dear Mr. Nastow:

        I am happy to recommend Ms. Tracy Budd for whatever position
    she thinks she can handle. She will not disappoint you.

        It has been a joy to have Tracy work in the Student Aid Office for
    the past two years. Not only is she prompt and dependable, but she
    has taken a personal interest in all of her co-workers. We do not
    have provisions for overtime pay for our student help, but Tracy
    has volunteered to stay far beyond the time she was paid for on
    several occasions when we were shorthanded.

        What is more to the point, she seems to take an interest in her
    work, even though it is often drudgery of a routine nature. She has
    not only brightened our office with her sunny personality, but she
    also brightened it physically, making curtains for the windows and
    bringing in several house plants for our pleasure.

        We have missed her greatly since her graduation, and wish her
    well wherever she goes.

                            Sincerely,

                            Mildred Suggs
                            Director, Student Aid
```

Figure 17–6

Contrast this letter with the one that follows. Which of the letters follows the
precepts we set down earlier?

House plants and window curtains may contribute to the pleasant atmosphere of an office, but they have little to do with Ms. Budd's performance of
her duties, which is what Mr. Nastow wanted to know. Be pleasant and courteous, but *get to the point* and *give the information that is requested.*

```
                        TECO UNIVERSITY
                        Palo, Texas, 77429

                        Student Aid Office
                                                    May 17, 198—
Mr. Jack Nastow
Larrapee, Inc.
400 Pecos Street
Houston, Texas, 77581

                        RE: Ms. Tracy Budd
                        Management Trainee applicant

Dear Mr. Nastow:

    Ms. Tracy Budd was employed by the Student Aid Office for two
academic years (1978–1980). She is a dependable worker, prompt
and efficient, and has made a number of contributions to this office's
efficiency.

    Ms. Budd studied our method of processing student loan appli-
cations, and made a suggestion that allowed us to expedite such
loans within less than one week, whereas the process had formerly
taken two weeks or more. All of her work is organized well.

    She has a pleasant personality, and gets along extremely well
with her fellow-workers. I am happy to recommend her for the
position as management trainee. Any other information will be
given with pleasure.

                        Sincerely,

                        Mildred Suggs
                        Director, Student Aid
```

Figure 17–7

## SUGGESTED CLASSROOM EXERCISES

1. Students will write resumés of themselves. After collecting and grading them, the instructor may select two or three of the better ones, and two or three of the poorer ones to present to the class (with names withheld) for discussion.
2. Students may be paired off, and each student will write a letter of recommendation for a job that the other student desires. In both these assignments the

instructor should ask that all students review the supplements to Chapter Sixteen, to judge how much "word fodder" or how many cliché expressions they may have used.

## FOOTNOTES FOR CHAPTER SEVENTEEN

[1]Virginia Lee Hallock, *Business Communications* (Providence, RI: P.A.R., Inc., 1974) p. 109.

[2]Leland Brown, *Communicating Facts and Ideas in Business,* 2nd ed. (Englewood Cliffs, N.J.: Prentice-Hall, 1970) p. 357.

[3]Robert M. Archer and Ruth P. Ames, *Basic Business Communications* (Englewood Cliffs, N.J.: Prentice-Hall, 1971) p. 284.

[4]Personal interview with Richard German, Vice-President of Bernard Haldane Associates, New York City, April 25, 1977.

# 18 | Internal Correspondence: Minutes, Memoranda, and Reports

He can compress the most words into the smallest ideas of any man I ever met.

A. Lincoln (1806–1865)

The boundaries of internal and external correspondence are sometimes blurred. Theoretically communication written for only a member, or members, of a company to read is strictly *internal;* communication for an outsider, or outsiders, to read is strictly *external*. A report to the stockholders, or a report about a change in operating procedure, may be meant for both outsiders and insiders to examine. Under extraordinary circumstances even the minutes of a meeting may be subpoenaed for the public to see.

## MINUTES

The minutes of a meeting are generally thought of as the lowest form of business writing. But minutes (whether of a general meeting or a committee meeting) are vastly underrated as a means of moving forward the business of a corporation.[1]

Taking the minutes of a meeting is usually relegated to the lowest person on the totem pole of a corporation. Minutes are too often thought of as being a waste of time and are dispensed with. One reason for this is that minutes are regarded by many people as being nothing more than a blow-by-blow account of

1. The time and place of present meeting
2. The number present to constitute a quorum
3. Disposal of minutes of previous meeting
4. Reports of treasurer and other officers
5. Reports of standing and *ad hoc* committees
6. Old business
7. New business
   Exact wording of each motion, amendment to it, discussion of it, and report on its passage or defeat
8. The time and place of next meeting
9. Adjournment.

All of the aspects just listed are essential, but they can just as easily be handled by a tape recorder. The skillful reporter of minutes will do more than a tape recorder possibly can.

Decisions that affect an entire company are often made on the bases of reports by committees that are appointed to study certain details governing those decisions. If, at the general meeting of the company's officers, it is necessary to wade through the mass of verbiage of each committee's meetings, it will waste thousands of dollars of the company's time doing so. If, on the other hand, the recorder of minutes can *summarize* the committee's findings and recommendations, those attending the general meeting can make decisions accurately and quickly.

So, the minutes of a meeting should be written, not as a complete transcript, but as a brief *report,* summarizing the attitudes expressed and the actions taken.[2]

In summarizing the attitudes expressed by committee members, the minutes recorder must avoid "loaded" adjectives and bias. The minutes must be absolutely objective. Note these two examples:

1. Ms. Koheen rudely interrupted the speaker by moving that employees of the company be given no time off with pay for any outside duties, civic or otherwise, ending her motion by stating, "We're a business, not a community charity!"

The chairman asked if Ms. Koheen wanted to include that last statement in her motion, and scornfully reminded her that parliamentary procedure required that the action of a motion be stated last.

Before the motion could be seconded, Mr. Lindquist (who is the worst offender in taking time off for outside duties), complained in a whining tone that the company has an image to present to the community.

Mr. Bergen shouted "Hogwash!" and seconded the motion. Ms. Jones protested vehemently that time was being wasted, and called the question loudly, before any time for discussion was allowed, contrary to parliamentary procedure. A vote was taken and the motion failed miserably.

2. Ms. Koheen moved that employees of the company be given no time off with pay for outside duties. Mr. Lindquist demurred on the grounds of the company's community image.

Mr. Bergen seconded the motion, and Ms. Jones called the question without discussion. The motion failed.

In the report of a committee meeting to a general meeting, even the details in Example #2 are not necessary. All that is needed is the statement that, "The committee failed to pass a motion that employees of the company be given no time off with pay for outside duties, civic or otherwise."

A blow-by-blow description *is* necessary for reference. As in Example #2, the names of those involved are desirable so that officials may know where various individuals stand. If a roll call on a motion is demanded, those voting for or against a motion must be named. However, for purposes of decision by higher echelons, the summation in the preceding paragraph is all that is necessary.

## Importance of a Minutes Recorder

There is no more important position for one who is trying to learn the inner workings of a corporation than that of a minutes recorder in a committee. This is particularly true if you are fortunate enough to serve as recorder for several different committees.

*First,* you can learn a great deal about group dynamics by observing how one or two members attempt to persuade the others, and how they react and capitulate to the more persuasive members. Being completely impartial—as you should be at all times—you can learn to judge when a group is nearing a consensus. You can do this better than the more active participants, because individual participants are so engaged in advancing their points of view that they are often unaware that an agreement is near—indeed, has often been reached.

*Second,* you can learn objective writing as no other school can teach it. Although your minutes may not be "published" in one sense, they will be scrutinized by those on both sides of an issue and criticized accordingly. If you dare make a remark that may seem favorable to one side, the other side will let you know.

*Third,* you can learn the skill of *summarizing,* which is a priceless quality in a business person. In a meeting while other members are fumbling or stumbling around to find words for their thoughts, you can capsule their thoughts into a simple, concise statement. We have known executives who, after reading the recording of committee meetings, have said, "That's exactly what I meant to say!" This can come only after you become an expert in *listening*.

Finally, as a recorder of procedures, you are often the *only* person who knows what is going on.[3] The committee members are so busy rehearsing their verbal contributions, while waiting to catch the chairman's attention, that they don't *listen*.


## MEMORANDA

Essentially a memorandum is a short letter, designed to be read by more than one person (though not always). It should provide clear, complete information in the shortest, simplest, and most understandable language possible.[4] The reason for its rigid format is to ensure brevity, conveying the necessary information without the usual social amenities of a letter. A bit of information buried in an avalanche of words is apt to remain buried. Paragraphing, spacing on the page, underlining, and numbering are important to make the vital information stand out.

Other than the body of the memo, requirements are (a) the date, (b) who sent it, (c) who it is meant to reach, and (d) a "telegram" of its subject. Figure 18-1 shows a good example of format and spacing. Sometimes a simple visual aid is attached to a memo for clarity, such as giving street directions or instructions for assembly of mechanical objects.

Memoranda are not signed. Some business people like to have each memo initialed personally by the person who originated it. Sending a memo to dozens of people is, in the opinion of some, a waste of time.[5] There are also differences of opinion as to whether FROM should precede TO in the format, and whether SUBJECT should be shortened to RE. These are minute details and are not nearly as important as brevity, clarity, and *purpose*.


### Purposes

The memorandum has many uses, but its chief purposes are

1. *To inform*. This includes everything from bits of general information, as shown in Figure 18-1, to detailed instructions for a particular department or individual. It may include confirming an oral agreement between two parties, or conveying feedback information from a previous conference.[6] Figures 18-2 and 18-3 are examples.

2. *To request*. In Figures 18-4 to 18-8,* you will notice that this type of memo may range from a mere suggestion, to a polite request for information or action, all the way to a flat command. The important thing is that *something is to be done*, and whoever receives the memo is supposed to do it.

---

*The sample memos in this section are not always consistent in capitalization and punctuation even though the format is rigid. For example, *all* of the words in the subject do not need to be capitalized; the abbreviations "2nd, 3rd, 4th" do not require a period; and, since most memos are current, the date of the year is rarely used in the body itself, but only at the top—the day of the week is more important.

```
                                                        May 10, 1980


    TO:        All Employees of Rayco
    FROM:      Dept. of Transportation
    SUBJECT:   New Shuttle Service to and from Wayzata

    Starting Monday, May 17, we will have a regular company bus
    service from the subway station in Wayzata to the Rayco plant and
    return, at 15-minute intervals:

      Leaving Wayzata subway station: 8:20, 8:35, 8:50 A.M.

    Buses will collect and discharge passengers at the front entrance
    of the Security Building, as it is protected from weather by passages
    to all other buildings.

      Returning to Wayzata subway station: 4:35, 4:50, 5:05 P.M.

    See your supervisor if there is any problem concerning these sched-
    ules.

    There is no charge for this service.

                                                              J.K.B.
```

Figure 18-1

If it is a detailed request, absolute clarity is essential on these points:

1. *What* is to be done
2. *Where* it is to be done
3. *When* it is to be done
4. Sometimes *how* it is to be done; the *why* should not be necessary.

Figures 18-7 and 18-8 deserve special attention. They deal with the same problem, and one question that arises is, "How much friendliness is allowed among employees, without destroying the strict discipline sometimes necessary?"

Because of plant security, the subject is a command, and tact takes second place to directness. The explanation given is sufficient, and the memo is as courteous as the situation demands.

```
                                                            Date

  TO:      All Employees
  FROM:    Director of Personnel Benefits
  RE:      Health Insurance for Dependent Parents

     We have received a letter from Fidelity Insurance Co. that parents
  of employees are not eligible for health coverage under our group
  policy, even though those parents are solely dependent upon the
  employee for support.

     Payments that have previously been made on premiums for those
  parents were in error, and will be refunded.

     Employees with dependent parents are urged to obtain coverage
  through another source; they cannot be insured under our group
  policy, as some of you believed.

                                                            MTS
```

Figure 18-2

Figure 18-7 is almost everything that a memorandum should *not* be: First, it is too long (364 words, compared with the 114 words in Figure 18-8); second, it is filled with "word fodder" while failing to mention government contracts—an essential reason for such tight security. Notice these useless expressions:

It has been brought to our attention (we have learned)
A small contingent (a few)
Have been negligent in the respect that (rush past)
Without following the procedure of (without showing)
Especially when those workers are apt to be late [cut this clause; who cares *why* they don't show their cards?]
It is incumbent (you must/we must)
Highly hazardous and potentially dangerous [repetitive; this entire sentence is unnecessary]
To facilitate your convenience (for your convenience).

Instead of referring to "the plant," "the laboratory," or simply "Loeb's," the writer uses "this facility," which is often used as a euphemism for "toilet."

Date

FROM:      Charles Jones, Executive Vice President
TO:        All Department Heads, Ersatz Company
SUBJECT:   Change in work schedule for November

Please make a note on your calendar of the following changes in the November work schedule:

1. Monday, Nov. 11th (Armed Forces Day), will *not* be a holiday. A survey of our employees tells us that they would prefer an extra day at Thanksgiving, instead. I am enclosing notices of this to be posted on your bulletin boards.

2. Friday, Nov. 15th, is the *new* final date for all semiannual reports on production and personnel to be turned in to my office.

3. Our Thanksgiving Holiday will begin on Wednesday, Nov. 27th, at 2:00 P.M., to allow those who need it extra travel time to their families.

4. Friday, Nov. 29th, will *not* be a work day. On Monday, Dec. 2nd, all work will resume full time at 9:00 A.M.

CJ

Enclosure

Figure 18-3

---

Date

TO:      All Second-Floor Employees
FROM:    Byron Danford, Office Manager
RE:      Untidy Employee Lounge

The Employee Lounge on the second floor is a mess!

Empty soft drink bottles, half-empty Styrofoam coffee cups, and wrappers from the snack dispensers litter the tables and chairs, while unfolded newspapers cover the carpet. Ashtrays never seem to be emptied.

Management maintains these lounges on each floor for the employees' convenience, and pays for normal janitorial services.

I suggest that the employees on the second floor get together and appoint one or two members to "police" the lounge each day for one week, on a rotating basis, and that the schedule be posted on the Lounge bulletin board.

This should be done at once. Unless some responsibility is taken on the part of employees to clear up their own litter, the second floor lounge will be closed at the end of next week.

BD

Figure 18-4

---

Date

TO:      Mary Balenkiwicz, Office Manager
FROM:  Adelaide Gray, Personnel Supervisor
RE:      New File clerk, Susan Shatner

The new file clerk, Susan Shatner, seems to have a lot on the ball, but has never before worked in an office that handles highly classified documents.

I would appreciate it if you will make yourself available to her for answering any questions, and let her know that you are ready to help in any way you can, for a couple of weeks.

You don't need to breathe down her neck, or give her preferential treatment, because she shows a lot of initiative and will not call upon you unless she really needs you.

I believe that this extra effort on your part will be worth the investment you make in time.

AG

Figure 18-5

Date

FROM:  Charles Bloodgore, Plant Executive
TO:  All Supervisors
RE:  Delinquent production reports

I expect all departmental production reports on my desk each Monday morning before noon. Thank you.

CB

Figure 18-6

Date

FROM:  Security Headquarters
TO:  All Employees of Loeb Laboratory
SUBJECT:  Security Identification Cards

It has been brought to our attention that a small contingent of workers at this facility have been negligent in the respect that they do not always bring their Security Identification Cards to work with them.

Mr. Harry Hawkins, the security guard at the front door of this facility, has been in our employ for ten years, and it has been reported that many of our workers give him a friendly greeting and rush by him without following the procedure of displaying their Security Identification Cards, especially when those workers are apt to be late for work in their respective departments.

At the time of your employment by this facility, all employees were briefed by their supervisors on security measures, and were issued Memorandum #43A-2711, which contains the following paragraphs:

> "As an employee of Loeb Laboratory it is incumbent upon you to carry your Security Identification Card at all times, whether on duty or off, in either your purse (if female) or in your wallet (if male). This is

to prevent the card from falling into the hands of undesirable persons, who may use it for counterfeiting or for infiltration of the plant for purposes of sabotage. *It is a pre-condition of your employment at Loeb* that you agree to this.

"Furthermore, you must present your Security Identification to any entrance guard, so that it can be seen clearly, and so that the guard may scrutinize it to assure its validity. This is also a pre-condition of your employment."

It is incumbent upon us that we insist that the foregoing procedure be followed rigidly, without exception.

As you must realize, we are working upon several highly sensitive projects in this facility. The mistaken identity of even *one* person who might infiltrate our plant could be highly hazardous—or potentially dangerous—to any one of these projects. This cannot be emphasized too strongly.

To this end, we are posting an additional security guard at the front entrance during the rush hour of 8:00—9:00 A.M., to facilitate your convenience in having your identification examined carefully and properly. We sincerely hope and trust that you will cooperate with us in this matter.

CBS

Figure 18-7

---

Date

FROM: Security Headquarters
TO: All Employees of Loeb Laboratory
SUBJECT: Security Identification Cards

We have learned that a few of our employees rush past the security guard each morning, without showing their Security Identification Cards, presuming that Mr. Harry Hawkins recognizes them. This practice must stop immediately.

Because of the highly sensitive nature of our Government contracts, it is a condition of your employment that you keep your Security Identification cards in your purse or wallet at *all times*, whether you are on duty or not (See Memo #42A-2711). You must present your S.I.C. each time you enter the premises.

For your convenience, we are posting *two* security guards at the main entrance to the building, starting tomorrow morning, from 8:00–9:00 A.M.

You are expected to cooperate.

                                                                    NBC

Figure 18-8

In Figure 18-7 the memo's forcefulness is weakened considerably by a plethora of words. Important information has been buried and is apt to remain buried.

## REPORTS

A business report is a factual presentation of data or information directed to a particular reader or audience for a specific business purpose.

                                                            Leland Brown[7]

The basic ingredient of a report is research. The researcher can be compared to a detective examining every clue in a mysterious murder. Research is Galileo, peering through the newly invented telescope* and confirming Copernicus's theory that the earth revolved around the sun and not the opposite; research is Leonardo, digging up dead bodies at night to see how the muscles were placed over the human frame; research rode with Jacques Cousteau on the *Calypso,* and is the reason for every satellite man sends into outer space. So, in discussing reports, we are not writing about the report in which one merely fills in the blanks on a printed form, but the report that involves true investigation and creative writing.

*Usually attributed to a Dutch spectacle maker, Hans Lippershey (1587–1619).

Reports may be external or internal. They are of many types, but we shall confine our discussion to internal reports that are needed for making decisions in business. Most of these reports are made to the people in charge of operating a company. They can be classified as informational, explanatory, or interpretative.[8]

## The Informative Report

These reports are made to inform management of what is going on in every department. Sometimes they are specifically requested, and often they are made on a regular basis: monthly, quarterly, or even semiannually, but rarely annually. (If the executives of a company find out what is happening only on a yearly basis, the business may deteriorate beyond all hope of saving it!) Informative reports come from every department—production, marketing (including advertising and sales), inventory, and personnel. Normally they do not carry an extreme sense of urgency; they are nonetheless vital to management in making decisions in a deliberate and competitive way.

## The Explanatory Report

This type of report may be topical (such as monthly or quarterly) but more often it is requested by management. It takes more time to prepare, because it deals not only with facts and figures but also with opinions. It attempts to explain *why* there is a sudden drop in sales, or a delay in a construction project. It tries to give the *reasons* for a healthy spurt in production, or a lowering of morale among personnel. It may even examine a competitor's manufacturing process and attempt to compare its efficiency with that of its own company. The explanatory report provides information and interprets it to give management a basis for making an immediate decision.

This type of report is invariably supported with subreports of statistics, surveys, opinions of key personnel, and even the statements of experts in the general field of the company's business.

## The Analytical Report

This type of report takes the explanatory report two steps further. It *evaluates* the data, so that management has almost all of the information it needs to make decisions; it also offers alternatives and provides an evaluation of them. Sometimes it may recommend a course of action. In theory a recommendation is made only when the report writer is specifically authorized to do so; in practice, a recommendation is almost always a part of the analytical report. Management is not obliged to *follow* the recommendation, but it seems that management almost always wants to know of the report writer, "What would *you* do, in the light of this report?"

Since the analytical report is the most complete, it is addressed in the following discussion. The first two types can be encompassed easily within its scope.

## Preparation

Reports are generally compiled to help management make a decision. When a decision must be made, it is usually the result of some problem. So, the first step is to isolate the problem and to state it succinctly. To illustrate, here is an imaginary case history.

> Apko is a relatively small plant that freezes and packages frozen vegetables, on the outskirts of Sarasota, Florida. Apko owns 1,200 acres of fertile land, on which it grows green beans, lima beans, okra, and tomatoes. Its processing plant is located at the edge of its farmland, and it takes an average of thirty minutes for a truck to make a round trip from the plant to the fields.
>
> Apko's closest competitor is Bambi, located about sixty miles east, near Lake Okeechobee. Bambi has the same size plant, owns the same acreage, and processes the same vegetables. However, Bambi has a considerably larger net income than Apko. Why?

1. *Isolating the specific problem from any surrounding ones:* Since the climate and rainfall are about the same on both the Apko and Bambi properties, natural causes can be ruled out as the reason for Bambi's edge over Apko. Preliminary investigations also show that (a) the type and amount of fertilizer used on the farmlands of both Apko and Bambi are the same, (b) both pay their workers the same wage scale, and (c) the type of seeds used are the same.

2. *Investigating the problem.* In investigating a problem, you may use *primary* or *secondary* research, or a combination of the two.

   A. *Primary research* consists of surveys, questionnaires, telephone inquiries, interviews with experts, direct observation, and carefully controlled experiments.

   B. *Secondary research* consists of reading carefully the printed material on the subject. This may be the general literature in the field,* minutes of board and committee meetings, company records, or informal reports on company operations (your own or some other company).

> Ben Hill, the Vice-President of Production at Apko, starts doing some detective work.
>
> First, he asks his Marketing and Advertising Manager (It's a small plant, and the two are the same) to find out how much Bambi spends on advertising, and how it is distributed among the media—print, radio, and television. The Marketing and Advertising Manager turns in his report that Bambi's advertising budget is smaller than Apko's, but that its distribution is about the same. *Smaller* budget for advertising, eh?
>
> Next, Ben asks his Shipping Supervisor to take a trip to Lake Okeechobee and examine the shipping records of Bambi from the carriers (truck and rail). Never mind

---

*In Supplement "A" at the end of this chapter, we have listed some of the sources of general literature in the field of business, industry, and management.

how he got the information, but the Shipping Supervisor reports that, during the busiest part of the season, Bambi shipped an average of *four more truckloads* per *day* than Apko shipped out of Sarasota. Ben Hill was puzzled: same acreage, same size plant, lower advertising budget, but four more truckloads per day!

Ben also asked his Labor Supervisor to take a trip to Lake Okeechobee to find out how many workers Bambi employed, and how many workshifts they operated. Since Bambi and Apko are competitors, such figures are usually kept secret, but the Florida State Department of Labor helped some. However, the Labor Supervisor was engaged mainly in primary research. He hung around the bars and bowling alleys and made friendly inquiries of the workers at Bambi, and he employed direct observation by counting the employees at Bambi when they reported to work and also when they left. Ben Hill was genuinely startled when the Labor Supervisor reported that Bambi employed 18% fewer workers than Apko!

So far, the reports to Apko have all been *informative*. They will follow the format and writing examples that are presented later in this section, and Ben Hill will incorporate them in the subreports that he will present to other company officers. Let us continue the investigation:

By the process of elimination Ben Hill decides that the secret of Bambi's margin of profit over Apko must lie in the actual plant operation. He does two things: First, he calls in Vic Clark, an efficiency expert in food plant operations. Second, he sends Ray Kune, a trained observer, to find work with Bambi. [Industrial "spying"? It's done all the time.]

Vic Clark breaks down Apko's operation to its smallest unit—that is, to each truckload of vegetables from the time the pickers go into the fields to harvest the crop, until the finished product is packaged. His time-motion study shows this. (See Figure 18-9.)

Meanwhile, Ray Kune, the industrial spy, reports that Bambi is using a new refrigeration truck that goes directly to the fields, and which will half-freeze a truckload

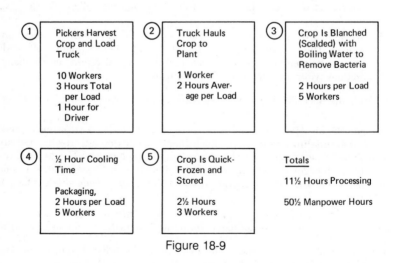

Figure 18-9

of vegetables in one hour. The truck is also equipped with a special microwave that will kill any bacteria on the vegetables, thereby eliminating the process of scalding; only a simple rinsing in cold water is necessary.

Clark has examined the packaging machine and knows of an attachment that will cut in half the time needed for packaging.

Vic Clark and Ben Hill together figure that the cost of this new equipment could be amortized over a period of time by (a) eliminating the cost of fuel to provide a constant supply of boiling water ready to scald the crops, and (b) eliminating *five* workers needed for the scalding process, in favor of only *two* workers necessary for the cold water rinsing. They also realize that the half hour for "cooling" is no longer required, which saves a half hour for *everybody* in the entire operation. The new flow of processing is shown in Figure 18-10.

It does not happen often, but sometimes—in the middle of your investigation of a problem—a hypothesis of the right solution may occur to you. This hypothesis should be noted and written down but not pursued any further until your investigation is complete. It may be valuable as an alternative, even if it does not turn out to be the *best* solution. It occurs more frequently—but not always—that, while working on a problem, some additional benefits may present themselves; this is what happened to Ben Hill:

Thus far, Ben had been interested in saving time and money, in order to meet the competition from Bambi. Now, he wondered if there were additional benefits in quick-freezing the crops in the fields. So, he traveled to Florida Technological University near Orlando (now the University of Central Florida), to consult with nutrition experts there. The nutrition experts had already been studying this possibility and had documented the results. It seemed that quick-frozen vegetables had a slight advantage in both nutrition and taste over the other processes. It was only

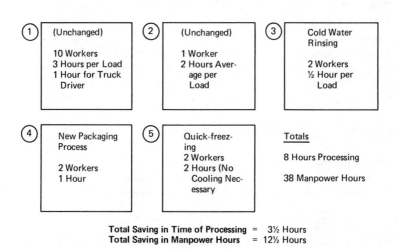

Figure 18-10

a slight advantage, but it was enough for Apko's purpose in launching an advertising campaign that proclaimed:

"UNIVERSITY TEST SHOWS THAT APKO'S FOODS ARE BEST!"

Too bad Bambi had not thought of that angle!

If this sounds like fiction, it is. However, it is not far-fetched, and it demonstrates how exciting research can be. Ben Hill and his staff still have a long way to go before they can present a final report to the other executives and the board members at Apko:

1. On the basis of the informational reports, they must show that the main problem of Bambi's margin of profit over Apko lies in the plant operations.
2. They must show that the outlay of new equipment, running into millions of dollars, can be amortized within a reasonable length of time.

In short, they must succeed in:

- *Identifying the possible solutions and selecting the best possible solution.* This has already been done to the satisfaction of Ben Hill and his staff. But, when several million dollars are involved, *all* of those informational reports must be put into order as backup material, when Ben presents his final report to the other executives and members of the board.

## Format and Writing

In a formal report running to many pages, the format may be formidable. It may contain the following[9]

| | |
|---|---|
| Cover | Introduction |
| Title page | Discussion |
| Letter of authorization | Conclusions |
| Letter of acceptance | Recommendations |
| Letter of approval | Supplementary reports |
| Letter of transmittal | Charts, diagrams, tables |
| Acknowledgments | Bibliography |
| Table of contents | Index |

In Ben Hill's report to Apko the contents may be shortened to

| | |
|---|---|
| Title page (with contents) | Conclusion |
| Introduction | Recommendations |
| Discussion (including charts) | Supplementary reports. |

The title page might look like Figure 18-11.

**Introduction.** In his introduction Ben will summarize the problem as described at the beginning of this section, that is, that Bambi, with the same

*Improving Plant Operations in Apko Frozen Foods, Sarasota, Florida*

A comparison of two frozen food processors as applied specifically to Apko's operation in Sarasota

*Prepared for:* The President, Executive Directors, and Board of Directors, Apko Frozen Foods

*Prepared by:* Benjamin Hill, Vice-President of Production

*Supplementary reports by:*
Victor Clark, Consultant, Juneau Corporation, Inc.
William Postum, Marketing & Advertising
Claude Bedichek, Shipping Supervisor Apko Frozen Foods
Michael Meany, Labor Supervisor
Mavis St. John, Cost Accountant
Dr. Isaac Schwartz, Professor of Nutritional Biology, University of Central Florida at Orlando.

January 16, 198-

Figure 18-11

acreage and approximately the same size plant, shows a greater margin of profit than Apko. He can do this in one paragraph.

**Discussion.** Ben will devote one paragraph each to the reports of Advertising, Shipping, Labor, and Kunes "the observer," showing that

(a) Bambi and Apko have about the same advertising budget.
(b) Bambi ships four more truckloads than Apko per day, with 18 percent fewer workers in the plant, and that
(c) Bambi has superior equipment in its refrigeration trucks and packaging machine.

He will devote perhaps one-half page to the calculations of Vic Clark, the efficiency expert, and will include the before-and-after flowcharts (shown in Figures 18-9 and 18-10). He will then summarize the estimate of the Cost Accountant, showing that the cost of new equipment can be amortized within a reasonable time.

**Conclusion.** Ben Hill will conclude that the reason Apko does not show the same margin of profit as Bambi is that its equipment and plant operation are out of date.

**Recommendations.**    Hill will recommend that (a) new refrigeration trucks be purchased, and (b) that an attachment for the present packaging machine be bought.

If Ben is clever, he will have saved the supplementary report from Dr. Schwartz at the University of Central Florida, to give added weight to his recommendations. By doing this, he can show that Apko will actually have an *advantage* over Bambi in advertising that "University test shows that Apko is best."

At most, the body of Ben Hill's report should cover two pages. Busy executives should not be expected to wade through a mass of petty details. If they want that, they can examine the supplementary reports. The supplementary reports should be replete with accurate details.[10]

There is a minor controversy on the part of business writers as to whether or not the recommendations should be at the beginning or end of the report. Leland Brown[11] suggests that if the recommendation is a pleasant one, it should be placed at the beginning; if it is unpleasant, it should be placed at the end, after all of the reasons leading up to it have been detailed. The authors advocate placing it at the beginning of the report, *if* the main body of the report totals no more than three or four paragraphs; if it runs to two or more pages, it should be placed at the end, since it will be the last item and therefore more easily recalled. There is no arbitrary position.

*Supplementary reports* should follow the same format as the main report.[12] That is, there should be a brief summary of the report on the second page, with details such as figures, charts, and secondary sources on the pages that follow. (Ben Hill may need to delete some details from primary sources, submitted to him by Michael Meany, the Labor Supervisor; bowling alleys and bars are not usually regarded as reliable sources of business information.)

*Visual aids* can be of major importance in a report. Edward Hodnett devotes almost one-third of his book to visuals in *Effective Presentations,*[13] and Leland Brown places great emphasis on them in both *Effective Business Report Writing*[14] and *Communicating Facts and Ideas in Business.*[15] *Visual aids should be simple and accurate (see Chapter 7).*

## Establishing Probability

A report recommending a change in policy must be credible; it must have support. Following are five ways to establish probability; three of them are definitely *fallible,* but reasonable.

1. *Association.* Let us assume that Apko is trying to establish a policy addressing how much time its employees may devote to civic duties without losing any of their salary. In your report, you cite this example: "Birdseye and Green Giant frozen foods allow each of their employees with the rank of supervisor or above to spend an average of one hour per week, with pay, working for local charities and civic enterprises." That implies that Apko, which is also a frozen food op-

eration, should do the same, since Birdseye and Green Giant have grown into such successful corporations. Of course, it does not consider the size of Apko by comparison, its location, or its profit margin. Some of the favorite television commercials for edible products depend for their appeal on association: "Koolwhip Topping tastes like the *real* thing—only fresher," "*Grandma* would have loved Mellow Roast," and "Tastes like the *good, old-fashioned* recipe my *mother* used." Association may persuade the unthinking person, but it will not give your report credibility.

2. *Analogy.* "Bindlestick Products, Sweepover Manufacturers, and Topsy Toys are all manufacturing firms about the size of Apko. They are all located in towns of about the same size as the town where Apko is located. Allowing a limited number of hours on company time to engage in civic duties has greatly increased their employee morale, resulting in increased production. If it works for those firms, it will work for Apko." Not necessarily. Analogy consists of showing that if two things are alike in a number of *known* ways, they will also be alike in an *unknown* way. It's one of the most common forms of reasoning. In fact, experience is comprised of analogies, but it is never reliable as proof. Why? Because no two things are *exactly* alike. Yes, it's reasonable, but fallible.

3. *Authority.* Too many people believe anything that finds its way into print, as can be witnessed by the tremendous sales of the *National Enquirer,* a thoroughly unreliable periodical. If we read that "Benjamin Dismukes, Ph.D., a noted labor-management consultant, says that participation in community affairs can almost totally destroy a worker's concentration on the job at hand," are we going to believe it? Not without inquiring a bit more into "Dr. Dismukes'" background:

   A. What qualifies him to be an expert? Is his doctoral degree an earned degree, or was it bought from a diploma mill?
   B. Is he in a position to know the facts? Has he done research on the relationship between a worker's concentration and the worker's involvement in civic affairs?
   C. Is he biased? Does he have something to *gain* or *lose* by his statement?

   "Authority" can definitely strengthen the support of your report, but be sure it is a *reliable* authority.

4. *Instances.* "Jones Building Products allowed their workers to devote two hours per week to community affairs, and it wrecked their business, because the workers interpreted 'community affairs' to mean that they could spend those two hours in a bowling alley or a bar." That's one example of an "instance." Here is another: "Bekwik Grocery Chain allowed every employee an average of two hours per week to engage in community activities, and their sales jumped upward by 20 percent, because the townspeople helped them launch a nationwide advertising campaign." And still another: "Super Insurance *requests* that their employees engage in some form of civic duty, whether it be the chamber of commerce, the school board, the parks planning commission, or the local hospital volunteers association. They claim that their sales have increased because of the new image projected by Super Insurance."

   "Instances" are a form of inductive reasoning (see Chapter Thirteen) and must be strictly regulated. They are valuable in a report that involves decision making, and *reliable* if used with caution.

5. *Cause to effect, or effect to cause.* This is the backbone of scientific and legal proof, but *only* under the strictest scientific conditions. To say, "Participation in community affairs caused Apko productivity to increase by 18 percent in the past

six months" is an irresponsible statement. It is a rare thing for *one* cause to produce the *same* effect, time after time, and it almost never happens in human affairs. Yet, it is an effective way of establishing probability in your report for decision making. Ask yourself these three questions before you use it:

A. Was the cause in operation *prior* to the effect? Sometimes a cause and an apparent effect can happen so close together that one is mistaken for the other.

B. Was the cause *sufficient* to produce the effect?

    1) There is a court record of an ignorant young girl who thought that she had become pregnant simply because she allowed her boy friend to kiss her.

    2) In 1979 the Shah of Iran caused destructive and bloody riots—and was eventually deposed—because of his disregard for human rights, and the fear of his secret police, the SAVAK.

Was either of those causes sufficient to produce the resulting effects?

C. Could *other causes* have produced the effect? We can get the same effect by mixing lemon juice with bicarbonate of soda (a foaming reaction) as we can by mixing vinegar with bicarbonate of soda (again, a foaming reaction). So, let's examine the causes in the foregoing paragraph:

    1) Obviously in the case of the pregnant young girl, a kiss is not sufficient cause for pregnancy, so there had to be other causes.

    2) While suppression of human rights is a justifiable cause for rioting, there were many other causes for the Shah of Iran's downfall. Among them were the powerful influence of the Moslems (who resented the Shah's "modernization" of Iran), and the importation of foreigners who got most of the highly paid jobs in the oil industry.

These tests of credibility apply not only to reports, but also to almost every form of human discourse. In a report they are especially important because decision making may be the difference between success and failure in a business.

## SUGGESTED CLASSROOM EXERCISES

1. *Minutes.* The instructor may assign one class member to prepare minutes of each class discussion (not the instructor's lectures) and present them at the next class session for approval. This assignment can be scheduled in advance, and the schedule can be posted on the classroom bulletin board; each student takes a turn until the entire class has had an opportunity.

2. *Memoranda.* Each student will compose a memorandum consisting of at least three items of instruction or information. The memos will be evaluated on the basis of format, neatness, clarity, and brevity.

3. *Reports.*

    A. A student will read a current news item and will interview five other students (not in the classroom) about their opinions of the item. He will then report on the item itself and the students' views on it.

B. The instructor may divide the class into groups of three to act as committees. Each committee will investigate a current problem, conduct research on it (including interviews), and report its findings and recommendations.

## Supplement A

The library card catalog lists books in the library by author, title, and subject; the *subject* index is separate from the title and author index. Following are indexes that list *periodicals* pertaining to the subjects indicated:

*Business Periodical Index* lists articles pertaining to business, accounting, banking, insurance, labor and management, public administration, and various trades. Cumulative from 1958.

*The Applied Science and Technology Index* lists articles pertaining to science, industry, and technical fields. Cumulative since 1958.

*Applied Arts Index* lists articles on architecture, engineering, and applied science. Cumulative since 1957.

*Reader's Guide to Periodical Literature* indexes more than 100 periodicals monthly, mostly of popular and general nature.

Special indexes in particular fields. Among them are *The Accountant's Index, Engineering Index, Index to Legal Periodicals,* and *The Management Index.*

## FOOTNOTES FOR CHAPTER EIGHTEEN

[1] Nelda Lawrence, *Writing Communications in Business and Industry* (Englewood Cliffs, N.J.: Prentice-Hall, 1974), p. 157.

[2] Norman G. Shidle, *The Art of Successful Communication* (New York: McGraw-Hill, 1965), p. 183 ff.

[3] Patricia Weaver and Robert G. Weaver, *Persuasive Writing* (New York: The Free Press—Macmillan, 1977), p. 140.

[4] Luther A. Brock, *How to Communicate by Letter and Memo* (New York: McGraw-Hill, 1974), p. 109.

[5] Auren Uris, *Memos for Managers* (New York: Thomas P. Crowell Co., 1975), pp. 36–37.

[6] Robert M. Archer and Ruth P. Ames, *Basic Business Communications* (Englewood Cliffs, N.J.: Prentice-Hall, 1971), p. 320.

[7] Leland Brown, *Effective Business Report Writing,* 3rd ed. (Englewood Cliffs, N.J.: Prentice-Hall, 1973), p. 7.

[8] Jessamon Dawe and William Jackson Lord, Jr., *Functional Business Communication* (Englewood Cliffs, N. J.: Prentice-Hall, 1968), p. 282.

[9] Leland Brown, *Effective Business Report Writing,* pp. 238–239, pp. 271 ff.

[10] Robert M. Archer and Ruth P. Ames, *Basic Business Communications,* p. 359.

[11] Leland Brown, *Effective Business Report Writing,* p. 281.

[12] Patricia Weaver and Robert G. Weaver, *Persuasive Writing,* pp. 66–82.

[13] Edward Hodnett, *Effective Presentations* (West Nyack, N.Y.: Parker Publishing Co., 1967).

[14] Leland Brown, *Effective Business Report Writing.*

[15] Leland Brown, *Communicating Facts and Ideas in Business* (Englewood Cliffs, N.J.: Prentice-Hall, 1970), pp. 341–344.

# External Correspondence:
# 19 Special Requests, Sales, Complaints, and Credit

Kind words will never die—neither will they buy groceries.
Edgar Wilson ("Bill") Nye (1850–1896)

You are representing your business firm when anything you have written is seen by an outsider. If the format of your correspondence is sloppy, if your vocabulary is limited, and if your choice of words is poor, an outsider will have a low opinion of your company—even if that outsider could do no better! Misspelled words and incorrect grammar are not to be tolerated. That lesson was brought home to this author vividly, upon receiving a letter from a local attorney. The stationery was expensive—heavy vellum in a beige tint; the letterhead was impressively engraved (raised type) in Old English style. The opening sentence was, "I have been retained by Barbara Loewe in regard to certain agreements between yourself and she concerning . . ." At the bottom of the text were the initials of the lawyer PHH/kd, indicating that it had been dictated to a secretary. I showed the letter to my cleaning woman, whose education was stopped before she reached the sixth grade in grammar school. Her comment was, "He must not be much of a lawyer; that ain't even good grammar, is it?"

Routine business letters are usually executed by a business official's secretary. The secretary knows the format and the style of the employer and can usually compose and respond to letters concerning (a) orders, (b) acknowledgments, (c) routine inquiries, (d) transmittal, (e) miscellaneous information, and (f) good will. There are other letters that must convey the personality of the writer; they are (a) letters of special requests, (b) letters handling complaints, and (c) letters of credit and collection. The sales letter should also appear to be a personal letter if it is addressed to a specific person.

## SPECIAL REQUESTS FOR INFORMATION OR SERVICES

Figure 19-1 shows a letter requesting services, which the authors believe is the most audacious and the most rewarding they have seen. The names and identities have been withheld for obvious reasons, but the facts are a matter of record.

The outcome of that letter was that Zieglar consented to take Catherine Corners as his pupil and even provided living space for her. She remained in Hollywood for eighteen months, and two years after she returned to Upper Delta University she and her cameraman developed a device for splicing sound tracks that is used by all movie studios to this day!

When making a request for information or services, remember that you are asking a favor.[1] In the foregoing letter, note that as president of Upper Delta University, Jon Johannson is a big fish in a little pond, but he is very humble in his praise of Zieglar. Keep in mind your reader's relationship with you. Is the reader a customer? a supplier? a fellow professional? a lodge brother? or what?

Make your request as early as possible—preferably in the first paragraph—and express why you are asking it. It is best if you give some reason for the reader's *need* in granting your request, but needs are not always mutual. The important thing is not to go on and on until your request comes at the close of your letter. Give as many details as may be necessary to show the importance of your request.

If information is desired, be *specific* about what you want. When possible, put the specifics in the form of questions, so that it will be easy for the reader to answer them.[2]

> *Poor:* "We should like to have the reactions of your employees to your recent changeover to computers."
>
> *Better:* "Have your employees expressed fear that the computers will take away some of their jobs?"
>
> *or*
>
> "Have your employees expressed pleasure in the fact that the computers relieve them of the drudgery of calculations?"

When the request for services or information involves payment, state plainly what you are willing to pay. Don't make the mistake of writing, "We will pay handsomely for this." Handsome may mean two entirely different things to you and the reader. Do not expect something for nothing, but you can state your limits: "Would you consider $500 adequate payment for this service?"

UPPER DELTA UNIVERSITY

Glenville, Tennessee

March 12, 197-

Mr. Saul Zieglar
(Address)
Hollywood, California

Dear Mr. Zieglar:

Through investigation I have learned that you are the finest producer-director of quality, low-budget motion pictures in Hollywood.

Will you take Catherine Corners, one of our graduates, as your protegee, and teach her *everything* you know about making movies?

We are a small, liberal arts university, and Jean Trudeau, the machine manufacturer, has given us two million dollars to set up a studio for making religious and educational motion pictures.

Frankly, we do not know where to start. We decided to pick out the *best* and go from there.

If you will take Miss Corners under your tutelage, we will gladly pay all of her expenses, and she can remain with you until you think she is ready to be "graduated." Catherine has a major in Drama, so she knows enough to keep out of your way when you are too busy for her.

You can realize how much it would mean for our little university to have its motion picture director trained by the "master." You will have contributed to education in a significant way.

Please let me have your decision by June 1, 197-.

Sincerely,

Jon Johannson
President

Figure 19-1

LETTERHEAD

September 5, 198-

Mr. Peter Borlund
Carbide Corporation of America
401 South Park Avenue
New York City

Dear Peter,*

Yours is the only firm I know of which has staggered employees'
work hours to avoid traffic problems. When you initiated this, you
wrote an article about your plan which appeared in *Business World.*
That was more than a year ago, and I am curious to know how it
worked out.

Most of our workers must drive in from the suburbs, and Washington, D.C. traffic has become intolerable, so we are considering
trying your plan. Now, my friend, how about giving me some further
information:

1. Has there been any decline in production since the plan was
   put into effect?
2. Do you still use the 7–3, 8–4, & 10–6 shifts?
3. Have you needed to add any part-time employees to take care
   of work at peak periods during the day?
4. Are the workers allowed to volunteer for the shift they prefer,
   or are they assigned arbitrarily?
5. Are the workers rotated among the different shifts, or is it a
   permanent arrangement?

Your plan seemed brilliant when it appeared in *Business World,*
and I'm sure that other companies are as eager as I am to know
how it worked out. Why not do a follow-up article for *Business
World?* I could lend you Miss Donnie Brooks for a couple of weeks
to help out on the writing; she has ghost-written several articles
for businessmen we both know.

Meanwhile, can you give me answers to the above questions by
October first? Surely would appreciate it!

Sincerely,

Sidney Burnopp

SB/sh

Figure 19-2

*The writer and Mr. Borlund were college fraternity brothers, so to address him as
"Mr. Borlund" would be inappropriate.

Finally, close with some concern about the reader's response to your request; you might even suggest a time for the reader to comply, as in Figure 19-1. Do not close with, "thanking you in advance." This presumes that the reader will agree to your request. Thank the reader afterward.

Figures 19-2 and 19-3 are two more examples of request letters for your comparison:

---

LETTERHEAD

September 17, 198-

Mr. Edmund Askins
Editor, *Business World*
Chicago, Illinois

Dear Mr. Askins:

Three years ago, a group of business men and women in Minneapolis got together and formed a social and business club which we call "The Clearing House." We meet over dinner every two weeks, and hold our meetings afterwards.

At each meeting, one member of the club is asked to present a problem that has arisen concerning his/her company, and the other members contribute suggestions for its solution. If the time allows, the members take turns, alphabetically, and present a *minor* problem that has arisen at work, and only two members volunteer a brief suggestion. In this way, we cover a lot of ground and several members get valuable suggestions from the group in each meeting.

"The Clearing House" grew to sixty members within a year, after which we closed the membership. Only if a regular member drops out is there an opening for a new member. Our attendance has averaged 90% over the past two years, so you can judge that there is a high degree of enthusiasm in the group.

Every six weeks, instead of a regular meeting, we meet in the small auditorium at the Town House and a speaker is presented on some topic that is of interest to the group. Members are then allowed to invite guests, and the 250 seats are most always filled to capacity.

All of us have been impressed by your fine editorship of *Business World*, and members of "The Clearing House" often discuss your weekly series on Public Television, "It's Your Choice." So, we are wondering if you would consent to be our guest speaker on the evening of September 25, 198-, or on some future date? Our guest speakers usually talk from 30—45 minutes, and conduct a brief question-and-answer period afterwards.

We know how busy you must be, with your responsibilities at *Business World*, plus the PBS series, but we hope that you can come down to visit us for some evening at your convenience.

Since we do not charge admission for our guest speakers, we do not pay a set fee, but we could take care of your expenses. And we do represent *twenty* different companies in the city of Minneapolis, so it would be excellent publicity for you.

Thanking you in advance,

Nora Olsen
Public Relations Officer

Figure 19-3

If you were Edmund Askins, would you accept Ms. Olsen's invitation to speak? Probably not.

Aside from the length of the letter (far too long!), the request is not made until the end of the fifth paragraph. Remember, we suggested that it be made at the *beginning*.

We also advised that, if any payment is to be made for the reader's granting a request, it should be a specified amount. Mr. Askins might hire a limousine to take him from Chicago to Minneapolis and return, stay overnight at an expensive hotel en route, put up both himself and the limousine's chauffeur at the most expensive suite of rooms in Minneapolis, and easily run "expenses" up to $2,000 or more.

The third gross error in the letter is that the writer made it too easy for Askins to say "no." When you are requesting something, don't give any reasons for refusal, such as, "We know how busy you must be . . ." The busiest of people can always find time to take on an added task—*if* they want to!

There are other things wrong; for instance, the advance notice given. The letter was written on September 17th, and probably did not reach Askins until two or three days later; that means he has only six days to rearrange his busy schedule. Such requests should be made at least three weeks in advance—one month is better. Finally, the writer asks for some other *indefinite* date. Suppose Askins consents to be the speaker and gives Olsen a definite date of October 4th as the *only time* he can appear. Can Olsen be sure that the auditorium at the Town House is available on October 4th? If not, the entire negotiations must be repeated. Be *explicit* in your request!

## SALES LETTERS

Through commercials on radio and television, printed advertisements in periodicals, and the junk mail that reaches us constantly, selling has become associated with a gimmick. These advertisements are all calculated to hook the reader (or listener or viewer) into giving undivided attention to the sales pitch that follows. One should not underestimate the effectiveness of such gimmicks; direct mail must bring some benefits to the seller, since upward of *three billion dollars* per year is spent on it.[3] However, this text is not concerned with broadside advertising but with letters which are targeted to a *particular* person or business. Therefore, we suggest that a sales letter be free of gimmicks and offer a genuine, competitive service. Figure 19-4 is an example.

### Aim at a Specific Reader

Unless your product or service is something that *everyone* uses, you should address it to someone who *does* use it, or at least to someone who *can* use it.

In every chamber of commerce there are directories of club groups of special interest, and the yellow pages in the telephone directory can help you in eliminating people to whom it would be of no possible use. If you do this, you can save your company many dollars in printing and postage. Even if the sales letter you send is a printed form, it should carry the name of the firm in the inside address. For example, The writer of Figure 19-4 did not know whether Floriland Bakeries *had* a title "Director, Plant Operations," but he guessed that it was not the personnel director or the secretary who runs the stenographic pool. If it is a local company you wish to reach, a simple phone call asking,

BAKER'S UNIFORM SERVICE

3604 34th Street
Tampa, Florida, 33605

April 25, 198-

Director, Plant Operations
Floriland Bakeries
Tampa, Florida

Dear Director:

Have you had problems with your employees' uniforms?

Since 1884, Baker's Uniform Service has specialized in solving the problems of companies who provide uniforms for their workers. That must be why we're still in business after nearly 100 years.

We sell uniforms for all types of workers. Because we also RENT them—and must maintain those which we rent—we tailor our uniforms of the finest and most durable materials, in a variety of colors which are fade-proof. That's why, when you *buy* or *rent* Baker's Uniforms, you can be assured of the best quality.

We also specialize in extra personal services, such as (a) not charging for a uniform when a worker is on vacation, (b) alterations without extra charge, and (c) furnishing your company's trade-mark and the name of the employee without extra charge.

Your employees will take pride in their personalized uniforms, and you will take pride in the economy and style of Baker's Uniforms—whether you *buy* or *rent* them.

Give us a call (collect, if you're out of town), and we will do our best to see that you *never* have problems again with your employees' uniforms. Our telephone is (813) 248-4414.

Sincerely,

Lucian C. Reed
Sales Manager

Enc: Card "A"

Figure 19-4

"Who is in charge of renting or purchasing the uniforms for your workers?" will give you the exact name. A title is better than nothing, but the *name* of a person is infinitely preferable to "Gentlemen" or "Dear Sir or Madam."

In the foregoing case it turned out that Mrs. Malloy was in charge of uniforms at Floriland Bakeries and invited the Baker's Uniforms salesman to call on her, by returning the card that was enclosed in the first letter (more about the card later). The salesman took her order and ten days later sent the follow-up letter shown in Figure 19-5.

---

LETTERHEAD

May 8, 198-

Mrs. Mary Malloy
Floriland Bakeries
Tampa, Florida

Dear Mrs. Malloy:

Thank you for your order of last April 28th. You will be happy to know that Baker's Uniforms now has a policy of one extra change in uniform per week for each worker, with no extra charge. This means that, if you order five changes of uniform for one employee, we will furnish that worker with a sixth at no cost to you, just in case the employee has a mishap. Now, aren't you glad you chose Baker's?

Your uniform order is well on its way to being filled but our design department has come up with a second design for coveralls. We are sending over one of the old design and one of the new design by special messenger, to see which your male workers prefer. There is no difference in price, but some of our clients believe that the new design has some advantage over the old one.

Your order will be complete, as promised, on May 14th.

Sincerely,

Lucian C. Reed
Sales Manager

---

Figure 19-5

There are two motives behind the letter shown in Figure 19-5. The first is to let the client know that the order is being filled, just about halfway between the time the order was taken and the time for delivery; this reassures the client, although in businesses with huge volumes this may be impractical. The second motive is one that could be called sly. Baker's *always* makes a practice of giving a worker an extra change of uniform without charge; it is one of its chief selling points. However, if the salesman can make his sale without it, he has a bonus to offer the customer at a later date, thereby surprising the customer pleasantly. Many business firms are more forthright by saying, "Order *now*, and get this free bonus gift!" Tauck Tours, one of the oldest and most successful packagers of combined airplane and motor coach tours in the U.S.A., uses the "surprise bonus" constantly:

1. Our bus pulls into Grand Lake, Colorado, a little before 11:00 A.M. The driver stops the coach on the ridge for the passengers to admire the lake, 1,000 feet below. While they are exclaiming over the beauty of the scene, the tour director says, "We have a few minutes before lunch; how would you like to take a boat-ride on that beautiful lake? . . . O.K., *we'll treat* you to one." Now the passengers have already paid for the boat-ride, and the boats on the lake have already been reserved, but nothing has been mentioned about it in the advertising brochure, so the passengers enjoy it twice as much . . .

2. Leaving Yosemite, we arrive in Merced, where we join again the Tauck Tour Coach. From Merced west, there is not much to see except rich farmland and vineyards, so the tour director is briefing the passengers on points of interest to visit in San Francisco during their free time. Meals are not furnished by Tauck in San Francisco; so, after giving the passengers some tips on where to dine, the tour director announces, "Now, save tomorrow evening's dinner for Tauck Tours, because we're giving you a free cocktail party and a farewell dinner in one of the most magnificent dining spots in the City—The Garden Court of the old Palace Hotel."[4]

—Hugh P. Fellows*

## Use Persuasive Techniques

Perhaps the main difference between a persuasive speech and a persuasive sales letter is that the persuasive letter must be shorter. Because of this, it must tailor its appeal to a specific person, rather than to an audience made up of people with varied interests. Here are some of the elements of persuasion:

1. *Attention.* Any fool can get attention by being blatant. Only a wise person can get that attention and *focus* it on his *purpose.* "The entire California Coast, between Sacramento and San Diego, will slide into the Pacific Ocean because of earthquakes!" is not *nearly* as important to the farmer in Lubbock, Texas, as the statement, "If you cannot irrigate your wheat, you will have a crop failure."

*Fellows was a tour director for Tauck Tours for fourteen summers. Some of those itineraries have now been changed.

2. *Interest.* Attention must be achieved before once can become *interested.* While blaring headlines in newspapers and startling statements on television may attract *attention*, a person is *interested* only in what concerns *that person.* Furthermore, the person's interest is divided into two categories:

    A. *Emotional appeal,* which is centered around self-preservation, sex, ego and altruism.**

    B. *Rational appeal,* which is centered around economy, durability, efficiency, and profits.

        Example: This refrigerator will outlast three automobiles, two vacuum cleaners, and goodness knows how many teenagers! (Durability)

        Example: Wear the after-shave that will make *you* the man in her life. (Sex)

        Example: Wear the after-shave that makes a man smell like a *man!* (Ego)

3. *Creating a desire* for your product or service is necessary in a sales letter. People have individual desires, but they also have group, or class, desires. How would you classify these appeals?

    A. Get your husband out of that hot cement jungle, and waft him away to the cool north woods.

    B. Loving is giving; give your wife security for the rest of her life, with this annuity.

    C. All busy executives have this loud-speaker attachment for their telephones, so they can listen and write in comfort.

    D. You can enter the world of tomorrow, while your competitors are lagging behind yesterday, with this new, time-saving computer.

4. *Making it easy* for your reader to respond is important.[5] In the case of Baker's Uniforms a card was enclosed in the sales letter; one side was prestamped and bore the address of Baker's Uniforms; the other side looked like Figure 19-6.

---

YES, I am interested in learning more about
BAKER'S UNIFORM'S unique service. Your
representative may call on me _____
                              (Date)
at _____
    (Time)
                    (Signed)_____
                  (Company)_____

---

Figure 19-6

**Appealing to *fright* is related to self-preservation. Strangely enough, it has *little impact*, as witnessed by labels on cigarette packs, "The Surgeon General has determined that cigarette smoking is dangerous to your health."

You will note that people who fill out the card do not even need to bother inserting the address of their company; Baker's already *has* that, and the telephone number as well. If there is a conflict between the time one prospect and another expects the representative to call, it can be resolved by a simple telephone call.

In television commercials, how many times have you been invited to make a toll-free telephone call if you are interested in a certain product? The vendor is simply making it *easy* for you to respond.

5. *Some "Don'ts."* Here are some pitfalls that writers of sales letters are likely to fall into:

A. Avoid implied criticism at all costs. "Are you tired of serving the same food to your family day in and day out?" implies a lack of culinary knowledge on the part of the housewife. "Why return to the same vacation spot, year after year? Why not try something different?" implies that the reader lacks imagination. Besides, "different" is not always "better."

B. Respect your readers' intelligence, and *don't* tell them what they think or feel—or what they *should* think or feel.[6] "I'm sure that you've often felt that life is not worthwhile; here is something that will change all that!" is insulting: The reader may be an incurable optimist and does not want to change "all that." The same applies to this passage, "All intelligent people believe that waste produces want." Benjamin Franklin said it long ago, and I'm sure that you'll agree that his was one of the greatest minds in all of our history.

C. Don't use an old bromide, such as, "Where there's a will there's a way," or, "He who hesitates is lost." They've been tired for decades!

D. Avoid gimmicks and exaggeration, such as, "There is ONE MILLION DOLLARS waiting for YOU!—and *no strings attached!*"

If you have a worthwhile product to sell, try to show it in its best light, but don't pretend that Night of Layo is going to transform an old hag overnight into a raving beauty!

## LETTERS OF COMPLAINT AND ADJUSTMENT

To abide faithfully by the slogan, "The customer is always right," will destroy your business as thoroughly as a tornado. Nevertheless, you should aim for satisfied customers, and you cannot ignore their complaints. Some people are chronic complainers, but they are in the minority. Here is an incident that seems hard to believe:

United Airlines had oversold the seats in tourist class on a certain flight from San Francisco to New York by six spaces. The airline promptly offered to place the six passengers into *first class* on another flight, that would get them into New York thirty minutes *ahead* of the one they had booked on originally. There were bitter complaints from four of the six passengers! "I'll have to hang around Kennedy Airport for thirty whole minutes, until my folks come to get me!" one passenger complained. Another snorted indignantly, "If I had wanted first class, I'd have *booked* first class!"

Most customers complain in good faith, and they should be replied to in equally good faith. When a customer complains, it is usually about:[7]

1. Faulty merchandise
2. Poor services
3. Overcharges
4. Others (such as company policy) are in the minority.

However minor the complaint may be, once the customer has taken the trouble to call by telephone or write a letter, the customer *magnifies* that complaint out of all logical proportion. The customer is concerned with only two things:[8]

1. Something is wrong!
2. What are you going to do about it?

Business people sometimes tend to decimate customer complaints. Complaints are often regarded as a criticism of company efficiency, and some poorly managed businesses will bristle with indignation when a customer complains, because complaints appear to be a threat to profits or job security. But, even Rolls Royce makes mistakes. Benjamin Franklin wrote, "Love your enemies, for they tell you your faults." A customer with a complaint is only temporarily an enemy. Your job is to turn that enemy into a friend. Nevertheless, as a practical business person, you must be concerned with three things:

1. Something is apparently wrong, and one of our customers is upset.
2. Who is at fault?
3. What can I do about it to keep the customer's trade, without its costing my business too much money?

Before you do anything, *investigate!* If the investigation is going to take more than a day or two, let the dissatisfied customer know that you care and are investigating the trouble. Use the telephone, rather than writing a letter, if this is feasible. The longer the complainant waits, the more he or she will magnify the complaint.

While some complaints and adjustments may involve thousands of dollars, the discussion in this text is confined to the most common (although not always the simplest!) type between the customer and the retailer.

## When to Say "Yes" and When to Say "No"

Obviously when a customer complains about something that is clearly the fault of your company, you always say "yes" to the customer's complaint, and try to make a satisfactory adjustment. Beyond that, there is no hard and fast rule for refusing or agreeing to make an adjustment. Even when you suspect that the customer is at fault, you sometimes say "yes," depending upon (a) how long the customer has been doing a substantial volume of business with you, and (b) how much money it will cost your company. This is always accompanied by a clear statement of exactly *why* you are saying "yes." When the customer is at fault, you often have to say "no." When a third party is at fault (a carrier, for instance), it is up to *you* to make an investigation of that third party. After all, the customer bought the merchandise or service from you, and it is no fault of the customer that you did not select a carrier who could be depended upon. Note the examples in Figures 19-7 to 19-9.

It is difficult to believe that anyone in business would write a letter such as that in Figure 19-8. The phrase "you claim" is insulting (so are phrases such as, "your mistake," "your complaint," and "you state"). The grossest error, however, is in trying to defend Johnson; whether or not Mrs. Medlow "misinterpreted" Johnson is irrelevant; so far as she is concerned, he was rude to her. Such a letter is calculated to drive away a $6,000-a-year customer.

In Figure 19-9, the writer is doing everything he can to save money for the store. The important thing is to get Mrs. Medlow back into the store. If Bixby simply agrees to credit her account with the amount paid for the shoes, she is not apt to return to Bimbel's after her unhappy experience with Johnson. If Bixby can get her into his office and be exceptionally pleasant to her, it does not really matter whether or not she finally accepts the stretched shoes; she will probably select another pair of shoes from Bimbel's, but Bixby had better make sure that Johnson is *not* in the shoe department when Mrs. Medlow visits it! He should send Johnson for a coffee break, or find some other pretext to get him off the floor temporarily. Time will heal Mrs. Medlow's wounded pride, but it will take time.

Figures 19-10, 19-11, 19-12 show three letters illustrating an instance where a third party (the carrier) is at fault. In Figure 19-12, Mr. Oaks not only has a satisfied customer, but he may also sell another set of crystal for $150.00! There are times when you, as a business person, must say "no" and refuse to satisfy a customer's complaint. Figures 19-13 and 19-14 are examples. Under normal circumstances, one would not write such a long letter as in Figure 19-14. In a city as small as Santa Fe,* where the townspeople get to know the tradesmen by name (and frequently by reputation!), it is not too much to expect. You will note that Mr. Church did not refer to the competition by name, a tactful omission. You will also note that Church did not overlook the slight prevarication in Thatcher's letter (that is, holding the coat until "the winter social season"), and recalled that Thatcher needed the coat for a trip to Canada. Was this tactful? No, but Thatcher implied that he had not worn the coat, while the probability was that he had. It was simply Church's way of reminding Thatcher that "I'll be fair with you, if you'll be fair with me."

---

*45,941, according to the 1976 census estimate.

Store Manager
Bimbel's Department Store
Seattle, Washington

Dear Mr. Bixby:

I am sending *to your office* a pair of beige-and-burgundy lady's shoes. I paid $45.00 for them, and wish it credited to my account.

When I came into Bimbel's three weeks ago, looking for a pair of dressy daytime shoes, I did not particularly like the style of these shoes, but your salesman, Mr. Johnson, insisted that beige-and-burgundy was the latest color combination, and it's true that they harmonize well with some of my daytime outfits. Johnson fitted me, and came up with a size 3½. I insisted that I had always worn a size 4, but I let him talk me into buying them.

Within two days of wearing the shoes, my feet began to hurt, because the shoes were obviously too small. When I attempted to return the shoes to Mr. Johnson, he was insufferably rude, and refused to exchange them. He implied that I was the sort of person who bought things, soon became tired of them, and then wanted to return them and get my money back. He informed me, snobbishly, that every intelligent person knows that one cannot return articles of clothing that have been worn.

I have had a charge account at Bimbel's for *nine years,* and spend an average of $6,000 a year for my family in your store, but cannot remember ever returning anything before.

Now, you should fire Mr. Johnson, who hasn't the first notion of tact, and credit me with the $45.00 to which I am entitled.

Angrily,

Mrs. Andrew Medlow

Figure 19-7

BIMBEL'S DEPARTMENT STORE
"Only the Finest"
777 Broad Street
Seattle, Washington (98109)

Date

Mrs. Andrew Medlow
(Address)

Dear Mrs. Medlow,

I am indeed sorry that you had an unpleasant experience in Bimbel's shoe department.

You claim that Mr. Hal Johnson fitted you with the wrong shoe size. You may recall that we use an X-ray machine, which the customer can look into and see whether or not a shoe is fitted properly, so I don't know how Mr. Johnson could have been inaccurate.

What you may have interpreted as rudeness on Mr. Johnson's part was beyond his control. You see, State Law forbids our accepting wearing apparel for re-sale that has been worn. The law is especially strict where footwear and wigs are concerned. Mrs. Medlow, Hal Johnson has been in our employ for twelve years, and is known as the *soul* of courtesy. I am sorry that you misunderstood him.

We regret that we cannot possibly make any adjustment in this instance; we suggest that, in the future, you make sure that your shoes are comfortable before leaving the place of purchase.

Regrettably,

John Bixby
Store manager

Figure 19-8

LETTERHEAD

Date

(Internal address)

Dear Mrs. Medlow:

I regret deeply that you had an unfortunate experience in purchasing shoes at Bimbel's. Of course we will credit your account with the $45.00 as you requested. However, may I offer an alternative?

Shoe sizes—even in the most exclusive brands—are sometimes a fraction "off." We have a special water-stretcher which insures absolute comfort up to two sizes above that which appears on the label. Since it *is* a water-process, and since pure leather is so malleable, the stretching process is guaranteed not to revert to a tighter fit. We have put your shoes onto these stretchers, and they will be ready in two days. It is indeed against the law for us to sell already-worn shoes, but that is inconsequential in comparison with your patronage of Bimbel's.

Since you like the beige-and-burgundy color which goes well with your daytime dressy clothes, why don't you come into my office at your convenience, and we will see how comfortable the shoes are? If you are not completely happy with them, we will credit your account with the amount, and hope that you will select another pair of shoes from our stylish line of footwear, which is the finest in the city.

Sincerely,

John Bixby

Figure 19-9

```
┌──────────────────────────────────────────────────────────────────┐
│                                                     Address        │
│                                                     Date           │
│                                                                    │
│   Mail Order Dept.                                                 │
│   Marisol-Shield Glassware                                         │
│   Chicago, Ill.                                                    │
│                                                                    │
│   Gentlemen:                                                       │
│                                                                    │
│      On October 4th I ordered six Waterford Crystal goblets (catalog│
│   number 12G4417) @ $25.00 each. I explained that it was imper-    │
│   ative that the goblets reach me by October 25th, as they are to be│
│   an anniversary present to my wife. Your catalog states that two  │
│   weeks is ample time for delivery in the State of Illinois, but the│
│   crystal has not arrived.                                         │
│                                                                    │
│      If the crystal goblets do not arrive by October 25, I shall have to│
│   return them, as they are a match for others which we have, and   │
│   we are giving a party to celebrate our anniversary.              │
│                                                                    │
│      Please give this matter your immediate attention.            │
│                                                                    │
│                                    Yours truly,                    │
│                                                                    │
│                                    W. Edgewood                     │
│                                                                    │
└──────────────────────────────────────────────────────────────────┘
```

Figure 19-10

## How to Say "Yes"

You can lose customers by saying "yes" to their complaints just as easily as you can by saying "no".[9] If the customer is at fault, and you make concessions, the customer may feel, "Well, I got by with it this time, but I probably won't get by with it next time, so I'd better trade somewhere else." Cynical? No, just realistic. Always explain *why* you are making the concession, even though the client was at fault. (See Figure 19-9, paragraph 2)

*First,* apologize for the customer's inconvenience, and tell him/her what adjustment you are going to make. *Do this in your opening sentences.*

*Second,* explain how the inconvenience occurred, and tell what steps you have taken to see that it does not happen again.

```
┌─────────────────────────────────────────────────────────────────┐
│                                                                   │
│                  MARISOL-SHIELD GLASSWARE                         │
│                     Exclusive Imports                             │
│                  2870 North Sheridan Road                         │
│                  Chicago, Illinois (60657)                        │
│                                                                   │
│                                          October 20, 198-         │
│                                                                   │
│         Mr. W. Edgewood                                           │
│         1713 Forward Street                                       │
│         Urbana, Illinois                                          │
│                                                                   │
│                                    RE: Order # 1337547-I          │
│                                                                   │
│         Dear Mr. Edgewood:                                        │
│                                                                   │
│         Thank you for your order of October 4, 198-. We note that │
│         it was shipped via insured parcel post on October 11th,   │
│         and should reach you in plenty of time for your party.    │
│                                                                   │
│                       Happy Anniversary!                          │
│                                                                   │
│                       Sherman Oaks                                │
│                       Mail Order Supervisor                       │
│                                                                   │
└─────────────────────────────────────────────────────────────────┘
```

Figure 19-11

Example:

Our computer billing system is new, and one of our programmers failed to delete your name from the list of customers who had paid. Our accounting system is extremely accurate, so that you were never *charged* for the bills you have been receiving. We are now using two programmers for the billing computer, to double check, and this should not happen again.

*Third,* thank the customer for his/her patronage, and look foward to future business.

## How to Say "No"

It is difficult to refuse a customer with a complaint, even though that customer is at fault, but it is necessary. Here are the steps to take:

*First,* cushion the bad news with a pleasant opening (see Figure 19-14, first

October 20, 198-

(Internal address)

Re: Order # 1337547-I

Dear Mr. Edgewood:

Thank you for your order of October 4, 198-. We note that it was shipped via insured parcel post on October 11th, and should have reached you by now. We have put a tracer on the shipment.

However, to assure that you will not be disappointed on your anniversary, we have today sent you a duplicate set of six Waterford crystal goblets (12G4417) by Overnight Express. The crystal will probably reach you before you receive this letter.

When the original order shows up, please return it to us. All you need do is to scratch out your address and mark the parcel "return to sender"; a "return postage guaranteed" is printed in the upper lefthand corner of the parcel.

Or, if you wish to keep both sets of goblets, simply mail us your check for the extra set. Waterford crystal will never depreciate in value, and can be a valuable family heirloom!

Happy Anniversary!

Sherman Oaks
Mail Order Supervisor

Figure 19-12

paragraph), but do not mislead the writer into thinking you are going to grant his or her request.

*Second,* explain *why* you must refuse the request. This should be done in some detail, and not by the cowardly phrase of, "it is against company policy."

*Third,* offer an alternative if there is a logical one (see Figure 19-9 paragraph 2). One of the best replies offering an alternative we have seen concerns a

```
                                          2509 Pachenko Dr.
                                          Santa Fe, NM
                                          September 26, 198-

     Mr. Grady Church
     EL Pueblo Men's Furnishing
     200 Mercado Plaza
     Santa Fe, NM

     Dear Mr Church:

        Three weeks ago (Sept. 5th, to be exact) I bought a cashmere
     topcoat from your store, to hold it until the winter social season.
     I paid $280.00 for the coat. Yesterday, I was in Albuquerque and
     found the exact same cashmere coat on sale at Delman's for only
     $260.00. Of course I could not pass up such a bargain, and had
     Delman's put away the coat for me on their lay-away plan.

        I have traded at El Pueblo for seven years, and I wonder what
     you propse to do about this contrast in price. Will you meet Delman's
     price of $260.00, or shall I return the topcoat to your store and
     have the $280.00 credited to my account? I await your decision.

                                          Yours truly,

                                          Hubert Thatcher
```

Figure 19-13

woman who returned an electric toaster to the manufacturer, complaining that the toaster stopped working the *very day* after her warranty had expired. The manufacturer replied:

> Although your warranty has expired, Procter-Silex toasters have the record of lasting many years beyond their warranty. We have found a small coil that is the cause of the problem, and will gladly replace the coil at its cost to us, which is $4.50; there is no labor charge.
>
> If you wish this done, please sign the stamped card that is enclosed and mail it to us. In a very few days you will have your toaster in perfect working order.

*Fourth,* appeal to the customer's sense of fair play. While we have advocated throughout this text, "Put yourself in the place of the reader," this is one

EL PUEBLO MEN'S FURNISHINGS
"Eastern Style with Western Comfort"
200 Mercado Plaza
Santa Fe, New Mexico
87501

September 28, 198-

(Internal address)

Dear Mr. Thatcher,

You have indeed been a valued customer at El Pueblo for several years, and our salesmen say that you have impeccable taste.

All retail stores have sales for the purpose of clearing away seasonal merchandise, or for disposing of items which are no longer carried by their suppliers. The store offers an item or two at cost—or even below cost—as a "leader" to draw in customers. El Pueblo has such sales, and the reasons are no secret. You can certainly get lower prices if you buy *only* during these sales.

El Pueblo has never pretended to have the lowest *prices* in this area, but always to give the highest *quality* of men's furnishings, when you need them. As we recall, you needed a topcoat for a trip to Montreal, Canada, at the time you bought your coat from us.

You can understand that, if stores listed merchandise at "sales prices" all year 'round, it would simply mean that their *overall* prices would be higher. It is for this reason that we cannot meet the sales price of a store whose *quality* of merchandise is unknown to us.

You can also understand that we cannot alter our price on an item that was sold three weeks ago.

We hope that we can continue to serve you with the finest quality of men's furnishings, at the lowest possible cost to you.

Sincerely,

Grady Church
Manager

Figure 19-14

instance where you, as a business person, should ask the customer to put himself or herself in *your* position!

Finally, look forward to future business. Point out your past record of service, and close cordially. That is as much as can be expected of you.

## Nonadjustment Complaints

There are complaint letters that require no adjustment by the company to whom they are addressed. These letters fall into two categories: The (1) "I'm-just-mad!" letter and (2) the letter of constructive criticism. Newspaper and magazine editors get more of the first type, especially if the periodical publishes editorials and articles on current events. However, business firms get their share, and they should be replied to, even though the reply may be a brief one. Two samples of the first type are shown in Figures 19-15 and 19-16.

---

Tauck Tours, Inc.
Westport, CT.

Dear Mr. Tauck,

    I have taken Tauck Tours for several summers and they have always been first-rate. My recent tour to Ontario, Canada was spoiled for me because I got almost no sleep for three nights.

    In Niagara Falls, in Kingston, and in Ottawa, I was put into rooms on the second or third floor, and there were large trees growing outside my window. I like fresh air, and the nights were cool enough that I did not need air conditioning. At the crack of dawn, those trees were filled with birds who carried on such a screeching that there was no hope of sleep. After it happened to me in Niagara, I forgot about it, although I was so sleepy the next day that I couldn't enjoy the scenery. Then it happened again in Kingston and Ottawa! Three of my seven-day tour was spoiled by those damned birds.

                                                 Sincerely,

                                             Mrs. Hall Phrate

Figure 19-15

Date

(Internal address)

Dear Mrs. Phrate:

We always demand outside rooms for all of our Tauck Tour guests because of the view. The air-conditioning usually shuts out street noises and other sounds. If you had told Mr. Rother, your tour director, of your problem, he could have taken care of it easily.

We are always glad to honor special requests. The next time you take a Tauck Tour, go to your tour director at the *beginning of the trip* and explain your preference; he will make a note on his rooming sheet which will automatically insure your special request for the remainder of the tour.

Tauck Tours has a slogan, "We can fix everything but the weather!" While that is a slight exaggeration, your problem would have been a very easy one to fix. So, just let us know!

Looking forward to seeing you on future Tauck Tours.

Sincerely,

Arthur C. Tauck, Jr.
President

Figure 19-16

As we wrote earlier, business people often resent complaints because they construe it as a criticism of their efficiency, or as an actual job threat. Uninvited criticism—even when it is constructive—often meets the same resistance.

The late Julian Goldner had been active in restaurants for fifty-five years— as everything from a busboy to the *maître d'hôtel* of some of the finest dining spots across the continent. After he retired, Julian traveled in order to visit as many of the world's fine restaurants as possible. He came to Central West Florida and paid a visit to the most lavish dining spot on the "sun coast,"

Weingardner's.* The place had been open for six months, but the service was chaotic, and the fine food was ruined by the time it reached its destination. Mind you, several million dollars had been spent on this restaurant to make it the most luxurious dining spot in all Florida, yet it took at least two hours to get a dinner that was not fit to eat! Julian kept murmuring all evening, "What a pity! And such a *beautiful* place. What a pity!" After spending an evening there, Julian sat down and wrote a painstaking 3-page letter, explaining how the operation could be improved. He received a scathing letter from the owner's wife, telling him to mind his own business, and asking him never to attempt to get a reservation there again, because it would be refused! However, one of Julian Goldner's letters had happier results. We have permission to reproduce it (see Figure 19-17).

---

Date

Ms. Leslie Gordon*
Champlain Inn
Lake Champlain, N. Y.

My dear Ms. Gordon,

I am happily a guest in your inn. My room is beautiful, and the view from it is spectacular. My late wife would have loved the fine antiques with which you have tastefully decorated the lounges and parlors.

As one who has been in the restaurant business for more than fifty years, I am hesitant to say this, but your dining room leaves something to be desired. I realize that you are using inexperienced college students to supplement your regular help during the summer, and they are a joy to behold, with their bright young faces and sense of humor. *That* is *not* your problem.

The secret of a crowded—but well-run—dining room lies in one word: Bussing.**

Now, you have four lines of six tables each, excluding the large banquet table at the rear, and you have three bus-boys. Apparently,

---

*The actual name has been changed.

**"Bussing" is the clearing of tables when guests have finished eating, putting a clean table cloth on the table, and taking the dishes and utensils to the kitchen for the dishwasher.

the dining-room manager has assigned each of the bus-boys to look constantly for *any* table that is not cleared and re-set, and to get busy and do it immediately; there will be no standing around idly on the part of the bus-boys! *That* is your problem!

Each bus-boy should be assigned to a certain eight tables, and *only* to those tables. It doesn't matter if one boy stands idly for 15 minutes, while waiting for certain guests to finish; you will save time in the long run. There should also be aisles reserved for *only* the bus-boys and *only* the waitresses; then they don't get into each other's way. I have drawn a crude diagram to show you what I mean:

| Bus-boy only | B-1 | Waitresses only | B-1 | Waitresses only | B-2 | Bus-boy only | B-2 | Waitresses only | B-3 | Waitresses only | B-3 | Bus-boy only |
|---|---|---|---|---|---|---|---|---|---|---|---|---|
| | B-1 | | B-1 | | B-2 | | B-2 | | B-3 | | B-3 | |
| | B-1 | | B-1 | | B-2 | | B-2 | | B-3 | | B-3 | |
| | B-1 | | B-1 | | B-2 | | B-2 | | B-3 | | B-3 | |
| | B-1 | | B-1 | | B-2 | | B-2 | | B-3 | | B-3 | |

There are also four waitresses (six at dinner), and I have drawn a diagram showing how their tables could be apportioned for greater efficiency, both at breakfast, lunch and dinner.

Sincerely,

Julian Goldner

Figure 19-17

The letter is too long to reproduce it here entirely, but it brought forth the response from Ms. Gordon shown in Figure 19-18. Julian Goldner did not charge Leslie *anything* for helping to get her dining room organized; in fact, he spent one week at the beginning of each summer as a guest of the Champlain Inn until he passed away. He *loved* seeing people comfortable and happy in a dining room, and the Champlain Inn became his grandbaby!

We cannot report such a happy ending to all business letters, but they *do* happen.

## Some "Don'ts"

Remember that dissatisfied customers believe that they have been wounded, so don't rub salt into the wound. Treat it gently.

```
                        (LETTERHEAD)

                                                       Date

Dear Mr. Goldner,

    What a dear man you are, to offer to help with the organization
of our dining room!

    You must have been sent by Heaven, because our headwaiter left
us two weeks ago, just before the start of the summer rush. One of
our waitresses has attempted to fill in, but—although she is a very
good waitress—she doesn't know much about organization.

    If you will help us get organized, I shall certainly pay you. Would
$300.00 help you to get us started?

                                             Gratefully,

                                             Leslie Gordon
                                             Proprietor
```

Figure 19-18

1. *Avoid undesirable overtones,* which the phrases, "your unfortunate error," "your mistake," or "your complaint" imply.

2. *Don't be flippant* by using such sentences as, "That's the way the cookie crumbles; "sorry!" or, "There's many a slip twixt the hip and the lip."

3. *Don't be arrogant or critical,* and don't be condescending or sarcastic.[10] A jeweler once replied to a customer whose expensive watch needed repair, "Your Executive Watch *is* shockproof, but it won't run if you use it as a hammer."

4. *Don't hide behind company policy;* each complaint letter deserves an individual explanation. Even multimillion-dollar companies must value each customer.

Every answer to a letter of complaint should be courteous and honest, and should not try to compromise the dignity of the writer or receiver.

"Although a dissatisfied customer may be an enemy, a dissatisfied customer who is treated with honesty and courtesy can be transformed into a satisfied and staunch supporter."[11]

                                             Archer and Ames

# LETTERS OF CREDIT AND COLLECTION

More than 90 percent of the commercial transactions in this country are conducted on credit, and approximately 50 percent of consumer goods are bought on credit. From the mid 1960s until late in the 1970s almost every large chain store was begging customers to open a charge account with its local outlet. Credit card operations proliferated to five times their original number; some of them amalgamated, and the giants of the newcomers emerged as Master Charge and Visa. At first, Master Charge gave out cards indiscriminately—even to permanent unemployables! Everyone was invited to *buy*, whether or not the person could *pay*. At the time of this writing, it is no longer as convenient to use Master Charge, because the cashiers must go through a long list of cards that are delinquent (7,000 in Florida alone!) before accepting the charge.

## Extending Consumer Credit

When you are in business, you want as many customers as you can take care of, on both a cash and credit basis. When a potential customer asks for credit, you examine the request in the light of what we call the *Three R's*—resources, reputation, and recent performance.

1. *Resources.* How much property does the individual own? Does the person own a home? Other real estate? Does the person own a car—make and model? A boat? How much life insurance does the person have? Its cash value? Does the person have a savings account—if so, how large? A checking account? How much is the person's salary? What is the size of the person's family?

2. *Reputation.* What is the person's reputation among other people in the community? Does the person's family have a reputation for living above their income? Does the person have a reputation for changing jobs often under questionable circumstances? Is the person a stable citizen?

3. *Recent performance.* What is the person's recent record (four years is as far back as you need go) for borrowing and repaying money? Does the person pay bills on time?

Most businesses (all of the larger ones) have a credit application form that asks all of these questions and more; the form also requires references. Even when a potential customer writes a letter asking for credit and answering most of these questions, it is advisable to require the person to fill out the form. Write a short, courteous note such as that shown in Figure 19-19.

It is customary to "spot check" two or more of the references given on the application. This is usually done by phone, unless the references given are from another city. Most firms have printed forms for this purpose, which require only the name and address of the reference and the name and address of the

Dear Mr. Alcott:

Thank you for applying to Dale's Department Store for a charge account in your name and that of your wife and daughter. Your business and credit records are impressive, and we appreciate your patronage.

However, all of our charge accounts are mechanized, so we know that you will not mind taking a few minutes to fill out the enclosed application form. Within a few days after we receive it, we feel certain that all three members of your family will receive their charge-a-plates.

Sincerely,

Figure 19-19

applicant to be filled in. We have enclosed in brackets the portions that need filling in on the suggested form. Credit managers from another firm will almost always supply this information, because they may need to get the same information from *you* at some time (see Figure 19-20).

Once you have decided to grant a person credit, you should write a short letter enclosing the charge-a-plate and delineating specific rules for payment. Although these rules have been stated on the application, they may be in language so confusing that only a lawyer could interpret them. Let the customer *know* what to expect, as shown in Figure 19-21.

## Refusing Credit

If, after your investigation of an applicant, you know that the person is a poor credit risk, you must *tell* the applicant. It is true that a one-sentence card or letter saying only, "We regret that, in view of the information we have received, we cannot extend the credit you requested," sounds cold and tactless. Some writers on the subject do not object to it. Others do object, and here are some of their suggestions:

1. Tell the applicant that, according to your marketing experts, the particular item he wishes to buy on credit (a TV color set, or a bedroom suite, for example) will be reduced in price within six months, and suggest that he wait until then to reapply. (Suppose he is not asking for credit to buy any one item?)[12]
2. Tell the applicant that, as soon as he gets a little more settled in his new job, or in the new city to which he has just moved, that he should reapply. (Suppose

```
CONFIDENTIAL

[Credit Manager
Barnum's Metal Supply
Kansas City, MO.]

Your name has been given as a credit reference by:

                    [Mr. J. W. Alcott
                     2250 Golftee Blvd.
                        Peoria, IL.]

Will you please supply the following CONFIDENTIAL information:

How long was the above-named person a customer of yours?


_____

What was his average monthly account?_____
Did he always pay the full amount on time?_____
If not, please give brief details:_____

_____

Other comments:_____

_____

Your signature and position:_____

_____
```

Figure 19-20

he has *not* just recently moved, or has been holding the same job for fifteen years?)[13]

3. Explain to the applicant that your bookkeeping department has all of the charge accounts they can handle, and ask him to reapply in six months. (Suppose a friend of his, with a very *good* credit rating, applies *after* the applicant in question has been refused, and receives a charge card immediately?)[14]

We do not subscribe to any of these "dodges," which are made on the pretext that the poor credit risk may change in the future, and you may have lost his business forever if you are blunt. We believe applicants should know where they stand with regard to credit, so that they can begin to do something about it. (See Figure 19-22.)

Dear Mr. Alcott:

Dale's Department Store is pleased to open a charge account in the names of

Mrs. J. W. Alcott
Miss Nancy Alcott
Mr. J. W. Alcott

Your charge-a-plates are enclosed. You will need to present them each time you make a purchase.

Each month an itemized bill will be sent to you of purchases made during the past 30 days. The bills will be mailed on the 20th of each month, and will show any purchases made up until 2:00 P.M. on the 18th of that same month. Full payment is expected within 30 days, and will carry no finance charge. A schedule of minimum payments and finance charges for amounts that are unpaid after 30 days is enclosed.

We are sure that you will enjoy shopping at Dale's.

Sincerely,

Encs.

Figure 19-21

---

Dear Mr. Alcott:

In view of the information we have received, we do not think it advisable to extend you credit *at this time.*

However, circumstances change, and you may simply have had a streak of bad luck that gives you such a poor credit rating. We suggest that you not be discouraged, and invite you cordially to discuss the matter of credit with us within the next few months.

Figure 19-22

```
PERHAPS IT SLIPPED YOUR MIND?

Your account with us is overdue. If you have paid it in the past few
days, please disregard this reminder and accept our thanks.

                                          Dale's Department Store
```

Figure 19-23

## Collecting

An elderly credit manager we know uses this analogy: "Collecting money owed
on charge accounts is very much like harvesting apples. Some get ripe and fall
to the ground naturally; those are the customers who pay their debts on time
as soon as a bill is sent to them. With others, you have to give the tree a gentle
shake; those are the customers who have to be reminded to pay. To get more
apples, you have to shake the tree and the *branches* real hard; those are the
customers who have to be sent a slightly threatening letter. To get the rest of
the apples, you have to climb out onto the limbs and pull them off with an
apple-picker; those are the customers who have to be turned over to a collection
agency, and aren't worth having."

*The first reminder,* when an account is overdue, need be no more than a
printed card (enclosed in an envelope) and can read something like that shown
in Figure 19-23.

*The second reminder* should be a little stronger, but should consider that
there might be extenuating circumstances which have caused nonpayment. It
can also be a printed card (see Figure 19-24).

*The third reminder* should not be a printed card, but a letter written on the
firm's letterhead, although the *wording* could be the same for all delinquent

```
This is the second time we have reminded you that your account
is overdue. If some development has made prompt payment difficult
for you, please let us know. We'll be glad to discuss the matter and
try to work out something.

                                          Dale's Department Store
```

Figure 19-24

customers. If, receiving the card shown in Figure 19-24, the customer responds with payment, the chances are that the person is a good customer, although a slow-paying one. However, if you get no response from the second reminder, don't delay any further (see Figure 19-25).

If, after the first or second reminder, the customer calls or writes, expressing intent and willingness to pay, your firm should try to make arrangements for the person to do so. Unless such people are living chronically beyond their means, they will be grateful to you, and will become staunch supporters and word-of-mouth advertisements of your business. Figure 19-26 shows the type of letter we mean. Of course you will allow Mr. Bender to pay off his account in fifty-dollar installments. If you are a good public relations person, you will not tack on an added finance charge; the word of your being willing to help a customer who has had a streak of bad luck will get around, and will be worth more than the finance charge!

Credit is serious business, but the letters shown in Figures 19-27 and 19-28 are amusing. It is doubtful that they were ever sent.

In all business writing, the most important thing to remember is that you are writing to *one person*, not a general population. Keep your words simple and your sentences varied, and try to write as if that person has invited you for a cup of coffee—for which that person is paying!

---

LETTERHEAD

Date

(Internal address)

Dear Mr. Alcott:

You have not responded in any way to our recent reminders that your account with us is long overdue. We dislike resorting to legal action, but unless you make some sort of satisfactory arrangement with us within *three days*, you will force us to do so.

(Signed)
Credit Manager
Dale's Department Store

---

Figure 19-25

Dear Mr. Mendez,

I have had a charge account with Dale's Department Store for six years, and have always paid my bills on time. My account No. is 12G4867-B.

I still owe Dale's $300 on the furniture and TV set we purchased, and intend paying it.

I was in the hospital for three weeks, and lost a month's wages. My worker's compensation did not do much more than buy food for my family. I am back on my feet now and able to work.

My installments on the furniture and TV are $75.00 a month, but I wonder if I could pay you $50.00 a month (maybe I can pay more later) until I get the $300 paid off?

I surely would appreciate this help.

Ralph Bender

Figure 19-26

LETTERHEAD

Date

(Internal address)

Dear Mr. Jameson:

Your account with us for $93.00 is now three months overdue, and you have not responded to our reminders.

We have learned that you have accounts all over town that are also delinquent.

Now, unless you square our account within the next week, we are going to tell all of the other merchants in town that you have PAID US!

Figure 19-27

Dear Squaroff Company:

My wife and I are honest people, and try to pay all of our bills on time, but—in these hard times—there isn't always money enough to go around.

So, we take all of our monthly bills and put them in my wife's old sewing basket and mix them up. Then we take out one bill at a time and pay it, until our money runs out. We keep the bills we can't pay, and put them back into the sewing basket the *next* month, along with the *new* bills that come in, so that the people who haven't been paid last month will have a 2-to-1 chance of getting paid *this* month. Now, you must agree that this is a fair way of dealing with the people we owe money to.

However, if you persist in writing us those insulting letters you've been sending us, *we won't even put your bills into the basket!*

Faithfully yours,

Figure 19-28

## SUGGESTED CLASSROOM EXERCISES

1. *Requests.* The instructor may assign each student to write a request letter, for either information or services. The letter will then be passed on to another student to edit for suggestions before the instructor collects them. Both the writer and the editor will receive grades.

[There are several methods of passing a student's work to another student, without one student ever getting the same work twice, as explained in the Instructor's Handbook.]

2. *Sales Letters.* Students may write a sales letter, directed to a particular business, about a product with which they are familiar. They must know their product well enough to answer questions from other classmates.

3. *Complaints-Adjustments.* Students write letters complaining about goods, services, or charges. The letters will be passed to other students who will then make the proper adjustments in a letter.

4. *Credits-Collections.* Divide students into groups. Each group will write letters (a) requesting credit, giving details of his/her reliability, (b) granting credit, but stating terms of payment and limitations, (c) trying to collect on a promissory note from an old friend, and (d) asking for lower payments, with an extension of time in which to pay.

# FOOTNOTES FOR CHAPTER NINETEEN

[1]Nelda R. Lawrence, *Writing Communications in Business and Industry* (Englewood Cliffs, N.J.: Prentice-Hall, 1971), p. 70.

[2]Virginia Lee Hallock, *Business Communication* (Providence, R.I.: P.A.R., Inc., 1974), p. 34.

[3]Luther A. Brock, *How to Communicate by Letter and Memo* (New York: McGraw-Hill, 1974), p. 78.

[4]From personal experience by the author (Fellows), after having been a Tour Director for Tauck Tours, Westport, Conn., for fourteen summers. (1954–1967).

[5]Patricia Weaver and Robert G. Weaver, *Persuasive Writing* (New York: The Free Press—Macmillan, 1977), p. 18.

[6]Jessamon Dawe and William Jackson Lord, Jr., *Functional Business Communication* (Englewood Cliffs, N.J.: Prentice-Hall, 1968), p. 145.

[7]Robert M. Archer and Ruth P. Ames, *Basic Business Communication* (Englewood Cliffs, N.J.: Prentice-Hall, 1971), p. 145.

[8]Hugh Fellows, *The Art and Skill of Talking with People* (Englewood Cliffs, N.J.: Prentice-Hall, 1964), pp. 137 ff.

[9]*Ibid.*

[10]Luther A. Brock, *How to Communicate by Letter and Memo*, pp. 70 ff.

[11]Robert M. Archer and Ruth P. Ames, *Basic Business Communication,* p. 205.

[12]*250 Tested Credit and Collection Letters* (Chicago: The Dartnell Corporation, 1966), p. 147.

[13]R. Bartels, *Credit Management* (New York: The Ronald Press Co., 1967), pp. 113 ff.

[14] W. H. Butterfield, *Credit Letters that Win Friends* (Norman, Okla.: University of Oklahoma Press, 1964), pp. 124 ff.

# Appendix A

## MEETINGS

Whether or not you belong to an organization that meets on a regular schedule, you are almost sure to participate in or preside over a meeting at one time or another. Knowing how to do either is an asset.

### THE CONSTITUTION

Many organizations have not only a constitution, but also bylaws, standing rules, and rules of order. Some organizations have only bylaws and standing rules. The complexity of the organization determines what is needed. The books by Demeter,[1] O'Brien[2] and Sturgis[3] contain models of all four written documents. This brief appendix will only outline what each should contain. Here is what comprises the constitution:

1. Name of the organization
2. Purposes and functions
3. Membership
   A. Qualifications
   B. Classes of membership (such as life or honorary), if any
   C. Provision for dues (usually stated in bylaws)
4. Officers
   A. Number and titles
   B. Selection procedure (elective or appointive)
   C. Duties and terms of office

5. Board of directors or executive committee (if any)
   A. Number on board, and qualifications for serving
   B. Duties and terms of office
   C. Selection procedure for presiding officer and other members
6. Elections
   A. Nominating procedures (by committee or from the floor)
   B. Time and method of elections (such as secret ballot or standing vote)
   C. Votes required to elect
   D. Provision for election by acclamation of unopposed nominees
7. Provisions for amending the constitution
   A. Written advance notice to members
   B. Quorum required to amend (if different from quorum required to legally conduct business, as stated in bylaws)
   C. Vote required to amend.

## THE BYLAWS

The bylaws usually contain details that the constitution does not. They are as binding upon members as the constitution but may often be more easily amended. They provide for the following details:

1. Meetings
   A. Regularly scheduled meetings (see Standing Rules)
   B. Provisions for special meetings
   C. Provisions for agenda items requiring prior notice to members
   D. Rules for protection of absentee members
2. Committees
   A. Standing Committees
      (1) Membership qualifications, if any
      (2) Selection procedure for presiding officer (chairman) and other members
      (3) Duties and terms of office
   B. Special (ad hoc) committees
      (1) Selection procedure
      (2) Provision for termination
   C. Committee reports
3. Quorum
   A. For assembly meetings
   B. For committees
4. Organizational discipline
   A. Dues, and penalties for late or nonpayment
   B. Discipline of members for other reasons
   C. Procedures for conducting hearings, bringing charges, impeaching or suspending members
   D. Reinstatement provisions
   E. Selection of parliamentary authority
5. Procedure for amending bylaws.

## STANDING RULES

There is no reason why standing rules should not be included in the bylaws except that they may be more easily amended *if* so provided by the constitution. One advantage is that both the bylaws and the standing rules are less cumbersome when they are separated; thus each is more easily referred to. Standing rules provide for such items as

1. Location of regular meetings
2. Time for meetings to begin
3. Policy on guests at meetings, and meetings closed to them
4. Guest speakers
5. Responsibility for refreshments
6. Responsibility for comfort in the meeting place: public address system, heating, lighting, noise control
7. Procedure for amending standing rules

## RULES OF ORDER

Rules of Order concern the meeting itself. Sometimes they are contained in the bylaws. When kept separate, they are more easily referred to. They include such details as

1. The order of business ("Orders of the day")
2. Special rules governing length of speeches, if any
3. Methods of voting, including provisions for mail ballots, proxies, and preferential ballots*
4. Conditions (if any) under which a plurality vote, rather than a majority vote, is acceptable**
5. Procedural rules that vary from the parliamentary authority adopted (see bylaw # 3–A)
6. Provisions for amending rules of order.

*The preferential ballot provides for the election of several nominees on one ballot. For example, if three members are to be elected to the board, each voter ranks the nominees first, second, third, fourth, and so forth. The candidates who get the highest ranking for the three offices are elected. The system is somewhat elaborate in tallying but saves time for the members in general.

**If Dall, Bangs, and Chase are nominated for the same office, and votes are Dall–10, Bangs–8, and Chase–4, Dall wins under this system, without a majority. The bylaws or rules of order *must* specify when a plurality vote is allowable.

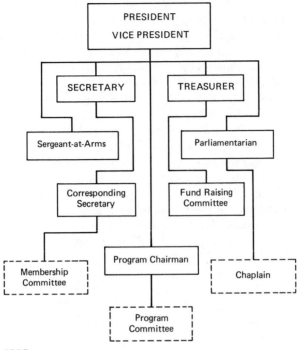

CLUB OR SOCIETY ORGANIZATION CHART

CODE:

1. Solid line enclosures are elected
2. Dotted line enclosures are usually appointed
3. Connecting lines show chain of command

Figure A-1

## OFFICERS

The officers required in an organization vary according to the needs and purposes of the organization. Figure A-1 shows the officers usually found in an organization and indicates whether they are elected or appointed. Some of these may be dispensed within an organization; others may need to be added. This brief appendix will discuss the qualifications only of the president and the secretary.

### The President, Chairman, or Presiding Officer

The president of an organization usually acts as chairman of all meetings, except committee meetings. In the president's absence the vice-president takes the chair, and in the absence of the vice-president, the secretary, the treasurer, the parliamentarian, or the sergeant-at-arms, in that order, preside. However, this order of precedence may be changed according to an organization's bylaws.

The chairman must be tactful, firm, and impartial. While, as a member in good standing, the chairman may vote on any motion brought before the assembly, he or she does not usually do so. As referee between any two factions that may develop, the chairman's impartiality is difficult to sustain if he or she has voted consistently with one faction or the other. In case of a tie vote, the chairman may vote to break the tie; in cases where a two-thirds majority is needed, the chairman may vote to prevent or make possible a two-thirds vote. The chairman always votes when there is a secret ballot.

If the chairman wishes to discuss or debate a motion, he or she asks some other member to take the chair and preside while he or she is discussing the motion, but resumes his or her position when the vote is taken.

The president should have a basic working knowledge of parliamentary procedure, and should have at hand at all times a chart indicating the precedence of motions, or have them firmly committed to memory. The chairman must insist that the assembly entertain only one main motion at a time and must be patient with fools and tactful with tyrants. It goes without saying that the chairman should memorize the organization's order of business.

While the president of an organization usually officiates at all public occasions, he or she may appoint a toastmaster to serve in his or her stead on social occasions. If empowered to do so by the organization's bylaws, the chairman appoints all *ad hoc* committees. The chairman's chief duty, however, is conducting the meeting in an orderly manner in order to get things done. Here are a few pointers for the chairman on form and conduct in a meeting:

1. Always refer to yourself as "The Chair," not as "I."
2. Refer to each speaker by name. If the name has slipped from your mind (It shouldn't!), ask, "Will the member please state his/her name?"
3. Keep at hand a list of all committees, so that you can refer to their personnel by name.
4. Restate each motion loudly and clearly, so that all will know what is under consideration. Make sure that you state the motion exactly as the member who made it has done.
5. Announce clearly the results of each motion voted on: "The motion is carried," or "The motion is lost."
6. Keep business moving by avoiding useless voting. If the assembly apparently is in accord on an issue, the chairman may simply say, "It has been moved that our club send flowers to Mrs. Donavan, who is hospitalized. If there are no objections [Pause], flowers will be sent."

## The Secretary

For this demanding position in an organization someone should be chosen for ability, rather than popularity or personality. Unless your organization has a parliamentarian, the secretary should be thoroughly conversant with its rules.

The secretary must be able to take notes rapidly, and to read the notes when they get cold. The secretary should be able to read aloud correspondence and records of business to the assembly in a loud, clear voice and to preside over the meeting if necessary.

After each meeting, the secretary puts the minutes into final form, for approval or correction at the next meeting. The minutes should include

1. Name of organization, presiding officer, date and place of meeting, and type of meeting (regular or special).
   Example:   The monthly meeting of the Board of Directors of Everhold Stocks, Inc., with Vice President Otto B. Kild presiding, met in the Ennui Room on Friday, May 13th, 1982, at 2:30 P. M.
2. All formal actions of the organization, with all main motions and their disposal.
   Example:   The minutes of the previous meeting were read and approved as corrected.

The motion to share all profits of the Everhold Stocks Corp., made by Mr. Kom U. Nist, was asked to be amended by Ms. Soshi List, to read, "all profits above those of 10%."
The amendment to the main motion was passed.
The main motion failed.
[Amendments are always voted on before the main motion.]

The secretary keeps at hand a copy of the constitution, bylaws, and all pertinent documents pertaining to the organization.

When the minutes are approved, the following should be noted: "Approved as read," or "Approved as corrected." The minutes are signed by the secretary, and often countersigned by the presiding officer.

The secretary keeps on hand a copy of the constitution, the bylaws, and all documents of the organization. The secretary keeps handy a roster of all members, and calls the roll when required. At the beginning of each meeting, the secretary presents the chairman with the order of business of that meeting (what business is unfinished, and what *ad hoc* committees must be heard).

In addition to all of the duties just stated, the secretary handles all official correspondence of the organization. If the mail is heavy, it is usually assigned to a corresponding secretary.


## COMMITTEES

Standing committees are those which function over a long period of time, usually from one election to another. Temporary *(ad hoc)* committees are those which cease to exist when they have accomplished their purpose. Standing committees might be membership, program, finance (of which the treasurer is usually the chairman), scholarship, and publications. Temporary *(ad hoc)* committees are nominating, investigating, and such others as are needed to perform a certain task.

Members of a committee usually number three or five. Standing committees are usually elected by the membership; *ad hoc* committees are usually appointed by the president. If committees are to be elected by the membership of your organization, we urge you to try the preferential ballot method (see the section on Rules of Order). There is another method that some large (forty or more members) organizations use, call the "single vote method." In this procedure no nominations for committee candidates are made, but each member writes on a slip of paper his or her preferred candidate for the five members of the committee. In theory, the majority will elect three of the five members, while the minority will elect the other two. But there is the possibility that each member will put his or her own name on the slip of paper and that no one will receive even a plurality.

## ORDER OF BUSINESS

While the order of business in an organization is traditional, it is not prescribed by parliamentary law. It should be definitely described in the standing rules or the rules of order. The standing committees do not necessarily need to report at every meeting; the treasurer may be required to report every quarter, and a nominating committee only when an election is imminent. However, neither the presiding officer nor any member is allowed to alter the Order of the Day without the consent of the membership.

> Example:    Because of a special program that is available to us only at this time, The Chair proposes that the Club dispense with reports from committees at this meeting. Are there any objections? [Pause] Since there is no objection, we will proceed with the program.

Following are two formats for the order of business in a meeting; they are more detailed than is necessary in most organizations. The steps marked with an asterisk (*) are not often included in the agenda.

### Format of Meeting Without a Program

1. Call to order
*2. Invocation (if opening prayer is customary)
*3. Roll call (only if it is questionable whether a quorum** is present)
4. Reading of minutes (corrections if needed) and approval

*Denotes steps not often included in the agenda.

**A quorum is the minimum number of members who must be present to legally transact business. It is usually fixed in an organization's bylaws as a certain percentage of the total membership. If a quorum is not present, the members may *discuss* any issues that are in question but may not vote on them.

5. Appointment of *pro tem* officials vital to the meeting, if regular officers are absent: acting secretary, sergeant-at-arms, and so forth
6. Reports of committees
7. Old or unfinished business
8. New business
9. Announcements
10. Adjournment

## Format of Meeting With Program

1. Call to order
2. Reading of minutes
3. Urgent business—new or old
4. Program
5. Announcements
6. Adjournment

## FOOTNOTES FOR APPENDIX A

[1]George Demeter, *Demeter's Manual of Parliamentary Law and Procedure,* blue book edition (Boston: Little, Brown, and Co., 1969).
[2]Joseph F. O'Brien, *Parliamentary Law for the Layman* (New York: Harper and Brothers, 1952).
[3]Alice Sturgis, *Sturgis Standard Code of Parliamentary Procedure,* 2nd Ed. (New York: McGraw-Hill, 1966).

# Appendix B

## PARLIAMENTARY PROCEDURE

Evidence exists that procedural rules for meetings of governance date back as far as the fifth century B. C. in Athens.[1] There is also evidence that the Roman Senate used a similar form of procedure for its deliberations. However, parliamentary procedure and its name evolved in England from around the thirteenth to the eighteenth centuries. In 1776 John Hatsell, a clerk in the House of Commons, published his first volume of the rulings of the British Parliament, followed by a second volume in 1781. *Hatsell's Precedents*, as they were referred to, were later expanded into four volumes.

In this country, Thomas Jefferson recognized the necessity of rules of governance in any deliberative body, so he devised a system which he thought appropriate, based largely on *Hatsell's Precedents*. These were used in the Senate when Jefferson was Vice-President. Later, when Jefferson became President of the United States, he published a *Manual of Parliamentary Practice* (1801).

Two other landmarks in parliamentary procedure were written in the United States during the nineteenth century. The first was published by Luther Stearns Cushing. Drawing on his experiences as a clerk in the Massachusetts House of Representatives (1832–1834), Cushing wrote *A Manual of Parliamentary Practice; Rules of Proceedings and Debate in Deliberative Assemblies*. It is commonly known as *Cushing's Manual*. The second, and by far the most widely known, is *Robert's Rules of Order*. First published in 1876, the original title was *Pocket Manual of Rules of Order*. Henry M. Robert, an army engineer, was such a successful promoter of his *Manual* that the book has gone through six revisions and expansions, and the 1970 edition, *Robert's Rules of Order Newly Revised,* is 594 pages long.

There have been numerous attempts at streamlining Robert's work and that of his successors. Some of the more successful ones appear in an annotated bibliography at the end of this appendix.

## VALUES

Parliamentary procedure, although it carries the same name in a number of instances, has no *one* fixed set of rules. The United States Senate, the House of Representatives, the House of Lords, and the House of Commons each uses a slightly different set of rules. A social club or a faculty meeting may each use rules that differ from the aforementioned. Yet the rules should not be so different as to negate the principal values of parliamentary procedure, which are:

1. Equality of membership, whether that membership be ordinary members or officers in the organization.
2. Rule of the majority in a democratic society.
3. Respect and protection of the minority, with no restriction of the minority's right to be heard.
4. Free and full discussion of any motion, except those which are made purely to waste time.
5. Consideration and disposition of only one matter at a time.
6. Discussion of topics (or issues) rather than personalities.

The overall principle is that in a democracy the majority should rule, but the minority must be heard.

## ORDINARY MOTIONS

The motion is the means of getting business done. Some motions take *precedence* over others, and the individual organization may make this decision as to the rank of *ordinary* motions. However, in normal parliamentary procedure, motions take the following order of precedence:

1. To adjourn
2. To recess
*3. To close debate
*4. To limit or to extend the limits, of debate

*Denotes motions requiring a two-thirds majority of the members present. All other ordinary motions are carried by vote of a simple majority.

5. To postpone
6. To refer
7. To amend

The main motion ranks lower than any of the foregoing seven.

## Example 1.

Allen:   Mr. Chairman, I move that all members be assessed five dollars for next month's party.

Bates:   Mr. Chairman, I move that we amend Ms. Allen's motion to read ten dollars for next month's party.

Cole:    Mr. Chairman, I move that we refer the matter to the Finance Committee to determine what amount should be assessed for next month's party.

Chair:   It has been moved that we refer the amount of assessments for next month's party to the Finance Committee to determine the amount of the assessment. Is there any discussion?

Because Cole's motion takes precedence over those of Allen and Bates, Cole's motion is voted on first. Only if it fails to carry is Bates' motion for amendment voted upon.

## Example 2.

Allen:   Mr. Chairman, I move that all members be assessed five dollars for next month's party.

Cole:    Mr. Chairman, I move that we refer the matter to the Finance Committee to determine what amount should be assessed for next month's party.

Bates:   Mr. Chairman, I move that we amend Ms. Allen's motion to read ten dollars for next month's party.

Chair:   You are out of order, Mr. Bates. Miss Cole's motion to refer the matter to the Finance Committee takes precedence over any motion to amend.

Bates:   Then I would like to amend Miss Cole's motion to ask that the Finance Committee make its recommendation to us at our next weekly meeting.

Chair:   Is there any discussion on the proposed amendment to ask the Finance Committee to make its recommendation at our next weekly meeting?

Amendments are voted on *before* the main motion. However, in a matter as trivial as this, to save time Miss Cole would probably respond as follows:

Cole:    Mr. Chairman, I withdraw my original motion and offer this one instead. I move that we refer the matter of assessment to the Finance Committee and ask that the Finance Committee make its recommendation at our next regular weekly meeting.

Ordinary motions are the only motions that take rank in order of precedence, and it is fairly easy for the chairman to memorize them.

### Seconding the Motion

Theoretically, requiring the seconding of all motions was to prevent members of an organization from proposing a frivolous move. The authors of this text propose doing away with seconding of motions. The authors believe that if a foolish motion is made by a member, the chairman should be allowed to rule it out of order as being frivolous or irrelevant, and that seconding motions is a waste of time. Others agree with this, among them Ray E. Keesey in his book *Modern Parliamentary Procedure*.[2]

## SPECIAL MOTIONS

Special motions have no rank in relation to each other; one does not take precedence over another. Their objective is to make procedure run smoothly in considering an ordinary motion, with the exceptions of *To Reconsider* and *To Rescind*. Only one of them, *To Suspend the Rules,* requires a two-thirds majority (*). Special motions include:

Point of Order
To Appeal
To Withdraw (a motion)
*To Suspend the rules
To Reconsider
To Rescind

*In Summary:* In addition to the main motion, there are *seven* ordinary motions and *six* special motions. Only three of the thirteen require a two-thirds majority to pass. We shall now define each motion and give examples of each.

## DEFINITIONS AND EXAMPLES

*Main Motion.* This is the move taken by any member to initiate a concerted action by the organization.

Allen:  Mr. Chairman?
Chair:  Ms. Allen. [It is not necessary to say, "The Chair recognizes Ms. Allen."]
Allen:  I move that we donate five thousand dollars to the United Fund.

*Requires a two-thirds majority.

Chair:    Ms. Allen has moved that we donate five thousand dollars to The United Fund. Is there any discussion?

## TO AMEND

Bates:    Mr. Chairman?

Chair:    Mr. Bates.

Bates:    Our Foundation is approached constantly for donations to various charities. It takes a great deal of time and effort to investigate them. The United Fund has already made its investigation of many of these same charities. I move that we amend Ms. Allen's motion, so that we donate ten thousand dollars to the United Fund and let that be an end to our donations for the year.

Chair:    Mr. Bates has moved to amend Ms. Allen's motion to donate ten thousand dollars to the United Fund and let that end our charitable donations for the year. Is there any discussion?

## TO WITHDRAW [No recognition from The Chair is needed.]

Allen:    I wish to withdraw my motion in order to reword it.

Chair:    Ms. Allen wishes to withdraw her motion. Is there any objection? . . . Hearing no objection, I declare the motion withdrawn.
[If there is an objection, a simple majority vote must be taken.]

## TO REFER

Allen:    Mr. Chairman?

Chair:    Ms. Allen.

Allen:    I move that we limit our charitable donations for this year to ten thousand dollars, to be donated to the United Fund.

Cole:    Mr. Chairman?

Chair:    Miss Cole.

Cole:    I move that we refer Ms. Allen's motion to the Funding Committee, and ask that they report their recommendations at our next monthly meeting.

Chair:    Miss Cole has moved that we refer Ms. Allen's motion to the Funding Committee, and ask them to give us their recommendations at our next monthly meeting. Is there any discussion?

## TO LIMIT

Bates:    Mr. Chairman?

Chair:    Mr. Bates.

Bates:    I move that we limit discussion on Miss Cole's motion to three speakers on each side.

Cole: Mr. Chairman?

Chair: Miss Cole.

Cole: I move to amend Mr. Bates' motion to limit each speaker discussing my motion to three minutes.

To Limit can be amended only so far as time restrictions are concerned.

Chair: Miss Cole has moved that Mr. Bates' motion be limited to three minutes for each speaker. Is there any discussion? . . . . . If there is no discussion, all in favor of Miss Cole's amendment, say "Aye." . . . All opposed, say "No."

A two-thirds majority is required to limit discussion in any way.

Chair: Is there any discussion on Mr. Bates' motion to limit discussion to three members on each side of the question? . . . . Since there is none, all in favor of the motion say "Aye.". . . . All opposed, say "No."

TO POSTPONE. This motion should state a definite time for the postponement to expire. Consideration of a motion may be postponed for fifteen minutes to allow some member of the organization to obtain material from the files in another room, or to allow a brief conference of some members. A motion may be postponed until the next meeting, to allow an *ad hoc* committee to study it more thoroughly. When this is done, the secretary makes a note of it and brings up the motion at the next meeting when unfinished business is called for.

Allen: Mr. Chairman?

Chair: Ms. Allen.

Allen: I move that the pending motion be postponed until the quarterly report comes in from the Finance Committee.

Chair: A move has been made to postpone the pending motion until the Financial Committee makes its quarterly report, which will be at the end of this month. Is there any discussion?

If there is no discussion, The Chair takes a vote. A simple majority is all that is called for.

TO CLOSE DEBATE. This motion means that all discussion on the pending motion (or motions) is to be terminated, and the assembly will vote immediately on the pending motion. It is not debatable and may not be amended, and it usually* requires a two-thirds majority vote to pass.

This motion should be used sparingly and must not be abused. For example,

*Most authorities agree on the two-thirds majority vote to close debate. However, if a particular organization wishes to use a simple majority vote for this purpose, it should be plainly stated in that organization's rules of order.

on a controversial motion three members who are in favor of the motion may speak in rapid succession, and a fourth member who favors the motion may move to close debate. If the fourth member's motion is carried, this deprives the opposition of its freedom to speak, which goes against the principles of parliamentary procedure. If, however, discussion over a trivial matter has gone on endlessly (a filibuster), it may serve to prevent the filibusterers from wasting any more of the assembly's time.

Allen:  Mr. Chairman, I move to close debate (understood to apply to only the immediate motion pending).

or

Allen:  Mr. Chairman, I move to close debate on all pending debatable motions (applicable to a pending main motion, a pending amendment to that motion; also applicable to *To Refer* and *To Postpone,* depending on what motions are pending at the time).

The person moving *To Close Debate* does not need recognition from The Chair but must not interrupt another speaker. The *Move to Close Debate* is not amendable and not debatable. Without further ado The Chair must call for a vote.

TO RECESS. This is a motion to interrupt a meeting. Sometimes its purpose is to give the members of the assembly a respite from a tiring session. It may often be for the purpose of refreshments, for counting ballots, or for waiting for a witness or speaker to arrive. At times a meeting will recess until the following day. It should always state the time when the meeting reconvenes.

Bates:  I move we recess until ten o'clock in the morning. (This does not mean that the meeting is adjourned.)

or

Chair:  If there is no objection, we shall recess for refreshments, reconvening at 10:45 A. M. (If there is no objection, the recess begins immediately.)

TO ADJOURN. This motion has precedence over any ordinary motion. It may be made before any business is transacted if the mover has determined that a quorum is not present. It is not debatable nor amendable and requires only a majority vote. In some organizations it does not even require a vote but does require a "second." It is *not* in order if a motion *To Adjourn* has just been defeated, but it can be made in the same meeting by the same person. It is also not in order if the mover interrupts a speaker, or interferes with the taking or counting of a vote.

It is in order even when a motion is pending. The pending motion will be carried forward to the next meeting as unfinished business. It can come from any member of the assembly or from the presiding officer.

Cole:   I move that we adjourn.

or

Chair:   Since there is no further business, if there is no objection, this meeting is adjourned.

In the first example, a simple majority vote is required. In the second example, no vote is required if there is no objection.

POINT OF ORDER. This is a powerful call, although its name appears trivial. It is used to (a) call attention to any unusual situation that requires immediate attention, such as danger or discomfort to any or all members of the assembly, or (b) to call The Chair's attention to a violation of the rules or a mistake in proper parliamentary procedure. The member who raises the *Point of Order* may interrupt a speaker in order to do so. It is used only in matters of extreme urgency.

Estes:   Madam Chairwoman, I rise to a Point of Order.

Chair:   State your point.

Estes:   We cannot hear the speaker.

Chair:   Your point is well taken. Will the speaker please speak loudly enough so that all the members can hear.

or

Funt:   Madam Chairwoman, I rise to a Point of Order.

Chair:   State your point.

Funt:   This room is so hot and stuffy that all of us are extremely uncomfortable.

Chair:   Your point is well taken. Will the Sergeant-at-Arms please see that the air conditioning is turned on. If there is no objection, we shall recess for ten minutes. Mr. Johnson will still have the floor when we return.

or

Garth:   Madam Chairwoman, I rise to a Point of Order.

Chair:   State your point.

Garth:   I deplore Mr. Johnson's name-calling of those who oppose his motion, and his insulting insinuations that we are all Marxists.

Chair:   I do not find anything the speaker [Johnson] has said to cause resentment, or to give umbrage to any member of this organization. Therefore, your point is not well taken.

TO APPEAL. Any member may appeal The Chair's ruling on a matter, and having that ruling overturned or substantiated by the assembly. This is a safeguard against The Chair's arbitrary use of power.

Garth:   I appeal to the membership on my Point of Order.

Chair:   All of those members who find Mr. Johnson's language deplorable and insulting to those opposing his motion, please say "Aye." . . . All those who think his language does *not* deserve censure, please say "No."

Whatever the decision of the assembly, it must be abided by. *To Appeal* is debatable, but it may not be amended, postponed, or referred to a committee.

TO SUSPEND THE RULES. This motion is used to set aside *temporarily* the normal order of business. It may not be used for the purpose of setting aside the constitution of the organization, or its bylaws. It gives flexibility to the Order of the Day. For instance, a program normally comes after the business meeting is finished, but the assembly has the opportunity to hear an expert speaker on a subject in which all are interested, and the expert must catch a plane and can speak only at the beginning of the meeting; therefore, after the meeting has been called to order, The Chair or some other member may call for a suspension of the rules so that the business meeting will take place *after* the program instead of before it. It requires a two-thirds majority vote.

Estes:   Madam Chairwoman, I move To Suspend the Rules in order to hear the report on the *ad hoc* committee on costs of the new building before the regular standing committee reports.

Chair:   If there is no objection [Pause] the rules will be suspended to permit us to hear the special committee on costs of the new building. Will the chairperson of that committee please proceed?

*but*

Funt:   Madam Chairwoman, I move To Suspend the Rule requiring a quorum so that we can get some work done.

Chair:   The rule requiring a quorum to conduct business legally is in our bylaws, and may not be suspended. Therefore, the motion is out of order.

TO RECONSIDER. This motion enables an assembly to correct a vote taken earlier in the same meeting, because its members were under a misapprehension or lacked adequate information at the time. For instance, the members voted to hold their annual outing on Sunday, April 25th. Then Garth recalls that The Toastmasters Club has scheduled its all-day outing somewhere near the first of May, so he excuses himself from the meeting to telephone a fellow member of The Toastmasters and get the exact date. Sure enough, April 25th is the date, and nearly half of the members belong to The Toastmasters.

Garth:   Madam Chairwoman, I move To Reconsider the motion that we hold our annual outing on April 25th, because that is the date previously set by The Toastmasters for their picnic, and many of our members also belong to that organization.

Chair:   A move to reconsider the vote on the motion to hold our annual outing on April 25th is before you for consideration. [Discussion] All those in favor of setting another date for our annual outing say "Aye." . . . All opposed say "No."

The motion *To Reconsider* must be made at the same meeting during which the motion being reconsidered has been voted upon (see *To Rescind*). It may be made only once on the same motion, and the motion *To Reconsider* may not be reconsidered. This is to prevent a group which loses a motion from using it for purely heckling purposes or from wasting time after losing any motion, by asking that it be reconsidered.

TO RESCIND. This motion allows an organization to nullify a motion that was passed in a previous meeting, and which the organization now considers was imprudent or ill-advised. It does not matter how long ago the motion to be rescinded was passed, provided no irreversible action has been taken.

Estes: Madam Chairwoman, I move To Rescind the motion passed three months ago appointing Mr. Perry Mason as our legal representative.

Chair: The motion To Rescind the motion passed three months ago, appointing Mr. Perry Mason as our legal representative, is before you for discussion.

Funt: Madam Chairwoman, the motion To Rescind is out of order. This assembly has paid Mr. Mason a retainer fee for one year's service. This is a contract, and we are bound to it, unless Mrs. Estes can show that Mr. Mason has acted unethically or unsatisfactorily.

Chair: Can you show such cause, Mrs. Estes?

Estes: No, but I do think we could find a lawyer who would be more active on our behalf.

Chair: That is not sufficient reason for breaking our contract, and your motion is out of order. The next item on our agenda is . . .

or

Garth: Madam Chairwoman, I move to rescind the amendment passed three years ago, requiring students to start repaying their loans immediately upon graduation.

Chair: State your position.

Garth: Well, only two students have taken out loans from our Scholarship Fund since that amendment was added. As Chairman of the Scholarship Loan Fund, I have talked to many students, and they say that to start repaying their loans immediately upon graduation is too soon. They need time to get a job and start earning some money . . .

[Note that the *entire* motion need not necessarily be rescinded; even a *portion* of the motion (that is, an amendment) is rescindable.]

Ordinarily a move *To Rescind* requires only a majority vote to pass. However, if the original motion to be rescinded has required a two-thirds majority to pass, then the move to rescind that motion must also require a two-thirds majority.

## SUPERFLUOUS MOTIONS

One reason why parliamentary procedure is cumbersome and difficult to master is that some guides on the subject are cluttered with motions that are rarely used or useless. Other motions will serve to handle almost every situation the average organization may encounter. Following are some of the motions we have deleted (arranged alphabetically), and the reasons for doing so.

1. To AMEND THE AMENDMENT. This gets confusing for the layman, or even for some people who have studied parliamentary procedure. It is also time consuming to vote three times to approve a main motion, a motion to amend, and a motion to amend the amendment.
   There is an easier way of handling this same procedure. If, after discussing a main motion, the members assembled wish it amended, the mover of the main motion simply withdraws the motion and rewords it.

2. To CALL FOR A DIVISION OF THE ASSEMBLY. This expression is not only archaic, but a misnomer, since the assembly does not divide. It is used to determine the accuracy of a vote.
   Instead of using "Aye's" and "No's," a member may call in advance for a show of hands on the vote, or may ask that all opposing or in favor of the motion rise at separate times.

3. To CALL FOR THE ORDERS OF THE DAY. The purpose of this is to remind the presiding officer to return to the agenda, from which the assembly has strayed. All that a member of the assembly needs to say is something such as, "Mr. Chairman, I believe we omitted the reports of the Standing Committees" (or whatever). If a stronger measure is needed, a member may rise to a Point of Order to remind The Chair to return to the agenda.

4. To CLOSE NOMINATIONS. This motion was never intended to deprive a member of his or her right to nominate the candidate of his or her choice, and The Chair must not permit such to happen by entertaining a premature motion by another member *To Close Nominations*. That being the case, the motion is superfluous. All that an alert presiding officer need say is, "If there are no further nominations [Pause], we will proceed with voting for the office of . . ."

5. To DISPENSE WITH THE READING OF THE MINUTES. "To dispense with" usually means "to do without," and that may violate the agenda that is set down in the bylaws of the organization. Some bylaws specify that the minutes of the previous meeting must be read and approved by the membership. More accurate ways of handling this situation are

   A. Have the minutes of the previous meeting printed and distributed in the call for this meeting, at which time they simply need be approved.
   B. Postpone reading of the minutes of the previous meeting, and have them printed and distributed to members for approval at the next meeting.
   C. Refer the minutes to either the Executive Committee or the Organization and Rules Committee, which can be authorized to approve the minutes or to make any changes which are necessary for accuracy.
   D. Postpone reading the minutes from the last meeting until the next meeting.

6. To EXPUNGE FROM THE RECORD. This is much more accurately taken care of by the motion *To Rescind*, since the motion rescinded gives reason for its being rescinded.

7. To FIX THE TIME TO WHICH TO ADJOURN. Cumbersome and awkwardly stated. A motion *To Adjourn* is all that is necessary. Or, if no time is set in the

bylaws for regular meetings, the motion *To Recess* until (state date and time) is sufficient.

8. To LAY ON THE TABLE or TO TABLE. The purpose of this motion is to put aside temporarily a motion, while other motions are considered, or until further information can be obtained concerning it. The motions *To Postpone* and *To Recess* serve the same purpose. In the U.S. Congress and in other organizations *To Table* a motion usually has the effect of killing it. If the purpose is to kill a motion, *To Withdraw* is much more accurate.

9. To MAKE A GENERAL or a SPECIAL ORDER. This motion is one of the chief stumbling blocks in parliamentary procedure. *Robert's Rules of Order Newly Revised* spends seven pages (fine print) detailing how questions become *General Orders* and *Special Orders,* and the authors of this text still do not understand them. However, you must remember that Robert was an army engineer, and—up until recently—the military were notorious for writing prose that was obfuscating. Sturgis[3] does manage to untangle the mess, and presents it clearly, but it is still unnecessary for the successful conduct of a business or of a meeting. All that is necessary for one to know is that items postponed until a meeting of a definite date in the future must be considered at that particular meeting. One can trust a secretary to have a calendar, and to be sure that those items are considered at that particular meeting. There is nothing in this motion that cannot be handled by a motion *To Postpone,* with a definite date mentioned in the postponement.

10. To OBJECT TO THE CONSIDERATION. The original purpose of this motion was to prevent frivolous, irrelevant, or *embarrassing* motions from being considered. We submit that The Chair should be able to handle frivolous or irrelevant motions by ruling them out of order. However, what kind of motion could be *embarrassing* to a group if it is *concerned* with that group? This seems to the authors an abridgment of freedom of speech. The *Motion to Withdraw* is all that is needed in a democracy, and the authors believe this motion should be eliminated from parliamentary procedure.

11. To POSTPONE INDEFINITELY. Originally this motion was designed for two purposes: (a) To get rid of a motion that was unworthy of consideration, without ever dignifying the motion by voting on it, or (b) to take a *straw vote* in order to judge the strength of the opposition.
As for the former purpose, The Chair should rule any unworthy motion out of order; as for the latter, cliques and gamesmanship have no place in a serious deliberative assembly. The motion *To Withdraw* will serve nicely instead of the vague motion *To Postpone Indefinitely.*

12. The PREVIOUS QUESTION. What this actually means is "to end the discussion and vote." The motion *To Close Debate* serves the same purpose. Why confuse people by having two motions which mean the same thing? Scrap it!

13. To RAISE QUESTION OF PRIVILEGE
To RISE TO A PARLIAMENTARY INQUIRY
To RISE TO A POINT OF PERSONAL PRIVILEGE
All of the above procedures (they are not motions) allow a member to interrupt when another speaker has the floor, thereby disrupting the meeting and destroying its continuity. The Chair is required to give the interrupting member immediate attention. The only one that *might* be justifiable is the last named, when a member is forced to leave the assembly by some urgent matter, such

as a trip to the toilet or having a subpoena served on him or her. There is hardly any question—whether it is asked for clarification or to insure that parliamentary procedure is being followed—that cannot wait until a speaker has finished. Any matter that requires immediate attention can be handled by *Point of Order*, although that was not its original intent.

14. To RECONSIDER AND HAVE IT ENTERED ON THE MINUTES. This is another motion that allows "wheeling and dealing" on the part of a minority and should have no place in an assembly. It may work like this:

A minority group in the Omega Club wishes to have the meeting place changed from the east side of town to the west side, since that minority has so far to travel. According to *Robert's Rules of Order* (page 242), a member must have voted on the *prevailing* side of the motion, to be eligible to make the motion To Reconsider and Have It Entered on the Minutes.

Felton, who is one of the minority who want the meeting place changed, votes with the majority, who are *against* a change. Felton is then eligible to move To Reconsider and Have It Entered on the Minutes, thus blocking any action on the motion until the next meeting.

This wastes the time of the assembly and violates a basic principle of parliamentary procedure, that of majority rule.

15. To REFER TO A COMMITTEE OF THE WHOLE or TO CONSIDER AS IF IN A COMMITTEE OF THE WHOLE.
Confused? So are most people. These motions, which are almost never used, simply mean that the assembly should act as a committee, instead of as a meeting. The idea that a large body can function on the same level as a small group is ridiculous, and—when put into practice—borders on anarchy. It becomes laughable, when the "Committee of the Whole" (all members) reports back to the assembly or meeting (again, all members)! We deign to mention it only because it is still found in some manuals on parliamentary procedure; a member of your organization may come across it and wonder why it was omitted from this appendix.

## CHARTS FOR REFERENCE

We have prepared two charts for a quick reference on various motions, with the privileges and restrictions governing them. The presiding officer may wish to copy them and keep them before him or her. We must emphasize that this brief appendix is by no means a complete treatment of parliamentary procedure, with its many ramifications, but we believe that it will serve to familiarize it to many organizations. At the end of this appendix we have listed further books that should be of help for those who wish to make a deeper study of the subject.

| Motion | Debatable | Amendable | Vote | May be Withdrawn | May Close or Limit Debate | May be Postponed | May be Referred |
|---|---|---|---|---|---|---|---|
| 1. To Adjourn | No | No | Majority | Yes | x | x | x |
| 2. To Recess | No | Yes* | Maj. | Yes | x | x | x |
| 3. To Close Debate | No | No | 2/3 | Yes | x | x | x |
| 4. To Limit (or extend the limits of) Debate | No | Yes* | 2/3 | Yes | x | x | x |
| 5. To Postpone | Yes | Yes | Maj. | Yes | Yes | x | x |
| 6. To Refer | Yes | Yes | Maj. | Yes | Yes | x | x |
| 7. To Amend | Yes | Yes | Maj. | Yes | Yes | x | x |
| 8. MAIN MOTION | Yes | Yes | Maj. | Yes | Yes | Yes | Yes |

May be Rescinded - Yes    May be Reconsidered - Yes

*When ordinary motions are made, with no main motion on the floor, they are treated like main motions.
*Only regarding time limitations may this be amended.

Figure B-1
ORDINARY MOTIONS—IN ORDER OF RANK. X = not applicable.

| Motion | Debatable | Amendable | Vote | May be Withdrawn | May Close or Limit Debate | May be Postponed | May be Referred |
|---|---|---|---|---|---|---|---|
| Point of Order | No | No | None | X | X | X | X |
| To Appeal* | Yes | No | Major-ity | Yes | Yes | X | X |
| To Withdraw | No | No | Maj. | X | X | X | X |
| To Suspend the Rules | No | No | 2/3 | Yes | X | X | X |
| To Reconsider** | Yes | No | Maj. | Yes | X | X | X |
| To Rescind*** | Yes | Yes | Maj.**** | Yes | Yes | Yes | Yes |

* Must be made *immediately* after a ruling by The Chair. *Only* judgments and opinions by The Chair may be appealed, and *not* known facts, existing laws, or established rules.

** Must be made during the same meeting, or convention, at which the vote was taken on the motion to be reconsidered. May not be made if some irreversible action has taken place.

*** Used to nullify an action taken in a *previous* meeting, no matter how far back that meeting may go. However, if some irreversible action has taken place—such as payment of money or promises fulfilled—the action may not be rescinded.

**** Some organizations require a two-thirds majority to rescind an action; if so, it must be stated in the organization's bylaws. However, if the original motion required a two-thirds majority to *pass*, then a two-thirds majority vote must be required to rescind it.

Figure B-2
SPECIAL MOTIONS—NO ORDER OF RANK. X = not applicable

# FOOTNOTES FOR APPENDIX B

[1] J. F. O'Brien, "Historical Development of Parliamentary Discussion," *The Thomas Jefferson Parliamentarian,* IV (Nov., 1960) 3–19, and V (May, 1961) 1–20.

[2] Ray E. Keesey, *Modern Parliamentary Procedure* (Boston: Houghton Mifflin Co., 1974).

[3] Alice Sturgis, *Sturgis Standard Code of Parliamentary Procedure,* 2nd ed. (New York: McGraw-Hill, 1966).

# ANNOTATED BIBLIOGRAPHY

GEORGE DEMETER, *Demeter's Manual of Parliamentary Law and Procedure,* blue book edition (Boston: Little, Brown, and Co., 1969).
Thorough, but unattractive, book because of its fine print and overly lengthy legal examples. It *is* authoritative but tends to adhere strictly to *Robert's Rules,* with no attempt to modernize them.

HUGO HELLMAN, *Parliamentary Procedure* (New York: Macmillan Company, 1966).
This short textbook (113 pages) is organized around three topics: (1) Participating as a Member, (2) Presiding as Chairman, and (3) Broadening Your Knowledge. There is an effective attempt to simplify *Robert's Rules.*

RAY E. KEESEY, *Modern Parliamentary Procedure* (Boston: Houghton Mifflin Co., 1974).
In our opinion, the best of the streamlined versions. As the "blurb" on the back cover claims, it (a) emphasizes majority rule, (b) requires less memorization of rules, and (c) eliminates most of the complicated motions and situations that cause confusion.

JOSEPH F. O'BRIEN, *Parliamentary Law for the Layman* (New York: Harper and Brothers, 1952).
Chief value is its clear, informal style and its specific examples. Makes a plea for no more formal use of *Robert's Rules* than is necessary. A special value is advocating a varying degree of formality to various groups.

HENRY M. ROBERT, *Robert's Rules of Order Newly Revised* (Glenview, Ill.: Scott, Foresman and Co., 1970).
The "granddaddy" of the subject in this country. Thorough, often archaic, but useful if a point on parliamentary procedure cannot be answered by others.

ALICE STURGIS, *Sturgis Standard Code of Parliamentary Procedure,* 2nd ed., (New York: McGraw-Hill, 1966).
Definitely not streamlined, but compendious. A modernized version of *Robert's Rules.* Excellent guide for professional parliamentarians. Readable, with clear examples.

# Appendix C

## ANSWERS TO Vocabulary Study for Chapter Two

1. – B
2. – B & C
3. – C
4. – A
5. – B

6. – C
7. – B
8. – C
9. – B
10. – C

11. – A & C
12. – B
13. – C
14. – C

## ANSWERS TO Vocabulary Study for Chapter Two

1. – A
2. – C
3. – A
4. – A
5. – B
6. – C

7. – B
8. – A
9. – C
10. – A
11. – B
12. – C

13. – A
14. – B
15. – A
16. – C
17. – B
18. – B

## ANSWERS to Jargon List: Chapter Three

### List I

1. – E.
2. – F.
3. – A.
4. – J.
5. – C.

### List II

1. – I.
2. – C.
3. – A.
4. – G.
5. – J.

### List III

1. – I.
2. – D.
3. – G.
4. – F.
5. – A.

6. – I.
7. – H.
8. – D.
9. – G.
10. – B.

6. – B.
7. – H.
8. – D.
9. – E.
10. – F.

6. – H.
7. – J.
8. – C.
9. – E.
10. – B.

## List IV

1. – H.
2. – D.
3. – J.
4. – A.
5. – I.
6. – B.
7. – C.
8. – E.
9. – G.
10. – K.
11. – F.

## List V

1. – H.
2. – F.
3. – G.
4. – K.
5. – I.
6. – J.
7. – C.
8. – E.
9. – A.
10. – D.
11. – B.

## ANSWERS to Vocabulary Study for Chapter Four

1. – B
2. – A
3. – C
4. – B
5. – C

6. – B
7. – A
8. – B
9. – C
10. – B

## Answers to Vocabulary Study for Chapter Five

1. – C
2. – B
3. – B
4. – C
5. – A
6. – B

7. – A
8. – B
9. – A
10. – C
11. – C
12. – B

## Answers to Vocabulary Study for Chapter Six

1. – A
2. – B
3. – A
4. – A
5. – A

6. – C
7. – C
8. – C
9. – C
10. – A & C

354    *Appendix C*

## Answers to Vocabulary Study for Chapter Ten

1. – L
2. – J
3. – H
4. – F
5. – D
6. – B

7. – A
8. – C
9. – E
10. – G
11. – I
12. – K

## Answers to Vocabulary Study for Chapter Eleven

1. – C
2. – B
3. – A
4. – B
5. – B
6. – C

7. – A
8. – B
9. – B
10. – C
11. – B

## Answers to the Crossword Puzzle in Chapter Twelve

### Across

1. Ice
5. Is
8. Omniscient
11. I.G.U.
12. Duct
13. Are
14. Pi
15. Impetuous
18. Dissonance
22. Veer
23. Cut
24. Vendetta
27. Hoop

### Down

2. Cognitive
3. Emu
4. Kid
5. I.C.C.
6. Sit
7. Snaps
9. Sultan
10. Tri
16. Posed
17. Own
19. Sent
20. Ore
21. Echo
25. Ta
26. Ah

## Answers to Vocabulary Study for Chapter Thirteen

1. – B
2. – A
3. – B
4. – B
5. – C
6. – A
7. – C
8. – B

9. – B
10. – C
11. – A
12. – A
13. – C
14. – B
15. – C

*Answers to How Perceptive Are You? exercise in Chapter Thirteen*

## I. Basic Drives

| | | |
|---|---|---|
| 1. – SP | 8. – SX | 15. – CH |
| 2. – SX | 9. – AL | 16. – AL |
| 3. – E | 10. – CH | 17. – SP |
| 4. – AL | 11. – E | 18. – E |
| 5. – AL | 12. – SQ | 19. – SQ |
| 6. – SX | 13. – E | 20. – SP, SX, CH, |
| 7. – E | 14. – SP | SQ, E, AI |

## II. Answers to Inductive and Deductive Reasoning exercise in Chapter Thirteen

| | |
|---|---|
| 1. – I | 6. – I |
| 2. – D | 7. – D |
| 3. – D | 8. – I |
| 4. – I | 9. – D |
| 5. – D | 10. – I |

# Author Index

Names in the bibliographies at the end of chapters have not been included, unless otherwise mentioned.

## A

Academy Awards, motion picture, 205
Antoinette Perry Awards ("Tony"), 205
Aristotle, 185, 186
Armed forces, 8, 36
Arnold, Oren, 96
Aspin, Representative Les, 112

## B

Baruch (Bernard) School of Business, 107, 219
Barzun, Jacques (quoted), 219
Bernard Haldane Associates, 95–96
Bible, the
    Mark 14:38, 25
    Song of Solomon 2:15, 54
Bob Jones College/University, 208
Borchers, Gladys, 257
Brigance, William Norwood, 175
Bruyére, Jean de la, 224
Bukeley, Lucinda, 24
Bureau of Naval Weapons, 251
Burton, Supreme Court Justice, Harold H., 148
Byron, Lord (see Gordon)

## C

Calypso, 278
Capote, Truman, 233
Carnegie, Dale, 220
Carroll, Lewis (quoted), 35
Central Florida, University of, 285–86
Christina, Queen of Sweden, 24
Chrysler Corporation, 6
Churchill, Winston, 173
Civil Aeronautics Board, 253
Cobb, Irvin S. (quoted), 71
Coca-Cola, 134–35, 191
Coolidge, Calvin (quoted), 3
Corbin, Mallie, 130
Cornell University, 221
Cousteau, Jacques, 278
Crane, Clarence (quoted), 43
Cross, Bert S., 158–59
Crum, George, 43
Cushing, Luther Stearns, 336
Cushing's Manual, 336

## D

Davis, Commander Judson, 14
Delsarte, Francois, 192

# E

*Economics Press Magazine,* 252, 257
Emmy Awards, 205
*Encyclopedia Britannica,* 211


# F

Federal Communications Commission, 191
Fellows, Hugh, 130–31, 177, 183, 222,
    227–28
Feuchtwanger, Arnold, 43
Fort Lee, N. J., 190
Franklin, Benjamin (quoted), 304
Frost, Robert (quoted), 87


# G

Galileo, 278
General Services Administration, 251
German, Richard, 266
Gordon, George (Lord Byron), 233
Grammy Awards, 205
Gregory, Marvin G., 252, 257
Gunning, Robert (quoted), 240


# H

Haight, Grace, 208
Haldane, Bernard Associates, 95, 96, 266
Hall, Grover C., 232
Hall, Joseph, 207
Hamwi, Ernest A., 43
Hatsell, John, 336
*Hatsell's Precedents,* 336
Hayakawa, S. I., 26
Henie, Sonja, 54
Hillsborough Community College, 79
Hirschhorn, Jack, 221
Hubbard, Ken (quoted), 226
Hunt, Mrs. Ramsey, 230
Hutchins, Robert, 221
Huxley, Aldous (quoted), 258


# I

Indiana, 191
Iran, Shah of, 290


# J

Jefferson, Thomas, 336


# K

Kahn, Alfred E., 252–53
Kingry, Irene, 130
*Kiwanis Magazine,* 96


# L

Lake Okeechobee, FL, 283–84
Landers, Ann, 231
Lee, Irving, 40
Lee, Irving and Laura, 8
Leonardo (da Vinci), 278
Light, George, 206, 208
Light, Mark, 206, 208
Lincoln, Abraham, 181, (quoted) 271
Lincoln-Douglas debate, 229
Lippershey, Hans, 278 (footnote)
Loewe, Barbara, 292


# M

Macauley, Thomas Babington (quoted), 142
McCarthy, Senator Eugene, 222
McHugh, Frank J., 71–72
McKim, Martena, 131
*Manual of Parliamentary Practice,* 336
Masson, Tom (quoted), 47
Master Charge, 319
Maugham, W. Somerset, 211
Meyer, Adolf, 131
Milne, A. A. (quoted), 157
Morgan, Arvel, 206, 208–9
Morley, John (quoted), 57
Morris, Desmond, 90, 191
Murrow, Edward R., 39


# N

New Jersey, 225–26
New York University, 38, 53
Nichols, Beverley, 90
Nobel Peace Prize, 208
Nye, Edgar Wilson ("Bill"), (quoted), 292

**O**

Orlando, FL, 285
Orr, Bill, 193

**P**

Pei, Mario, 29
Perry, Antoinette, 208
Plato, 171
Postman, Neil (quoted), 141
Price, Alan, 54, 176, 193, 219
Pulitzer Prizes, 205

**R**

Rarig, Frank, 197
Raubicheck, Letitia, 131
Rauschelback, E. M., 110
*Reader's Guide to Periodical Literature*, 174
Riker's Island, 221
Robert, Henry M., 336
*Robert's Rules of Order*, 336–37, 348
Rochefoucauld, La, 232, 237
Rolls Royce, 304
Roosevelt, Eleanor, 106
Ryan, Earl, 24

**S**

Sales Executive Club, 211
Salmasius, 24
Santa Fe, NM, 305
Sarasota, FL, 283
Sarett, Lew, 131, 197
SAVAK, 290
Seaman, Paul, 211
Service Clubs, 193
Shakespeare, 171–72, 195, 208
Shaw, George Bernard, 5
Siepmann, Charles, 42
Sister Teresa of Calcutta, 208

Socrates, 15
Steele, Addison, 74
Swift, Jonathan (quoted), 99

**T**

Tauck, Arthur C., Jr., 314–15
Tauck Tours, Inc., 300–301
Technifax Corp., 72
Tilden, Bill, 6
Tony Awards, 205, 208
Turkenheimer, Judge Frank, 17
Twain, Mark, 40, 199, 222

**U**

Union Carbide and Carbon Company, 110
United Airlines, 303
Ustinov, Peter, 240

**V**

Vicary, James, 190
Visa, 319

**W**

Wallace, DeWitt and Lila, 53
Walters, Barbara, 224, 229, 233
Ward, Artemus, 40
Warner Brothers, 191
Welles, Orson, 190
Wells, Carolyn (quoted), 57
Wisconsin, University of, 257

**Y**

Yurka, Blanche, 57

# Subject Index

## A

Abstract/concrete terms, 181
Actions, covert, 190–91
Actions, overt, 190–91
Adaptability, 6–7, 187
Adjustment letters (*see* Letters of complaint/
 adjustment)
Adrenal glands/adrenalin, 52
After-dinner speaking, 209–11
 chairman's duties, 209–10
 occasion, 209
 physical set-up, 209–10
 purposes, 209
 time allotted, 209
Altruism, 178–80 (*see* Basic Drives)
Anxiety, speech, 52–55
 causes, 52–53
 controls, 53–54
 fear, conditioned, 52, 53
 fear, instantaneous, 52
 value, 54–55
Aphasia, 18
Appeals, 9–10
Application letters, 258–66
 follow-up, 266
 form, 265
 format, 259
 samples, 259–62
Appraisal interviews, 113–17
 counseling, 116–17
 the interviewee, 114–15
 the interviewer, 115–16
 purposes, 113–14
 time periods, 113
Articulation, 62, 63–64
Attention, 175–76, 301
 holding, 73
Attitude, positive, 90–92
 towards others, 4–5, 55
 towards self, 4–5
Audience analysis, 187
Authority, distributing, 157
Award:
 presenting (*see* Presenting an award)
 receiving (*see* Receiving an award)

## B

Basic drives, 10, 178–80
"Big Why," the, 121–22
Body language, 189, 191
Brain:
 functions diagrammed, 19
 left/right lobes, 17–19
Breathing:
 controlled, 53–54
 diaphragmatic, 59–61
Buccal cavity, 189
Business writing, general
 accuracy, 243–44
 concealed assumptions, 244
 grammar, punctuation, spelling, 243–44
 illogicality, 244
 prejudices, 244

clarity, 245–49
  condense, simplify, support, 245
  numbering, labeling details, 243
  simple vs. complex words, 247–48, 256
  topic sentence, 245–46
  "Word fodder," 246–47
expression (style), 249–52
  active vs. passive, 250–51
  clichés, 252
  try it on yourself, 251
  use of synonyms, 250
  variety in sentences, 249–50
purpose, early statement, 241–43
Business writing vs. journalism, 240

**C**

Central idea:
  listening for, 40
  recognizing, 41–44
Chain of command, 95, 331
Change, desire for, 10, 179–80
Clarify/simplify, 73 (#4)
Clubs, organizations (*see* Meetings)
Collection letters (*see* Letters of credit and
    collection)
Committees, 329, 333
Complaints, customer, 99–106
  adversary roles, 105–6
  case histories, 101–4
  company at fault, 104
  considerations, company, 101
  considerations, customer, 100
  customer at fault, 105
  diagnosing, 100–101
  fair play, justice, 105
  handling, 104–6
  intimidation, 106
  third party at fault, 104–5
Complaint letters (*see* Letters of complaint)
Concrete/abstract terms, 181
Conferences:
  causes of failure, 166–68
  format, 159–60
  Four D's, the, 160–62
  leader, 162–65
  participants, 165–66
  procedure, 159–62
  purpose, 157
  reflective thinking, 158
  values, 158–59
Connotations, 23, 25, 247
Consonants, 58, 63–64
Conversation:
  active preparation, 223–24
  acute observation, 222

bluffing, "namedropping", 224–25
bores, 233
breaking into groups, 232–33
changing topics, 232
criticism, suspension of, 231–32
format, poor, 220
interjecting self, 234
introductions, 235
need for, in business, 219–20
openers, good, 227–30
openers, poor, 226–27
personal equipment, 221–22
remembering names, 234–35
responsibility, 230–31
seating arrangements, 235
*Corpus callosum*, 18
Correspondence:
  external, importance, 292–93
  internal, boundaries, 271
Credit letters (*see* Letters of credit)
Critiques, training, 136–38
Curiosity, creating, 176

**D**

Discussion:
  audience questions, 147–48
  autonomy/harmony, 144
  backgrounds, individual, 143
  ballot (form), 149
  case histories, exercises, 150–53
  characteristics, small group, 143–44
  courtesy, 143–44, 147
  critique, 153
  defined, 142
  evaluation of, 148
  individual rights, 142
  moderator, requirements of, 145, 146–47
  participants, requirements of, 144
  seating arrangement, 145
  size, structure, 145–46
  topics, nature of, 142
  topics, properties of, 145
  values, 141–142
Dissonance, 159, 161
  cognitive, 159
"Dodges" and subterfuges (credit), 320–21
Dyad, dyadic, 14

**E**

Ego, 178–80 (*see also* Basic drives)
Empathy, defined, 189
Emphasis, 17
  achieving, 64–65, 67

Employee grievances, 113
Employment interviewee:
    clothes, grooming, 88–89
    deportment, 89–90
    fears, anxieties, 88
    questions, conditions, 95
Employment interviewer:
    attitude, 90–92
    deportment, 87–88
    understanding, 90–92
Encoding, 16
English language:
    richness, 23
    phonics, 23
    pronunciation, 23
Enunciation, 62–63
Epilepsy, 18
*Esprit de corps*, 95
*Ethos*, 185
Eye contact, 193


**F**


Feedback, 7–8
Flow chart, 74
Follow-up letters, 96, 266, 300
Fringe benefits, 95
Funny story, telling of, 211–16
    bases of humor, 212
    climax, knowledge of, 215
    dialect, use of, 216
    naming/placing characters, 212–15
    things to avoid, 216
Future action, determining, 157


**G**


General semantics (*see* Semantics, general)
Gestures, 192
Gimmicks, 264, 298, 303
Graphology, 90
Grievances, employee (*see* Employee
    grievances)


**H**


Handwriting analysis, 90
Hypothesis, 285


**I**


Immediacy/closeness, 6, 177–78, 188
Impromptu speech, 173
    materials for, 199–200

Inflection, 17, 65–66
Information, passing to others, 8–9
Instruction:
    adaptability needed, 129
    formula
        ask for questions, 135
        demonstrate, 135–36
        demonstrations, trainee, 135–38
        overall objective, 135
    techniques of, 129–35
        ability recognition, 132
        achievement recognition, 132
        analysis and organization, 132–35
        aptitude recognition, 132
        evaluating methods, 132
        reinforce key points, 131–32
        speech clarity, 131
        step by step, 134
Instructors' case histories, 130–31
Intensity, vocal, 64–65
Interest, 129, 177–79, 302
    diagrams, 178, 180
Interpretive response, 93–94
Interview, second, 95–96
Interviews (*see* Appraisal interviews,
        Employment interviewer)
Intonation, 17, 65–66
Introducing speaker, 200–204
    classroom exercises, 202–4
    do's and don'ts, 201
    questions and answers, 201–2
Introductions, social, 235
Isolation/self-centeredness, 233


**J**


Jargon, 23, 29


**K**


Kinesics, 8


**L**


Language, closed/open, 14
Leading question, 92
Learning:
    difficulties, 137–38
    discoveries, 128–29
    interest essential, 129
    mind not muscle, 128
    motivation essential, 129
    past conditioning, 129
    patterns differ, 129
    senses involved, 129
    sensory, 71

transfer of skills, 128
uncomfortable effort, 129
Learning/remembering, association, impact,
    recency, repetition, 134–35
Letters, nonadjustment, 314–17
    sales (*see* Sales letters)
Letters of complaint/adjustment, 303–18
    business firm's consideration, 304
    common complaints, 304
    customer's consideration, 304
    saying "no," 304–5, 310–14
    saying "yes," 304–5, 309–10
    things to avoid, 317–18
    third party at fault, 305, 311
Letters of credit and collection, 319–26
    collecting, 323–26
    credit references, 319, 321
    extending consumer credit, 319–20
    refusing credit, 320–21
    reminders, 323–24
    willingness to pay, 324
Lie detector, 90
*Limen*, 191
Listening:
    active, 37–38
    barriers to, 38–39
    "blackout" areas, 38–39
    central idea, 40
    concentration, energy, 38
    distractions, 38–39
    hearing and, 36
    to oneself, 57, 58
    percentage of time spent, 36
    perils of poor —, 36–37
    reading ability and —, 37
    sensory medium, 7
    structure, 41
    taking notes, 40
    training, 39–40
Listening response, 93, 115
Logical, 9
*Logos*, 185
Lungs, 59–60

**M**

Meanings (*see* Semantics, general)
Medium, sensory, 7–8
Meetings, 328–35
    ballot, preferential, 330 (footnote)
    bylaws, contents, 329
    committees
        *ad hoc*, 334
        appointed/elected, 334
        number of members, 334
        standing, 333
    constitution, contents, 328–29

officers, 331–33
    president, 331–32
    secretary, 332–33
    order of business, 334
        format, no program, 334–35
        format with program, 335
    organization chart (diagram), 331
    rules, standing, 330
    rules of order, 330
Memoranda, 274–81
    purposes, 274
    requirements, 274
    samples, 275–81
    signature of, 274
Memorized presentations, 53, 173
Memory aids, 73
Minutes:
    dispense with, 346
    essentials of, 272
    meetings, 333
    objectivity of, 272–73
    report as, 272
Minutes recorder, 273–74
Mnemonic(s), 134
Moderator, critique, 154
Monorate, 58, 67–68
Monotone, 58, 64–66

**N**

Nasality, 58
Noise, intermittent vs. steady, 39
Noise interference, 15
Non-directive techniques, 93–95, 115
Nonverbal communication, 5–6, 16, 191

**O**

Opportunity, promotion, 95
Oral reports, 117–22
    accuracy, brevity, organization, 117
    the "Big Why," 121–22
    policy, 117, 118–19
    process, 117, 120
    progress, 117, 120–21
    visual aids, 117, 120–21
Order (*see* Structure)

**P**

Paralinguistics, 16
Parliamentary procedure, 336–51
    early history/values, 336–37
    motions, definitions and examples, 337–39

Parliamentary procedure (*cont.*)
  motions, definitions and examples (*cont.*)
    adjourn, 342–43
    amend, 340
    appeal, 343–44
    close debate, 341–42
    limit, 340–41
    main motion, 339–40
    point of order, 343
    postpone, 341
    recess, 342
    reconsider, 344–45
    refer, 340
    rescind, 345
    suspend rules, 344
    withdraw, 340
  motions, ordinary, 337–38
    charted, 349
    examples, 338
  motions, precedence of, 337–38, 339
  motions, seconding of, 339
  motions, special, 339
    charted, 350
  motions, superfluous, 345–48
  motions summarized, 339
Participants, conference (*see* Conferences
    participants)
*Pathos,* 185
Perception, tests for, 193–95
Personal data/record (*see* Resumé(s))
Persuasion, 184–92
  antagonism, 188–89
  audience analysis, 187–88
  body language, 189–92
  deductive reasoning, 185–86
    tests for, 186–87
  emotion and logic, 184
  empathy, 189
  ethics, 184
  *ethos, logos, pathos,* 185
  formula for presentation, 188
  inductive reasoning, 185
    tests for, 186
  judgment and value, 184
  policy, 184
  syllogism, 187
Phrasing, pauses, 64, 67–68
Pictures (*see* Visual aids)
Pictures vs. words, 72
Pitch, 58, 64–66
Platform conduct, rules for, 3
Policy formulation, 157
Polygraph, 90
Posture, 189–90
Prejudices, 94
Presentations, persuasive (*see* Persuasion)
Presenting an award, 205–8
  formula for, 205–6

  sample speeches, 206–7
  two types, 205
Principles vs. rules, 3–4
Projectors (*see* Visual aids)
Proxemics, 8
Public speaking
  attention, getting, 175–77
  delivery, methods, 172–73
  development of body, 180–83
  gestures, posture, walking, 190, 192
  interest, arousing, 175–77, 180
  limitation, 181, 183
  outlining, 175–84
  persuasion, 184–89, 190–91
  preparation, 173–75
  purposes, 171–72
  structure, 180–81
  summarizing, 183–84, 188
  support, 181–83
    diagrammed, 182
Purposeful speech, 4

**Q**

Qualifications record (*see* Resumé(s))
Questions:
  answering, asking, 90–93
  from audience, 147–48
  type, 92–93
Quorum, assembly/committee, 329
  defined, 334
Quotations, apt, 177

**R**

Reading aloud:
  importance of, 66–67
  practice, 68
  preparation for, 67–68
Receiving an award, 208–9
Recommendations, 267–69
References
  credit, 319–20
  employment, 258, 263, 265–66
  special categories, 265
Reflective response, 93, 115
Remembering names, 234–35
Repertory of speeches, 4
Reports, oral/written (*see* Oral reports,
    Written reports)
Research, primary/secondary, 283
Resonance, 58, 61–62
  diagrammed, 61
Responses, non-directive, 93–94

Responsibility, distributing, 157
Resumé(s), 258–60
    format, 263
    personality in, 263–64
    samples, 259–60, 262
    selectivity, 264
Retention:
    hearing/seeing, 71–72
    sight/sound, 72–73
Rules vs. principles, 3–4

**S**

Sales letters, 298–303
    aim at specific reader, 298–300
    appeal to fright, 302 (footnote)
    avoid gimmicks, 298, 303
    avoid implied criticism, 303
    follow-up letter, 300
    make response easy, 302
    persuasive techniques, 301–2
    respect reader's intelligence, 303
"Searchlight" technique, 193
Seating arrangements
    after-dinner speaking, 210
    conferences, 168
    discussions, 145
    parties, 235
Self as communicator, 50–51
Self-image, 47
Self-inventory, 48–49
Self-preservation, 178–80
Semantic difficulties, 160, 191
Semantics, general, 26–29
Sex drive, 178–80
Sick leave, 95
Sight plus sound, 7–8
"Six-day plan" (public speaking), 173–75
Slang, 28
Smell, sensory medium, 8
Sound:
    duration of, 64–65
    as sensory medium, 7
    speed of, 61
Special requests (written)
    information and services, 293–98
    payment and early request, 293, 296
    specifics, 293, 298
    timing, 295, 298
Speech, speed of, 164 (footnote)
Stage fright (*see* Anxiety, speech)
Statement, startling, 176–77
*Status quo*, 10, 178–80
Steps, vocal, 65–66
Stereognosis, 19
Stereotypes, 163

Stimuli:
    subliminal, 190–91
    supraliminal, 190–91
Story telling, 176, 211–16
Structures, 41, 180, 183–84
Style (writing), 249–52
Suggestion, post-hypnotic, 191
Supervisory responsibilities, 95
Supportive response, 94
Syllogism, 187

**T**

Talking:
    sensory medium, as, 7
    "up/down," 187
Talk-show hosts, 220
Telephone communication, 106–25
    anonymity, 108
    case histories, exercises, 123–25
    limitations and use, 106–7
    noise/signal ratio, 106
    selling, 112
    sending-receiving, 108–12
Tension, relief of, 73
Testimonial question, 93
Thinking, reflective, 158
Thought, speed of, 164 (footnote)
Timing, vocal, 64–65, 68
Time-motion study, 284
Trainee, barriers to reception, 137–38
Transmissions, acoustical, verbal, visible, 16

**U**

Understanding job, 90

**V**

Verbal communication, 5–6
Verbal-visual retention, 72–73
Visual aids
    actual/factual, 74–75
    bar graphs, 72–73, 75
    chalkboard, 77–78
    combination sight/hearing, 71–72
    film strips, 75, 78
    flannel board, 76
    flip cards, 77, 81, 82–84
    grid graphs, 75–76
    hearing/seeing, 71–72
    "mock-ups," 75
    pictographs, 76–77
    pictures, 73–74, 75

Visual aids (*cont.*)
    pie graphs, 76
    projectors, 78–79
    reports, importance of, 288
    requisites of, 73–74, 77
    SAMPLE SPEECH, 80–84
    seating arrangements, 78–79
    slides, 75–78
    values, 73
Vita (*see* Resumés)
Vocabulary, 24–25
Vocal variety, 64–66

Voice and diction, 96
Voice, requisites for good, 58
Volume (voice), 62, 64
Votes, secret, tie, two-thirds, 332
Vowels, 58, 63

**W**

"Word fodder," 276
Working conditions, 95
Written reports, 277–90